Lord's 1787–1945

LORD'S 1787–1945

SIR PELHAM WARNER

Introduction by Roy Hattersley

THE PAVILION LIBRARY

First published in Great Britain 1946

First published in the Pavilion Library in 1987 by
Pavilion Books Limited
196 Shaftesbury Avenue, London WC2H 8JL
in association with Michael Joseph Limited
27 Wrights Lane, Kensington, London W8 5TZ

Consulting Editor: Steve Dobell

British Library Cataloguing in Publication Data
Warner, Pelham
Lord's 1787–1945
1. Lord's Cricket Ground (London, England)—History
I. Title
796.35'8'06842132 GV928.G7

ISBN 1-85145-140-4
ISBN 1-85145-112-9 Pbk

Printed and bound in Great Britain by
Billing & Sons Limited, Worcester

INTRODUCTION

I was fifteen years old when I first saw Lord's. It was 1948 – the year of Don Bradman's final tour and the summer of Lindwall and Miller. But when I got off the 'bus in St John's Wood on that sunny distant afternoon, the Australians were batting elsewhere. All that Lord's had to offer was the MCC versus one of those club sides of whom boys from the north and their fathers have never heard. Knowing that we wanted no more than to see the ground, the gateman at the nursery end let us in free. We walked across the practice ground, past the nets and the carpenter's shop and climbed up the back of the free stand to the topmost row of free seats. I suppose that, since then, I have made that same journey a thousand times.

Forty years ago, I thought that Lord's was the most beautiful cricket ground in the world. My experience was, admittedly, limited. I had been brought up on the great urban arenas – Bramall Lane, Headingley, Old Trafford and Park Avenue. And I had yet to discover that, despite their romantic names, rural grounds in Kent and Somerset had concrete stands with corrugated iron roofs. But even now, although I have seen the Moat Park and the Meads (as well as incomparable Worcester), I see no reason to change that judgement. The sight of Lord's spread out from sight screen to sight screen filled me with awe and wonder. Cortez, silent upon a peak in Darian, could not have been more impressed by the sudden sight of the Pacific Ocean.

The Lord's which stretched out below me was, of course, not quite the ground which I visit now. And architecturally, it has certainly deteriorated. My views on all such matters are deeply suspect, for I use cricket to exorcise the devil Reaction which lurks in even the most progressive soul. I prefer the old days. I have not adjusted to limited overs, batting helmets, sponsorships and Ian Botham. Nor do I intend to. But I think that I can make an objective defence of the view that Lord's looked better then. The Mound Stand had not quite recovered from its war wounds. And the Tavern was still proclaiming the Edwardian virtues of self-confidence and uninhibited vulgarity. It ran like a curving cloister, which joined the outside world to the *sanctum sanctorium* of the pavilion.

The Tavern has been gone so long that this year's little boys will not even know that once a real tavern stood on the spot which is now unattractively filled by private boxes and a fair imitation of a railway station buffet. But the pavilion remains intact, demonstrating (by its close proximity to the aerial bunker which is the Middlesex members' stand) that whatever else has improved during the last hundred years, architecture is in decline. But then, it is an unlucky building which is compared with the pavilion at Lord's.

The Lord's pavilion is of the classic kind – straight out of India and the Raj. It would be wholly at home at a durbar. Some of England's great pavilions have been ravaged by progress. At Headingley the players have been relegated to a prefabricated box at mid-wicket and the old minarets and cupolas have been squared off under a covering of breeze block and white paint. But at Lord's the pavilion steps are still suitable for the swift ascent of the old-style modest batsman who removed his cap and ran up into the dressing-room in order to minimise the applause for his century.

I do not know why I always think of Lord's as the home of W. G. Grace. The good doctor lived in Kent and played, most of his life, for Gloucestershire. Perhaps it is only natural to associate the home of the game with its first national hero. Whatever the reason, the great bearded presence is one of the images that always flash across my mind whenever Lord's is mentioned. The others, of course, include the turf brought – to the original site of Thomas Lord's ground in Marylebone – all the way from his (and my) native Yorkshire. The most vivid image of all comes from the last decade covered by Sir Pelham Warner's history. For all its clarity, it is in double focus – Denis

Compton and Bill Edrich walking out to bat.

These days we talk too much as if their glorious careers were all compressed into the extraordinary summer of 1947. In fact, they were beginning to build the partnerships and the legends well before the Second World War. In 1938 Bill Edrich achieved the most romantic of all cricket distinctions – a thousand runs before the end of May. He scored all of them at Lord's.

Of course the single word denotes a great deal more than a single cricket ground. Lord's is not just a place. It is an institution in both senses of the word – on one hand venerable and enduring, and on the other for years the home of cricket's ruling body and therefore the shorthand description for the final authority over the game. It was to 'Lord's' – not a postal address but cricket's senate – to which Pelham Warner had to send his anguished telegrams during the Bodyline tour of 1932–33. When the Laws of Cricket were changed it was 'Lord's' that changed. In a very real sense, its history is the history of the game.

Pelham Warner's own part in that history is almost unique. Player, county and England captain, tour manager and President of the MCC (when that private club still ran world cricket), he did more and lasted longer than any other player of his age. He writes about Lord's with the knowledge of fifty years' inside experience – and with the special insight that comes from deep affection. When I made my first visit to the ground in 1948, the kindly gateman pointed out the Warner Stand. I hope that the MCC has no plans to pull it down and replace it with a bowling alley or supermarket. But even if they do, one Warner monument will remain – his account of one hundred and fifty-eight years in the life of Lord's.

London, 1987 — Roy Hattersley

Sir Pelham Warner

Lord's

1787–1945

TO
CRICKETERS
THE
WORLD OVER

FOREWORD

by

H. S. Altham

Sir Pelham Warner has done me the honour of asking me to write a foreword to this the latest and greatest of his many contributions to cricket literature. It is altogether fitting that the year of its publication should also have seen him accorded two of the highest honours within the gift of the M.C.C.—election to the life office of a Trustee and the painting of his portrait to hang in the Valhalla of cricket, the Long Room at Lord's. For his services to cricket in general, of which Lord's is the epitome, can hardly be greater than his knowledge of and devotion to the ground which is its focus.

His qualifications for writing the story of Lord's are, of course, incomparable: he has read everything that bears on his subject; for more than fifty years he has known intimately all the great figures who have made its history; and he has made no inconsiderable contribution to the history himself, not only as a great batsman and a great captain, but as a selector of unsurpassed experience, and, let me add, success, and as a member for very many years of those M.C.C. committees who have handled so wisely the ever-changing problems of the game's development and the kaleidoscopic variety of issues which the welfare of that great institution and property—Lord's—must involve.

No wonder, then, that the field of this book is all-embracing, and his verdicts authoritative, and, as one might expect from one who is by courtesy "my learned friend," judicious; and that the great canvas of famous players and matches which he presents is full of life and colour. Where there is criticism—and he has not shrunk from making it where he felt the need—it is always constructive and kindly, for it springs never from rancour, but always from his conviction that there should be only one standard for the conduct of cricket, the highest.

If he has been able to steep his book in the traditions and atmosphere of Lord's it is surely because he has loved the ground with a single-minded enthusiasm and pride which is as wholehearted now as on the day when he first fell under its spell. I believe he would ask no better reward for his labour than that he might convey that enthusiasm and pride to others, so that they may feel, as I know he does each time that he turns into the St John's Wood Road,

Ille terrarum mihi præter omnes angulus ridet.

PREFACE

In 1851 the Rev. James Pycroft gave to the world his *Cricket Field*, and in the Preface thereto he wrote:

> We have been long expecting to hear of some chronicler, aided and abetted by the noblemen and gentlemen of the Marylebone Club—one who should combine, with all the resources of a ready writer, traditional lore and practical experience. But time is fast thinning the ranks of the veterans. Lord Frederick Beauclerk and the once celebrated player, the Hon. John Henry Tufton, afterwards Earl of Thanet, have both passed away; and probably Sparks, of the Edinburgh Ground, and Mr John Goldham, hereinafter mentioned, are the only surviving players who have witnessed both the formation and the jubilee of the Marylebone Club, following, as it has, the fortunes of the Pavilion and of the enterprising Thomas Lord, literally through "three removes" and "one fire," from White Conduit Fields to the present Lord's.
>
> How, then, it will be asked, do *we* presume to save from oblivion the records of Cricket?

Nearly a hundred years have passed, and cricket to-day possesses an immense literature, so that there is no question of "saving from oblivion" the history of the Marylebone Club, which has already been ably recorded up to 1914 by the late Lord Harris and F. S. Ashley-Cooper.

It would seem, however, that there is now room for a history, brought down to the present day, dealing not only with the Club itself, but also with the great matches which have taken place at its headquarters. And I hope, with all modesty, that as one of the "ranks of the veterans," as a player, as a student, and as a writer on the game, I can bring to the task of writing such a history certain qualifications of experience and memory that should be recorded before I too pass on to join Lord Frederick Beauclerk and the Earl of Thanet.

It is fifty-nine years since I saw my first match at Lord's—M.C.C. *v.* Sussex, in 1887—and fifty-seven years since I made my first appearance 'in the middle'—for Rugby against Marlborough.

Since that day Lord's as a ground and the M.C.C. as a club have held pride of place in my devotion to cricket, "the most catholic and diffused, the most innocent, kindly, and manly of popular pleasures." So it has been a labour of love for me to write this book, indeed "aided and abetted by the noblemen and gentlemen of the Marylebone Club."

I must thank particularly the Committee of the M.C.C. for giving me full access to the Club's records, and above all Colonel R. S. Rait Kerr, our present Secretary—assisted by his daughter Diana—for his great help and interest. I am indebted to Viscount Ullswater for his scholarly contribution on the Club's pictures; to Mr H. S. Altham, with his unrivalled knowledge of cricket and its history, for reading the proofs—and approving what I had written; to Mr R. Aird for his generous assistance, especially with the Tennis and Rackets and Refreshment Department sections of the Appendices; to Mr W. Bowring for his enthusiastic help and research on my behalf; to the Portman Estate Office; and to the Marylebone Borough Council and their librarian for bringing valuable material to my notice, and for giving me access to their records.

Messrs Harrap have shown themselves the most considerate of publishers, and I would like to mark especially my appreciation of the unfailing co-operation of Mr A. J. White and Mr D. D. Bird in the preparation of this book, and of Mr R. A. Maynard in the work upon the illustrations.

Finally, my thanks are due to my son Esmond for much help and advice.

P. F. W.

ACKNOWLEDGMENT

For permission to reproduce the colour plates in this edition I acknowledge with gratitude my indebtedness to:

The Committee of the M.C.C., for "Tossing for Innings," "George Parr," "A Cricket Match," "Thomas Lord," "Alfred Mynn," "N. Felix," "The Cricket Match," "William Beldham," "The Scorer," and "England *v.* Australia, 1938"; Mrs Vera Dick-Cunyngham, for "Lord Frederick Beauclerk in Fancy Dress"; and the Borough Librarian, for "The Consecration of the Colours," a coloured lithograph in the Ashbridge Collection, Marylebone Public Library.

In the case of the monochrome plates acknowledgment appears beneath each subject.

I wish also to express my gratitude to the Editor of *The Spectator*, for permission to reproduce an account of the 1918 England *v.* Dominions match, first published in that journal under the initials "E.B."; Messrs Longmans Green and Co., Ltd., for R. H. Lyttelton's description of "Cobden's Match," from the Badminton *Cricket*; Messrs Methuen and Co., Ltd., for Lieutenant-Colonel C. P. Foley's account of the Eton *v.* Harrow match of 1910, from *Autumn Foliage*; Messrs Williams and Norgate, Ltd., for a quotation from Edward Rutter's *Cricket Memories*; Messrs Hutchinson and Co., Ltd., for permission to reproduce my Introduction to *Don Bradman's Book*; the Editor of *The Times* for Lord Harris's message on his eightieth birthday and the obituary notice of the late Sir Kynaston Studd; Messrs Spottiswoode, Ballantyne and Co., Ltd., for the Eton *v.* Harrow (1910) verses, by W. D. Eggar, from *A Song of Lord's and Poems for the Mag*; and, finally, Messrs Chatto and Windus, who have allowed me to draw freely on my *Cricket between Two Wars* for the accounts of the matches in Chapters XII and XIII of this book.

P. F. W.

CONTENTS

CHAPTER I

The Birth of Lord's

Thomas Lord—The White Conduit Club—Founding of the M.C.C.—Dorset Square—St John's Wood—The Present Ground—First Match—J. H. Dark—Lord Frederick, E. H. Budd, William Ward, and the "Squire"—Walker, Beldham, and Lambert

MANY who are not familiar with cricket believe that the name Lord's has some connexion with the peerage:[1] nothing could be further from the truth. The name comes from Thomas Lord, the pivot round whom the formation of the Marylebone Club turned. Lord was born at Thirsk, in Yorkshire, on November 23, 1755, and his father, who was a substantial yeoman of Roman Catholic stock, had his lands sequestrated when he espoused the Stuart cause in the rising of 1745, so that he had to work as a labourer on the very farm that once belonged to him. The Lord family moved south to Diss, in Norfolk, where Thomas Lord was brought up, and from here, on reaching manhood, he migrated to London and found employment at the White Conduit Club as a bowler and sort of general attendant.

This club, only a few of whose scores are extant, deserves always to be remembered affectionately by cricketers as "the acorn that blossomed into the gigantic oak known as the Marylebone Club."[2] Formed in 1782, it was an offshoot of a West End convivial club called the "Je-ne-sais-quoi," some of whose members took to frequenting the White Conduit House and playing their matches in the adjoining fields near Islington.

In 1786 the members were tiring of this site, and the Earl of Winchilsea,[3] a great patron of cricket, and Charles Lennox, later

[1] In a recent conversation Mr H. Douglas Bessemer told me that when his nephew Gordon Johnston—a prisoner in Italian hands—was elected a member of the M.C.C. in 1942 Johnston's relatives were able to send him a message through the Vatican. In case, however, the Italian authorities should attach a sinister meaning to the letters 'M.C.C.,' the message just stated that he had been elected to Lord's. The Italian interpreter at his camp, apparently unaware of the existence of the well-known institution at St John's Wood, concluded that one of the prisoners had been raised to the peerage. From that moment Johnston was treated with great respect, and was allowed many concessions, much to his own and to his fellow-prisoners' advantage.

[2] A. D. Taylor, *Annals of Lord's and History of the M.C.C.* (Arrowsmith, 1903).

[3] Lord Winchilsea, the ninth Earl (1752–1826), may be considered the founder of the M.C.C.—"the urbane and loyal Winchilsea," as Lord Frederick Beauclerk called him.

fourth Duke of Richmond, offered to Lord their guarantee against loss if he would start a new private ground. White Conduit played several matches at Marylebone in 1787, but it seems almost certain that at the end of the season the old club was merged into the newly formed Marylebone Cricket Club. The M.C.C. had been born.

Lord, being assured of support, quickly got to work, with the result that in May 1787 he opened his first ground on what is now Dorset Square, on the Portman Estate. In the Portman Estate Office is a map of 1780 which shows the site of the field of seven acres which Lord secured for his ground. It was at the time leased to one Samuel Adams: whether Lord obtained a sub-lease from him or a new lease cannot be said, as the Portman Estate records all went to salvage during the Second German War.[1]

The first great match at Dorset Square was on May 31 and June 1, 1787, when Middlesex beat Essex by 93 runs in a game played for 200 guineas, and the earliest recorded M.C.C. match was against the White Conduit Club on June 27, 1788, the M.C.C. winning by 83 runs. The first thing Lord did was to put a fence round the ground, thereby ensuring privacy for the Club. It is possible also that no gate money was charged at Islington, and Lord instituted an entrance-fee of sixpence to the public. Lord's quickly became popular, and the matches were well attended,[2] but during its early existence the M.C.C. played very few games. However, all went well with the ground until 1810,[3] when the last game was played on August 17 of that year, the Old (over thirty-eight) beating the Young by 90 runs.

In that year whatever lease there was apparently ended, and the site was let on building leases, with ground rents of over £600

[1] In J. Stockdale's plan of London (1797) the ground is shown as "Prince of Wales's Cricket Ground." The Rate Books of St Marylebone indicate that Lord was lessee of the Allsop Arms in 1785, which suggests that he acquired the ground adjoining at the same time. However, it was not ready for play until two years later. The Allsop Arms (now called Allsop House) to-day stands on the corner on the opposite side of Upper Gloucester Place. Moon's garage occupies the site where the inn stood. There is a tradition that the players used to change in the old inn.

[2] "Colonel Greville had his pocket picked on Monday last at Lord's ground of cash to the amount of £30. The pickpockets were so daring on Monday evening in the vicinity of Lord's Cricket Ground that they actually took the umbrellas of men and women by force, and even their watches and purses, threatening to stab those who made resistance. They were in gangs of between twenty to thirty, and behaved in a manner the most audacious."—Extract from the Press, 1802.

[3] An interesting and important event took place on June 29, 1799, when colours were presented to the Royal East India Volunteers.

a year, its value during the twenty-one years' tenancy of Lord having reached a figure far beyond his resources.

Lord had foreseen that he would have to leave his original ground, so as early as October 15, 1808, he rented two fields—the Brick Field and the Great Field, at North Bank, on the St John's Wood Estate—for a term of eighty years, free of land-tax and tithe, at £54 a year. The new ground was ready in 1809, and therefore for two seasons Lord had two grounds on his hands, the St John's Wood C.C. using the new enclosure. This club was afterwards incorporated in the M.C.C.

The new Lord's was officially taken over on May 8, 1811, the turf having been removed from the original ground in Dorset Square, so that "the noblemen and Gentlemen of the M.C.C." should be able "to play on the same footing as before." The move was not popular with many of the members of the M.C.C., and the Club did not play a single match there in 1811 or 1812—and only three during the following year.

In that year another move became necessary, as Parliament had decreed that the Regent's Canal should be cut through the centre of the ground. The Eyre family, on whose estate the second ground was situated, were willing to grant Lord another plot, which enabled the Club to make its headquarters on the site it has ever since occupied. And so Lord once again transferred his turf to his third ground (at a rent of £100), in time for the opening of the 1814 season. He was now a person of some importance in the parish of Marylebone, for he was made a member of the Marylebone Vestry in 1807 and also conducted a wine-and-spirit business.

Four days before the ground was due to be opened there was a big explosion in the "Cricket-ground public-house," which did considerable damage.[1] Despite this inauspicious start the third Lord's soon began to attract the public, and appropriately enough in the first great match recorded on the new site the M.C.C. beat Hertfordshire by an innings and 27 runs.

Although the ground was a success, Lord was apparently not altogether satisfied with the pecuniary results, and he obtained

[1] "A shocking incident occurred on Thursday at New Lord's Cricket-ground public-house, Marylebone Fields. The landlady of the house had occasion to use a small quantity of gunpowder, and whilst in the act of taking the same from a paper, containing a pound weight, a spark from the fire caught it, and it went off with a great explosion. The landlady, her sister, and four little girls were seriously burnt. The two former are in a dangerous way."—Extract from the Press, 1814.

power from the Eyre Estate to develop the ground as a building site to enhance the value of the sixty-eight years remaining of the lease, and plans for building houses were actually drawn up which limited the playing area to 150 square yards. William Ward, a director of the Bank of England, and later M.P. for the City of London, saved the situation by buying Lord's interest in the ground for £5000.

Lord's contact with the famous ground thus ceased in 1825, but he continued to live in the St John's Wood Road until 1830, when he retired to West Meon, in Hampshire, where he died on January 13, 1832, aged seventy-six.

In 1835 Ward and his four daughters, who joined in the lease to bind any interest they had in the property, transferred it to J. H. Dark, who, on the advice of Benjamin Aislabie, gave £2000 for it, and undertook to pay an annuity of £425 to the Ward family during the unexpired term of the lease, which was for fifty-nine years from Midsummer Day, 1834, at a yearly rental of £150. In his book *Recollections of Lord's and the Marylebone Cricket Club*[1] W. H. Slatter, whose family had a long connexion with Lord's, says that when Dark first leased Lord's there were two ponds, one in front of the centre portion of the present Mound Stand, and the other at the west end of the ground. From time to time these ponds were filled with brick rubbish and gradually disappeared to some extent, but for years the wickets and outfield were very rough. Dark himself lived in a house near the present members' luncheon-room.

Among the early M.C.C. members there is no more striking personality than the Rev. Lord Frederick Beauclerk, D.D. He was born in 1773, and in 1787 his father became fifth Duke of St Albans, succeeding his cousin the fourth Duke. Both these Dukes were grandsons of his Majesty King Charles II and the pretty, witty actress Nell Gwyn. Of royal lineage—albeit with a bar sinister—and son of a duke, Lord Frederick was an aristocrat in an age when a deference amounting almost to obeisance was paid to persons of exalted rank, and in course of time he became an autocrat at Lord's. As player and captain he strode the cricket field a dominant figure, and he was equally dominant in the pavilion in the affairs of the Club.

As to his ability as a cricketer, there can be no dispute: he was regarded as the finest all-round amateur of his day. Some thought

[1] Published privately in 1914.

E. H. Budd a better bowler, but as a batsman Lord Frederick was the former's superior, his play being more scientific, in the then more orthodox style of the professionals, and he never gave his wicket away. He made eight centuries on the first Lord's—a large number in those early days. His highest score in cricket was 170 for the Homerton Club against Montpelier in 1806. He kept up his form well beyond middle age, scoring, in 1824, 99 for the B's against England, and in 1827, when fifty-four, playing an innings of 78 against W. Ashby, slow right-hand, the best bowler of the day. This score is reminiscent of W. G. Grace's 74 in his last Gentlemen *v.* Players match, at the Oval in 1906, when he was fifty-eight. What the famous Doctor was to a later generation, so was Lord Frederick to his generation.

As to Lord Frederick's merits as a man, he must be judged in the light of the times in which he was born and in which his early life was spent. Anyone who reads the correspondence of that incomparable letter-writer Horace Walpole can see how widespread was gambling in the eighteenth century. At Almack's and White's thousands were won and lost at cards or dice in a night. Nothing was too absurd on which to have a bet. One instance will suffice. Writing in 1756 to Sir Horace Mann, Walpole says, "My Lord Rockingham and my nephew Lord Orford have made a match of five hundred pounds, between five turkeys and five geese, to run from Norwich to London." It was not to be expected that cricket would be immune from the gambling fever.

In earlier days cricket had been regarded as a game confined to the lower classes, but when men of quality began playing it in increasing numbers matches were arranged for stakes up to a thousand guineas, and there was much betting on the result. At any rate in a cricket match a backer had a longer run for his money than a throw of the dice provided, and as the match proceeded there was the opportunity both for hedging and for side-bets. Lord Frederick was one of the greatest single-wicket players of his day, and it is not surprising that in such an age he sought to turn his cricketing prowess to monetary gain. He frankly stated that he expected to make £600 a season by playing matches for stakes. It must be admitted that matches were sometimes sold. There are whispers that have come down through the years that Lord Frederick was a party to such roguery, and though he did things which would not be tolerated to-day, there is no evidence of it. One can imagine that when a crucial catch was dropped or a batsman failed to score a disgruntled backer said unpleasant things, and, like all dictators, Lord Frederick had his enemies. When he died in 1850 *The Times* gave no obituary notice, and the *Annual Register* dismissed the event in four lines, from which we learn that he died in Grosvenor Street.

An account of his prowess appears in *Celebrities I have known*,[1] by Lord William Lennox, son of the Duke of Richmond, who was so prominent in forming the M.C.C. This was the Duke who fought a famous duel with the Duke of York, grazing his head with a bullet, after which he was posted to Edinburgh, where he spent much of his time playing cricket with the soldiers, which in those days was considered a great condescension for an officer. Lord William Lennox, with his brother George, had been playing in a cricket match in Goodwood Park, for Boxgrove against Bersted, and as the match reached its end he described the following scene:

> A party sallied forth from the house, headed by my father, including Lord Winchelsea, Lord Frederick Beauclerk, Sir Horace Mann, General Bligh, the Honourable Henry and John Tufton, and Richard Leigh. They had quitted the dining-room after imbibing a fair quantity of port wine, leaving instructions with the butler that clean glasses, devilled biscuits, and a magnum of "beeswing" should be ready on their return from the cricket field. . . .
>
> "How stands the match, youngsters?" said Lord Frederick. . . .
>
> "Oh, we've beat them by twenty runs," I responded.
>
> "I suppose you Westminster fellows are in pretty good form."
>
> Of course we answered "Yes."
>
> "Look here," he added, "I'll put you to the test . . . if you get me out I'll tip you a guinea."
>
> We agreed, upon which he doffed his coat, borrowed a bat from Lillywhite, our umpire, and stood manfully up at his wicket. . . . Undoubtedly Lord Frederick was the first gentleman cricketer of his day, for although he could not equal David Harris in bowling, surpass Tom Walker in batting, or Hammond in wicket-keeping, he united in his own person all those three great points in the game to such a considerable degree as to be pronounced the Crichton of cricket. My brother and myself soon found that we might as well have endeavoured to bowl down the Monument as Lord Frederick's wicket, and we were in despair that we should never see the golden reward, when fortunately . . . he was caught out, bowled by myself.

---

[1] Four vols.; London, 1876–77.

"Well bowled, well caught," he exclaimed, "there's a guinea apiece for you, you have earned it fairly."

Lord William adds:

> Lord Frederick was one of the best bowlers of his day at Cambridge. . . . His bowling, though extremely slow, was very effective; knowing exactly where to pitch the ball, he so delivered it as to cause a quick and abrupt rise. At the period I write of [Lord William was born in 1799] the members of the Marylebone Cricket Club always appeared in their sky blue club dress.

There is something very pleasant about this picture of Lord Frederick, as there is something pathetic about the last picture of him, sitting in his brougham at Lord's, with a nurse beside him, watching the cricket and surveying a scene where for so long he reigned supreme.

Before his last illness, and when his playing days were over, he had his regular seat just inside the wicket of the pavilion, where he sat with cigar in mouth and his little white snappish dog, who barked every one in and out. Woe betide the hound that ventures to-day to put even half a nose inside Lord's!

A contemporary of Lord Frederick was E. H. Budd, who was born in 1785. He made his first appearance at Lord's in 1802, and his last for the M.C.C. against Marlborough College, at Marlborough, fifty years later. He was a very hard hitter, and once hit a ball out of the original Lord's in Dorset Square. For this feat Lord had offered a reward of £20, which Budd announced he would distribute among the players, but Lord refused to pay. Budd was also a magnificent fieldsman and a bowler of pace—and a great all-round sportsman.

The honour of the first century on the present Lord's belongs to him—105 for his eleven against Osbaldeston's in 1816. Budd played with a bat weighing three pounds, which is to be seen in the pavilion to-day.

William Ward, who 'saved' the ground in the twenties, was probably the most powerful batsman of his day, and his 278 for the Club against Norfolk in 1820 held the record at Lord's for over a hundred years.[1]

So long an innings was an almost unheard-of feat in those early days, but perhaps what is more interesting is the fact that

[1] Ward's record was broken by P. Holmes, of Yorkshire, against Middlesex in 1925, with 315, not out. This was beaten by J. B. Hobbs for Surrey *v.* Middlesex in 1926, with 316, not out.

Ward's bat weighed no less than *four* pounds, and that it was used by him for *fifty* years! Many years later Albert Trott ruined his batting by trying to carry pavilions with a three-pound bat like that of Budd's, so Mr Ward was evidently no mean weight-lifter!

Closely associated with Lord Frederick was George Osbaldeston, who played his first match on the original Lord's in 1808. He was invariably referred to as "the Squire," and Sir Theodore Cook, editor of *The Field*, in his Introduction to the Squire's autobiography,[1] recounts the following story. Two old friends met, and *A* mentioned the old Squire. *B:* "What old Squire?" *A:* "George Osbaldeston, of course." *B:* "What is he Squire of?" *A:* "Why, he's Squire of England!"

The Squire was the son of George Osbaldeston, of Hutton Bushall, Yorkshire, by Jane, only daughter of Sir Thomas Head, Bart., and was born in Wimpole Street on December 26, 1787. His father was a son of the Rev. John Wickens, Rector of Petworth, who assumed the name of Osbaldeston on his wife Philadelphia, in 1770, inheriting half the estates of Fountayne Osbaldeston, M.P. for Scarborough. The Squire was educated at Eton and Brasenose College, Oxford, and left without taking a degree. Master of the Quorn from 1817 to 1821, and again from 1823 to 1828, with the famous Tom Sebright as his huntsman, he was later Master of the Pytchley and the Atherstone. There was no finer man to hounds or over a steeplechase course. He was also a great shot—he once killed ninety-eight pheasants in a hundred shots—as well as being an expert fisherman, and was pretty handy with his fists, promoting many a fight. A small man, about 5 feet 6 inches in height, he was, however, of great strength, with a tremendous chest, and weighed eleven stone. He had charming manners, and was very good-humoured and gay, and "never spoke harshly or in an unkind way of any human being." A great gambler, he is said to have lost £200,000 on the Turf, while he played whist for very high stakes, both on the tricks and on the rubber. In 1831, at the age of forty-four, he made a wager that he would ride two hundred miles in ten hours, and won with an hour and eighteen minutes to spare, using a horse for every four miles.

In 1800 the Squire won a bet of 200 guineas from Lord George Bentinck, but Bentinck, on paying the bet, let slip from his lips,

[1] *Squire Osbaldeston: his Autobiography*, edited by E. D. Cuming (Lane, 1926).

"This is robbery." "This will not stop here," said Osbaldeston, and a challenge to a duel followed, which took place at Wormwood Scrubs. Two versions are given of this encounter—one that Osbaldeston fired in the air, the other that a ball went through Bentinck's hat, missing his brain by two inches.

All Osbaldeston's friends were firm in their opinion that the Squire would never claim the recovery of a dishonest bet, and a reconciliation with Lord George was later effected.

As a cricketer Osbaldeston, though a splendid hard-hitting batsman, was best known as a bowler, said to be the fastest who had yet appeared, and in conjunction with William Lambert he was ready to challenge any other pair in England. He challenged for a match of fifty guineas Lord Frederick Beauclerk and T. C. Howard, to decide who were the stronger pair. Just before the match Osbaldeston was taken ill, and suggested a postponement. "No! Play or forfeit!" said Lord Frederick. "I won't forfeit. Lambert shall play you both, and if he wins have the money," was Osbaldeston's reply. Lord Frederick argued that such a match was nonsense, but Osbaldeston held his ground, and said, "If you don't play we shall claim the stakes." In the result Lambert made 56 in the first innings and 24 in the second—total 80. He dismissed Lord Frederick and Howard for 24 and 44—total 66—and so won by 14 runs. Lambert, however, showed great guile. Lord Frederick had an irascible temperament, and, wides not counting, Lambert bowled them to him till he lost his temper, and then bowled him with a straight one. Lord Frederick was not too magnanimous, and took a revenge that does not redound to his credit. In a moment of pique Osbaldeston removed his name from the list of members at Lord's. Later in life he came to live at 2 Grove Road, St John's Wood, and sought re-election. Lord Frederick prevented his readmission as a member by his determined opposition, though both Budd and Ward pleaded for his reinstatement.

In the first recorded match on the present Lord's ground on June 22, 1814—M.C.C. *v.* Hertfordshire—Osbaldeston, Lord Frederick, E. H. Budd, and W. Ward all took part—the four most celebrated amateurs of the day.

The Squire died at 2 Grove Road on August 1, 1866, in his eightieth year.

Other contemporaries of Lord Frederick Beauclerk and the Squire were three famous professionals—Tom Walker, William

Beldham, and, as we have seen, William Lambert. The first two were members of the Hambledon Club, and have been immortalized by John Nyren. Walker was a bony, muscular rustic, leisurely in his movements, with a dogged defence. He once played 170 balls from David Harris for one run, and was nicknamed "Old Everlasting." He used to exasperate Lord Frederick, who, dashing the ball on the ground, would hurl epithets at him down the pitch. Walker made the first century on Dorset Square—107 for the M.C.C. *v.* Middlesex in 1792—and four other centuries on the first Lord's ground. When playing for Hambledon he was the first bowler to raise the arm above the elbow, but the method was at once prohibited as "foul play."

Beldham's batting has been described in glowing and idyllic language by Nyren, who speaks of his majestic attitude at the wicket, his fine hitting, and his splendid cutting, which he likens to "the speed of thought." He made 144 on Dorset Square in 1792, in the same match in which Walker obtained the first century on the ground, and, for Surrey, two other centuries on the first Lord's. He only just missed the credit of the first century at Dorset Square, scoring for Hambledon in one of their last matches 94 against a Thirteen of England, in 1789. He was nicknamed "Silver Billy,"[1] and died at the great age of ninety-eight. The Rev. James Pycroft visited him in 1837, Beldham being then seventy-one, and his conversation with this great veteran is given at length in Pycroft's historic book *The Cricket Field.*[2] On the wall in the cottage hung, black with age, Beldham's most cherished possession, his trusty bat.

Lambert was a fine batsman. In his position at the wicket he stood with his legs rather far apart—the "Harrow stradle," as it was called—and he was of the forward school, a powerful hitter, with a long swing of the bat. His skill with the bat and his effective bowling and fielding made him one of the great all-round players of his day. His hands were huge, and the Squire said of him that he was "the most wonderful man that ever existed at catching a ball." He made two centuries on the first Lord's ground against Lord Frederick's side, but his greatest feat was on the present ground, when playing for Sussex against Epsom in 1817: he was the first batsman in cricket history to score a hundred in each innings—107, not out, and 157. This remained a record for seventy-six years, until equalled by A. E. Stoddart, with 195, not

[1] A reference to the colour of his hair. [2] St James's Press, 1922.

out, and 124 for Middlesex against Nottinghamshire. But 1817, the year of Lambert's feat, also saw his eclipse, for he was "warned off the Turf" at Lord's on the charge of having "sold the match" England *v.* Nottinghamshire by not playing his best. It may be the charge was false. A cricketer's skill is not always at one level of excellence: he has his off-days, and even weeks when out of form. Should these coincide with an important match, on which there was heavy wagering, the atmosphere created by disappointment and anger might well preclude an accurate judgment on a particular player's failure. In the case of so fine a cricketer one prefers to think that the decision was based on surmise and supposition rather than on indisputable evidence. In the racing world charges are sometimes made against jockeys, and on inquiry as often disproved. The incident, however, proves the evils then caused by betting on cricket.

The year before (1816) Lambert dedicated a book on cricket to the M.C.C., "appearing with great diffidence before them in the novel character of an author."

CHAPTER II

The Development of the Ground

First Pavilion—Fire in 1825—New Pavilion—"Jubilee" Match—The Ground in the Forties—Eton, Winchester, and Harrow—Purchase of the Freehold—The "Nursery"—Threat to the Ground—Present Pavilion—Mound Stand—New Grand Stand—"Father Time"—Car Park

LORD's a hundred and thirty years ago had a very rural appearance. There were, as already mentioned, two ponds on it, and "Steevie" Slatter, an employee on the ground for forty years, taught himself to swim in one of them! In the very early days of the present Lord's stabling was provided for those who had ridden or driven in from a distance.

A wooden pavilion was built in 1814, and later enlarged and improved by William Ward; but unfortunately, on the night of July 28, 1825, a few hours after the Winchester *v.* Harrow match, it was destroyed by fire, and thus perished all the Club's original possessions, records, score-books, and trophies.

A new pavilion was built during the ensuing winter, and members used it for the first time at the Anniversary Dinner on May 11, 1826. This building was enlarged in 1865, and in 1889 the first stone of the present pavilion was laid. Benjamin Aislabie laid the foundation-stone of the tennis court on October 15, 1838. The tennis prizes were established in 1867, and the court was pulled down in 1898 to make way for the Mound Stand. The present tennis and rackets courts, behind the pavilion, were then built. The rackets court dates from 1844.

The year 1837—historical as the year of accession of Queen Victoria—also saw the Jubilee of the Club, to celebrate which a Grand Match was played between North and South. The North team included Box, of Sussex—"in his day probably the best wicket-keeper that has yet appeared," says Caffyn, in his *Seventy-one Not Out*[1]—and Cobbett, of Surrey, a good all-rounder.

Here is the score of what was called the "Jubilee" Match:

[1] Blackwood, 1899.

NORTH *v.* SOUTH

Played at Lord's, July 10 *and* 11, 1837

Result: The South won by five wickets

THE NORTH, *with* BOX *and* COBBETT

First Innings		*Second Innings*	
W. Garrat, run out	5	b. Lillywhite	25
H. Hall, b. Lillywhite	14	b. Lillywhite	0
T. Barker, c. Dorrington, b. Millyard	1	st. Wenman, b. Lillywhite	0
G. Jarvis, c. Dorrington, b. Lillywhite	17	c. Wenman, b. Lillywhite	0
J. Cobbett, b. Lillywhite	0	b. Lillywhite	15
E. Vincent, b. Lillywhite	7	b. Lillywhite	0
T. Marsden, st. Wenman, b. Millyard	5	c. Lillywhite, b. Adams	1
J. Dearman, b. Millyard	8	not out	7
T. Box, c. Adams, b. Lillywhite	4	ht. wkt., b. Lillywhite	0
S. Redgate, c. Pilch, b. Lillywhite	2	c. Pilch, b. Adams	12
G. Rothera, not out	0	b. Lillywhite	0
Bye	1	Byes	5
Total	64	Total	65

THE SOUTH

T. Beagley, b. Redgate	5		
J. Broadbridge, st. Box, b. Redgate	0	c. Redgate, b. Cobbett	8
W. Ward, c. Box, b. Redgate	0	not out	0
E. G. Wenman, b. Cobbett	4	not out	7
F. Pilch, c. Box, b. Redgate	13		
J. Taylor, b. Cobbett	14		
G. Millyard, b. Redgate	5	b. Redgate	23
T. Adams, b. Cobbett	0	b. Redgate	1
W. Clifford, not out	6	b. Redgate	26
W. Dorrington, b. Redgate	0	b. Cobbett	0
W. Lillywhite, b. Cobbett	0		
Byes 12, wide 1	13	Byes 4, wide 1	5
Total	60	Total (5 wkts.)	70

By 1838 the pavilion had been lighted by gas, and the Tavern, which had been erected by Lord when he opened the new ground in 1814, had an assembly-room built over it, while a billiard-room had also been provided. At the west end of the ground a bowling-green had been laid down.

Here is a description of the ground as it appeared in 1841. It had a

> cottage-like pavilion with a few shrubs in front of it. Sandwiches and beer were the only refreshments except an ordinary at a tavern which gentlemen never went to. There was a miniature hill ana valley between the farthest corner of the pavilion and the lower wicket, and Lord's was more like a field pure and simple; but the

rigour of the game was insisted on, and that was the ground to test a man's batting ability.

In 1840 the first match between the M.C.C. and Rugby was played at Lord's. The next year the scene was transferred to Rugby—the famous Tom Brown match—but from time to time the match was on the Lord's programme. Since 1888, however, the fixture has always been at Rugby.

At the Winchester *v.* Harrow match in 1841

> there might have been a thousand present in the afternoon; in the morning there was no one there hardly, except the Harrow boys, who then numbered only about 80 in the school, a few members of the M.C.C. and old public school men, a few Winchester fellows who lived near London, and a most critical knot of professionals under the trees in front of the tavern, and a drunken Harrow vendor of fish who called himself "Lord Warner of Harrer,"[1] who came drunk and kept drunk and offered to fight anyone who said a word against his boys.

Eton also produced their 'cad,' one "Picky" Powell, who used to irritate Warner by saying, "All the good I sees in 'Arrow is that you can see Eton from it if ye go up into the Churchyard."[2] The result: a prearranged scrap, after which the hat went round!

As far back as 1825 Eton, Winchester, and Harrow used to meet at Lord's, and continued to do so until 1854. But in the autumn of that year the headmaster of Winchester refused his consent to the fixture, and this caused great disappointment, especially annoying Mr F. Gale, who wrote, "It is a remembrance too sad for tears. Dr Moberly, the Headmaster, afterwards Bishop of Salisbury, was the chief conspirator with the Provost of Eton in stopping these matches." Gale is said to have written several articles on the matter, the earliest, according to *Lord's and the M.C.C.*, by Lord Harris and F. S. Ashley-Cooper,[3] being a pamphlet privately circulated entitled

IN MEMORIAM
GLORIOSAM LUDORUM
ETONIENSIUM HARROVIENSIUM
WYKEHAMICORUMQUE
NUPER INTERMISSORUM ANNO 1854

[1] I can claim no kinship to this bibulous, if patriotic, individual!
[2] A. G. Coleridge, *Eton in the Forties* (Bentley, 1896). [3] Jenkins, 1920.

So far as Winchester was concerned, the matches were stopped because of complaints made by some of the parents of the temptations their sons incurred in London. Even the Eton *v.* Harrow match was in abeyance in 1857, and when in 1858 it was announced that Eton and Harrow would play again the older Wykehamists in London made another attempt to revive Winchester *v.* Harrow at Lord's,[1] but nothing came of it.

At the end of the forties and early in the fifties there were Galloway Pony Races round the ground after the cricket season was over. The starting-point was near the Tavern, and the finish about twenty yards south of the pavilion.

The roughness of the Lord's wicket in the early days was notorious. For many years the grass was 'kept down' by bringing sheep on to the ground a day or two before a match was due to begin. A small roller was used in the preparation of the wicket, but it was a long time before a mowing-machine appeared, and its use was strongly objected to by the Hon. R. Grimston.[2] In September 1864 the M.C.C. engaged their first groundsman, David Jordan, at a salary of 25*s.* a week. Before that a few odd men on the ground prepared (!) the wickets.

The Club celebrated their purchase of the freehold by beginning the building of the Grand Stand that winter. It was later added to from time to time, and finally pulled down in 1929–30 to make way for the present building. In the winter of 1867–68 the present Hotel replaced the old Tavern.

A serious crisis arose in 1860, when the Eyre Estate sold the freehold of Lord's at public auction. Dark and others urged the Club to bid, but, with a strange lack of vision, they declined to do so, and the ground was bought by Mr Isaac Moses for £7000. When eventually the ground became the property of the Club on August 22, 1866, a sum of £18,333 6*s.* 8*d.* had to be paid to Moses for the freehold. This large sum was most generously advanced by an old Harrovian, Mr William Nicholson, to whom, therefore, the Club owes a very great debt. He was a good enough cricketer to play for the Gentlemen as a batsman and wicket-keeper from 1846 to 1858, and was President of the Club in 1879. Mr Nicholson was born on September 2, 1824, and died on July 25, 1909. At one time he was M.P. for Petersfield, in Hampshire.

[1] The Captain of the Winchester Eleven is still called "Captain of Lord's," and the members of the Eleven "Lord's men."

[2] Though "averse to change of all kinds," Grimston, a great sportsman, was firmly opposed to every form of gambling. A barrister, he was President of the Club in 1883.

In 1872 the clock, which is now placed in what is known as the South Clock Tower, was presented to the Club by Lord Ebury, and erected in the centre of the side-lights of the old tennis court. In 1881 the present luncheon-rooms on the west side of the Hotel were added to the amenities of the ground. Hitherto the players had lunched in the pavilion.

A considerable addition was made to the ground in 1887 by the purchase, for £18,500, of the 3½ acres of Henderson's Nursery (or the "Pine Apples," the best pineapples in England being grown there; it was also famous for its tulips), which stood in what is now the northern portion of the practice ground. Hence the 'Nursery' end, as opposed to the 'Pavilion' end.

Up to that time the practice nets had been pitched on the outskirts of the match ground. Four years later the M.C.C. acquired the Clergy Female Orphan School, which stood at the corner of the St John's Wood and Wellington Roads, from the then Manchester and Sheffield Railway, in exchange for leave to tunnel under the practice ground. To-day the L.N.E.R. own a strip of ground forty yards wide where the arbours are situated, for which the M.C.C. pay an annual rent of £200. The 99-year lease dates from May 1897.

In 1888 the Great Central promoted a Bill in Parliament to acquire Lord's in order to run their line through it. This would, of course, have meant the end of Lord's, and cricketers—and not only cricketers—were immediately up in arms, with the result that that part of the Bill was withdrawn.

There was a famous cartoon in *Punch* in which W.G. on a charger, with pads on and bat in hand, advanced at the head of a 'battalion' of cricketers to drive off the 'enemy,' who was depicted by a railway engine puffing furiously.

On September 17, 1889, Sir Spencer Ponsonby-Fane laid the foundation-stone of the present pavilion, which was ready in time for the General Meeting on May 17, 1890, the architect being F. T. Verity. The cost, including furniture and extras, was £21,000. There have been several internal improvements since then, but to all intents and purposes the pavilion is as it was when first built, the only appreciable alteration being the accommodation added in 1906, when provision was made for the Press and players at the north end of the building.

The Mound Stand, which replaced the old tennis and rackets courts, was ready for use in 1899.

After the First German War the M.C.C. spent considerable sums, the most notable improvements being the new Grand Stand, which was ready for the Australians' visit of 1930, and the cantilever stands on the east side of the ground. In 1934 an additional stand for members and their friends was built between the south Clock Tower and the pavilion—of useful capacity, but devoid of architectural merit. The Grand Stand balcony affords a magnificent view of the game, but the structural arrangements behind it would seem to demand attention, being badly designed, with a maze of staircases and with some seats affording less than a full view of the cricket. It cost £46,000, including the balcony.[1] Never in the history of cricket has so large a stand held so few people.

For many years the M.C.C. have owned property adjoining the ground. At one time it consisted of two leasehold houses in Grove End Road, two freeholds and one leasehold in Elm Tree Road, and a leasehold in Cavendish Road West. Now the M.C.C. own as freehold all the houses abutting on the ground from the south corner of Grove End Road to No. 22 Elm Tree Road, the Secretary's official residence. Flats for some of the Club staff have been erected within recent years on the north side of the practice ground, and in 1937 a car park, which was much needed, was made on a part of the practice ground—a great boon both to the members and the public.

With the great increase in the interest of cricket, it is clear that further accommodation for the public will have to be undertaken so soon as labour and materials are available and Government permission is obtained. On no fewer than four occasions in 1945 the gates were shut before luncheon. Thousands had to be refused admission, and this is detrimental to the interests of the game and of the Club: it damps enthusiasm. The problem is not an easy one, for there is little room for expansion. Block *A* could be heightened and widened. It has been in existence for more than seventy years, and is unsuited to modern requirements. Again, the Mound Stand might be joined up to the side of the Hotel, and a few hundred seats might also be obtained by filling

[1] "Father Time" was a surprise on the part of Sir Herbert Baker, the architect. No one on the Committee knew that he was to be placed on the top of the Grand Stand. During one of the early raids, in November 1940, he was 'yorked' by a cable of the balloon barrage, and slid gently down, practically undamaged, on to the balcony seats. He spent the rest of the War in the Committee Room, but is now back on his old perch, dominating the scene, a loved and venerated landmark.

up the space behind the screen at the Nursery end. But, whatever is done, the atmosphere of Lord's and its charm *must* be preserved. No one wishes to see huge, skyscraping stands, which would turn the ground into something approaching a cockpit, and to cut down the trees, which give to Lord's a beauty of its own, would be almost sacrilege. However, careful planning should in due course provide an addition of some 5000 to 6000 seats. At the present time Lord's, packed tight, can hold only about 32,000 spectators. We may eventually hope for, say, 37,000 to 38,000. Beyond that it is not possible, so far as one can see at present, to go.

CHAPTER III

Early Personalities

N. Felix—Alfred Mynn—Herbert Jenner-Fust—Fuller Pilch—William Lillywhite—Benjamin Aislabie—Arthur Haygarth—Sir Spencer Ponsonby-Fane—Harvey Fellows—Sir Edward Chandos Leigh

DURING the first quarter and middle half of the nineteenth century many arresting figures pass across the cricket stage, N. Felix, Alfred Mynn, H. Jenner, Fuller Pilch, and William Lillywhite among them.

Felix, whose real name was Nicholas Wanostrocht, was of Flemish descent, and was born on October 5, 1804, at Camberwell, in a spot very convenient on account of the coaches going to and from London every hour. Here his great-uncle, Nicholas Wanostrocht, a distinguished man of letters, founded a school known as the Alfred House Academy, which Felix's father, Vincent, helped to run. On the death of his great-uncle his father took control, but died at the early age of forty-three, and young Nicholas, only twenty, found himself head of the school. He had learned cricket on a ground at Camberwell kept by Harry Hampton, and his love of it was thought "detrimental to the more strictly academic portion of the curriculum." However, in spite of his new and heavy duties, he continued to play, but under the pseudonym of Felix, "in deference, it was supposed, to the feelings of parents." Cricket was still identified with gambling.

Felix was a fine left-handed bat and fieldsman at point, and played in nearly all the Gentlemen *v.* Players matches for many years. Though he lacked his inches, he seems to have resembled F. E. Woolley in style, for his off-drives went flashing to the ring, and he was a beautiful late-cutter. Against fast bowling he was at his best. In 1842, when the Gentlemen won their first game on even terms since 1822, it was Felix's score of 88 in their second innings that won the match. He was very popular at Lord's, where on June 1–3, 1846, a match, attended by the Prince

Consort,[1] was played in his honour—Felix's Eleven against Fuller Pilch's Eleven—but his side lost. In the same month, before another large crowd at Lord's, he was beaten in a single-wicket match by Alfred Mynn, and also lost a return match at Bromley.

Felix moved his school to Blackheath in 1832, and so played for Kent, but retired from first-class cricket in 1853, when he was given a handsome testimonial from old friends and pupils. His was a happy school, where the rudiments of cricket were as important as any other tuition. Felix was a very versatile man—inventor, writer, musician, classical scholar, and accomplished artist. He invented the catapulta and also tubular index batting-gloves, the patent of which he sold to Robert Dark at Lord's, and was the author of the well-known *Felix on the Bat* and the *History and Use of the Catapulta.* He retired to Brighton, and spent his time painting portraits and animals, until on his second marriage he went to live at Blandford, in Dorset. In 1876 he died, and was buried at Wimborne Minster, not, as the *Dictionary of National Biography* states, at Montpelier Road, Brighton. His bat and ball were for long in the pavilion at the St Lawrence Ground, Canterbury, and when the pavilion was raided by the Suffragettes they were rescued, and are now in the Beaney Institute in Canterbury.

That he was a man of charming character we have the Rev. Pycroft's testimony. Writing of Mynn and Felix, he says, "Their amiability and good nature were perfect sunshine on the cricket field."

G. F. Watts made six sketches of Felix, which can be seen to-day in the M.C.C. collection. Recently Felix's All England Eleven Diary, with pencil and water-colour sketches, has come into possession of the M.C.C., the gift of Colonel N. C. King.

Until W. G. Grace appeared Alfred Mynn was the greatest personality in cricket. Standing six feet one inch and weighing some seventeen or eighteen stone, he took a short run to the crease, and, bringing his arm over with a nice, easy swing, kept a length on the leg stump, making the ball go with his arm. With his enormous hands, he was also a superb short slip.

[1] In *Lillywhite* we read: "He came on horseback, attended by some of the *élite* of the land; he was enthusiastically received, and was invited to see the Pavilion, and to inspect the implements of war, etc., etc., peculiar to the noble game. . . . He turned and left the spot, saw a little more of the passing game, thanked the noblemen and gentlemen of the M.C.C. for their attention, and remounted his horse, and every head was uncovered as he left the ground."

According to *Scores and Biographies*, Mynn once scored 283 in four consecutive innings—no small affair then—and when he bowled —at a terrific pace, pure round-arm—"it was considered one of the grandest sights at cricket to see him advance and deliver the ball." Denison, writing in 1846, after stating that Mynn was "signalized for possessing one of the most even dispositions that man has ever been gifted with," was even more complimentary. "If a stranger," he said, "were to ask the author to introduce him to a match wherein he could see the finest display of person and play, he would usher him to Lord's just at that moment when the Giant of Kent was in the act of walking up to the bowling-crease to deliver the ball."[1]

Mynn was born on January 19, 1807, and died on November 1, 1861. Having been a Kentish Volunteer, he was given a military funeral, and the whole county went into mourning. He is buried at Thurnham, near Maidstone, and when I lived in that part of the world I more than once took my cricketing friends on a pilgrimage to his grave. He played many a match at Bearsted, where he had a house looking on the green. He was called "the Lion of Kent," and the following verses by "Nicholas" Prowse are known to many:

With his tall and stately presence, with his nobly moulded form,
His broad hand was ever open, his brave heart was ever warm.
All were proud of him, all loved him. As the changing seasons pass,
As our Champion lies a-sleeping underneath the Kentish grass,
Proudly, sadly, we will name him—to forget him were a sin:
Lightly lie the turf upon thee, kind and manly Alfred Mynn.

Herbert Jenner, afterwards Jenner-Fust, was born on February 23, 1806, and died in 1904, in his ninety-ninth year. He played his first match at Lord's on August 1, 1822, for Eton *v.* Harrow. In his prime he was the finest amateur in the country. He could bat and bowl, but his forte was wicket-keeping. In *Old English Cricketers*, by Old Ebor (A. W. Pullin),[2] there is an interview with him in which he recalls: "I stood up (a little behind the wicket) without gloves or pads; in fact, pads were not heard of in my days, and the player would be laughed at who attempted to protect his shins. I used to keep wicket to Alfred Mynn, but I don't mind confessing that I was sometimes glad when the umpire called over." In 1833 Jenner-Fust was President of the M.C.C. In those far-away days, when there were very few members—200

[1] W. Denison, *Cricket: Sketches of the Players.* [2] Blackwood, 1900.

or 300 at most—the Presidents were often young and active players.

Jenner-Fust captained Cambridge in the first University Match at Lord's, on June 4, 1827, and played for Gentlemen *v.* Players from 1827 until 1836. In his interview with Old Ebor he said that he fielded "nips"[1] in the Eton *v.* Harrow match, in the position which we now call point.

Fuller Pilch was a great stylist, the Lionel Palairet of his day. He was probably the first forward player, and not only drove the half-volleys, but forced the good-length ball on the off side. He flourished between 1825 and 1849, and to a very great extent mastered the new school of round-arm bowling, "his bat going down the wicket like the pendulum of a clock." Pilch was tall, just over six feet, and powerfully built. "He was a remarkably quiet man, with no conversation, and never seemed happier than when behind a churchwarden pipe, all by himself," says William Caffyn, in *Seventy-one Not Out*. He played for the Players at Lord's between 1827 and 1849, and for Kent from 1836 to 1854. Kent were a great side in those days, and it was no idle boast when the poet wrote:

> And with five such mighty cricketers 'twas but natural to win
> As Felix, Wenman, Hillyer, Fuller Pilch and Alfred Mynn.

About 1820 round-arm bowling was introduced by John Willes, of Sutton Valence, and there was much argument over what was at that time called a revolutionary proposal. The reformers, however, eventually had their way, and the "new" bowling had become firmly established some time before 1835, when the M.C.C. gave it official sanction so as to admit of the arm being raised as high as the elbow, but not above the shoulder. The mantle of Willes fell on William Lillywhite, and in a lesser degree on John Broadbridge, "a fox-headed fellow," both of Sussex.

"The Nonpareil," as Lillywhite was called, was born in 1792. He was only five feet four inches in height, and "always played in a tall hat and broad cotton braces, with a Gladstone collar and deep black tie." He was noted for his accuracy of length—his pace was slow medium to slow—and invariably bowled round the wicket. Lillywhite's first match for the Players at Lord's was in 1820, and his last in 1849. He was fifty-two when he joined the ground staff at Lord's. He died in 1854, and the M.C.C. put

[1] There were also cover nips and long nips.

up a handsome memorial, with only his surname—no initials—at the top, followed by a long eulogy, over his grave in Highgate Cemetery. As he said of himself, "I bowl the best ball in England," which, if not exactly modest, was quite true.

Another personality, and none more charming, was Benjamin Aislabie. A member of the Homerton Club, which amalgamated with the M.C.C. in 1808, he was not an outstanding cricketer, but was devoted to the game, and for forty years was closely connected with the M.C.C., acting as Honorary Secretary from 1822 until his death, twenty years later. He weighed between nineteen and twenty stone at the end of his life, and was allowed to have a man to run for him. He delighted in playing against the schools, and is immortalized in the pages of *Tom Brown's Schooldays*, where we are told that "old Mr Aislebie stood by looking on in his white hat, leaning on a bat, in benevolent enjoyment," and after luncheon in the Fourth Form room "made the best speeches that ever were heard." It will be recalled that Tom bowled "slow cobs" to him when he came in to bat. Aislabie was a most delightful companion, and radiated charm and happiness. He was the author of several cricket verses and songs, and often sang at the Anniversary Dinners. There is a bust of him at Lord's, and two oil paintings, one of them in a pink coat on horseback, when he was a young and, apparently, slim man. He was described by John Mitford, himself a very good cricketer, as "the Father of Cricket." His name lives, and will always live, in the annals of the M.C.C., and should be added to those of Beauclerk, Budd, Osbaldeston, and Ward as the men to whom the initial success of the Club was mainly due. Aislabie is buried in a vault beneath the Parish Church of St Marylebone.

It is impossible to recall all those who made notable the early history of Lord's and the M.C.C., but we cannot pass by Arthur Haygarth. As a batsman he was decidedly unattractive, and in 1844 it is recorded that he *batted three hours for 16* for the M.C.C. *v.* Hampshire, but won the match at Lord's for the Gentlemen *v.* Players in 1846, when he was in *four hours for 26*, the Gentlemen winning by one wicket. He will always be remembered as the compiler of *Scores and Biographies*. He was elected a life member of the M.C.C. in 1864, and loved Lord's with such fervour that it was facetiously suggested that he slept under the pavilion! He died in 1903.

Sir Spencer Ponsonby-Fane, who was born on March 14, 1824,

and died on December 1, 1915, was elected a member in 1840, when only sixteen. Treasurer for many years, he was the most charming and courteous of men, with a wonderful manner, loved and respected by all. On several occasions he declined the Presidency of the Club. To him the M.C.C. largely owe the collection of paintings, engravings, and prints in the Long Room, and he was co-founder of I Zingari with his brother, Lord Bessborough, and J. Loraine Baldwin. He was a nephew by marriage of Lord Frederick Beauclerk.

In the Eton Elevens of 1841 and 1842 we find the name of Harvey Fellows, who developed into a tremendously fast bowler, and on the rough wickets of that period must have been very unpleasant to face. It was said that he "could make the ball hum like a top," and in the annual Gentlemen *v.* Players matches frightened out many a good batsman. When Hillyer was stumped off him by Redding in the Gentlemen *v.* Players match of 1849 this was thought a great feat.

Harvey Fellows, who died in 1907, and was buried in his I Z. tie, lived in the days of long-stops, and it so happened that on one occasion when he was bowling at Canterbury the long-stop was the Hon. Sir Edward Chandos Leigh, K.C., one of the greatest characters the M.C.C. has ever known.[1] As we have seen, Fellows was extremely fast, and, according to Sir Edward, was "showing off before the ladies on Ladies' Day" by endeavouring to bowl faster than ever. Poor Chandos Leigh had a bad time at long-stop, and when he returned home after the match, battered and bruised, his man said to him, "I beg your pardon, sir, but have you noticed your finger?" "Finger? Which finger?" "This one, sir. It's broken." "Good heavens, man! Quick! Get me an arnica bath!" And that was why in after-years Sir Edward often shook hands with half a hand.

The story goes that Chandos Leigh almost insisted on being given a place in the Oxford Eleven. That, possibly, is a little unkind, but the fact remains that he was by no means an outstanding cricketer, and we can, therefore, understand why H. D. G. Leveson-Gower, his nephew, replied, "Heaven forbid, Uncle Eddy!" when Chandos said to him during the Varsity Match of 1895, "Well played, Henwy [he had difficulty with his *r's*], my boy! You bat just as I did."

On one occasion at Scarborough the following conversation

[1] Sir Edward was President in 1887.

took place: "Tell me, Warner; do your people object to your being called 'Plum' as much as my sister Sophie objects to my nephew Henwy being called 'Shwimp'?" "As a matter of fact, I am never called 'Plum' at home—always Pelham." "Very good; I shall call you Pelham in future"—and he did.

During his long life—he died in May 1915, at the age of eighty-two—there can have been few better-known men at Headquarters than Sir Edward. He often wore a grey bowler hat, with an I Z. ribbon round it, tilted over his nose, and he had a superb swagger, which, I hasten to add, was such a pleasant swagger that no one could possibly be offended by it. He was altogether a most charming personality; but, such is fame, he had failed to impress himself on one of the attendants at Lord's, who demanded to see his ticket.

"Ticket!" said Sir Edward in a horror-struck voice. "Ticket! Don't you know me, fellow?"

"Ticket, please, sir. That's the rule, sir."

"Who is this fellow who does not know me?" he asked of quite a number of members who had by this time crowded round him. "My good fellow, I was Pwesident of the M.C.C., and Pwesident, moreover, in the Jubilee year."

Despite all protests, however, the attendant was obdurate, and in the end Chandos was forced to sign his name in the book.

He was very fond of the word 'capitally': "How capitally you batted, Henwy!"

I don't know who admired him more, his nephew or myself. He was indeed a delightful character, whose conversation was worth listening to, as he had touched life at many points.

CHAPTER IV

The Forties and Fifties

A. J. Lowth, Redgate, and Hillyer—Sir Frederick Bathurst—William Clarke—The All England Eleven—The United England Eleven—The United South of England—George Parr—Decline in Amateur Cricket—Gentlemen and Players—Some Great Professionals—V. E. Walker—Richard Daft—University Cricket

BEFORE giving some idea of the cricket at Lord's in the forties and fifties something must be said of A. J. Lowth, S. Redgate, and W. Hillyer.

A. J. Lowth, who played for the Gentlemen in 1836, was a Winchester man, whose reputation was so great that some M.C.C. members went down to have a look at him. Result: an invitation to play for the amateurs—eighteen of them on this occasion against eleven professionals. "He danced up to the wicket on his toes, and his bowling hand [his left] went through a full quarter-circle very quickly; he put a lot of spin on the ball and broke back very fast."[1] Lowth was a pocket Hercules, 5 feet 6 inches in height, and had a most beautiful natural round-arm left-handed delivery from the height of the shoulder. He was in the Oxford Elevens of 1838 and 1840–41, and played again for the Gentlemen in 1841, but, his sight failing him, he soon gave up the game. So far as I can discover, he and G. T. S. Stevens, who played at Lord's in 1919, are the only two cricketers who have represented the Gentlemen while still at school.

S. Redgate, of Nottinghamshire, was described by Pycroft as "the finest bowler within my memory." He had both pace and spin, and could hold the ball back in the air. He clean bowled the great Fuller Pilch for a pair of spectacles in the Gentlemen *v.* Players match at Lord's in 1835. This was Redgate's first appearance at Lord's, and he was playing as a given man for the Gentlemen. Four years later, at Town Malling, he sent down perhaps the most famous over in "medieval" history—as H. S.

[1] From J. A. Fort's Introduction to *Winchester College Cricket*, by E. B. Noel (Williams and Norgate, 1926).

Altham puts it.[1] The first ball shaved Pilch's wicket, the second bowled him, the third bowled Alfred Mynn, and the fourth Shearman. Unfortunately Redgate was a thirsty soul, and his career, which began so brilliantly, came to an end in 1846.

W. Hillyer, who was engaged at Lord's for several seasons, was a medium-paced right-handed bowler with a break from leg, who obtained many of his wickets by catches in the slips. "I used to find him terribly difficult, as his ball went off the pitch so quickly. He could make the ball get up, too, more than most bowlers of his time. He was a middle-sized, well-made man, who towards the latter part of his time was a martyr to rheumatism and gout in his feet."[2]

In 1841 the Hon. Frederick Ponsonby announced that, the Gentlemen *v.* Players match not being considered of sufficient interest to warrant the Committee of the M.C.C. offering it their support, he proposed to raise a subscription so that it might be played. The judgment he had formed with Charles Taylor proved correct, sufficient funds were forthcoming, and Dark, having in the following year most liberally taken on himself the whole expense, the Gentlemen having on that occasion broken the spell of years, this became an annual M.C.C. match.

In the forties the Gentlemen defeated the Players in 1842, 1843, 1846, 1848, and 1849, playing on even terms. Previously they had had only one victory on level terms—in 1822.

Alfred Mynn's skill was now supported by Sir Frederick Bathurst's bowling, Felix's batting, and the all-round play of C. G. Taylor. In 1843 the latter made 89, and was then given out "hat knocked on wicket," the highest score for the Gentlemen since William Ward's 102 in 1825—the first century for the Gentlemen. In 1846, when the Gentlemen won by one wicket, Taylor's 44 gave the main support to Haygarth's historic innings of 26, which, as we have seen, continued for four hours. When the last man, Mynn, came in but 2 runs were required.[3]

Sir Frederick Bathurst was one of the mainstays of the Gentlemen's bowling for some twenty years—1833–54—during which he obtained 73 wickets. He was one of the great fast bowlers of

[1] See *A History of Cricket* (Allen and Unwin, 1926).

[2] William Caffyn, *Seventy-one Not Out.*

[3] A scoring, or telegraph, board was first used at Lord's in 1846, showing runs, wickets down, and the score of the last man out. On June 26, 1848, a printing tent was in working order, and the public, for the first time, could buy a "card of the match."

his day, a useful cross-bat hitter, who made an occasional huge drive, and a splendid fieldsman.

A fine figure of a man, standing six feet, he was powerfully built and a great personality on the field. A Wykehamist, he was never in the Eleven, as he left young to join the Guards. In 1857 he was President of the M.C.C.

William Clarke (1798–1856) made his first appearance for the Players at Lord's in 1846, and of the M.C.C. he wrote:

> The Marylebone ranks first of all:
> It's they who do our laws control;
> And then I Zingari, those tramps with bat and ball,
> And the Eleven of All England composed of great and small.

He was the founder of the All England Eleven, sole manager of its fixtures and finances, and captain of a closely knit band of brothers. He was a great underhand bowler, bowling from the hip, and a superb judge of the game, but he was not selected for the Players until he was forty-seven years of age. The All England Eleven began playing in 1846, when there were few professionals, and these were hard put to it to earn a livelihood, owing to there being so few matches. Their matches later spread all over England, mostly against Eighteens, Twenties, and Twenty-two's, the railway helping their travels, though there was still a certain amount of coaching. Clarke paid his professionals between £4 and £6 a week, and later three amateurs—the great Mynn, Felix, and V. C. Smith, of Winchester and Oxford fame[1] —joined the team. Clarke maintained good discipline, and, says William Caffyn, "did more than anyone else to popularise our great national game." Many a young cricketer owed his subsequent prowess to the encouragement Clarke gave him. Felix was President of the All England Club until his last first-class match in 1853.

Clarke had the reputation, however, of being dictatorial, arbitrary, and close-fisted, and in 1852 John Wisden broke away from him and formed the United England Eleven.

When the Cricketers' Fund Friendly Society was founded in 1857 the two sides met at Lord's for the benefit of the fund, and this match was played there for ten years, at Whitsuntide.

In 1865 the Northern professionals declined to play with the

[1] V. C. Smith was five years in the Winchester Eleven, and was nearly twenty-two when he last played for his school. He was Captain for three years—a record—and for two years Captain of Oxford, in 1846–47.

Southern, which led to the formation of United South of England, which meant that the players of the All England and United England teams were all Northern professionals. In 1867, therefore, their annual match for the benefit of the Cricketers' Fund was played at Manchester.

The M.C.C. then passed the following resolution:

> Taking into consideration the conduct of certain of the professionals of England during the season of 1866, it is no longer desirable to extend the patronage of the Marylebone Club to the Cricketers' Fund exclusively; but a fund has now been formed which shall be called "The Marylebone Professional Fund," which shall have for its object the support of the professional players who during their career shall have conducted themselves to the entire satisfaction of the Committee of the M.C.C.

The first match on behalf of this new fund was played at Lord's on June 10 and 11, 1867, between England and Middlesex.

The United England Eleven disbanded in 1869, the All England Eleven after 1876, when it played three matches, and the United South Eleven in 1880. Lack of gate support and the rise of county cricket caused these sides to disappear.

On Clarke's death George Parr took over the management and captaincy of the All England Eleven. Both Clarke and Parr had played in Gentlemen *v.* Players at Lord's in the exciting match of 1846, their first appearance in this fixture.

George Parr played his first game at Lord's for the North *v.* the M.C.C. in 1845. He was then in his twentieth year. He was called "the Lion of the North," and captained the first touring side to leave England, to the United States and Canada in 1859, and also led the second side to Australia in 1864. His last match at Lord's was in 1870, when he scored a brilliant 41 for North *v.* South. In the same year he resigned the captaincy of the All England Eleven and played his last match for Nottinghamshire. He was the greatest professional batsman of his day, and excelled in hitting to leg. There is a tree at Trent Bridge—"Parr's Tree"—to this day, into which he hit many a ball. When he died a branch of this tree was laid on his grave. His father had been a gentleman farmer, and he retired to his home, whose acres his ancestors had farmed for over two hundred years. An attempt was made, without success, to establish a relationship between George and the famous Thomas Parr, who, at the reputed age of a hundred and fifty-two, was brought to London and presented to Charles I, but died through being over-fêted and -feasted. He was buried in Westminster Abbey, after living in ten reigns.

In George Parr's last game for the Players, in 1865, he scored 60. This was W.G.'s first game at Lord's for the Gentlemen—a remarkable link between two great players.

The fifties saw a marked decline in amateur cricket. The Gentlemen lost nine matches at Lord's, and the first three ever played at the Oval. They won the match at Lord's in 1853 by 60 runs, when Sir Frederick Bathurst and Mat Kempson bowled unchanged through both innings of the Players.[1]

In 1857 the Gentlemen ran the Players to a close finish, losing by only 13 runs. In this game R. Hankey played a great innings of 70, hitting the Players' bowling all over Lord's in the first innings, while Arthur Haygarth, going in first wicket, carried his bat for 53, batting for upward of four hours. R. T. Drake, with a score of 58, made a great effort in the second innings. The win in 1853 and the close finish in 1857 were the only games in the fifties in which the Gentlemen enjoyed any success, but Mynn and Felix had played in their last Gentlemen and Players match in 1852, and Bathurst in 1854, and there was no one to take their places. During the fifties Richard Daft, who afterwards played as a professional, and V. E. Walker made their début at Lord's for the Gentlemen, but the Players could point to a long list of new and famous cricketers—H. H. Stephenson, Julius Cæsar, William Caffyn, Edgar Willsher, John Jackson, Robert Carpenter, James Grundy, R. C. Tinley, Tom Lockyer, who replaced T. Box as wicket-keeper, and T. Nixon, who, if not an outstanding player, was the inventor of cane handles for bats and cork leg-guards. This cavalcade overwhelmed the Gentlemen, who did not win again at Lord's till 1865, after losing nineteen games in succession. The match of 1854 was preceded by an unfortunate dispute between Clarke and the M.C.C. Clarke declined to play or to permit Caffyn, Cæsar, and Parr to take part in the match, claiming control over them as manager of the All England Eleven. It is a pity that Clarke's great services to cricket were marred by an over-tenacity in asserting his rights, real or otherwise.

[1] In 1894 S. M. J. Woods and F. S. Jackson also bowled unchanged for the Gentlemen.

H. H. Stephenson was a fine all-rounder—batsman, fielder, wicket-keeper, and bowler—who, if he had his off-days, when in the mood bowled a devastating break-back, which with round-arm bowling was something of a novelty. Later he became coach at Uppingham, which under his rule turned out a succession of fine players. His influence at Uppingham was wide, and tradition has it that he could enter a classroom and say, "Mr ——, I want you in the nets," and no master liked to protest!

Caffyn uses the word 'brilliant' of Julius Cæsar's batting. About 5 feet 7 inches in height, Cæsar was very powerfully built. The on-drive was his best stroke, and he was quick on his feet. There is a match on record in which twelve Cæsars took the field. The family had long resided at Godalming. It is an interesting name, to put it mildly, over which genealogists might ponder; "but it was a real and not a feigned name, as many supposed," says *Scores and Biographies*.

John Jackson, of Nottinghamshire, was undoubtedly a great fast bowler. He stood 6 feet 1 inch and weighed fifteen stone, but was exceptionally active. His pace was "very fearful," and on the fiery wickets of his time (1855–66) he was a terror, causing many a good batsman to retire to square leg. His action, "true round-arm," was smooth and easy, and he made the ball go with his arm. Now, on any wicket a bowler who can make the ball run away from the bat must command respect, and Jackson was also accurate in both length and direction. His run to the crease was not more than three or four yards, and he "bowled like a machine, always well within his strength."[1] He never obtained ten wickets in an innings in first-class cricket, but once, at Nottingham, for North *v.* South, got nine, and lamed John Wisden so that he could not bat, which "was as good as ten, eh?" as he remarked in an interview with "Old Ebor." Richard Daft has recorded that every time he got a wicket he used to blow his nose: hence his nickname "Old Foghorn." This would look as if he suffered from a perpetual cold, and his nose was certainly "awry," due to a blow on it at the nets at Cambridge. He was also called "the Demon," as Spofforth was to be in later years. His first appearance for the Players at Lord's was in 1857, his last in 1864, and he was consistently successful. In 1859 he went to Canada and the United States with George Parr's team, and to Australia and America, also with Parr, in 1864. He died in great straits, for

[1] H. S. Altham, *A History of Cricket*.

he was practically penniless, except for an allowance of 6*s*. a week from the Cricketers' Fund Friendly Society. Thank heaven, we manage these things better to-day, the Cricketers' Fund Friendly Society and the Hornsby[1] Trust being in good funds and both sympathetic and generous in their disbursements.

Edgar Willsher was a fast left-handed bowler. He had great command of pitch, and could make the ball get up on almost any wicket. Before above-the-shoulder bowling was given official sanction in 1864 Willsher had often transgressed the law as it then stood, and his being no-balled six times in succession in the England *v.* Surrey match at the Oval in 1862 brought matters to a head, and cleared up a long-standing controversy to the benefit of the game. He was a delicate-looking man, and off the field "hardly looked like an athlete," says Caffyn. He was in the Players' Eleven between 1856 and 1875. In 1861 he and Jackson bowled unchanged in both innings, and in 1864 he and Tarrant performed the same feat. Wisden and Clarke had also bowled unchanged for the Players in 1850.

"John Wisden," says Caffyn,

> was the best fast bowler I ever saw for so small a man. His height was about 5 ft. 4 inches, and his weight under 10 stone. He was a remarkably good-tempered little fellow, with a most comical expression of face. He was a grand bowler, with, I think, the easiest delivery I ever saw, and great command of pitch. As a batsman he was first-rate, with a beautifully straight bat.

In *Scores and Biographies* he is described as "very fast and ripping."

Of William Caffyn Richard Daft, in his *Kings of Cricket*,[2] wrote, in 1893, "if Surrey ever possessed a finer player than William Caffyn I never saw him." He was a great cutter "from the wrist," a medium-paced round-arm bowler, with an easy delivery, and a fine fieldsman. A great favourite at the Oval, where he was called "the Surrey Pet," he went to Australia with Parr's team in 1863–64, and stayed there for seven years, where he did great work as a coach. His book *Seventy-one Not Out* is most

[1] J. H. J. Hornsby was educated at Fettes and Oxford, and played a good deal of cricket for the M.C.C., I Z., and the Butterflies, and on a few occasions for Middlesex. He was a slow-to-medium right-hand bowler, who could spin the ball, and a fair batsman. He was a member of Lord Hawke's teams to India, the United States, and Canada. He died on July 9, 1926, at the age of sixty-six, leaving some £30,000 for the benefit of professional cricketers who have fallen on hard times.

[2] Arrowsmith, 1893.

interesting, and gives a clear picture of the cricketers of his time both on and off the field.

Robert Carpenter, whose name is always linked with that of Tom Hayward, senior, though the latter was five years his junior, made his first appearance at Lord's for the Players *v.* the Gentlemen in 1859. He was essentially a back-player, but he was quick on his feet and had plenty of driving-power. He was better against slow than fast bowling, not that he was at all susceptible to pace, for in the All England Eleven *v.* the United England Eleven match at Lord's in 1858 he made a perfect 45, playing Jackson's terrific fast bowling particularly well.

James Grundy, of Nottinghamshire, was a steady bowler of quick-medium pace, but somewhat lacking in variety. "He could keep on dropping them on a cheese-plate."[1] R. C. Tinley, of Nottinghamshire, originally a fast bowler, developed into a lob bowler inferior to Clarke alone, say H. S. Altham and Caffyn. Tom Lockyer, of Surrey, was a great wicket-keeper, especially good on the leg side, who stood up even to Jackson, and a hard and powerful hitter. For twelve years he kept regularly for the Players.

Of the two amateurs already mentioned, V. E. Walker first appeared at Lord's in 1853, for Harrow *v.* Winchester, and played for the Gentlemen in 1856, when only nineteen years of age. He was a fine and powerful hitter, and one of the best of the slow underhand bowlers. He was not so accurate in his length as Clarke, "but his wonderful fielding to his own bowling on both sides of the wicket made him not much inferior.[2] He was also a splendid cover-point. He three times—in 1859, for England *v.* Surrey; in 1864, for the Gentlemen of Middlesex *v.* the Gentlemen of Kent; and in 1865, for Middlesex *v.* Lancashire—took all ten wickets in an innings. One of the founders of Middlesex cricket, President of the M.C.C. in 1891, and a brother of J., I. D., and R. D. Walker, he belonged to a family which may be ranked in cricketing distinction with the Graces, the Studds, the Steels, the Lytteltons, and the Fosters. A visit to his house, Arnos Grove, Southgate, in the year 1902, when A. J. Webbe was one of the party, stands out in my memory. He was the perfect host.

Richard Daft played his first match at Lord's for North *v.* South in 1858, and for the Gentlemen in the same year. In 1859 he

[1] William Caffyn, *Seventy-one Not Out.* [2] *Scores and Biographies*, vol. iv.

turned professional, but was an amateur again before retiring. To his contemporaries "he stood alone as a model of grace and commanding execution."[1] He had what Neville Cardus would call "the grand manner," for he was graceful in every movement he made and every attitude he assumed. Nimble on his feet, he had a perfectly proportioned figure, and he would frequently be out of his ground to "give a bowler the rush." Successful on every kind of wicket—bumpy, slow, or sticky—he was also a magnificent deep fieldsman. After ten years' absence from first-class cricket he appeared for Nottinghamshire *v.* Surrey at the Oval in 1891, at the age of fifty-six, and had a wonderful reception from the crowd. On a sticky wicket against Lohmann and Lockwood "he showed much of his old grace of style" in two small innings.

Writing of this period, W. G. Grace, in his book *Cricket*[2] says:

> But, undoubtedly, the contests of the year were the All-England XI *v.* The United XI, and the North *v.* South, at Lord's, especially the former. When the two famous Elevens met reputation was at stake, and both strove to put their best teams in the field. . . . It was the match of the year . . . and crowds testified to it by turning out in thousands. It was not always so in the North *v.* South matches.

The first University Match was played at Lord's in 1827, but the venue varied between Oxford and Lord's until 1851, since when it has always taken place at Headquarters, except during the First German War, when the two sides did not meet, and in 1940, during the Second German War. These war-time fixtures, however, were not official, and do not count in the general record. During the forties and fifties the best Oxford cricketers on university form appear to have been A. J. Lowth, W. Marcom, H. E. Moberley, V. C. Smith, C. E. Coleridge, R. Hankey, C. D. Marsham, and W. F. Traill.

Marcom "was one of the fastest, if not the fastest, bowler that has ever appeared. The pace was always terrific, always requiring two long-stops; nor was a wicket-keeper of the slightest use. The delivery was nearly underhand, and when at Oxford he broke a man's leg."[3]

But in these early years cricket at both universities was a casual

[1] H. S. Altham, *A History of Cricket.* [2] Arrowsmith, 1890.
[3] *Scores and Biographies,* vol. iii.

affair, and there were few good matches. Certainly some of the university authorities did not recognize the importance of the occasion. Nor did the players, for in 1841 Lord Ward failed to be present when his turn came to bat, and Oxford lost by 8 runs! The public, too, did not patronize the match, and the newspapers gave but little space to a description of the play.

CHAPTER V

The Sixties

Lean Days at Lord's—R. A. Fitzgerald—C. E. Green—W. G.—Eton and Harrow—A "Cricket Parliament"?—Boundaries—Varsity Cricketers—Rough Wickets—R. A. H. Mitchell—C. J. Ottaway—Tom Hayward Senior—Alfred Lubbock—The Summer of 1868—The Aboriginals—A Great Innings—C. K. Francis

EDWARD RUTTER,[1] who played for Rugby and Middlesex, and later was Secretary of the Free Foresters, wrote in his *Cricket Memories*:[2]

> The reader will be surprised to hear that the matches there [at Lord's] in the fifties and sixties were mostly of no interest except to the players themselves. Scratch teams of amateurs against the Club with bowlers and suchlike comprised most of them. . . . Lord's was a heavy clay and badly drained, and the outfielding was always rough and treacherous. There were no boundaries—except the pavilion—no stands or fixed seats of any kind, nothing but the small old pavilion and a line of loose benches running part of the way round the ground, and these were but little occupied save at the more important matches.
>
> The ground in most matches presented rather a dreary scene. To anyone but the Committee, as it was then constituted, it was becoming evident that the Club was in danger of losing its influence, and the man who best realized the situation was our admirable Secretary Bob Fitzgerald. He was full of energy, and enthusiastically keen on making Lord's the great centre of cricket, as it should be. But the Committee were deplorably lethargic and out of date, and the zealous Secretary could obtain little support. One of his schemes for advancing this desirable end was to attempt to induce Middlesex to play their matches at Lord's. For he could easily perceive that unless he could find something to attract the crowd to the ground it would soon become deserted. . . . But Middlesex in the meantime had found a suitable ground at Prince's, and Fitzgerald's offer was politely declined.

As we shall see later, the invitation by the M.C.C. was renewed,

[1] A member of the M.C.C. Committee from 1873 to 1876, from 1888 to 1891, from 1894 to 1897, and from 1902 to 1903.

[2] Williams and Norgate, 1925.

and ever since 1877 Middlesex have played all their home matches at Lord's. Fitzgerald was sagacious, cheery, and amusing, and above all an excellent Secretary, but his health failed, and Henry Perkins filled the vacancy.

> Fitzgerald, thoroughly realizing how much out of date the M.C.C. Committee had become, was extremely anxious to liven it up by the introduction of some young fresh blood. With this in view, he had C. E. Green[1] and myself nominated, and we proceeded to sit in conclave with our elderly and reactionary fellow-members. At first we were distinctly ignored, and Charlie Green was so utterly disgusted with the supercilious manner in which he was received that he declared he would never serve on the Committee again. Nor did he, but stuck to his resolve. Oddly enough the next official appearance he made in the Club was many years later (1905), when he was elected President.

Green himself was not altogether free of reactionary tendencies, for when I suggested early in the present century a wider screen at Lord's he remarked, "I never knew you were such a Radical, Warner!" However, the screen was widened.

Lord Harris, in *A Few Short Runs*,[2] suggests that some of the customs at Lord's in the sixties would not be allowed to-day—such as a pot-boy arrayed in a white jacket and apron, who used to go round the ground calling, "Give your order, gents!" and supplying thirsty ones with pots of beer. "I have even seen a fieldsman in a big match have a drink," says Harris.

One must omit from Edward Rutter's remarks the Gentlemen *v.* Players, Oxford *v.* Cambridge, and Eton *v.* Harrow matches—but until W. G. made his first appearance for the Gentlemen at Lord's in 1865 the Players invariably overwhelmed the Gentlemen. Grace's genius, however, entirely reversed the position, the Players gaining only one victory—in 1866—until 1874. Oxford and Cambridge and Eton and Harrow attracted the usual fashionable crowds, and in 1863 "carriages were five or six deep all round the ground, and besides that a ring of some 8000 spectators." This season the charge made by J. H. Dark of 7*s.* 6*d.* *to each boy playing in this match* (!) was discontinued, and next year Lord's became the property of the members, on Dark's retirement. In that year £570, an unprecedented amount at the time, was

[1] C. E. Green was the life and soul of Essex cricket, and a great Master of Hounds. He was Master of the Essex for nearly thirty years.

[2] Murray, 1921.

taken at the gate on the first day of Eton *v.* Harrow, and on the following Monday the state of the ground was described in these words: "The grass had been so ridden over and trodden down that it had nearly assumed the appearance and character of a highway road."

"In the early part of 1864," says W. G., in his *Cricket*,

> an agitation was set going in one of the leading sporting newspapers which had for its aim the formation of a "cricket Parliament" to depose the Marylebone Club from its position as the authority on the game; but it met with little countenance, and the old club, which had now played on its present ground for fifty years, was allowed to carry on the work which it, and it alone, seemed to be able to do with firmness and impartiality.

It may be that in the sixties and seventies the M.C.C. Committee were slow to move and to take responsibility, and held somewhat limited views. They probably reacted too slowly to changing circumstances, and the programme, except for three or four matches, was unimaginative and inspired little interest, while the wickets were unnecessarily rough. But what may be described as a certain complacency and a lack of consciousness of the great position the public expected the Club to occupy gradually disappeared, and in any event a "cricket Parliament" would have been a poor substitute for an institution of long standing which had grown up, so to speak, with the game and was mindful of its traditions. Probably the threat of such a "Parliament" did no harm, for it prompted certain questioning, and we may be sure that Fitzgerald, the Secretary, was not slow to appreciate that in the best interests of the Club a close and exhaustive examination of the position was essential. A study of the cricket literature of the period shows clearly that there were murmurings which it would have been fatal to ignore, but by the eighties the Club's position was secure, and was to become even more so in the early years of the present century.

Boundaries were not introduced before 1866, and Lord Harris[1] gives his version of an incident which led to so great a disturbance that "the Princess of Wales promptly drove away." A spectator sitting on the grass stopped a ball driven by E. Lubbock, the Eton Captain, and threw it to a Harrow fieldsman, who returned it to the wicket, and the batsman, J. W. Foley, who had stopped

[1] *A Few Short Runs.*

running on the assumption that the umpire would signal a boundary, was given run out by both umpires—T. Hearne and Alfred Shaw. Lubbock objected, and so great was the uproar and confusion that the game was stopped and stumps eventually drawn for the day. Next morning an offer that Foley should resume his innings was declined by the Eton Captain.

In University cricket of the sixties honours were divided, Oxford winning in 1863–65 (R. A. H. Mitchell's three years of captaincy) and 1866, and Cambridge in 1860–62 and 1867. Great players pass across the stage—R. Lang, the Hon. C. G. Lyttelton, J. Makinson, H. M. Plowden, and C. E. Green, of Cambridge, and R. D. Walker, R. A. H. Mitchell, the Hon. F. G. Pelham, C. G. Lane, C. D. Marsham, and R. Hankey, of Oxford. R. Lang was very fast and accurate; Alfred Lyttelton thought that C.G. was the best of that famous family; Joseph Makinson was a fine all-rounder; H. M. Plowden a medium-paced bowler; R. A. H. Mitchell a beautiful and powerful batsman; R. D. Walker an original player, who jumped about a good deal, causing George Pinder, the wicket-keeper, to inquire, "What's this Punch and Judy show?" to which Walker replied, "I am feeling very comfortable, thank you, Pinder." C. G. Lane was a great player of fast bowling, and was later an outstanding Surrey cricketer, of whom it was written:

> You may join with me in wishing that the Oval once again
> Shall resound with hearty plaudits to the praise of Mr Lane.

Richard Daft thought him one of the best amateur batsmen he ever saw. Lane rowed two years in the Oxford boat.

C. D. Marsham was one of the finest of amateur bowlers, medium pace round-arm, with an easy delivery and accuracy of length. Five years in the Oxford Eleven, he took forty wickets in the Varsity Matches. R. Hankey, who was a powerful hitter, and is described in *Scores and Biographies* as "one of the very best batsmen who has ever yet appeared," had a splendidly free style. His innings of 70 in the Gentlemen *v.* Players match of 1857 was talked of for years, the professionals saying "they had never seen anything like it." The bowlers opposed to him were Wisden, Willsher, Jackson, and Stephenson: he hit them to every corner of the ground. C. E. Green was a fine hitter. His innings of 51 for M.C.C. *v.* Yorkshire at Lord's in 1870 was perhaps the best he ever played. W. G. made 66, and both were badly battered about the body by Freeman and Emmett on a very rough wicket.

As we have seen, W. G. 'carried' the Gentlemen after 1865, while the foremost professional bowlers were Jackson, Tarrant, Grundy, Willsher, G. Wootton, and Alfred Shaw, who prior to this had suggested that the creases, instead of being cut in the turf, should be whitewashed—a much-needed innovation which, apart from helping the umpires, prevented damage to the turf—a necessity at a time when wickets were prepared in a rather haphazard manner. In 1864 the M.C.C. had given the bowler full liberty of action to bowl from what height he chose, though for a few years previously Willsher and one or two others had transgressed the law which forbade the bowler to raise the arm above the shoulder.

Of the professional bowlers Caffyn thought Willsher "*the* most difficult of all bowlers I had ever met."

George Tarrant was very fast right-hand, with a tear-away action, and took seven wickets for 17 runs in the Gentlemen's first innings in 1862, and in 1864 eleven wickets for 49 runs. He and Jackson must have been almost terrifying on the rough Lord's wicket of those days.

It should never be forgotten that our forefathers had to play on very bad wickets, and especially was this so at Lord's, where Surrey refused to play in 1859, as did Sussex four years later. On other grounds, such as the Oval, Fenner's, Brighton, and Trent Bridge, the wickets were good enough, but at the headquarters of the game there would appear to have been a sort of "what was good enough for my father is good enough for me" attitude. In judging, therefore, the performances of the batsmen of previous generations one must always bear in mind the conditions of the pitch and the array of fast bowlers like Jackson, Tarrant, and others. During Fitzgerald's Secretaryship, however, the wickets gradually began to improve, but they could hardly be described as perfect, or anything like perfect, until we come to the eighties. Even then the heavy clay and the inadequately drained ground produced sticky wickets of the type that bowlers dream of.

In a review of the season of 1865 Fred Lillywhite asked whether enormous totals are calculated to improve the game, and suggested that the height of the stumps should be increased by an inch or two to 28 or 29 inches. It was some seventy years before his proposal was carried into effect, when the stumps were both widened and heightened by an inch.

On July 5, 1865, immediately following their match against Marlborough, Rugby played Charterhouse at Lord's, the only occasion, so far as I can discover, on which the two schools have met at cricket.

There were many other great cricketers of this period. R. A. H. Mitchell played for Eton from 1858 to 1861, being Captain in his last year; for Oxford from 1862 to 1865 (Captain the last three years); and for Gentlemen *v.* Players at Lord's in 1862, 1863, 1865, and 1868. In 1861, while still at Eton, he was asked to play for the Gentlemen, but was unable to do so. That he was a great and polished batsman his contemporaries agree, and until W. G. arrived he was generally considered the best amateur batsman in England—W. G. himself had a high opinion of him—but owing to his work as a master at Eton, where he was the ruling spirit of cricket for over thirty years, his career in first-class cricket was limited. He is the only Oxonian or Cantab who has captained the University Eleven for three years—a tribute not only to his skill, but to his character and personality. The free forward strokes, the drive both on and off, and the late cut were the foundations of what used to be called the typical Eton style, but Mitchell did not, perhaps, always realize that batting on a fast, true wicket and on a sticky one are two different things. He was the arch-apostle of orthodoxy, and when on one occasion B. J. T. Bosanquet, when practising in the nets, hit a good-length off-break which pitched outside the off stump hard and wide to the on, he remarked, "Boy, I won't have you in the Eleven if you play like that." But that during his reign Eton produced such cricketers as C. T. Studd, Alfred Lyttelton, G. H. Longman, and W. F. Forbes, as well as several other lesser lights, is a tribute to his coaching.

Mitchell himself thought that C. J. Ottaway was the most reliable boy batsman he had ever seen. "He was not the most punishing batsman, but he was the most difficult to get out, and he had a great many strokes, though they were not hard ones." Ottaway was a remarkable athlete, winning the Public Schools Rackets Cup with E. W. Tritton in 1868, and with J. P. Rodger in 1869, and representing Oxford not only at cricket—he was Captain in 1873—but also at Association football and rackets, singles and doubles. He died on April 2, 1878, at the early age of twenty-seven.

Tom Hayward was rather on the short side, sparsely built, and of a dark complexion. His style was attractive, and he held his bat at the top of the handle so lightly that it looked as if a fast ball would knock it out of his hands. He was a master at playing the rising ball, and had plenty of strokes. Richard Daft thought that Hayward was Carpenter's equal, but George Parr would have none of it, holding that Hayward was the more showy, but inferior to Carpenter. Whether Parr was right or not matters little: both of them scored many runs against the best bowling, and often on rough wickets. Hayward made his first appearance at Lord's in 1860, scoring 132, and played for the Players from 1860 to 1871, making another century (112, not out) in 1863. There is a well-known photograph of these two famous Cambridgeshire cricketers in billycock hats, spotted print shirts, and belts with a snake clasp in the middle. They also adorned themselves with what was called a Newgate fringe, a combination of whiskers and beard, but with the upper lip and just below the mouth clean-shaven.

Alfred Lubbock, who, like Mitchell, gave up first-class cricket very early in life, was another fine batsman, with a beautiful style, whose all-round athletic record at Eton was surpassed only by Alfred Lyttelton's some ten years later. He was in the Gentlemen's Eleven at Lord's between 1866 and 1871, and was perhaps at his best in 1867, when he scored 129 for England *v.* Middlesex at Lord's and 107, not out, for Gentlemen *v.* Players at the Oval. He was also a brilliant fieldsman at cover-point and in the deep. He was one of the founders of the Eton Ramblers, whose colours —purple, crimson, and green—are attributed to him. "He was," writes Lord Harris, in *A Few Short Runs*, "to my fancy, the *beau idéal* of athletic form and beauty. . . . If he had gone to a university when he left Eton, instead of into business, I can imagine his equalling that Admirable Crichton of athletic society, Alfred Lyttelton."

Two of Lubbock's sons—A. B. and R. Lubbock—played in the Eton Eleven, the former in 1894 and 1895, and R. in 1896 and 1897. A. B.—Basil—was the author of the famous *Round the Horn before the Mast*.

The summer of 1868 was one of the finest England has ever known, with very little rain, except for a period in August. There were some notable matches at Lord's—M.C.C. *v.* England and, of course, Gentlemen *v.* Players, in which W. G. scored a wonderful 134 out of a total of 201 on a very fiery wicket. He also obtained ten wickets for 81 runs, and he was not yet twenty years of age! In the Eton *v.* Harrow match C. I. Thornton (Eton) hit a ball over the pavilion, the ball flying high and out of the ground for six. Lord Harris, in *A Few Short Runs*, writes:

> I was in with him at the time. He had just previously hit one against the old Armoury, which occupied the site of the members' luncheon-room, and one over *D* Block, and when he followed these big hits—very big for a boy—by that astounding drive over the pavilion I thought it was all right for Eton, but he was bowled by a shooter almost the next ball.

This exploit was all but repeated in 1877 by H. E. Meek (Harrow), who hit a ball on to the top of the pavilion, whence it bounced over. Thornton's went clean over.

A team of Australian Aboriginals, the first Colonial team to visit this country, met the M.C.C. and were beaten by 55 runs. They had been coached by Charles Lawrence, a Surrey player, who remained behind in Australia after the visit of H. H. Stephenson's team in 1861–62—the first English side to visit Australia. The Aboriginals played no fewer than forty-seven matches, the last as late as October 15, 16, and 17, against Surrey at the Oval. Their names make interesting reading—"Tiger," "Redcap," "King Cole," "Dick-a-Dick," and "Twopenny"—and in the field each man wore a different-coloured scarf—pink, yellow, magenta, etc. Their batting, except for Mullagh, a very neat batsman, who scored 1679 runs, was poor; Mullagh and Cuzens bowled fairly well. During intervals of a match they often gave exhibitions of throwing the boomerang, and when the first Australian team under D. W. Gregory visited us ten years later many people were so ignorant of Australia itself, to say nothing of its inhabitants, that, says A. G. Steel, in the Badminton *Cricket*,

> they fully expected to find the members of Gregory's team black as the Aboriginals. We remember the late Rev. Arthur Ward 'putting his foot into it' on this subject before some of the Australians. One day in the pavilion at Lord's the writer, who had been chosen to represent the Gentlemen of England against the visitors in a forthcoming match, was sitting beside Spofforth watching a game in which neither was taking part. Mr Ward, coming up, accosted the writer: "Well, Mr Steel, so I hear you are going to play against the

niggers on Monday." His face was a picture when Spofforth was introduced to him as the "demon nigger bowler."

I often wonder whether an Oxonian would have shown such ignorance!

But in those days Englishmen generally were pretty vague as to our Empire, and when I arrived at Rugby some nine years later another new boy, seeing the label "Trinidad" on my bag, said, "But you're not black." I replied, "No, I am not," to which he added, "Anyway, you do not look it!"

And this boomerang-throwing by the Aboriginals was not forgotten over twenty-five years later, at least by the great Cecil Rhodes. In March of 1895 he and Dr Jameson stayed at Oriel with the Provost of the College, Dr Monro, and on Sunday morning some eight or ten of the undergraduates were asked to breakfast to meet them. I was fortunate enough to sit next to Rhodes, and the conversation turned on the first visit, during the previous summer (1894), of a South African team to England. Rhodes had had a good deal to do with the financing of this side, and he remarked, "They wanted me to send a black fellow called Hendricks to England." I said I had heard that he was a good bowler, and he replied, "Yes, but I would not have it. They would have expected him to throw boomerangs during the luncheon interval."[1]

W. G. played probably as great an innings as even he ever played in the Gentlemen *v.* Players match at Lord's.[2] Going in first wicket down, after his brother, E. M., had been run out for a single, he scored 134 out of a total of 201, of which 8 were extras. And on what a wicket! F. Gale describes it thus:

> Had I been a wicket-keeper or batsman at Lord's I should have liked (*plus* my gloves and pads) to have worn a single-stick mask, a Life Guardsman's cuirass, and a tin stomach-warmer. The wicket reminded me of a middle-aged gentleman's head of hair, when the middle-aged gentleman, to conceal the baldness of his crown, applies a pair of wet brushes to some favourite long locks and brushes them across the top of his head. So with the wicket. The place where the ball pitched was covered with rough grass wetted and rolled down. It never had been, and never could be, good turf. I have no hesitation in saying that in nine cricket grounds out of ten within

[1] Major C. H. B. Pridham tells me he has in his possession a letter from a man who saw the boomerang thrown at Hove, when "it went far out of the ground, over the sea, returning to the thrower's feet, and even his hand."

[2] As we have seen, he also took ten wickets for 81 runs in this match.

twenty miles of London, whether village green or county club ground, a local club could find a better wicket, in spite of drought, and in spite of their poverty, than Marylebone Club supplied to the Players of England.

The season of 1869 at Lord's was not particularly noteworthy, except for the feat of C. K. Francis, afterwards the well-known Metropolitan magistrate, who for Rugby against Marlborough obtained all ten wickets, nine bowled, in Marlborough's second innings. He was a fast right-handed bowler, who played on several occasions for the Gentlemen and for Middlesex.

Thanks to a beautiful innings of 108 by C. J. Ottaway and effective bowling by S. E. Butler and J. Maude, Eton beat Harrow by an innings, for the first time since 1862, and at the end of the match

> there was an orgy of wild excitement such as I had never dreamed of and have never witnessed since; and in the thick of it, as I afterwards remembered, I saw the Provost of Eton, Dr Goodford, transformed into a Bachanal, dancing bare-headed, and waving his hat like the maddest of us all.[1]

[1] Henry S. Salt, *Memories of Bygone Eton* (Hutchinson, 1928).

CHAPTER VI

The Seventies

Thrilling Finishes—Cobden's Famous Over—Eton *v.* Harrow—George Freeman—W. Yardley—David Buchanan—A Sad Accident—Death of J. H. Dark—W. G. in Great Form—W. N. Powys—Allan Hill—A Lively Meeting—Resignation of Robert Fitzgerald—Long Scores—Tom Emmett—The M.C.C. and Middlesex—"The Glorious Match"—Australia's First Visit—Spofforth—Amateur Status—An Unhappy Season—Alfred Shaw—James Cannon

In contrast to the previous season, 1870 was a summer of very interesting cricket, and there were some thrilling finishes at Lord's, Cambridge defeating Oxford by 2 runs, the Gentlemen the Players by 4 runs, and Eton Harrow by 21 runs. This University Match is always referred to as Cobden's match. Oxford, set 179 to win, had scored 175 for seven wickets—4 to win with three wickets to fall. Then F. C. Cobden began his famous over. Off the first ball a single was made by F. H. Hill; off the second S. E. Butler was splendidly caught by A. A. Bourne at mid-off; the third and fourth balls bowled T. H. Belcher and W. A. Stewart.

But has not the Hon. R. H. Lyttelton told the story of this dramatic finish in the Badminton *Cricket*?

> We say with confidence that never can one over bowled by any bowler at any future time surpass the over that Cobden was about to deliver then, and it deserves a minute description. Cobden took a long run and bowled very fast, and was for his pace a straight bowler. But he bowled with little or no break, had not got a puzzling delivery, and, though effective against inferior bats, would never have succeeded in bowling out a man like Mr Ottaway if he had sent a thousand balls to him. However, on the present occasion Ottaway was out, those he had to bowl to were not first-rate batsmen, and Cobden could bowl a good yorker.
>
> You might almost have heard a pin drop as Cobden began his run and the ball whizzed from his hand. Mr Hill played the ball slowly to cover-point, and rather a sharp run was made. As the match stood, Oxford wanted 2 to tie and 3 to win, and three wickets to go down: Mr Butler to receive the ball. The second ball that

Cobden bowled was very similar to the first, straight and well up on the off stump. Mr Butler did what anybody else except Louis Hall or Shrewsbury would have done, namely, let drive vigorously. Unfortunately he did not keep the ball down, and it went straight and hard a catch to Mr Bourne, to whom everlasting credit is due, for he held it, and away went Mr Butler—amidst Cambridge shouts this time. The position was getting serious, for neither Mr Stewart nor Mr Belcher was renowned as a batsman. Rather pale, but with a jaunty air that cricketers are well aware frequently conceals a sickly feeling of nervousness, Mr Belcher walked to the wicket and took his guard. He felt that if only he could stop one ball and be bowled out the next, still Mr Hill would get another chance of a knock and the match would probably be won. Cobden had bowled two balls, and two more wickets had to be got; if, therefore, a wicket was got each ball the match would be won by Cambridge, and Mr Hill would have no further opportunity of distinguishing himself. In a dead silence Cobden again took the ball and bowled a fast ball well up on the batsman's legs. A vision of the winning hit flashed across Mr Belcher's brain, and he raised his bat preparatory to performing great things, hit at the ball and missed it, and he was bowled off his legs. There was still one more ball wanted to complete the over, and Mr Belcher, a sad man, walked away amid an uproarious storm of cheers.

Matters were becoming distinctly grave, and very irritating must it have been to Mr Hill, who was like a billiard-player watching his rival in the middle of a big break; he could say a good deal and think a lot, but he could do nothing. Mr Stewart, *spes ultima* of Oxford, with feelings that are utterly impossible to describe, padded and gloved, nervously took off his coat in the pavilion. If ever a man deserved pity, Mr Stewart deserved it on that occasion. He did not profess to be a good bat, and his friends did not claim so much for him; he was an excellent wicket-keeper, but he had to go in at a crisis that the best bat in England would not like to face. Mr Pauncefote, the Oxford Captain, was seen addressing a few words of earnest exhortation to him, and with a rather sick feeling Mr Stewart went to the wicket. Mr Hill looked at him cheerfully, but very earnestly did Mr Stewart wish the next ball well over. He took his guard and held his hands low on the bat handle, which was fixed fast as a tree on the block-hole; for Mr Pauncefote had earnestly entreated Mr Stewart to put the bat straight in the block-hole and keep it there without moving it. This was not by any means bad advice, for the bat covers a great deal of the wicket, and though it is a piece of counsel not likely to be offered to W. G. Grace or Stoddart, it might not have been inexpedient to offer it to Mr Stewart. Here, then, was the situation—Mr Stewart standing manfully up to the wicket, Mr Cobden beginning his run, and a perfectly dead silence in the crowd. Whiz went the ball; but alas!—as many other people, cricketers and politicians alike, have done—the good advice is neglected, and Stewart, instead of following his captain's exhortation to keep his bat still and upright in the block-hole, just lifted it: fly went the bails, and Cambridge had won the match by two runs! The situation was bewildering. Nobody could quite realize what had happened for a second or so, but then—— Up went Mr Absolom's hat, down the pavilion steps with miraculous rapidity flew the Rev. A. R. Ward, and smash went Mr Charles Marsham's umbrella against the pavilion brickwork.

In the Gentlemen *v.* Players match the scores were Gentlemen 187 (W. G. 109) and 87, the Players 121 (Carpenter 36) and 149 (Jupp 55). The Players wanted 154 runs to win, and when the ninth wicket fell they needed 10 runs. At this point W. Price, 'well in,' was joined by Southerton, and *Wisden* reported:

> No hands clapped, no voice cheered him as he walked to the wickets, so quiet, so strangely quiet, at that moment were the spectators, who, however, cheered wildly when Price by a cut for 2 made it 8 to win, and louder still when a leg bye, and a single by each batsman, brought it 5 to win; but there the match finished, as directly after a catch at cover-point settled Price [c. Absolom, b. G. F. Grace], and in this way at 7.30 the 1870 match ended in a victory for the Gentlemen by 4 runs.

It has been said that the ordinary fixtures at Lord's attracted few spectators, but such was seldom the case in Eton *v.* Harrow matches, and this year the attendance was larger than ever. Here is what *Wisden* said:

> The Grand Stand was thronged, a large majority of the occupants being ladies. The pavilion seats and roof were crowded with members and their friends. "The Ring" was deeper and more densely packed, and the outer ring of carriages more extensive, than at any preceding match. Such an assemblage of rank, fashion, and numbers has never before been seen even at Lord's. It was computed that quite 30,000 visitors attended the ground on those memorable two days. . . . Down by Mr Dark's house, up by the N.E. corner, and fronting the whole row of well-known dwarf chestnut-trees, the accidental but graceful grouping of ladies elegantly attired added a picturesque brilliancy to the old ground not seen at other matches. Two sights unusual on cricket grounds, and curious by contrast,

> were witnessed at this match: the first occurred on the Friday, when on "the boys" retiring to luncheon, the whole playing area of the ground was covered by a gay company promenading; the other on the Saturday, when on rain commencing falling at noon the youthful cricketers were suddenly surrounded by a dense ring of some thousands of opened umbrellas.

The scores of the match were Eton 189 and 151 (A. S. Tabor 50), Harrow 205 (F. C. Bailey 76) and 114.

> At the finish there gathered in front of the pavilion thousands of excited Eton and Harrow men; and amid shouting, cheering, and all that kind of thing, the captains and prominent players of the two Elevens were carried, jolted, tossed about from pavilion to wickets and back again.

Such large crowds now attended the Eton *v.* Harrow matches that this year, for the first time, no one was allowed into the ground on horseback.

Lord Harris, then the Hon. G. Harris, was Captain of Eton, and in Harrow's first innings C. A. Wallroth had been stealing runs by backing up before the bowler had delivered the ball. Whereupon Harris went on to bowl and promptly ran Wallroth out, breaking the wicket as he was in the act of delivering the ball. Harris told me the story years afterwards, and added, "There was quite a fuss about it." But he was surely acting quite correctly in what he did, seeing that Wallroth had been taking an unfair advantage.

A sister of Wallroth's, who later married Alfred Lubbock, the great Eton batsman of the sixties, was at Lord's on this occasion, and to the end of her long life—she died in 1943, at the age of ninety-five—used to wax indignant over this episode. When I ventured to suggest that what had been done was quite right she used to protest strongly and say, "That George Harris! I shall never forgive him!"

George Freeman played little more than five years' first-class cricket, but his name has been handed down to posterity as one of the greatest of fast bowlers; indeed, W. G. stated that he was the best he ever played. "When he hit you on the thigh it hurt. The ball seemed to sizzle into your leg, so much spin did he get on her," he once remarked to me. Freeman retired at the end of the 1871 season to go into business, and in that year made his first and only appearance for the Players at Lord's, and celebrated the occasion by clean bowling W. H. Hadow, A. Appleby, and S. E. Butler in four balls, but not in the same over.

W. Yardley was the first to score a century in the University Match, in 1870, and with H. J. Enthoven, A. Ratcliffe, and the Nawab of Pataudi one of the few to do so twice, his second century being in 1872. A Rugbeian, he was Captain of Cambridge in 1871, and batted consistently well for the Gentlemen at Lord's, for whom he appeared every year between 1869 and 1874. "Looking back now at all the fine bats I have played with and seen, I say unhesitatingly I have never seen a better natural or more brilliant bat than Yardley. He was so good that he needed no practice before playing the best bowlers in England."[1] Yardley was a prominent member of the Old Stagers at Canterbury, and a dramatic critic and author.

David Buchanan, like E. Peate, of Yorkshire, of later generation, began life as a fast left-handed bowler, and in 1871 made his first appearance at Lord's for the Gentlemen at the age of forty-one. He changed from fast to slow in 1864, and with plenty of spin, combined with length and feeding the batsmen on the off side, he met with great success, taking thirty-five wickets for 14 runs each in his four matches against the Players. He was no bat at all, and, if possible, a worse field, but he certainly worried the professional batsmen. He lived near Rugby, and was constantly bowling at the school, both in the nets and in matches, and it was written of him in the Badminton *Cricket* that "the only team that ever seemed to enjoy his bowling was the Rugby boys, and constant practice had robbed it of all terrors for them."

During the M.C.C. *v.* Nottinghamshire match there was a sad accident, a ball bowled by Platts getting up straight and hitting Summers, of Nottinghamshire, on the cheek. He retired, but the story goes that he was given brandy, the last thing to do in the circumstances, and, further, sat in a hot sun at Lord's the next day before returning to Nottingham that evening.[2] As a result he died a few days later, and was buried at Nottingham, where the M.C.C. put up this stone in his memory:

[1] Lord Harris.

[2] Alfred Shaw, in *Alfred Shaw, Cricketer* (Cassell, 1902), says that every care was taken of Summers, and that he did not leave his hotel until just before starting on his journey to Nottingham. The exact care that was taken of this unfortunate player after he had been hit seems, therefore, to have been in dispute, but I prefer to rely on Alfred Shaw's version. Shaw was a most reliable man, and is unlikely to have been incorrect in such a matter.

THIS TABLET
IS ERECTED TO THE MEMORY OF
GEORGE SUMMERS
BY THE
MARYLEBONE CRICKET CLUB
TO MARK THEIR SENSE OF HIS QUALITIES
AS A CRICKETER
AND TO TESTIFY THEIR REGRET AT THE
UNTIMELY ACCIDENT ON LORD'S GROUND
WHICH CUT SHORT A CAREER SO FULL
OF PROMISE
JUNE 19th 1870
IN THE 26th YEAR OF HIS AGE

Wisden records that "the wicket was excellent," but that the ball pitched on a pebble which had worked up. The next batsman, Richard Daft, went in with a towel round his head, and scored 53, following a beautiful first innings of 117.

On October 17, 1871, J. H. Dark passed away, at the age of seventy-six. He had been connected with Lord's for fifty-nine years (1805–64), "having, perhaps, done more for M.C.C. than any other individual," says Alfred D. Taylor, in his *Annals of Lord's and History of the M.C.C.* He was a somewhat taciturn, silent man, out of whom information was not easily extracted, but he was so much a part of the Club that at one period Lord's was often referred to as Dark's.

Dark was a good hitter and fieldsman, and a most capable umpire. He played once, in 1835, for the Gentlemen *v.* Players, in the match in which the Gentlemen were allowed to choose any two of the Players, except Lillywhite, to assist them. They chose J. Cobbett and S. Redgate, and the former bowled Dark for a 'duck.' The Players won by six wickets, Lillywhite taking in all twelve wickets.

Dark was known as "the Boss," and for many years selected the Players' team. He was born in the Edgware Road, on May 24, 1795, and died in a house in St John's Wood Road, which he built overlooking the ground. He had lived all his life within its hail, and his name is inseparably connected with Lord's.

His grave is in Kensal Green, and a red granite slab is inscribed: "Sacred to the Memory of Mr James Henry Dark, who died Oct. 17th, 1871, aged 76. For many years 'Proprietor of Lord's Cricket Ground.'"

In 1871 turnstiles were introduced at Lord's—or "the tell tales," as *Wisden* called them—in place of the old pay-boxes.

W.G. was in rare form at Lord's, scoring 181 for the M.C.C. *v.* Surrey, 23 and 98, run out, *v.* Yorkshire, 178 for South *v.* North, 49 and 34, not out, for Gloucestershire *v.* the M.C.C., 88 for the M.C.C. *v.* Middlesex, and 189, not out, for Single *v.* Married in Willsher's Benefit Match. He was always ready to play in a benefit match—a great asset financially to the professional in question.

The University Match was won by Oxford by eight wickets in a low-scoring game, S. E. Butler taking all ten wickets in the first innings of Cambridge for 38 runs, and five in the second for 57 runs.

At this period Cambridge possessed a very fast bowler, as fast as anyone, says Lord Harris, in W. N. Powys, left-handed, with the left-hander's natural break-back, who in his three Varsity Matches, in 1871, 1872, and 1874, obtained *twenty-four wickets for 153 runs*. Lord Harris had every reason to think highly of him, for in 1871 Powys clean bowled him for 0, and in the following year for 5 and 0. However, he appeared only once for the Gentlemen at Lord's, in 1872, and after his Cambridge days played very little cricket.

The summer of 1872 was very wet, and the slow bowlers took full advantage of the many sticky wickets which prevailed, and, says "Incog," in *Lillywhite*, "every one was glad when the season ended," the ground at Lord's being soaked.

The next year certain improvements were made, but the playing area was said to "lack decent attention and ordinary care," with the result that during the autumn and winter of 1873 the ground was relevelled, and "Lord's lost its proverbial reputation of being the most dangerous ground in the country."

In 1874 the gates were opened as early as five o'clock in the morning on the occasion of the University Match, and, for the first time, in order to reduce the crush, half a crown was charged for admission to the Eton *v.* Harrow match, instead of a shilling.

The Committee inveighed against "undue exhibitions of party feeling, hoisting being prohibited."

The Players defeated the Gentlemen by two wickets,[1] the Gentlemen's fielding at the crisis going to pieces. Allan Hill, of Yorkshire, a fast right-handed bowler with a somewhat low delivery, obtained nine wickets for 136 runs, performing the hat-trick—I. D. Walker, A. W. Ridley, and A. N. Hornby—in the second innings. This was his first appearance for the Players at Lord's, and for the next eight years he was one of the mainstays of the attack. He learned his cricket at the famous Lascelles Hall, then, as now, a great nursery of Yorkshire cricketers.

At the Annual General Meeting of the Club on May 5, 1875, a fierce attack was made, not for the first time, by Mr Willoughby, who criticized the expenditure on the Tavern, derided the match-list as rubbishing, and asserted that professionals were reluctant to play at Lord's, being better treated elsewhere. He objected strongly to the introduction of a lawn-tennis court, and criticized the attitude of the Secretary to members. Another member objected to the admission of carriages to Lord's. The Secretary—Robert Fitzgerald—declined to reply *seriatim* to Willoughby's strictures, and denied a lack of courtesy. J. M. Heathcote replied with equal warmth to these strictures, and defended lawn tennis as "an athletic and popular game." It would appear to have been a lively meeting, in which the cut and thrust of debate went too far, and at the subsequent dinner, which lasted until midnight, Fitzgerald said that he regretted the alleged lack of courtesy on his part, and added that if it was true it was excess of zeal for the interests of the Club. He offered to resign, but this brought general support for his retention of office, and the members separated in mellow mood, after the splendid dinner provided by Mr Crick, the caterer.

Oxford *v.* Cambridge was a very exciting game, Oxford winning by 6 runs, A. W. Ridley bowling the last Cambridge batsman with a lob. The enthusiasm was tremendous at the finish, and, says *Wisden*, Ridley was "forced down the pavilion steps on to the turf and hoisted on to men's shoulders and carried to and fro the wickets." There were two particularly fine catches during the match, one by A. J. Webbe, who ran twenty yards at long leg to dismiss Edward Lyttelton, and the other by W. W. Pulman at

[1] Their first victory since 1866.

long on, which got rid of H. M. Sims, who looked like winning the match for Cambridge.

The Gentlemen *v.* Players match was almost all W. G. He scored 7 and 152, run out, and took twelve wickets for 125 runs. He and A. J. Webbe put on 203 for the first wicket in the Gentlemen's second innings, the Gentlemen winning by 262 runs. This was one of the champion's greatest years, and *Lillywhite* wrote of him that "he still stands on a pedestal above the rest of his fellows."

In the following season (1876) W. G. again towered above his colleagues, one of his greatest innings being 169 for Gentlemen *v.* Players at Lord's,[1] in addition to which he took nine wickets for 122 runs, the Players being defeated by an innings and 98 runs.

Because of ill-health Fitzgerald resigned on October 2. He had held office for thirteen years, during which the number of members increased from 650 to 2080, "a result mainly attributed to his zeal, ability, and popularity." He had been an outstanding figure at Lord's. *Lillywhite* paid high tribute to him:

> No man did more to uphold the dignity of his position, no one had a better sense of what was due to or became the body which he practically guided. . . . It may be that to some he was a little brusque of manner, that he was apt to be hasty and needlessly sensitive; but he never forgot, nor did he ever neglect, the responsibilities of his office.

The year 1876 was remarkable for long scores, the summer being fine and warm until the end of August. W.G. "out-Heroded Herod," wrote *Lillywhite*. The membership of the Club was now over two thousand, and the Annual Report was one of optimism. Nine consecutive days were devoted to three Gentlemen *v.* Players matches at the Oval, Lord's, and Prince's.

Tom Emmett bowled W. G. at the Oval with the third ball of his first over for 0, and, reported *Wisden*, "a roar of deep, earnest cheers complimented the popular Yorkshireman." Years later at Rugby I asked Tom about this particular ball, and he said, "She pitched on the leg stump and hit the top of the off"—a "sostenueter," he called it—"but I won't say what he made in the second innings!" Actually W.G. got 90.

As we have seen, at Lord's W. G. took further revenge. This

[1] This was Arthur Shrewsbury's first match for the Players.

was the year in which Tom threatened to shoot W. G. in the interests of cricket, and "I know," he added, "that the professionals, anyway, will be glad!"

The Eton *v.* Harrow match was played in extremely hot weather, the temperature in the sun being 142 degrees on the first day and 135 to 140 degrees on the second, with a shade temperature of about 90 degrees. Eton overwhelmed Harrow, W. F. Forbes, the Eton Captain, scoring 113 out of 150 in 105 minutes.

Oxford came up against a good Cambridge Eleven, with A. P. Lucas, Edward and Alfred Lyttelton, W. S. Patterson, and H. T. Luddington, the last two pupils of the famous H. H. Stephenson at Uppingham, one of the best of cricket coaches, and were beaten by nine wickets.

In 1877 the now long association between the M.C.C. and Middlesex began. *Lillywhite* remarked that

> cricket at Lord's benefited greatly by the appearance there of the Middlesex Club, which had migrated from its former headquarters at Prince's, and the addition of a few county matches to the Marylebone programme will certainly strengthen it in a point where it has been undeniably weak of late years. For some time there has been a complaint that there was not so much first-class cricket at Lord's as the revenue and position of the Club warranted, and beyond all doubt, with the exception of the two fashionable meetings of the season, there had been for some time to the outside world an air of monotony and apathy about the cricket at Lord's. The addition of the Middlesex fixtures fitted a decided blank in the Marylebone programme, and there was certainly more life in the appearance of matters at headquarters than in the previous year.

There was no charge at that time for the use of the ground, but the county generally made a donation to the M.C.C., larger or smaller according to the state of its finances. These arrangements have varied from time to time, and to-day Middlesex pay a rent of £1100 a year and take the gate money, but no stand money, Middlesex paying all the expenses of the matches—professionals, umpires, scorers, gate-keepers, entertainment tax, luncheons and teas for the teams. Middlesex are limited to a membership of 1200, who have the *entrée* to the pavilion for Middlesex matches, and for all other matches at which a member of the M.C.C. is entitled to introduce a friend into the pavilion. This *modus operandi* has proved of advantage both to the Club and to the county. It has proved what may be called 'a happy marriage,' and those who criticize it can learn from the remarks of *Lillywhite* quoted above how Lord's before Middlesex played there had a meagre list of first-class fixtures.

There was a revival of the match M.C.C. *v.* England, first played in 1792. The weather was bad, and the pitch was described by F. Gale as "pasty as uncooked pudding crust," and "the cut-up wicket played very falsely." The feature of a low-scoring match, which the M.C.C. won by 24 runs, was the bowling of W. Mycroft, who took six wickets for 12 runs in England's second innings. At Whitsuntide, on another sticky wicket, the South won by three wickets, W. G. scoring 58 in the second innings and taking eleven wickets for 75 runs. A. W. Ridley, with his lobs, had the remarkable analysis of

O.	M.	R.	W.
34	17	21	7

in the North's first innings.

After a terrific fight the Gentlemen defeated the Players by one wicket, G. F. Grace and W. S. Patterson putting on 46 runs for the last wicket. The Gentlemen were so strong in batting that their Captain, I. D. Walker, put himself in last in the first innings. In the Players' second innings A. J. Webbe made no fewer than six catches, four at short slip and two in the deep field. *Wisden* described it as "the Glorious Match."

Oxford won the University Match by ten wickets, F. M. Buckland scoring 117, not out, and taking seven wickets for 52 runs. In Cambridge's second innings the Hon. Alfred Lyttelton was superbly caught low down at short leg by F. G. Jellicoe, a brother of the Admiral of the Fleet, a good left-arm bowler, but a notoriously bad fieldsman. Years afterwards at a Foreign Office reception Lyttelton and the Admiral met, and the first words Lyttelton said were, "How's that wretched brother of yours, who caught me out in such an outrageous way in the Varsity Match of '77?"

In Rugby *v.* Marlborough A. G. Steel, who was probably as good a bowler at school as ever afterwards, took twelve wickets for 59 runs and scored 128 in Marlborough's second innings. There have been few greater all-round cricketers.

The season of 1878 is a landmark in cricket history, for the Australians paid their first visit to this country, under the captaincy of D. W. Gregory, one of a family of seven brothers, five of whom played for New South Wales, and an uncle of S. E. and J. M. Gregory. James Southerton, in his description of the tour of James Lillywhite's Eleven in Australia in 1876–77, had written in high praise of several of the Australian cricketers, but little notice of his warnings had been taken, and our visitors arrived almost unheralded and certainly unsung. They started badly in bitterly cold weather at Nottingham, where they lost by an innings and 14 runs, but in their next match, against the M.C.C. at Lord's on May 27, they administered a severe shock to our complacency. In one day, in the short space of four and a half hours of actual play, on a very sticky wicket, they defeated a powerful side by nine wickets, and the fame of Australian cricket was established for all time. Nine of the M.C.C. Eleven were clean bowled in the second innings. The result created a great sensation, and *Punch* celebrated it in the following lines:

> The Australians came down like a wolf on the fold:
> The Marylebone cracks for a trifle were bowled;
> Our Grace before dinner was very soon done,
> And Grace after dinner did not get a run.

Wisden, in a long description of the game, said:

> This, one of the most remarkable matches ever played at Lord's, was commenced at three minutes past twelve, and concluded at twenty minutes past six the same day. Only 128 overs and 2 balls were bowled, and but 101 runs, from the bat, scored in the match.... Allan began; the first ball he delivered Grace hit to leg for 4, the second got Grace caught out at short square-leg, and thereupon out rang lusty cheers, and shouts of "Bravo, Allan! Well done, Australia!" ... At three minutes to four the second innings was commenced; at ten minutes to five that innings was over for 19 runs!
>
> A stream of at least 1000 men rushed frantically up to the pavilion, in front of which they clustered and lustily shouted, "Well done, Australia!" "Bravo, Spofforth!" "Boyle, Boyle!" the members of the M.C.C. keenly joining in the applause of that "maddened crowd," who shouted themselves hoarse before they left to scatter far and wide that evening the news how in one day the Australians had so easily defeated one of the strongest M.C.C. elevens that had ever played for the famous old club.

Here is the score of the match:

M.C.C. *v.* THE AUSTRALIANS

Played at Lord's, May 27, 1878

Result: The Australians won by nine wickets

M.C.C.

First Innings		*Second Innings*	
W. G. Grace, c. Midwinter, b. Allan	4	b. Spofforth	0
A. N. Hornby, b. Spofforth	19	b. Boyle	1
C. Booth, b. Boyle	0	b. Boyle	0
A. W. Ridley, c. A. Bannerman, b. Boyle	7	b. Boyle	0
A. J. Webbe, b. Spofforth	1	b. Spofforth	0
F. Wyld, b. Boyle	0	b. Boyle[1]	5
W. Flowers, c. and b. Spofforth	0	b. Boyle	11
G. G. Hearne, b. Spofforth	0	b. Spofforth	0
A. Shaw, st. Murdoch, b. Spofforth	0	not out	2
G. F. Vernon, st. Murdoch, b. Spofforth	0	b. Spofforth	0
F. Morley, not out	1	c. Horan, b. Boyle	0
Leg bye	1		
Total	33	Total	19

THE AUSTRALIANS

C. Bannerman, c. Hearne, b. Morley	0	b. Shaw	1
W. Midwinter, c. Wyld, b. Shaw	10	not out	4
T. Horan, c. Grace, b. Morley	4	not out	7
A. C. Bannerman, c. Booth, b. Morley	0		
T. W. Garrett, c. Ridley, b. Morley	6		
F. R. Spofforth, b. Shaw	1		
D. W. Gregory, b. Shaw	0		
H. F. Boyle, c. Wyld, b. Morley	2		
W. L. Murdoch, b. Shaw	9		
F. E. Allan, c. and b. Shaw	6		
G. H. Bailey, not out	3		
Total	41	Total (1 wkt.)	12

BOWLING ANALYSIS

THE AUSTRALIANS

First Innings	O.	M.	R.	W.	*Second Innings*	O.	M.	R.	W.
Boyle	14	7	14	3	Boyle	8.1	6	3	6
Spofforth	5.3	3	4	6	Spofforth	9	2	16	4
Allan	9	4	14	1					

M.C.C.

	O.	M.	R.	W.		O.	M.	R.	W.
Shaw	33.2	25	10	5	Shaw	8	6	4	1
Morley	33	19	31	5	Morley	8	4	8	0

Umpires: A. Rylott and M. Sherwin

[1] In W. H. Bettesworth's *Chats on the Cricket Field* (Merritt and Hatcher, 1910), p. 116, a note (written by F. S. Ashley-Cooper) confirms that in the M.C.C. second innings Wyld was bowled by Boyle, and not by Spofforth. He says, "This error is to be found in *Scores and Biographies*, *Wisden's Almanack*, Ayers' book on the tour, and even on the official score-card. The score was given correctly, however, in Lillywhite's *Companion and Annual* and in Conway. Boyle took six for 3."

The Australians played two other matches at Lord's—*v.* Middlesex, whom they beat by 98 runs, a game memorable for a magnificent innings of 113 by the Hon. E. Lyttelton, in honour of which Spofforth presented him with a walking-stick, which he used to point to with pride, and *v.* Cambridge University, under Edward Lyttelton's captaincy, who beat them by an innings and 72 runs. It was in this game that Charles Bannerman made an historic hit off the bowling of P. H. Morton, who was on at the Pavilion end. The ball pitched short of the ring, bounded over the low stand on the left of the pavilion, and cleared Lord Londesborough's drag, striking the wall behind with a lovely thud. Twenty-five years later I met Charles Bannerman in New Zealand, and in conversation with him I asked him if he remembered this hit, and he replied, "Lord bless you, sir! I can feel her on the bat now!"

If this Australian Eleven of 1878 could teach us little in the art of batting they certainly taught us a great deal in the matter of bowling, throwing, and wicket-keeping, in the hands of the great Blackham. Charles Bannerman was a beautiful natural hitter, and Murdoch and Horan were good batsmen, but the others were rough in style and method. It was the bowling of Spofforth, "the Demon"—so called not only because of his deadliness, but also because of a certain Mephistophelian cast of countenance—Boyle, Garrett, and Allan, a left-hander of medium pace, who in Australia was called "the bowler of a century," which caused our cricketers furiously to think. They introduced variety of pace into their attack, and their placing of the field was original, Boyle standing very close in at short leg and making many catches off Spofforth's break-back on the sticky wickets which prevailed that season.

The Australians undertook a large programme of thirty-seven matches, but only seventeen of these were against first-class sides, much of their time being spent in bowling out Eighteens and Twenty-twos. At this distance of time it seems extraordinary that there was no one of sufficient energy and imagination to urge a stronger fixture-list. We were, it would appear, sunk in complacency, and could not imagine that anyone but Englishmen could really play cricket. Modern cricket may be said to date from this Australian invasion, and that it did us no end of good cannot be doubted. In the circumstances it was much to be regretted that no fixture with England, or a return match with the M.C.C., was arranged. Such matches might well have taken the place of some of the minor and uninteresting games which formed a considerable part of the programme at Lord's, and could scarcely have upset the meagre county programme which was then in vogue. It would, too, have been at least a nice courtesy.

The Gentlemen beat the Players by 206 runs, no fewer than four of the Cambridge Eleven—Edward and Alfred Lyttelton, A. P. Lucas, and A. G. Steel—being in the side. This Cambridge team of 1878 is generally regarded as one of the best that has represented either university. They went through the season unbeaten, annihilating Oxford by 238 runs. A. G. Steel, in his first season of first-class cricket, actually obtained 164 wickets for an average of 9·66 runs. His slow leg-breaks, varied with an occasional off-break and a faster ball, were something of a novelty in those days.

There had been a great deal of controversy for some time past on the question of the status of certain amateur cricketers, and on November 2 the Committee of the M.C.C. passed the following resolution:

> That no gentleman ought to make a profit by his services in the cricket field, and that for the future no cricketer who takes more than his expenses in any match shall be qualified to play for the Gentlemen against the Players at Lord's; but that if any gentleman feels difficulty in joining in the match without pecuniary assistance, he shall not be debarred from playing as a Gentleman by having his actual expenses defrayed.

The M.C.C. has strictly observed this rule ever since the management of the finances of the Club has been in its own hands.

It is interesting to read in *Lillywhite*:

> Still making allowance for everything, it must be admitted that the charm of Mr W. G. Grace's marvellous scores with the bat seems at last to have been broken, and it is open to doubt whether he will regain his form of 1876 and 1877. Phenomenon as he has been, he cannot last for ever, and increasing weight with corresponding loss of elasticity must have a sensible effect on his powers of batting. . . . Whether he retires or not from all but county cricket, whether he be as successful as or less successful than of old, the public will remember him as not only for twelve years the best all-round player of his day, but the most wonderful cricketer that has ever lived.

This was written after the season of 1878, when W. G. was but thirty. Twenty years later he was still going in first for England!

The summer of 1879 was one of the wettest on record, for, with the exception of a very brief spell of fine weather in July, it rained almost unceasingly from early May to the end of August. Lord's, still badly drained, suffered terribly, and there were many blank days. The definition and qualification of amateurs and the infringement of Law X were again causes of controversy, and in the pages of *Wisden* we find some caustic comments, the M.C.C. Committee being accused of "tardy legislation," while "the practice of throwing has of late been allowed to degenerate into an abuse." Altogether it was a somewhat unhappy season, although the M.C.C. continued to increase its membership roll, which had now reached 2514, "with 570 candidates craving for admission." During the Under Thirty *v.* Over Thirty match at Lord's on July 22 W. G. was presented with a sum of money (some £1600), a marble clock, and two bronze ornaments representing Egyptian obelisks. Lord Fitzhardinge made the presentation, and Lord Charles Russell also spoke.

Alfred Shaw's bowling in Gentlemen *v.* Players at Lord's between 1870 and 1880 was one of the outstanding features of these games. No one seemed able to 'get at him' and to punish him—not even W. G.! He was called "the Emperor of Bowlers," a notable figure indeed at Lord's.

This season there arrived at Lord's a very small boy who was destined to serve the Club loyally for over sixty years. His name was James Cannon.

CHAPTER VII

The Eighties

The First Test—Three 'Live' Questions—A Curious Incident—The Studds—Law X—Recovery of the Ashes—Death of the Hon. Robert Grimston—First Test at Lord's—The Gentlemen of Philadelphia—Dearth of Fast Bowlers—Shrewsbury's Great Innings—George Lohmann—A 'Peculiar' Incident—The Parsees—My First Visit—The Centenary Match—F. S. Jackson and A. C. MacLaren—The Gentlemen of Canada—A Wet Summer—"A Gentleman's a-bowling"—Alterations in the Laws—My First Match at Lord's

THE summer of 1880, if not quite so wet as that of the previous year, saw enough rain to damp once more the enthusiasm of all but the keenest cricketers. Lord's was fortunate to this extent, that the University and Gentlemen and Players matches were favoured with fair weather. Middlesex played five matches at Lord's—against Surrey, Yorkshire, Gloucestershire, Nottinghamshire, and Oxford University—and there were two closely fought games between England and Daft's American Eleven and between Over Thirty and Under Thirty, but the feeling still prevailed that enough use was not being made of Lord's, many of the fixtures being of little interest.

The Australians, captained by W. L. Murdoch, were here again, but it was not until late in the spring that anyone knew for certain that their visit would take place. Consequently they played many games against odds, and not a single match at Lord's. At one time they were in the position of actually advertising for a fixture! It would appear that after the controversy which had arisen two years previously as to their status as amateurs, and the trouble over an umpire's decision which gave Murdoch run out at Sydney during the tour of Lord Harris's team, the atmosphere towards them was somewhat glacial. Matters would have been worse but for the intervention of Lord Harris himself, helped by C. W. Alcock, the Surrey Secretary, who arranged a match against England in September at the Oval—the first Test Match to be played in England. The Australians, greatly handicapped by the absence through an injury of Spofforth, were beaten by five wickets, after a game full of variety and incident.[1] Cricket owes much to Lord Harris, and never did he render greater service than on this occasion. The cloud which had darkened the horizon of cricket and had threatened even a wider sphere lifted.

There was a certain 'liveliness' in the cricket world in 1881, three questions—the status of Australian players, the competence of certain umpires, and the prevalence of throwing—being the causes of some agitation. In regard to the former, many of our professionals, led by Alfred Shaw and Shrewsbury, felt that the financial conditions under which the Australians had played here in 1878 and 1880 were inconsistent with the value placed on their own services. This led to a good deal of trouble between, in particular, the Nottinghamshire professionals and the committee of the county club. "Incog," in *Lillywhite*, criticized the M.C.C. in these words:

> The damage might have been checked had the M.C.C. made use of the immense influence it wields. . . . That it lasted so long without active interference by the Authorities at Lord's seems strange when it is considered that it was not merely the question of the welfare of the County, but it involved a distinct alteration in the relation between paid cricketers and their employers which vitally affected the interests of every club of any importance.

Eventually the action of the Secretary of the Marylebone Club brought about the submission of five of the Nottinghamshire players, though Shaw and Shrewsbury were not reinstated in the team. It is pertinent here to recall that Shaw, who had experienced harassing financial difficulties during a recently concluded tour with the Australians, was the first to suggest that all tours in Australia should be the responsibility of the M.C.C.

Lillywhite also, in dealing with umpires, quoted the remark of a distinguished cricketer: "A man has only to be a ground bowler at Lord's for a week, and he is competent to stand umpire in any match." It is obvious that the umpiring, generally speaking, was unsatisfactory, and it was suggested that the M.C.C. should be invited to give "Certificates of Competency."

There were, too, many complaints that Law X was frequently infringed by certain Northern players, and the general incompetence, or lack of courage, on the part of some umpires made the suppression of throwing all the more difficult.

[1] In this match W. G. scored 152, and W. L. Murdoch 153, not out.

Before the University Match began it was thought that "Oxford had not a ghost of a chance," but fine fast bowling by A. H. Evans, who took thirteen wickets for 130 runs on a fiery wicket, and a great innings of 107, not out, half of it with a badly damaged hand, by W. H. Patterson, who carried his bat through the second innings—ably backed up by C. F. H. Leslie (70)—gave Oxford a victory by 135 runs. Cambridge, on paper, with three Studds —G. B., C. T., and J. E. K.—A. G. Steel, and the Hon. Ivo Bligh were a strong side, but Evans dominated their batsmen, and Steel was, for once, in this match comparatively ineffective with the ball. There was one curious incident: when Leslie had made 8 he returned a ball hard to A. F. J. Ford, which the bowler held, high up, with one hand. Ford threw the ball up, amid the applause of his side, and Leslie, who was batting at the Pavilion end, retired. Patterson, at the other end, appealed to Farrands, the umpire at the bowler's end, and after reference to Price, the square-leg umpire, Leslie, who was on his way back to the pavilion, was recalled.

On a fast wicket, but one which quickly broke up, the Gentlemen beat the Players in a low-scoring match by five wickets, Evans, Steel, and Studd bowling well, as did Barlow and Peate for the Players.

The Australians had made such a great impression on their visits in 1878 and 1880 that it seems strange that only one Test Match was arranged when they came again in 1882, and that at the Oval. The Committee of the M.C.C. were certainly not thinking imperially. In 1880 the Australians did not play a single game at Lord's; on this occasion they were seen there on only two occasions—against Middlesex and against a powerful M.C.C. Eleven. Both matches were spoiled by rain.

G. B. and C. T. Studd were prominent this year, G. B. making 42 and 48 for Cambridge *v.* the Australians and 120 in the University Match, and C. T. 118 for Cambridge *v.* the Australians, 69 *v.* Oxford, 114 for M.C.C. *v.* the Australians, and 100 and 34, not out, for Gentlemen *v.* Players, a match the Gentlemen won by eight wickets. C. T. Studd was a fine all-round cricketer. He headed the batting averages, with an aggregate of 1249 and an average of 32·33, and obtained 128 wickets for 15·10 each. To this day it passeth understanding why A. N. Hornby, the Captain, put him in No. 10 in England's second innings at the Oval. He never received a ball, and England lost by 7 runs!

Lillywhite published an article, "The Decline of Fast Bowling," and suggested that the reason was that "the practice of fast bowling in our Schools and Colleges is sadly, almost cruelly, neglected." Of the few fast bowlers of that day more than one was suspected of throwing. The addition to the laws allowing the wicket to be rolled on the second and third mornings of a match was warmly welcomed. "Incog," in *Lillywhite*, had been urging this reform for some time, as he had the strict enforcement of Law X, which runs: "The ball must be bowled; if thrown or jerked either umpire shall call 'No Ball.'" In regard to this law, he did not blame the Committee of the M.C.C. for the disinclination shown by umpires generally to enforce their specific instructions—"Considerable ill-feeling was engendered last season, and is still likely to be evinced in the event of certain deliveries continuing to pass unchallenged"—and added of the bowlers who offended, "There was really no plea that the deliveries of certain bowlers were above suspicion." He records that Lord Harris had given notice that at the next General Meeting of the M.C.C. he would move that an addition be made to Law X enforcing an umpire, if he is not of opinion that a bowler's delivery is absolutely fair, to call no-ball.

In contrast to the previous year, the weather throughout the summer of 1883 was generally good, and a spur was given to our cricket before the season began by the recovery of the Ashes by the Hon. Ivo Bligh's[1] team, which defeated Murdoch's victorious 1882 Eleven by two matches to one. Ivo Bligh, however, was persuaded to play a fourth match against what was called United Australia, E. Evans and W. Midwinter taking the places of H. H. Massie and P. S. McDonnell, and was defeated by four wickets. The historians still argue as to whether in the circumstances he *did* regain the Ashes, but the fact remains that he was presented, in Australia, with a gold urn with the ashes of burnt cricket-stumps; and the urn, with the ashes inside, is to be seen in a glass case in the Long Room at Lord's.

There was some large scoring in Gentlemen *v.* Players—1098 runs for thirty-three wickets—the Gentlemen winning by seven wickets. And what a strong amateur side it was, with A. N.

[1] Later the eighth Earl of Darnley.

Hornby at No. 8, E. F. S. Tylecote to keep wicket—he also played a fine innings of 107—and H. Rotherham, W. F. Forbes, A. G. Steel, C. T. Studd, and W. G. to bowl! *Lillywhite* had recently complained of the decline of fast bowling, but here we had two really fast bowlers—H. Rotherham and W. F. Forbes, formerly of Uppingham and of Eton—and both contributed materially to the victory of their side, Rotherham taking four wickets and Forbes seven (for only 65 runs). The Players had as their fast bowler G. P. ("Shoey") Harrison, a very 'raw' lad from Yorkshire. When he received an invitation to play for the Colts of the North *v.* the Colts of the South earlier in the season he accepted, but asked Mr Perkins, Secretary of the M.C.C., "to meet him at the station, as he had never been in London before!"

On April 7, 1884, the Hon. Robert Grimston, President of the M.C.C., died, the first President to die in office. His name had been for many years closely connected with the Club, by which, says the Annual Report, "he was so justly esteemed as a true friend, a thorough sportsman, and the type of an honourable English gentleman."

The Australians paid us their fourth visit, and, at last, a Test Match was played at Lord's, England winning by an innings and 5 runs. A. G. Steel batted magnificently for 148, an innings which George Giffen talked of most enthusiastically as late as 1911 in conversation with me at Adelaide.

In reply to Australia's total of 229, England had lost five wickets for 135 runs, and Barlow, in his *Forty Seasons of First-class Cricket,*[1] recalls how Lord Harris, the England Captain, said to him as he was going in to bat, "For Heaven's sake, Barlow, stop this rot!" And stop it he did, for he scored 38 and helped Steel to add 98 runs. In Australia's second innings G. J. Bonnor, the six-foot-five fair, bearded giant, was caught and bowled right-handed by Ulyett off a terrific drive, one of the historic catches of cricket. Mr Stanley Christopherson is the sole survivor to-day of this match.

This was the second Test Match, the first, at Old Trafford, having been drawn, play being limited to two days owing to rain. England scored 95 and 180 for nine wickets, Australia 182. After our defeat at the Oval in 1882 this victory at Lord's was hailed with great enthusiasm. Here is the score:

[1] Heywood, 1908.

ENGLAND *v.* AUSTRALIA

Played at Lord's, July 21, 22, and 23, 1884

Result: England won by an innings and 5 runs

AUSTRALIA

First Innings		*Second Innings*	
P. S. McDonnell, b. Peate	0	b. Steel	20
A. C. Bannerman, b. Peate	12	c. and b. Ulyett	27
W. L. Murdoch (Capt.), l.b.w., b. Peate	10	c. Shrewsbury, b. Ulyett	17
G. Giffen, b. Peate	63	c. Peate, b. Ulyett	5
W. Midwinter, b. Peate	3	b. Ulyett	6
G. J. Bonnor, c. Grace, b. Christopherson	25	c. and b. Ulyett	4
J. McBlackham, run out	0	retired hurt	0
H. J. H. Scott, c. sub., b. Steel	75	not out	31
G. E. Palmer, c. Grace, b. Peate	7	b. Ulyett	13
F. R. Spofforth, c. Barlow, b. Grace	0	c. Shrewsbury, b. Barlow	11
H. F. Boyle, not out	26	b. Ulyett	10
Byes 5, leg byes 3	8	Bye	1
Total	229	Total	145

ENGLAND

W. G. Grace, c. Bonnor, b. Palmer	14
A. P. Lucas, c. Bonnor, b. Palmer	28
A. Shrewsbury, st. Blackham, b. Giffen	27
G. Ulyett, b. Palmer	32
A. G. Steel, b. Palmer	148
Lord Harris (Capt.), b. Spofforth	4
R. G. Barlow, c. Palmer, b. Bonnor	38
W. W. Read, b. Palmer	12
Hon. A. Lyttelton, b. Palmer	31
E. Peate, not out	8
S. Christopherson, c. Bonnor, b. Spofforth	17
Byes 15, leg byes 5	20
Total	379

BOWLING ANALYSIS

England

First Innings	O.	M.	R.	W.	*Second Innings*	O.	M.	R.	W.
Peate	40	14	85	6	Peate	16	4	34	0
Barlow	20	6	44	0	Barlow	21	8	31	1
Ulyett	11	3	21	0	Ulyett	39.1	23	36	7
Christopherson	26	10	52	1	Christopherson	8	3	17	0
Grace	7	4	13	1					
Steel	1.2	0	6	1	Steel	10	2	26	1

Australia

	O.	M.	R.	W.		O.	M.	R.	W.
Spofforth	55.1	19	112	2	Boyle	11	3	16	0
Palmer	75	28	111	6	Bonnor	8	1	23	1
Giffen	22	4	68	1	Midwinter	13	2	29	0

Umpires: F. H. Farrands and C. K. Pullin

The Australians also played the M.C.C., the Gentlemen of England, and Middlesex. They had by this time evidently come into favour, and it was a good move not only from the point of view of the game itself, but also from an imperial aspect. The rows and bickerings of the past were happily over and done with. The M.C.C. game was remarkable for the fact that W. G. (101), A. G. Steel (134), and W. Barnes (105, not out) scored centuries, the Club winning by an innings and 115 runs. The Gentlemen won by four wickets, but Middlesex came to grief before the splendid bowling of Spofforth—twelve wickets for 43 runs.

The Gentlemen defeated the Players by six wickets after a keenly fought game, and Oxford, who had previously achieved great renown by a seven-wicket victory over the Australians, were too good for Cambridge to the extent also of seven wickets. In this match T. C. O'Brien made 'a pair,' clean bowled in each innings, but so great was his reputation that ten days later he was in the England Eleven at Old Trafford, the Lancashire Committee, who selected the England side, remembering *Tom Brown*, with its "the goddess who presides over cricket loves to bring down the most skilful players." O'Brien was a remarkably fine batsman—a master on sticky wickets—and W. G. held him in high esteem.

The Gentlemen of Philadelphia paid their first visit to England this season, and appeared at Lord's *v.* the Gentlemen of M.C.C., but they found the bowling of Rotherham and C. T. Studd, who also scored 106, too much for them, and were beaten in an innings. Looking back, it seems to me that the season of 1884 marked something like the beginning of international cricket as we understand it to-day, though another fifteen to twenty years were to pass before the M.C.C. became the authority in which was centralized the organization of tours abroad.

The stimulus given to cricket by the events of 1884 was reflected in the following summer. "The more important matches never received better support," says *Lillywhite*, and with good weather the game flourished, and nowhere more so than at Lord's, where the membership passed 3000. For the M.C.C. *v.* Yorkshire W. Gunn and W. Barnes put on 330 runs for the fourth wicket in the Club's second innings, the match being limited to two days, because of the Derby, it being then the almost invariable custom to have no cricket at Lord's on Derby Day. There was nothing particularly exciting about either Gentlemen *v.* Players or Oxford *v.* Cambridge, but Eton *v.* Harrow was a glorious game, Harrow winning two minutes before time by three wickets, the winning hit, an on-drive for 4, being made by E. M. Butler, the Harrow Captain, off the bowling of H. W. Forster,[1] President of the M.C.C. in 1919, and in the following year Governor-General of Australia, where his cricket dinners are still remembered. Another future Pro-consul in the Eton Eleven was F. Thomas, the Captain, later Earl of Willingdon and Viceroy of India.[2] Looking through the teams, we find some traditional cricketing names—Foley, Lord George Scott, Brand, Bromley-Martin, and Gosling, of Eton, and Butler, Crawley, Kemp, Sanderson, and Ramsay, of Harrow.

One disturbing factor about first-class cricket was the continuing dearth of bowlers of any real pace, which *Lillywhite* had stressed three years previously. Christopherson was in the Gentlemen's Eleven, but the Players had no fast bowler on their side, and the leading bowlers of the year were all medium-paced or slow. This lack of pace was to continue for a few more years, but soon there was to come a flood of fast bowlers—and great bowlers too. Lord Harris was again on the war-path against unfair bowling, and of one bowler he wrote in *A Few Short Runs* that he "seemed to me to throw every ball." His persistency had its reward, for by the next season both Crossland, one of the chief offenders, and Nash disappeared from the Lancashire Eleven.

The Australian Eleven of 1886 came under the ægis and financial control of the Melbourne Club, and were heralded as the equals of the great elevens of 1882 and 1884. As it happened, their form here fell far below the expectations of their countrymen, and they lost each of the three Test Matches.

In the Lord's match Shrewsbury played a truly wonderful innings of 164 on a wicket which, fast and true for the first half-hour, subsequently became very difficult after rain. This innings is still regarded as one of the masterpieces of the art of batting under conditions favourable to the bowlers, one of whom was the redoubtable Spofforth, while in addition there were Palmer, Garrett, and Giffen. Briggs achieved a veritable triumph in his

[1] Later first Baron Forster.

[2] In the Winchester Eleven against Eton this year we find the name of the Hon. F. J. N. Thesiger, later third Baron and first Viscount Chelmsford, Governor of both Queensland and New South Wales, and Viceroy of India from 1916 to 1921. He was President of the M.C.C. in 1922.

first Test Match, taking eleven wickets for 74 runs. The England team was powerful in batting, but it lacked a fast bowler, for Ulyett could hardly be so considered at this stage of his career.

The Gentlemen, a weak side, were easily defeated by the Players by five wickets. Both teams, indeed, were below standard, but a new and glorious figure was seen for the first time in this match —George Lohmann, the greatest all-round cricketer Surrey has ever produced.

The University Match was memorable for a first-wicket stand by K. J. Key and W. W. Rashleigh, who, in just under three hours, put on 243 runs in Oxford's second innings. *Wisden's* comment was: "At twenty-five minutes to five, amid, perhaps, the heartiest cheering heard last season at Lord's ground, the 200 went up without the loss of a wicket."

A new telegraph board, which altered the batsmen's totals as the runs were made, was first used in the match between the Australians and an England Eleven on September 13, and appropriately the first run on it was credited to W. G. Part of the proceeds of the game, together with a diamond ring, was given as a testimonial to J. A. Murdoch, the Assistant Secretary of the M.C.C. He was a tall, well-built man with good features, who with his pointed grey beard, eyeglass, and good manners looked like a diplomat of the old school. Years later he was destined to be the manager of the first team the M.C.C. ever sent abroad, when his tact, courtesy, and resourcefulness were great assets.

A peculiar incident occurred in the fourth innings of the Rugby and Marlborough match, which Rugby won by 37 runs.

Law XIV ("The Over") then ran: "The bowler may not change ends more than twice in the same innings, nor bowl more than two overs in succession."

The law was altered in 1889 as follows: "The bowler may change ends as often as he pleases, provided that he shall not bowl two overs in succession in the same innings."

Wisden gave this version of the matter:

> Rugby *v.* Marlborough, played at Lord's, Wednesday, Thursday, July 28, 29. This proved to be one of the most interesting and well-contested of the public school matches played during the season of 1886, and it was made specially remarkable by a very singular incident which occurred late on the second afternoon. When Kitcat, the Marlborough Captain, was disposed of it was discovered that Bengough, the Rugby Captain, had by some oversight been allowed

to go on twice at each end, and in his first over from the pavilion wicket (the second time he had been on that end) he got Kitcat caught at cover-point. A long discussion ensued; but it was decided by the umpires that Kitcat, having been fairly caught, could not go in again. As a result, however, of the objection of the Marlborough Captain, Bengough was not allowed to bowl another ball in the innings after he had completed his over. The affair gave rise to a great deal of correspondence, and, indeed, it was not thoroughly settled at the time whether or not the umpires had acted rightly. Of course, it was a clear oversight on the part of the umpires that Bengough went on at this wrong end, but the universal opinion afterwards was that, Kitcat having been fairly caught, the umpires had no option but to give him out.

The decision given does not seem sound. The trouble arose through the umpires, T. Mycroft and Wheeler, failing to observe that Bengough, admittedly unwittingly, had broken the existing law. I agree entirely with the decision of the umpires that Kitcat was out, for the breach of the laws by Bengough in bowling again was the responsibility of the umpires, and of them alone, as "the sole judges of fair and unfair play," and no penalty should have been inflicted on the bowler. As it was, appeal was made to Mr Perkins, the Secretary of the M.C.C., who ruled that Kitcat was out, *but that Bengough should not bowl again.*

Thus at the Headquarters of the game a special penalty, unknown to the laws, was inflicted by a court, one of which was the Secretary of the Club, to whom no appeal lay; for the laws are quite clear that the umpires are the sole arbiters.

Appeal should not have been made to Mr Perkins, nor should he have entertained the same; but, having done so, it is remarkable that one who had been a successful barrister should have given an *ad hoc* decision both unknown to the laws and without precedent to sustain it.[1]

The Parsees sent a side this year—the first Indian team to visit England. They played the M.C.C. at Lord's, but were defeated in an innings; it must be said that they were not a strong side. They deserve, however, a page in any history of Lord's, for they were the pioneers of the fine Indian elevens we now know, and the forerunners of such cricketers as Ranji, Duleep, Pataudi, Nayudu, Merchant, and Amar Singh.

[1] I hope it is unnecessary to say that my opinion in this matter is 'judicial,' and not influenced by allegiance!

The first time I saw Lord's was on Friday, May 20, 1887. Only recently arrived in England from the West Indies, I had as a boy devoured the pages of *The Field*, which in those days gave a great deal of space to cricket, *Wisden*, and *The Times*. I had seen in the *Illustrated London News* a group of the Australian team, in which G. E. Palmer was wearing a stiff-fronted shirt, and nothing would satisfy me until I was given one exactly like his! The dramatic moments in the famous Test Match at the Oval in 1882, A. G. Steel's 148 at Lord's two years later, Ulyett's wonderful catch-and-bowl of G. J. Bonnor in the same match, and Shrewsbury's 164 on a sticky wicket for England against Australia at Lord's in 1886 were vivid in my imagination. I used to dream of cricket! It was, therefore, with a thrill of anticipation and delight that I passed through the turnstile at the main gate[1] and watched the play from a seat in front of the ivy-covered tennis court, with the great clock in the middle, where the Mound now stands. I can recall vividly even now the first wicket I ever saw taken at Lord's—C. A. Smith, from the Nursery end, clean bowling F. E. Lacey with what looked from the ring a very good one.

W. G. Grace was one of the Club side, and during the luncheon interval he passed near by, and I gazed with undisguised admiration, not to say awe, on the greatest personality the cricket world has ever known, or ever will know. With his black beard and giant figure, with an M.C.C. cap crowning his massive head, he bestrode the cricket world like some Colossus, and little did I dream then that one day I should play with and against him.

A month later my preparatory school was taken in a body to Lord's to see the M.C.C. play England during the Centenary week, in which nearly all the great cricketers of the day were taking part. Of the players in that match none survives to-day, but I can see Lord Hawke, with his cap worn back to front, and A. J. Webbe catching Louis Hall at short leg, right under the bat, as if it were but yesterday. I can recall, too, A. E. Stoddart's and Shrewsbury's great first-wicket partnership of 266; Ulyett's powerful hits over deep extra cover's head off Barnes, of Nottinghamshire, scattering the spectators in Block *A*; George Lohmann's artistic and cleverly flighted bowling; and Johnny Briggs at cover. It all comes back "quick like a shot through the brain."

Here is the score of this great match:

[1] The main entrance is still in the same place as it was when the present Lord's was opened.

M.C.C. CENTENARY MATCH

M.C.C. *v.* ENGLAND

Played at Lord's, June 13, 14, and 15, 1887

Result: England won by an innings and 117 runs

M.C.C.

First Innings		Second Innings	
Dr W. G. Grace, b. Lohmann	5	c. and b. Briggs	45
A. N. Hornby (Capt.), c. and b. Briggs	16	b. Bates	6
W. Barnes, b. Briggs	8	c. and b. Bates	53
A. J. Webbe, c. Briggs, b. Lohmann	0	c. Pilling, b. Bates	14
W. Gunn, b. Lohmann	61	c. Shrewsbury, b. Briggs	10
G. G. Hearne, b. Briggs	8	c. Barlow, b. Lohmann	6
J. G. Walker, c. Hall, b. Lohmann	3	b. Briggs	25
Hon. M. B. Hawke, b. Lohmann	16	b. Briggs	10
W. Flowers, b. Lohmann	19	c. Lohmann, b. Bates	43
J. T. Rawlin, not out	18	c. W. Read, b. Bates	4
M. Sherwin, b. Bates	17	not out	1
Byes 3, wide 1	4	Byes 4, leg bye 1	5
Total	175	Total	222

ENGLAND

A. Shrewsbury, c. Barnes, b. Rawlin	152
A. E. Stoddart, c. and b. Rawlin	151
R. G. Barlow, l.b.w., b. Rawlin	0
M. Read, c. Sherwin, b. Flowers	25
W. W. Read (Capt.), c. Webbe, b. Barnes	74
W. Bates, c. Hornby, b. Barnes	28
G. Ulyett, c. Sherwin, b. Barnes	46
L. Hall, c. Webbe, b. Barnes	0
J. Briggs, b. Barnes	9
G. A. Lohmann, not out	9
R. Pilling, c. Gunn, b. Barnes	0
Byes 8, leg byes 12	20
Total	514

BOWLING ANALYSIS

England

First Innings	O.	M.	R.	W.	Second Innings	O.	M.	R.	W.
Lohmann	57	29	62	6	Lohmann	32	13	60	1
Briggs	55	22	84	3	Briggs	39	8	77	4
Bates	5	2	5	1	Ulyett	21	8	34	0
Barlow	2	2	0	0	Bates	28.3	15	46	5
Ulyett	8	3	20	0					

M.C.C.

	O.	M.	R.	W.		O.	M.	R.	W.
Barnes	74.2	30	126	6	Flowers	74	29	122	1
Rawlin	90	39	140	3	Hearne	9	3	19	0
Grace	36	16	65	0	Webbe	13	5	22	0

Umpires: John West and T. Mycroft

How different was Lord's then from what it is to-day! Only three buildings remain—Block *A*, on the left of the pavilion as one looks at the wickets, the Hotel, and the members' luncheon room. The present pavilion was not built until 1890. There was no big scoring-board or "Father Time"; the stands were few and small, and there was nothing like the seating capacity we are accustomed to in these days. The northern end of the "Nursery" had only just been purchased by the M.C.C. But the atmosphere then was the same as now. Lord's was the home and the headquarters of cricket, with a tradition and history which no other ground in the world has ever quite succeeded in capturing.

In the Eton *v.* Harrow match of this year appeared two boys in the Harrow Eleven who were destined to play a very big part in English cricket—F. S. Jackson and A. C. MacLaren. Jackson was a tremendous 'swell' at Harrow, and, it was said, the friend and confidant of his headmaster, Dr Welldon. I remember Welldon saying to him after a dinner at Althorp Park, where Harrow and Rugby met two years later, "My dear Jackson, I do not know what we are going to do without you at Harrow." The match had been arranged by Earl Spencer, "the Red Earl," who was a Governor of both schools, and whose guests we were, and it was the first occasion on which I played cricket with Jackson; it has left a distinct impression on my mind.

As Captain of the Harrow Eleven he was seated at dinner, at what may be called the 'top table,' with the Red Earl, the two headmasters, and other prominent guests. To my intense surprise, I found myself sitting on Jackson's left. How it came about that I, only fifteen, a very small boy, and in my first year in the Rugby Eleven, was so honoured I cannot imagine. There had clearly been a mistake in the 'batting order,' but from that evening dates a friendship which has grown with the years, and which I prize. I can see him now, immaculately turned out, with a small, neat fair moustache—and how nice he was to me! I thrilled when he spoke to me, and every now and again I called him sir, which I think was right and proper. Many moons have waned since that evening, many games of cricket have I played with and against him, and often do we meet at Lord's, but somehow that first meeting with him is one of the most vivid of my cricketing life.

Years afterwards, when Bishop Welldon was 'Chaplain to the Forces' to the M.C.C. Australian team of 1903–4, he told me that "Jackson was a splendid boy, absolutely trustworthy and reliable"; and there can be no doubt that Jackson exercised a great influence for good over the Harrow of his day. He could even persuade his headmaster to allow a boy to escape an occasional lesson when assured that So-and-so's off-drive was not quite as it should be, or that he was playing back in the wrong way!

No school has ever had finer contemporary cricketers than Jackson and MacLaren. For years they were indispensable to an England Eleven. It was a thousand pities that Jackson was never able to go to Australia, but politics and the House of Commons claimed him. I can see him now in the Test Match at Lord's in 1899, wearing three different caps during the day—a Light Blue, I Z., and Yorkshire. He played no first-class cricket after the season of 1906.

A. C. MacLaren was a good-looking boy, as he was man, with a wonderful pair of eyes and a fine high-bridged nose. Many Australians aver that he is the finest batsman we have ever sent them. So highly was he thought of that there were to be found people who would lay even money that he would get a century every time he went in to bat at Sydney. But MacLaren made his hundreds for England not only in Australia, but in this country as well, and the best innings I ever saw him play was 88, not out, in the Test Match at Lord's in 1899. It was a sad day for England, Australia winning by ten wickets, but MacLaren's batting was something to console us. The Australians were very strong in bowling that year, with Jones, Trumble, Noble, and Howell all in their prime, but MacLaren, leading a forlorn hope, played magnificently. He was a perfect master in forcing good-length balls to the boundary, and also a great slip-fielder. He captained England in no fewer than twenty-two Test Matches.

The Right Hon. G. J. Goschen (afterwards first Viscount Goschen), at that time Chancellor of the Exchequer in Lord Salisbury's Government, was present at the dinner in the tennis court on June 15, 1887, to celebrate the Centenary, and in his speech remarked that so keen was his interest in cricket that, whatever the political situation, the first thing he looked at in *The Times* every morning was the cricket news. At the dinner was Monsieur Waddington,[1] Prime Minister of France in 1879,

[1] He rowed in the Cambridge Eight of 1849, the year of two races. The first was rowed on March 29, when all the Cambridge crew were Trinity men and beat Oxford by about eight lengths. Oxford, according to *The Story of the Inter-University Boat Race*, by Wadham Peacock (Grant Richards, 1901), were so disgusted with their defeat that they at once challenged Cambridge to row against them again in the same year. The second race took place on December 15, and was the only occasion when a foul

and French Ambassador to the Court of St James from 1883 to 1893. Curiously enough, he, like Goschen, was a Rugbeian, and, I believe, they were contemporaries at school.

During my Rugby days I used to play in Lord Goschen's cricket week at Seacox Heath, in Kent, with a fair amount of success, and he came hurrying from Downing Street to see me play my first match at Lord's for Middlesex in 1895. Unfortunately I got a 'duck,' and as I walked disconsolately up the pavilion steps he rose from his seat with "Oh, Pelham, how did it happen? You never did this sort of thing at Seacox!"

Lillywhite had some nice things to say about the M.C.C.:

> The fact that the year witnesses the Centenary of the Marylebone Cricket Club would have alone entitled it to be marked with a white stone in the Cricket Calendar. . . . Under its fostering care cricket has flourished . . . and those who have charge of its administration have not only good reason to look back on the work the M.C.C. has done during the first century of its existence, but also with every feeling of hope for the future.

The summer of 1887 was gloriously fine, and the batting averages, with Shrewsbury in the van with figures of 78·15, read like those of modern days, but "amateur bowling was never weaker. . . . The thinned and enfeebled ranks of amateur bowlers," records *Lillywhite*.

In these circumstances it is not surprising that the Gentlemen were beaten by an innings and 123 runs. The Players had no genuine fast bowler, but Lohmann, Briggs, W. Barnes, Peel, Flowers, and Bates formed a strong and varied combination, and the run-getting power of the side extended to No. 10 (Lohmann) in the batting order. No wonder that the Badminton *Cricket* wrote that they "reached the high-water mark of excellence"!

Wisden was critical of the selection of the Gentlemen's team, which contained seven men new to the match, while A. Appleby, who had not played for the Gentlemen at Lord's since 1878, was within ten days of his forty-fourth year, and had sent down only thirty-four overs (four balls each) for his county, Lancashire.

Oxford won the University Match by seven wickets, and it was a strange coincidence that the last choices on both sides—Lord George Scott, of Oxford, and E. Crawley, of Cambridge—

occurred. Cambridge won by a length, but Oxford appealed, and the decision went against Cambridge. On that occasion Waddington was not in the crew. I am indebted to Mr Valentine Heywood, of the *Sunday Times*, for this information.

should have been the most successful batsmen, Scott scoring 100 and 66, and Crawley 35 and 103, not out. Scott played only at the last moment, because of an accident to C. Wreford-Brown. But how often has a last choice more than justified his selection! Nine years later G. O. Smith was to emphasize this with his great innings of 132, which was one of the main factors in Oxford's famous four-wicket victory.

It was only fitting that in the Jubilee year of Queen Victoria's reign, when there was a remarkable gathering of imperial statesmen, soldiers, and sailors, Canada, our oldest Dominion, should send a team which played a drawn game against a fairly strong M.C.C. amateur side at Lord's. They had some good cricketers among them, notably D. W. Saunders, W. A. Henry, Dr E. R. Ogden, and A. C. Allan, a left-handed batsman. Saunders was the wicket-keeper, and years afterwards at a dinner at Lord's, at which he was present, he was referred to as "the Blackham of Canada." This was no exaggeration, for he was a wicket-keeper of the first order. Dr Ogden was a clever slow-medium-paced bowler, who kept a length and could spin the ball. In the M.C.C. match he obtained twelve wickets for 163 runs, including those of I. D. Walker, A. J. Webbe, A. E. Stoddart, C. I. Thornton, and T. C. O'Brien. *Wisden* wrote of the Gentlemen of Canada: "They fairly earned the respect and friendship of their opponents by their modesty in victory, their cheerfulness under defeat, and their good-fellowship always."

The summer of 1888 was one of the wettest on record. There were a few fine days in May, but from June to September rain fell pitilessly. Rugby *v.* Marlborough was abandoned without the stumps being pitched, though four days were given, and the University Match—again four days—had to be abandoned after three innings had been played. These extra days were agreed on during the course of the matches, the normal custom being two days for the Schools fixture and three for the University Match. There were, however, two days at Lord's with the weather fine and the wicket fast and true, when the Gentlemen of England met the Australians on May 28 and 29, no cricket being arranged for a third day because of the Derby. Up to this point C. T. B. Turner and J. J. Ferris had been bowling out sides for ridiculously small scores, and they had created something of a panic, Turner being called "the Terror." On this occasion, however, with the conditions all in favour of the batsmen, the Gentlemen of England scored 490 (W. G. 165, W.W. Read 109, and J. Shuter 71), though Turner bowled splendidly, sending down ninety-one overs (four balls each) and taking six wickets for 161 runs. The Australians made 179 and 213 for one wicket (Bonnor 119). But the Derby then was more important, and the game was drawn.

On a very sticky wicket the Australians defeated Middlesex, for whom the great J. T. Hearne made his first appearance, by eight wickets, and a fortnight later they won a small-scoring match against a strong M.C.C. Eleven by 14 runs. Then on July 16 and 17 came the Test Match, and England were beaten by 61 runs. The wicket was very difficult, the highest individual score being W. G.'s 24 in England's second innings. Australia made 116 and 60, England 53[1] and 62. England had a very powerful eleven on paper, the side bristling with famous names, but against Turner and Ferris they were helpless. Dare one suggest that the art of batting on a sticky wicket was not then so generally understood as it is to-day? And what would the modern critics have said of an England Eleven which failed so disastrously? I imagine their language would have been "frequent and painful and free." Arthur Shrewsbury had stayed in Australia after his tour there; he would have been worth his weight in gold, for there never was a greater batsman on false turf. This Australian Eleven were only a moderate batting side, but Blackham was the wicket-keeper, the fielding was splendid, and Turner and Ferris were one of the greatest pair of bowlers that the game has produced—the one, medium to fast medium, right; the other, medium left, with a longish run to the crease and bringing both hands above his head before delivering the ball, almost as if he was kissing his hands to the crowd. Turner obtained 314 wickets that season for 11·38 runs each, and Ferris 220 for 14·23.

Gentlemen *v.* Players produced a great finish, the Gentlemen winning by 5 runs in another very low-scoring match on yet another difficult wicket. The Players had only 8 runs to make to win and four wickets to fall when, says *Wisden*, "as a last resource Steel handed the ball to C. A. Smith. . . . With one added Smith clean bowled Attewell, Peel was bowled by Woods, Lohmann, in trying to score on the on side, was out l.b.w. to

[1] It is a strange coincidence that 53—the smallest score England has made in Test Matches against Australia at Lord's—was also Australia's lowest total in these matches at Lord's, made in 1896.

Smith, and Woods dismissed Flowers with a yorker." The respective totals were Gentlemen 84 and 100, Players 107 and 72.

Harrow beat Eton by 156 runs. R. B. Hoare scored 4 and 108 and took five wickets for 58 runs, but the feature of the match was F. S. Jackson's all-round cricket—21 and 59 and eleven wickets for 68 runs. His father[1] had offered to give him £5 for every wicket and £1 for every run—a most expensive match for him. He perhaps did not quite realize the sort of 'horse' he was backing, but I am certain that no debt was ever paid with greater pride and joy. Only the other day Sir Stanley told me that a cheque followed immediately on his return to Harrow. Jackson's performance produced an ode by E. E. Bowen,[2] entitled "A Gentleman's a-bowling":

A GENTLEMAN'S A-BOWLING

(*Dedicated to F. S. Jackson, Lord's,* 1888)

O Cabby, trot him faster;
  O hurry, engine, on,
Come glory or disaster
  Before the day be done!
Ten thousand folks are strolling,
  And streaming into view,
A gentleman's a-bowling
  (More accurately two).

With changes and with chances
  The innings come and go,
Alternating advances
  Of ecstasy and woe.
For now 'tis all condoling,
  And now—for who can tell—
A gentleman's a-bowling.
  It yet may all be well.

Light Blues are nimbly fielding,
  And scarce a hit can pass;
But those the willows wielding
  Have played on Harrow grass!
And there's the ball a-rolling,
  And all the people see
A gentleman's a-bowling,
  And we're a-hitting he.

[1] The Right Hon. William Lawies Jackson, Financial Secretary to the Treasury (January 1886 and July 1886–91), Chief Secretary for Ireland (November 1891 to August 1892), M.P. for Leeds (1880–1902), later first Baron Allerton.

[2] A devoted Harrovian, a master at the school, and the author of many of the famous "Harrow Songs."

Ten score to make, or yield her!
  Shall Eton save the match?
Bowl, bowler! Go it, fielder!
  Catch, wicket-keeper, catch!
Our vain attempts controlling,
  They drive the leather—no!
A gentleman's a-bowling,
  And down the wickets go.

And now that all is ended,
  Were I the Queen to-day,
I'd make a marquis splendid
  Of every one of they!
And still for their consoling,
  I'll cheer and cheer again
The gentleman a-bowling,
  And all the other ten!

At the Annual General Meeting of the M.C.C. on May 1, 1889, the Laws of Cricket[1] were altered in three respects: (i) the over was increased from four balls to five; (ii) the bowler was allowed to change ends as often as he liked, provided he did not bowl two overs in succession; and (iii) the captain of the batting side was given power to declare the innings closed on the last day of a three-day match, and in a one-day match at any time. As regards (i), Australia had been ahead of us, for the over there for some time had consisted of six balls. Four balls to the over sometimes gave the impression that an over was concluded almost as soon as it had begun, the changing of the fieldsmen between the overs wasted time, and some bowlers claimed that with only four balls they had not sufficient time in which to develop their attack. As for (ii), after the Bengough incident in the Rugby *v.* Marlborough match of 1886 a change was clearly necessary; while (iii) meant that the farcical knocking-down of wickets on purpose by the batsmen was abolished, and that drawn games would be fewer. These changes in the laws met with general approval. It is curious to recall that four balls to the over had been in vogue since the earliest days.[2]

[1] The Laws of Cricket appeared in the *New Universal Magazine* of 1752, and it is probable that these were printed somewhere between 1745 and 1750. There is also the 1755 edition, which was revised on February 25, 1774, at the Star and Garter, Pall Mall, by a Committee of Noblemen and Gentlemen of Kent, Hampshire, Surrey, Sussex, Middlesex, and London.

[2] In Lambert's *Introductions and Rules* of 1816 the following note appears: "It has been the custom in some matches to bowl six balls, which may be done provided both

The Gentlemen had the worst of the wicket at Lord's this year, but they were far inferior to the Players, their bowling, except for S. M. J. Woods, being moderate. Apart from Woods and Mold, a Northamptonshire man who had qualified for Lancashire, there was in England at this period no fast bowling of real quality. Woods for half a dozen years—from 1888 to 1894—was a great bowler, with a well-concealed slow ball to add variety to his pace, and Mold, with a few short strides to the crease and a smooth action, made the ball come even faster off the pitch than one would have expected from its pace through the air. His break-back was a very sudden affair, and when he hit you on the thigh you remembered it.

The Players' batting did not look too strong on paper, but the absence of Shrewsbury and Maurice Read, through injuries, upset the balance of the side. The eleven was overcrowded with bowlers —Lohmann, Briggs, Shacklock, Peel, Flowers, Attewell, and Barnes—but Sherwin, the Nottinghamshire and England wicket-keeper, used only the first three, Briggs and Lohmann taking seventeen wickets between them. The scores of the match were Players 280 (W. Barnes 130, not out), and 6 for no wicket, Gentlemen 148 and 137.

Woods' bowling (eleven wickets for 82 runs) really won the Varsity Match for Cambridge, for whom H. J. Mordaunt, a beautiful batsman on a true wicket, scored 127 and E. Crawley 54, by an innings and 105 runs.

Harrow defeated Eton by nine wickets a quarter of an hour before time. F. S. Jackson, now Captain of Harrow, scored 68 and took five wickets for 81 runs, but his father, remembering what had happened in the previous year, was more cautious on this occasion!

On July 31 I made my first appearance at Lord's for Rugby *v.* Marlborough. Little did I imagine then that fortune had decreed that I should play many hundreds of innings on the famous ground. I did not distinguish myself, scoring but 3 and 16. In the first innings, following Tom Emmett's advice that "if you come to her, come," I jumped out of my ground to drive, but missed the ball and was stumped by feet. In the second innings

parties are agreeable, but not without," and in John Nyren's *Young Cricketer's Tutor* there is a note to the same effect.

In Mexico the over at one time is said to have consisted of thirty (!) balls, and one of the West Indies bowlers, and a fast bowler too, remarked that so far as he was concerned, he would like the over to consist of twenty balls!

I hit my first boundary at Lord's. A. J. L. Hill, afterwards a member of the fine Cambridge elevens under the captaincy of MacGregor, Woods, and Jackson, and a heavy scorer for Hampshire, was on at the Pavilion end. I was a very small boy, but I leant on a ball outside the off-stump, and 'she' flew to the ring. Like Charles Bannerman, "I can feel her on the bat now," and I can still see the umpire signalling four. An idle and perhaps improper boast, but what would life be without its memories?

CHAPTER VIII

The Nineties

A Board of Control—J. J. Lyons—S. M. J. Woods—Shrewsbury and Stoddart—Great Varsity Matches—L. C. H. Palairet—C. J. Kortright—The "Follow-on" Incident—The Press—The South Africans—A Great Period—All out for 18!—Angry Scenes—A Change in the Laws—G. L. Jessop—F. E. Lacey as Secretary—The Mound Stand—W. G.'s Birthday Match—MacLaren as Captain—Australia's Great Victory—Trott's Historic Hit—G. H. Simpson-Hayward

Wisden tells us that "Mr Stoddart preferred playing for Middlesex against Kent at Tonbridge, instead of for England *v.* Australia at Lord's"—and Middlesex in 1890 were already closely allied to the M.C.C. Again, for the Test Match at the Oval "Yorkshire retained Ulyett and Peel to play against Middlesex at Bradford, and Mr Stoddart preferred to assist the latter county." Nowadays one reads such statements with astonishment, and it was this sort of thing which led to the formation of a Board of Control for Test Matches in England, though it took some years to do so: cricket authorities are, or were, apt to move slowly.

England won at Lord's by seven wickets. It was a keen fight for a long time, but, with England set 137 to win, W. G. settled the issue with a splendid 75, not out—an innings "entirely worthy of his reputation." Lyons had a great match, scoring *55 out of 66 in 45 minutes* and *33 in 25 minutes*, and taking five wickets for 30 runs in England's first innings. A man of granite strength, he was a great firm-footed hitter. He liked the accurate medium-paced bowler like Attewell, preferring the good-length ball for the exploitation of his tremendous drives, but seldom seemed at home on our wickets with slow left-handers like Peel and Briggs. He gave another example of his hitting powers at Lord's in September, when, against a strong M.C.C. team, he made *99 out of 117 in 75 minutes*. The M.C.C. Committee arranged no fewer than five matches for the Australians at Lord's—*v.* Middlesex, *v.* the Players, *v.* England, and two *v.* the M.C.C.—a complete reversal of their attitude in the early eighties—a welcome change indeed! In appreciation the Australians gave up their share of the gate of the second M.C.C. match—as did the M.C.C.—for the benefit of the Cricketers' Fund.

Cambridge, under the captaincy of Woods, were probably as good a side as either university has ever had, and they won the Varsity Match, played on a difficult wicket, by seven wickets. In *Wisden* for 1891 A. G. Steel, in an article, "Cambridge Memories," draws an interesting comparison between Woods' team and Edward Lyttelton's of 1878, of which Steel himself was such an outstanding figure.

Rain spoilt Gentlemen *v.* Players, as well as Eton *v.* Harrow, the feature of which was a magnificent innings of 76 by A. C. MacLaren.

One of the best things about the cricket at Lord's this year was a superb innings by A. E. Stoddart for South *v.* North, when on a sticky wicket he scored 115 out of 169 without the slightest mistake against Peel, Briggs, and Attewell. For the North Shrewsbury, an absolute master under such conditions, carried his bat through the North's first innings for 54 out of 83 runs from the bat, and made 34 in his second innings. Lohmann's analysis was eleven wickets for 110 runs, seven of them bowled in the second innings. In later years, when I was talking about cricket to Lohmann on a long railway journey in South Africa, he described Shrewsbury's batting on a sticky wicket. "He was not an attacking player, but he was always getting twos and threes. He often used his legs in playing an off-break, but it was difficult indeed to get a ball past his bat, and though he was accused of overdoing pad-play, it was curious how seldom he was out l.b.w. He was the best batsman I ever bowled to on a sticky wicket."

Stoddart was of an entirely different type. He used to take the bowler by the scruff of the neck and knock the stuffing out of him. He, Shrewsbury, and William Gunn taught their generation the art of batting on false turf—a lesson which many a fine batsman on good wickets at that time needed to learn.

The season of 1891 was very wet, and many matches at Lord's were spoilt. There was, however, a great Varsity Match. Oxford, on paper much the weaker side, running a Cambridge Eleven, which included such fine cricketers as MacGregor (Capt.), Woods, Jackson, Wells, and Streatfeild, to a desperate finish. Wanting 90 runs to win, Cambridge had scored 47 for two wickets when, in a bad light, G. F. H. Berkeley, slow-medium left, was put on to bowl at the Pavilion end. He quickly obtained two wickets, clean bowling R. N. Douglas and Jackson, while Hill was caught at slip, but, with five wickets in hand and only 12 runs to make, the match seemed a certainty for Cambridge. Berkeley, however, dismissed Foley, Streatfeild, and MacGregor in rapid succession. Visions of another Cobden match flashed through the minds of many, but down the pavilion steps strode the mighty Woods, bareheaded, without pads and gloves. He drove the first ball he received to the boundary, and Cambridge had won by two wickets. Foley made 41, and he was the last choice for Cambridge! The Oxford Captain was M. R. Jardine, father of D. R. A glorious fieldsman on the off side and a very good batsman, with a sound and attractive style, he was destined to achieve great distinction in his next Varsity Match. One of the best things about the match was the superb wicket-keeping of MacGregor, who stood up to Woods and took his fastest deliveries with perfect ease. He was "Sphinx-like in his calm fixity,"[1] and his keeping to Woods remains one of the great memories of cricket.

The best match of the season of 1892 was the University Match. Cambridge started hot favourites, and the odds on them strengthened when the first two Oxford batsmen were out without a run on the score-board. Then Jardine joined Fry, and a good stand was made until Fry was caught at the wicket. Five were down for 157 when V. T. Hill joined Jardine, and in an hour and forty minutes they put on 178 runs. Andrew Lang has written that "it is impossible to describe Hill's innings in prose." Hill was a left-hander, and hit no fewer than eighteen fours. Fortune was on his side, for he was missed three times in the deep—at 64, 96, and 103—before being caught off C. M. Wells for 114. Jardine played an innings which I remember to this day. He made 140 in four hours and three-quarters, without a chance of any sort. He was wonderfully good at either forcing the ball off his pads wide of mid-on or glancing it to leg, and every now and again he brought off a beautiful late cut.

I was at Rugby at the time, and the reader may wonder how I happened to be at Lord's, but I had been suffering from a strain, and a visit to a London surgeon was advised. Now Dr Percival was a great headmaster, if a somewhat grim man, with, however,

[1] *The Jubilee Book of Cricket,* by K. S. Ranjitsinhji (Blackwood, 1897).

a very pleasant smile, and when I asked for leave to go to London he said, "Yes," and added, "What about Thursday? The University Match begins on that day, doesn't it?" I caught an early train, saw the surgeon, and was at Lord's a few minutes after twelve. I wonder how many headmasters would have been so thoughtful—but then John Percival was fond of cricket, and had not failed to notice that I was even fonder! I bless that great man to this day!

Oxford scored 365, and Cambridge, all out for 160, had to follow on. Three Cambridge men were run out—Jackson, Wells, and Hill—and G. J. V. Weigall has been charged with running out all of them. This is a little unfair to him. He clearly was responsible for Jackson (34), who looked all over like making a century, and for Wells, but Hill ran himself out. Cambridge, 205 runs behind, had lost five wickets in their second innings for 179 runs when E. C. Streatfeild joined P. H. Latham, and at the close of play Cambridge were 300 for five (Streatfeild, who drove magnificently, not out 81, Latham, not out 61). On the third day Cambridge were all out for 388 (Streatfeild 116, Latham 69), and Oxford were set 184 to win. They had to fight hard. Four wickets were down for 99 when L. C. H. Palairet, who had not gone in in his usual place, first, because of a bruised hand, joined Fry. They stayed together until only 15 runs were needed, when Jackson sent Fry's off-stump flying. Palairet then finished the match with a series of lovely drives. His 71, not out, was a masterpiece of an innings. Everything Palairet did was gracefully done. He batted gracefully, he shot gracefully, he played golf gracefully, and he danced gracefully. He was a charming man, with a very gentle manner, and the memory of "Coo" Palairet does not fade even with the passing of the years.

Throughout a day and a half in the field the Oxford fielding was very good, Jardine being magnificent. These were the great days of the Varsity Match, when the ladies wore their loveliest frocks and no man dared to come to Lord's in anything less than a frock coat and top hat. And the crowd! 18,000 on the first day, 20,000 on the second, and some 14,000 on the third!

The season of 1893 was most enjoyable, the weather being fine and warm and the wickets of the kind to hold a fairly even balance between batsmen and bowlers. The Australians, under the captaincy of J. McBlackham, played four matches at Lord's—two *v.* the M.C.C., one *v.* Middlesex, and one *v.* England. The first M.C.C. match, which was drawn, will always be memorable for a wonderful second innings of 149 by Lyons, who completed his *100 in an hour*, and when out to a magnificent catch at long-off by L. Wilson, off Attewell, *had scored 149 in ninety minutes*. He hit twenty-two fours. It was one of the most remarkable displays of hitting ever seen. He revelled in the good-length bowling of Attewell, who was forced to place three, and sometimes four, men in the deep. W. G.'s captaincy came in for some criticism, *Wisden* remarking, "Strangely enough, it was not until 215 runs had been made that J. T. Hearne was put on to bowl at the Pavilion end, from which he had been very successful on Thursday, and again he proved effective." Hearne's analyses were:

First Innings				*Second Innings*			
O.	M.	R.	W.	O.	M.	R.	W.
25.1	10	59	4	36.1	14	74	6

Lyons seemed to like Lord's, for in the return match with the M.C.C. he played innings of 83 and 45. The M.C.C. won by seven wickets, the opening pair, W. G. and Stoddart,[1] putting on 120 runs when the Club went in with 175 to win.

C. J. Kortright obtained eight wickets for 129 runs, six of them clean bowled. He was very fast indeed, and almost invariably used a yorker with great effect against Nos. 9, 10, and 11. He was unlucky not to play for England this year, but Lockwood, Mold, and Richardson were about.

The Test Match at Lord's ended in a draw, rain on the third day spoiling what looked like a keen finish. England made 334 and 234 for eight wickets, innings declared, Australia 269. Jackson made a most successful first appearance for England, scoring 91 on a wicket which, after rain on the previous day, gave considerable help to Turner, who began by dismissing Stoddart and Gunn for 31 runs. Then Jackson joined Shrewsbury, and 137 runs were added before Jackson was out to a splendid catch at the wicket low down on the off side, off Turner, and as he walked away Blackham remarked, "Bad luck, young fellow! It was an awful fluke!" Jackson was missed at mid-on when he had scored 50, and gave two further possible chances, but his on-driving was superb, and anything short was hooked. He hit thirteen fours. Shrewsbury made 113, and also fell to Blackham

[1] It was in this season that Stoddart made a double century (195, not out, and 124) for Middlesex *v.* Nottinghamshire at Lord's.

off Turner, who had six wickets for 67 runs in thirty-six overs. Shrewsbury stood alone on a sticky wicket, and soon after Jackson had come in he advised him: "Back up with your legs, sir, or Charlie Turner will have you out." The pitch improved during the innings, but in the circumstances 334 was a fine total.

When the Australians went in Lockwood bowled superbly, and five wickets were down for 75, all to Lockwood, but Gregory (57) and Graham (107) put on 142 runs by brilliant stroke play and by fearless and rapid running. Lockwood's analysis was

O.	M.	R.	W.
45	11	101	6

and Mold's

20.1	7	44	3

On going in again England lost Stoddart for 13, but Shrewsbury (81) and Gunn (77) were at their greatest, and but for rain Shrewsbury would probably have had the then unique distinction of scoring two separate hundreds in an England *v.* Australia match. Owing to an injured finger W.G. was unable to play, and Stoddart captained the side.

It has nothing to do with the history of Lord's, but it is worth recording that for the third match, at Old Trafford, although it was distinctly agreed when the fixtures were made that the counties would release whichever men were required for these great games, Lord Hawke refused to give up Jackson, as Yorkshire were playing Sussex at Brighton. Naturally this did not go down too well at Old Trafford, and Lord Hawke's action met with a great deal of criticism.

The Gentlemen would probably have beaten the Players had not rain limited cricket to a little over an hour on the third day. The features of the match were the bowling of Kortright (seven wickets for 73 runs in the Players' first innings), the all-round cricket of C. M. Wells, Shrewsbury's second innings of 88, during which he played Kortright's terrific bowling with masterly ease, and the wicket-keeping of MacGregor, who, *standing up to Kortright*, caught Sugg on the off side from a ball which rose scarcely half-stump high. This was probably one of the greatest catches ever made by a wicket-keeper. Kortright's 'muzzle velocity,' to use a musketry term, was probably a hundred miles an hour down the pitch. When some years later, writing in the *Evening Standard*, I tried to compare the pace of various fast bowlers by using musketry terms the editor afterwards told me that he wished I had never written the article, as he had been inundated with letters from "every musketry expert from Hythe to Hong-Kong." He published, however, a letter from a correspondent which ran something like this:

> Has Mr Warner gone mad? Does he realize that to acquire such speed as he suggests the bowler's wrist would fly off, that the batsman would not see the ball, which would scatter death and destruction among the spectators in the pavilion and smash up the woodwork and brickwork?

Cambridge took full revenge for their unexpected defeat in the previous year, winning by 266 runs in two days, during which the crowd was estimated at 39,000. The long spell of fine weather during May and June had caused the pitch to be on the worn side, and the scoring was only moderate—Cambridge 182 and 254 (of which 47 came from extras), Oxford 106 and 64. Jackson, with 38 and 57 and four wickets for 57 runs, finished his Cambridge career in brilliant fashion. Latham played a very good second innings of 54, and Bromley-Davenport (five wickets for 11 runs), Streatfeild (four for 19), and Wells (seven for 66) bowled extremely well, as did Berkeley (nine for 94) for Oxford. *Wisden* reported the match as follows:

> Nine wickets were down for 95 [in Oxford's first innings], and then, on T. S. B. Wilson, the last man, joining W. H. Brain, an incident occurred which is likely to be talked about for a good many years to come. Three runs were added, making the score 98, or 84 short of Cambridge's total, and Oxford thus required only 5 runs to save the follow-on. The two batsmen were then seen to consult together between the wickets, and it was at once evident to those who had grasped the situation that the Dark Blues were going to throw away a wicket in order that their side might go in again. Had one of them acted on his own account, it is probable that the object would have been gained, but Wells, who was bowling from the Pavilion end, saw at once what was intended and promptly set to work to frustrate it. Going over the crease, he bowled a ball wide to the boundary, and then, after an unsuccessful effort to bowl a wide all along the ground, sent another round-arm ball to the ropes, thus giving away eight runs, but preventing Oxford from going in a second time. The incident gave rise to a great deal of talk and discussion, to say nothing of special articles in various newspapers. We are inclined to think, however, that in some quarters the matter was treated far too seriously, the point being overlooked that all the

players immediately concerned were actuated entirely by the desire to do the best thing possible for their side. Particularly would we wish to exonerate Wells from all blame. He saw clearly that Oxford, with the idea of securing an advantage, meant to throw away a wicket, and we hold that he was perfectly justified in taking any means to prevent them that the law permitted. Whatever may be thought of the incident, it had the immediate effect of bringing the question of the follow-on under the consideration of the M.C.C. Committee.

Cambridge had good cause to be apprehensive of a law which made it *compulsory* for the side which was 80 runs, or more, behind on the first innings to follow on, for in their match with the Australians that season at Fenner's they had led by 94 runs on the first innings. The wicket was almost certain to crumble on the third day, and had they been able to choose they would certainly have gone in again to bat. As it was, the Australians made 319 in their second innings, and on the last day, on a broken wicket, Cambridge were all out for 108. Thus the law penalized the side which had, up to half-time, played the better cricket.

During the winter of 1893–94 this law was the subject of much discussion, and at the Annual General Meeting of the M.C.C. on May 2, 1894, the following alteration was proposed: "The side which goes in second *may be required* to follow their innings if they shall have scored 80 runs less than the opposite side"; but, though the Hon. Alfred Lyttelton, in an able and vigorous speech, protested against postponement, on the proposition of the Chairman, the Earl of Dartmouth, it was resolved to refer the matter to the Committee to inquire into and collect the various opinions and report to a special meeting to be held in July. At this meeting, on July 10, the Committee proposed an increase to 100 runs in a three-day match, or 80 runs in a two days' match. This was carried, and came into operation in 1895. The law, be it noted, still made the follow-on compulsory. There was to be a dramatic sequel in the following year.

Until a grand stand was built during the winter of 1867–68 there was no accommodation for the Press. Previous to this the reporters had to stand their chance of getting a seat anywhere. There were shrubberies at each end of the pavilion, and Mr Knight,[1] the only recognized newspaper representative, stood all

[1] Mr Knight wrote for *Bell's Life* in London, which later changed its name to *The Sporting Life*.

day in the bushes inside the rails, this being the only place from which to view the cricket on a crowded day, with no score-board or cards to tell him the state of the game, and having to record the score of the whole of the match in his own score-book!

Even in the nineties we find in an article by C. S. C.—"Hints from the Press Box," in *Wisden* of 1893—the following remarks:

> At Lord's the arrangements for Press men are far from adequate, and, I imagine, it is only the uniform courtesy which one experiences from every one connected with the Headquarters of cricket that has prevented strong representations being made to the M.C.C. The accommodation is far too rough and limited, and, indeed, quite unworthy of Lord's Cricket Ground.

With no visit from the Australians and the weather less favourable, the cricket in 1894 was not so interesting as in the previous season. The Gentlemen *v.* Players match was finished in two days, Woods and Jackson bowling unchanged through both innings of the Players, their analyses being:

	First Innings				*Second Innings*			
	O.	M.	R.	W.	O.	M.	R.	W.
Woods.................	24.2	8	61	4	21.4	6	63	2
Jackson	24	8	36	5	21	7	41	7

Jackson (63) also made the best individual score in the match, the Gentlemen winning by an innings and 39 runs.

Oxford were clearly the better side, and won the Varsity Match by eight wickets, C. B. Fry scoring 100, not out. When the last man, R. P. Lewis, came in—a fine wicket-keeper, but so poor a batsman that in *Lillywhite* it was written of him, "As a bat, backs up well"—Fry was 17 short of his century. He then 'let fly,' and scored the necessary runs in a couple of overs. Fry also made three smart catches at slip, and managed his bowlers, of whom L. C. V. Bathurst and G. R. Bardswell stood out, with admirable judgment.

Very late in the season Gentlemen of the South met Players of the South for the benefit of G. F. Hearne, the pavilion clerk at Lord's. It was a batsman's wicket, and the game was drawn, W. L. Murdoch, W. Newham, and Abel scoring centuries.

The South Africans paid their first visit to England, played 24 matches, won 12, lost 5, and drew 7. They did not meet any strong sides, but they made a good impression, and in E. A. Halliwell, C. O. H. Sewell, G. Rowe, and J. Middleton they had four very good cricketers. Halliwell was a great wicket-keeper, Sewell a most attractive and able batsman and a beautiful fieldsman, who, making his home in England, subsequently distinguished himself for Gloucestershire. Here were instances of heredity, which is somewhat rare in cricket, for Halliwell's father kept wicket for the Gentlemen at Lord's in 1870, 1872, and 1873, and Sewell's father was a successful batsman for Middlesex in the sixties. Rowe and Middleton were left-handed bowlers. Rowe, quite a boy, obtained 136 wickets for 12 each and Middleton 83 for 15 each. The tour, if a severe financial loss, which the great Cecil Rhodes shouldered, was the beginning of subsequent big things. Within ten years South Africa were becoming a power in the world of cricket. The South Africans, who were captained by H. H. Castens, another good wicket-keeper, played one game at Lord's, and beat rather a weak M.C.C. side, which, however, included, W. G., O'Brien, and Mead, of Essex, in a thrilling finish by 11 runs.

I always think that the intense interest which nowadays is evinced in the matches between England and Australia began with the tour of Stoddart's team in Australia during the winter of 1894–95. The Australians of 1880, 1882, and 1884 were great sides, but there was a distinct falling off for some years afterwards, and this had had a discouraging effect in their own country, with a consequent loss of enthusiasm which was reflected in the smaller number of spectators. Lord Sheffield's visit in 1891–92 had done much to alter this, and, in spite of their losing the rubber, the 1893 Australian side were a strong and attractive side, with obvious future possibilities of real greatness. Stoddart won the rubber by three to two, after being two-all, and the tour ended in a crescendo of excitement. It was during this tour that the word 'Test' was applied to these matches, the *Pall Mall Gazette* being the first to coin the word.

There are periods in all walks of life when great names abound, and in the history of English cricket we find such a period between 1895 and 1914. Among amateur batsmen, with Ranjitsinhji, Jackson, MacLaren, Fry, Stoddart, O'Brien, A. O. Jones, Palairet, Jessop, H. K. Foster, R. E. Foster, Spooner, Perrin, and Hutchings, and, of course, W. G., there was a plethora of talent, which coincided with a great revival of fast bowling in Richardson, Mold, Lockwood, Kortright, Woodcock, Brearley, Hirst, Knox,

Buckenham, Fielder, Gill, Bradley, Warren, and Wass; medium to fast-medium bowlers included J. T. Hearne, S. F. Barnes, W. Mead, Pougher, and A. E. Relf; and when the great slow left-handers Peel and Briggs dropped out immediate successors were found in Rhodes and Blythe, followed later by Dean. Among the cricketers mentioned Jackson, Jessop, and Hirst were all-rounders of the highest class, as were Mason, Rhodes, J. N. Crawford, C. L. Townsend, Arnold, Bosanquet, Braund, J. W. H. T. Douglas, and F. R. Foster. Of professional batsmen, Shrewsbury, William Gunn, Abel, Hayward, J. T. Tyldesley, Hobbs, Woolley, J. W. Hearne, P. Mead, George Gunn, J. T. Brown, Denton, and W. G. Quaife stood out. In such an era of talent some of these found only a very occasional place in an England Eleven. So strong was amateur batting that the England teams at Lord's and at Birmingham against the Australians in 1902 included only one professional played solely for his batting—J. T. Tyldesley. All these cricketers were gifted with genius and personality, and a spectator had no need to consult the score-card: he knew who was batting or bowling because of that player's outstanding individuality.

Fast bowlers had a great season in 1895. Six weeks' frost from January 21 to March 3 was followed by continual sunshine from the beginning of May until the middle of July, and on the sun-baked wickets fast bowling was more successful than in probably any other season, with Richardson foremost among its exponents. Bowling 1690 overs (five balls), he took 290 wickets for 14 runs each. The editor of *Wisden* wrote, "Whether his skill or remarkable stamina be most admired, it is probable that no bowler of anything like the same speed has ever made the ball break back so frequently." Fast bowlers all over the country had fine figures —Mold 213 wickets for 15 runs each, Kortright 76 for 15 each, Hirst 150 wickets for 17 each, Woodcock 102 for 19 each. Eleven fast bowlers took *1266* wickets between them.

The Gentlemen *v.* Players match at Lord's on a lively pitch had a remarkable finish, the great opening start of 151 (Grace 118 and Stoddart 71) in the first innings of the Gentlemen being followed by the equally memorable partnership of E. Smith (40, not out) and C. B. Fry (60) for the last wicket in the second innings. In a glorious attempt to win the match Smith and Fry made 72 runs in thirty-five minutes, and victory for the

Gentlemen seemed in sight when, off Peel, Storer stumped Fry, with but 32 runs required.

Oxford started strong favourites for the University Match, for they had been making plenty of runs and defeating such strong sides as Yorkshire, Gentlemen of England (with Mold), and Kent (twice), but on the day they were not at their best, the double failure of Fry and G. J. Mordaunt, who in their four innings scored only 12 runs between them, making a fearful hole among a powerful array of batsmen. Also they batted in a shocking light on the first day, during which they lost six wickets for 67 runs. The light, indeed, was so poor that from the pitch one could see the gas-jets burning in the bar under the grand stand. Numerous appeals were made, but Phillips and W. A. J. West, the umpires, were adamant. Cambridge, splendidly captained by W. G. Druce, played determined and consistent cricket. The feature of the match was a glorious second innings by H. K. Foster, who made 121 out of 159 runs scored while he was at the wickets. He hit twenty fours, his off-driving and cutting being magnificent and his style perfect in its easy grace.

In 1896 the Australians were here again, a powerful side under the astute captaincy of H. Trott. *The Times* of Saturday, June 20, wrote, "The Marylebone Club Committee are making much unnecessary mystery about the constitution of the England Eleven to meet Australia at Lord's on Monday," but when the side was finally announced it was generally admitted to be a very powerful one. Here it is in the order of batting: W. G. Grace (Capt.), A. E. Stoddart, R. Abel, J. T. Brown, W. Gunn, F. S. Jackson, T. Hayward, A. A. Lilley, G. Lohmann, J. T. Hearne, and T. Richardson. The attendance on the first day, June 22, was estimated at nearly 30,000, and "Lord's," wrote *The Times* on the next day, "has scarcely ever before been the scene of so much noisiness and rowdyism as was displayed yesterday when the crowds encroached on the ground." Lord Harris, in *A Few Short Runs*, made this comment: "It was a dreadful sight for those who love the strictness of first-class cricket as played at Lord's; and the Committee felt that every effort must be made to prevent the repetition of a scene so deplorable."

Whether it was that their dismissal for 18—one short, Giffen being absent ill—by the M.C.C. ten days previously had shaken their morale—a most unusual trait in Australian cricketers!—it is, of course, impossible to say, and I personally doubt it, but on winning the toss they were all out for 53[1] on a perfect wicket, Richardson taking six wickets for 39 runs and Lohmann three for 13 runs. England replied with 292, Abel, missed in the slips at 9, scoring 94, W. G. 66, and Jackson 44. Going in again, the Australians lost three wickets for 62 runs, and then Trott and Gregory, by cricket of the finest possible description, put on 221 runs in two hours and three-quarters. W. G., during this long stand, was seen at times to be plucking his beard, always a sure sign that he was anxious, but Richardson came again, and, ably assisted by Hearne, the innings closed for 347. Before the close of play on the second day England lost Abel for 16. During the night it rained heavily, and England had to struggle hard on the third morning. Had all the catches been held there might have been a desperate finish, but Jones had two or three chances missed off him, and England won by six wickets.

This was the match in which Jones bowled a ball, the first sent down in England's first innings, through W. G.'s beard. The ball in question was very short and very fast, and got up quickly. J. J. Kelly, the Australian wicket-keeper, lost sight of it in Grace's beard, and it went to the screen. W. G. walked up the pitch and said, "Where the h—l are you bowling, Jonah?" to which Jones replied, "Sorry, Doctor; she slipped!" Jones was a magnificently built man, and active on his feet—he was one of the greatest mid-off's of all time—and if his analyses are examined it will be found that over and over again he got out the best batsmen on the other side. This was Lohmann's last match for England. Consumption had laid its fell hand on him, and though he subsequently went to South Africa in the hope of a cure in that lovely climate, he died on December 1, 1901, at Matjesfontein, at the early age of thirty-five. He was a great cricketer, who loved the game with all his soul, and to hear him talk on cricket was well worth while.

Of the two elevens who played in this Lord's match F. S. Jackson is the sole survivor to-day.

Reverting to the sensational match between the M.C.C. and the Australians, a few facts may be recalled. The M.C.C. batted first on a wicket affected by rain, and, thanks to two or three missed catches, scored 219. On the Australians going in W.G. began the bowling with Attewell and J. T. Hearne (Pavilion end),

[1] See p. 94*n*.

but with the score at 18 for three wickets he put on Pougher instead of Attewell, and not another run was made. Think of it—three for 18, all out 18! The score of this remarkable match is reproduced in full:

M.C.C. *v.* AUSTRALIANS

Played at Lord's, June 11 *and* 12, 1896

Result: M.C.C. won by an innings and 18 *runs*

M.C.C.

W. G. Grace, b. Trumble	15
A. E. Stoddart, st. Kelly, b. Trott	54
K. S. Ranjitsinhji, b. Trumble	7
F. S. Jackson, c. and b. Trumble	51
W. Gunn, b. M'Kibbin	39
G. MacGregor, b. Trumble	0
G. Davidson, b. Trumble	0
F. Marchant, b. M'Kibbin	20
A. D. Pougher, not out	9
W. Attewell, b. Trumble	7
J. T. Hearne, b. M'Kibbin	1
Byes 13, leg byes 2, no-ball 1	16
Total	219

AUSTRALIANS

First Innings		*Second Innings*	
J. J. Kelly, c. and b. Pougher	8	b. Hearne	0
H. Graham, b. Hearne	4	b. Hearne	5
H. Trott, b. Hearne	6	c. MacGregor, b. Hearne	14
S. E. Gregory, b. Hearne	0	c. MacGregor, b. Hearne	28
F. A. Iredale, b. Hearne	0	b. Hearne	0
C. Hill, b. Pougher	0	b. Hearne	4
H. Trumble, b. Pougher	0	b. Hearne	0
J. Darling, not out	0	c. Stoddart, b. Hearne	76
C. J. Eady, b. Pougher	0	c. Grace, b. Hearne	42
T. R. M'Kibbin, c. Davidson, b. Pougher	0	not out	3
G. Giffen, absent ill	0	absent ill	0
		Byes	11
Total	18	Total	183

BOWLING ANALYSIS

AUSTRALIANS

	O.	M.	R.	W.		O.	M.	R.	W.
Trumble	34	8	84	6	Trott	13	1	35	1
Giffen	9	0	22	0	Eady	8	2	11	0
M'Kibbin	19.2	2	51	3					

M.C.C.

First Innings	O.	M.	R.	W.	*Second Innings*	O.	M.	R.	W.
Hearne	11	9	4	4	Hearne	50.3	22	73	9
Attewell	8	5	14	0	Attewell	10	4	14	0
Pougher	3	3	0	5	Pougher	28	15	33	0
					Jackson	10	3	16	0
					Davidson	7	3	15	0
					Grace	8	1	21	0

Umpires: W. A. J. West and J. Phillips

The return game was drawn, M.C.C. wanting 68 runs to win with seven wickets to fall. The Club had a powerful side, for, although W. G. was too lame to play, the first five batsmen were Stoddart, MacLaren, Ranjitsinhji, Gunn, and Captain E. G. Wynyard, in great form this season, and a fine fieldsman.

Mr Pardon had some severe strictures on the Australian bowling. Of Jones he wrote: "Jones's bowling is to our mind radically unfair, as we cannot conceive a ball being fairly bowled at the pace of an express train with a bent arm." He also denounced M'Kibbin's off-break as a "continual throw." He was glad, however, that they passed unchallenged, as he thought by our supine attitude to illegal bowling we had brought the trouble on our own heads.

It had been feared by many that when the follow-on law was kept on a compulsory basis trouble would follow. Those who opposed making the follow-on voluntary stressed overmuch the advantage of winning the toss, and did not realize sufficiently that the side which had gained a lead on the first innings was being penalized for having played the better cricket. The climax came in the University Match. When F. Mitchell, the Cambridge Captain, in order to avoid Oxford's following on, instructed E. B. Shine, as Jackson had instructed Wells three years before, to send down three balls—two of them no-balls—to the boundary there was a very hostile demonstration. On returning to the pavilion the Cambridge Eleven were hooted at by the members of the M.C.C., and in the pavilion itself there were angry scenes, many members losing all control over themselves. Winged words were given and returned, Cantab was divided against Cantab, and brother against brother. The reader will remember that Alfred Lyttelton had pleaded for a voluntary follow-on, but now Lord Cobham supported Mitchell, and his brother, Edward Lyttelton, condemned him. When Oxford took the field they were greeted with loud and prolonged cheering, and when F. H. E. Cunliffe, from the Pavilion end, in his first over, clean bowled W. G. Grace, junior, for 0 his dismissal was greeted with a yell of delight. Young W. G., however, made a 'pair,' and both Dark and Light Blue partisans were genuinely sorry, and the Oxford team, even at a moment of extreme tension, did not forget to say so. We thought of the Grand Old Man and how deeply he would feel it. Six Cambridge wickets fell for 61 before the splendid bowling of Cunliffe and J. C. Hartley, but N. F. Druce played a beautiful innings, though I should have caught him at backward point, off Hartley, when he had scored some 20 or 30 runs. Had I been a six-footer I might have done so, but a hard cut touched only the tips of my fingers, though I jumped for the ball like a rough-haired fox-terrier I once owned, who put all other high-jumping dogs into the shade! E. H. Bray, P. W. Cobbold, and E. B. Shine gave Druce strong support, and Oxford were set 330 runs to make to win, a tremendous task in a fourth innings. But the wicket, which had shown definite signs of crumbling on the second afternoon—the reason for Mitchell's action—benefited, from an Oxford point of view, by rain during the night, and played easily enough. We had lost three wickets—Mordaunt, Foster, and myself—for 60 at lunch-time, but Leveson-Gower (41) and C. C. Pilkington (44) added 84 runs for the fourth partnership, and Leveson-Gower and G. O. Smith 97, when Leveson-Gower was caught at the wicket. 89 runs were wanted with five wickets to fall, and Cambridge still had a chance; but Bardswell never looked like getting out, and we were within 2 runs of victory when Smith jumped out to drive Cobbold and was caught at slip. As he came up the pavilion steps the members rose to him and took off their hats. He had played a magnificent innings of 132, and as long as there is a history of Oxford and Cambridge cricket the name of G. O. Smith will be emblazoned on its rolls.

Soon after Leveson-Gower had gone in to bat his mother, unable to stand the tension, left the ground, got into a hansom, and drove about Regent's Park. After an hour she returned, and as she walked through the entrance the gate attendant remarked, "It's all right, ma'am. He's still there." Leveson-Gower was a splendid captain. Always cheerful and encouraging, he managed his somewhat limited bowling most skilfully. He was a quick and smart fieldsman at cover-point, and a great man at a crisis as a batsman. Over and over again he came to the rescue and made runs when they were wanted.

It was not until the Annual General Meeting on May 2, 1900, that the law was changed to read as follows: "The side which leads by 150 runs in a three-day match, by 100 runs in a two-day match, and by 75 runs in a one-day match shall have the *option* of calling on the other side to follow its innings." To some it might appear that the M.C.C. Committee moved slowly, but it should always be remembered that the M.C.C., very wisely, are generally reluctant to propose any new legislation until the opinions of cricketers all over the world have been ascertained, and this naturally takes time. At the same meeting the over was increased from five balls to six, and a declaration of the innings was made permissible at or after the luncheon interval on the second day.

The Gentlemen defeated the Players. They had a great batting side—Grace, Stoddart, Ranjitsinhji, Palairet, Jackson, MacLaren, O'Brien, Woods, Jones, E. Smith, and MacGregor—and though they were set 222 runs to win on a wicket which had crumbled, they won by six wickets, a remarkable achievement against bowlers of the skill of Richardson, Briggs, Lohmann, and J. T. Hearne. It is probable that this was the best batting side which has ever represented the Gentlemen. When the Players batted MacGregor caught four and stumped one. The scores were: Gentlemen 268 and 224 for four, Players 116 and 373.

One of the finest in the long series of Gentlemen *v.* Players matches, which dates back to 1806, was that at Lord's in 1897, the Players winning by 78 runs, with totals of 358 and 279 against 286 and 273. Shrewsbury played a beautiful first innings of 125, run out, and, hitting nineteen fours, scored faster than usual, while W. G.'s 66 on a broken wicket in the second innings was one of his best. The most notable performance, however, was that of G. L. Jessop. Joining F. G. J. Ford when six wickets had fallen for 136 runs in the Gentlemen's second innings, he made 39 out of 44 in a quarter of an hour, and altogether 67 out of 88 in thirty-five minutes, hitting one five and eleven fours.[1] He made Ford, who played two fine innings of 50, not out, and 79, not out, look like a veritable stonewaller![2] For once Jackson and Ranjitsinhji failed in this match, scoring only 21 runs between them, and Jackson not taking a wicket in either innings. Hayward clean bowled both of them in the first innings, while Richardson did so in the second. Hayward is renowned as a batsman, but about this period he was a pretty good bowler, and Jessop, in his interesting book *A Cricketer's Log*,[3] says, "My particular *bêtes noires* (as bowlers) were M. A. Noble, Blythe, and Tom Hayward.

[1] In the University Match this year Jessop, in the second innings, scored 42 out of 51 in eighteen minutes.

[2] Ford was really a fast-scoring left-hander, with a beautiful style. He was described as "six foot two of don't care," he played so easily, almost casually. In general method he was not unlike F. E. Woolley, but not so great a batsman.

[3] Hodder and Stoughton, 1922.

Hayward possessed a most lively nip from the pitch, and could turn the ball from the off even on a plumb wicket." Describing the match, Jessop, "the Human Catapault who wrecks the roofs of distant towns when set in his assault," as the Philadelphia bard, R. D. Paine, put it, pays high tribute to Ford, Shrewsbury, and Richardson, saying of the last, "No bowler has ever compelled my admiration to such an extent as did Tom Richardson."

What a great cricketer Jessop was, and what a draw! *Sui generis* as a batsman, he was by far the greatest cutter of all the famous hitters, and his drives had a very long carry. If he was unorthodox he was a genius, and a genius may do as he likes—and, a point which has often been overlooked, no one watched the ball more closely than he did. As a cover or extra-cover he was unsurpassed, and for a few years he was a very fast bowler from round the wicket.

Jessop was on the short side, but he possessed long arms, had a barrel of a chest, like Squire Osbaldeston, and was as active as a cat. He gave the impression of great physical strength, but his health was not always of the best. He was a terribly bad sailor, and a voyage to Australia was one long agony to him.

> At the Annual Meeting of the M.C.C. it was reported that Sir Edward Grey had become the holder of the Gold Tennis Prize, having beaten the Hon. Alfred Lyttelton. The Committee have decided to present Mr Lyttelton with a replica of the Gold Prize in recognition of his great skill as a tennis-player, and of his having won the Gold Prize on twelve different occasions.

A special General Meeting of the M.C.C. was held at the Queen's Hall, Langham Place, on February 28, 1898. Lord Lichfield,[1] the President, was in the Chair, and some 1500 members were present. The chief business of the meeting was the appointment of a Secretary to succeed Henry Perkins. The Committee, after consideration of the many candidates for the post, were unanimous in recommending Mr F. E. Lacey, but one of the unsuccessful candidates, Mr J. S. Russell, declined to be bound by the Committee's decision. At the last minute, however, Russell withdrew his candidature, and the meeting passed off amicably. The Committee, sitting on the stage of the Queen's Hall in almost a semicircle, like a band of Christy Minstrels, were an impressive lot of men, many of them being of

[1] Thomas Francis, third Earl of Lichfield.

uncommon good-looks, and Lord Lichfield was tactfulness itself. The result was that Lacey was unanimously elected Secretary, and a pension of £400 a year was unanimously awarded to Perkins, who was also elected an honorary life member of the Club.

At the Annual General Meeting held in the pavilion on May 4 Rule XVII was altered, the words "including the appointment, dismissal, and fixing the salary of the Secretary" being added to the original "The Committee shall have the entire management of the property, funds, and affairs of the Club." The report also stated that it had been decided to pull down the existing tennis and rackets courts and the two houses Nos. 43 and 45 St John's Wood Road, in order to provide more accommodation for the public, necessitated by the scenes which had taken place at the England *v.* Australia match in 1896. The line of seats would be thrown back, which would increase the area of the ground. Thus the Mound Stand was born.

On July 18, 1898, W. G. was fifty, and the M.C.C. Committee, with a gracious gesture, fixed the dates of Gentlemen *v.* Players a week later than usual, so that the opening day should coincide with the Champion's birthday. Two fine sides were selected, though *Wisden* did not agree that Haigh, of Yorkshire, admittedly a great bowler on false turf, should have been preferred to Richardson, of Surrey, on a hard wicket. The choice of two wicket-keepers—Storer and Lilley—in the Players' team was also criticized, nor did the omission of L. C. H. Palairet appeal to the editor of the famous almanack. There was a great crowd when, on losing the toss, W. G. led the Gentlemen into the field, the members in the pavilion and the spectators round the ground standing up and giving him a reception which even he had seldom received. What a game it was, the Players winning by 137 runs a few minutes before time! And how splendidly the Old Man batted, in spite of lameness and an injured hand which compelled him to go in No. 9 in the second innings! And how thoroughly he enjoyed it all! During the three days 41,558 people paid gate money, not counting members of the M.C.C. and their friends. The match excited uncommon interest, and for a graphic description of it *Wisden* is well worth reading. *The Times* and other daily newspapers also devoted considerable space to it, and W. G.'s name was on every one's lips. A game worthy to be included among the best of these classic contests, and the full score is therefore given.

GENTLEMEN *v.* PLAYERS

Played at Lord's, July 18, 19, *and* 20, 1898

Result: Players won by 137 *runs*

PLAYERS

First Innings		*Second Innings*	
A. Shrewsbury (Capt.), c. Kortright, b. Townsend	18	b. Woods	11
R. Abel, b. Kortright	7	b. Kortright	5
W. Gunn, b. Woods	139	c. MacGregor, b. Mason	56
W. Storer, c. Woods, b. Mason	59	c. sub., b. Townsend	73
J. Tunnicliffe, c. MacGregor, b. Grace	9	c. sub., b. Mason	44
W. Brockwell, c. Woods, b. Townsend	47	c. and b. Woods	5
A. Hearne, b. Woods	17	c. MacGregor, b. Mason	11
A. A. Lilley, not out	17	c. Stoddart, b. Mason	10
W. H. Lockwood, b. Townsend	4	b. Kortright	6
S. Haigh, l.b.w., b. Townsend	9	not out	12
J. T. Hearne, b. Woods	1	c. Stoddart, b. Woods	13
Bye 1, leg byes 7	8	Byes 9, leg byes 8	17
Total	335	Total	263

GENTLEMEN

W. G. Grace (Capt.), c. Lilley, b. Lockwood	43	not out	31
A. E. Stoddart, c. A. Hearne, b. Lockwood	21	c. Tunnicliffe, b. Lockwood	4
F. S. Jackson, c. Lilley, b. J. T. Hearne	48	b. J. T. Hearne	33
C. L. Townsend, c. and b. Lockwood	2	c. Tunnicliffe, b. J. T. Hearne	17
A. C. MacLaren, c. Abel, b. Haigh	50	b. J. T. Hearne	10
J. R. Mason, c. Tunnicliffe, b. J. T. Hearne	35	b. Lockwood	0
J. A. Dixon, c. Storer, b. Lockwood	31	b. Haigh	4
S. M. J. Woods, b. J. T. Hearne	13	b. J. T. Hearne	9
Capt. E. G. Wynyard, c. Brockwell, b. J. T. Hearne	12	b. J. T. Hearne	0
G. MacGregor, c. Lilley, b. J. T. Hearne	16	b. J. T. Hearne	1
C. J. Kortright, not out	17	c. Haigh, b. Lockwood	46
Byes 11, leg byes 4	15	Byes 2, leg bye 1	3
Total	303	Total	158

BOWLING ANALYSIS

Gentlemen

First Innings	O.	M.	R.	W.	*Second Innings*	O.	M.	R.	W.
Kortright	37	13	90	1	Kortright	36	8	83	2
Jackson	28	12	48	0	Jackson	9	4	21	0
Townsend	25	8	58	4	Townsend	15	4	33	1
Grace	12	2	34	1					
Woods	20.1	4	49	3	Woods	26	9	62	3
Mason	11	3	30	1	Mason	17	8	47	4
Dixon	5	0	18	0					

PLAYERS

First Innings	O.	M.	R.	W.	Second Innings	O.	M.	R.	W.
J. T. Hearne	33	10	87	5	J. T. Hearne	27	10	65	6
Lockwood	32.4	9	82	4	Lockwood	20.3	6	39	3
Haigh	31	12	64	1	Haigh	10	1	21	1
A. Hearne	11	2	36	0	A. Hearne	4	1	9	0
Brockwell	6	1	19	0	Brockwell	6	3	7	0
					Storer	2	0	10	0
					Abel	2	1	4	0

Umpires: J. Phillips and W. A. J. West

The England teams for the Test Matches *v.* Australia in England had hitherto been selected by the committees of the clubs on whose grounds the matches were played—Lord's, the Oval, and Old Trafford—but at the request of the counties a Board of Control was formed by the M.C.C. and came into being in 1899. The Board was composed of the President of the M.C.C. (in the Chair), five of the Club Committee, one representative from each of the ten first-class counties at the top of the last season's list, and one representative from each county on whose ground a Test Match is to be played, subject to such county not already being represented. The Board made rules and regulations as to finance, payment of professionals, hours of play, umpires, etc., etc., and appointed a Selection Sub-committee of three, who, having chosen a captain, were to co-opt him as a member.

In 1899, for the first time in this country, five Test Matches were played with the Australians—at Trent Bridge, Lord's, Leeds, Old Trafford, and the Oval—and the responsibility for choosing the England elevens was entrusted to Lord Hawke (Yorkshire), H. W. Bainbridge (Warwickshire), and W. G. Grace (Gloucestershire). W. G., who was nearly fifty-one years of age, was invited to captain England in the first Test at Trent Bridge, but after the game decided that his Test Match days were over, and MacLaren was asked to be captain. Jackson was MacLaren's senior, but the choice fell on MacLaren. Whether the Selectors acted wisely is open to question, for though MacLaren was a magnificent batsman and an extremely fine tactician on the field, he was not a good strategist. Strategy is the art of choosing an eleven, and somehow he never seemed to get on with his committee, or they with him; and a captain who cannot obtain the confidence of his committee and persuade them of the soundness of his plans, or dissuade them from unsound strategy, or who quarrels with them, may forfeit both fame and victory. MacLaren was a pessimist by nature, and did not inspire his men to believe in their own prowess; and to make your men believe in themselves is a very important factor in cricket leadership. Moreover, he was unlucky. No cricketer likes to attribute his defeats to lack of good-fortune, but MacLaren, not once or twice, but on several occasions, found Fortune frowning on him in the shape of illness and accidents to his men after a match had begun. In this year, for example, Briggs was taken ill at the end of the first day at Sheffield and took no further part in the match, and there were other instances of this sort, both here and in Australia, during MacLaren's years of leadership. He could well claim, therefore, that the gods fought against him, and there is no question that he was a superb manager of his bowling and most skilful in placing the field. He is thus to be sympathized with, but much of his trouble arose from the friction between him and the Selectors. He captained England here and in Australia in twenty-two Test Matches, and won only four—and never the rubber. Was it not Napoleon who said, "Give me a lucky General"?

The Australian team of 1899 was one of the strongest that has visited this country, and they won the Test Match at Lord's by ten wickets. The first, at Trent Bridge, had been drawn in Australia's favour, England wanting 135 runs to win with three wickets to fall. The Selectors had a difficult problem to solve in regard to the fast bowling, for Lockwood and Kortright were both injured, and Richardson was but a shadow of his former greatness. So they chose Jessop as the fast bowler, and preferred Mead, of Essex, to J. T. Hearne. Jessop was the only fast bowler available, but to discard Hearne for a match at Lord's, his favourite ground, for Mead was a dangerous experiment which was far from being justified by events.

The match was really lost in the first hour and a half, when six wickets fell for 66 runs on a perfect wicket. Jones was in his finest form, clean bowling MacLaren and having Fry, Ranjitsinhji, and Tyldesley caught. For the whole innings his analysis was seven wickets for 88 runs. His pace was tremendous. Jackson's 73 was a superb innings, and Jessop made a good 51. Australia headed England's total of 206 by 215 runs, Hill (135) and Trumper (135, not out) being the highest scorers, both batting magnificently.

England scored 240 in the second innings (MacLaren 88, not out, Hayward 77, Jackson 37). Throughout the game the Australian bowling was of the highest class, and the fielding could not have been better. We were completely outplayed under even conditions for both sides. It was a sad day for English cricket, though MacLaren's masterly innings will never be forgotten by those who saw it.

The Australians defeated the M.C.C. twice at Lord's, winning the first match by eight and the second by nine wickets. The left-handers Hill (132) and Darling (71 and 53), for the Australians, and C. L. Townsend (37, run out, and 78), for the M.C.C., took the batting honours, and it is interesting to note that W. G., who made 50 in his first innings, clean bowled Trumper and Kelly and had Hill caught. And he a mere colt approaching fifty-one!

The return match will always be famous for Albert Trott's hit over the pavilion off Noble on the first day (July 31), the only occasion on which this has been done. Trott began with a 'sighter' on to the first balcony, and then came this stupendous straight drive, the ball landing in a garden of one of the houses. Trott was unlucky not to have done this before, for on May 4 of the same year, playing for the M.C.C. *v.* Sussex, he on-drove a ball from F. W. Tate which struck the cornice of the south-west corner of the pavilion and bounced back on to the seats in front of the Committee Room. This was undoubtedly the bigger hit of the two, for the cornice is several feet higher than the centre of the pavilion.

A typical Australian recovery enabled them to win the second match by nine wickets, Darling playing a great innings of 128, one of his finest efforts in England. They held a lead of 61, and the M.C.C. failed badly in their second innings, though C. L. Townsend, at No. 3, carried his bat for 69. In the first innings Ranjitsinhji gave one of his best displays in scoring 92.

Jones was almost invariably successful at Lord's, taking ten wickets for 137 runs in the first and five for 125 in the second M.C.C. match, ten for 164 in the Test Match, and ten for 84 *v.* Middlesex—in all, thirty-five wickets for 14 runs each. On the first day of the Middlesex match there was an unseemly demonstration on the part of the spectators, "happily without precedent at Lord's ground," says *Wisden.* Darling, the Australian Captain, who eventually scored 111, took three hours to make his first 38 runs, and the spectators in the Mound Stand whistled the *Dead March in "Saul,"* and kept time by stamping with their feet. Darling was suffering from a badly bruised heel, and the Middlesex bowling—J. T. Hearne, Trott, Wells, Rawlin, and Roche—was good, as was the fielding and the wicket-keeping of MacGregor.

We had our best August side, but Jones and C. E. MacLeod, who bowled unchanged, dismissed us for totals of 105 and 110 on a pitch which was a trifle worn.

Pardon, writing on Jones's bowling, while finding his delivery far from satisfactory in the opening match at the Crystal Palace and the England match at Manchester, thought "that he strove to keep within the law, and, this being the case, it was gratifying to find he had lost nothing in pace or effectiveness."

Although the Players were without Shrewsbury, W. Gunn, and Lilley, the Gentlemen's victory by an innings and 59 runs was a fine performance. Against Lockwood, Hirst, Albert Trott, W. Mead, and Rhodes the Gentlemen made 480 (Fry 104, W. G. 78, J. R. Mason 72, Jackson 44, Ranjitsinhji 38, MacLaren 31), and the Players 196 and 225, the wicket in this last innings being affected by rain. The match will always be memorable for D. L. A. Jephson's lob bowling—six wickets for 21 runs in the Players' first innings. He was backed up by magnificent fielding, MacLaren making a marvellous catch at deep square leg. Hirst hit a ball from Jephson very hard, and MacLaren, running fully twenty yards, held it just short of the boundary while moving at full speed. He was cheered to the echo, and the cheering was renewed when W. G. walked across and shook him by the hand, saying, "You caught it finely, Archie." This was the Old Man's last appearance at Lord's for the Gentlemen, and he was unlucky not to crown it with a century: he was run out through no fault of his own. Jephson's success brought back memories of the old lob bowlers, Clarke, Tinley, and V. E. Walker, but comparison with them is difficult. Of the more modern lob bowlers—Humphreys, of Sussex, G. H. Simpson-Hayward, and Jephson himself—Simpson-Hayward, perhaps, was the best. Humphreys got a lot of work on the ball from leg, and was undoubtedly a very clever bowler, as was Jephson, who turned the ball both ways. But Simpson-Hayward flighted the ball very cleverly and spun it tremendously from the off. Though he bowled a straight one, he seldom, if ever, bowled a leg break. On the then matting wicket at Johannesburg he was particularly hard to play.

The University Match was drawn, the batting being far superior to the bowling. In Cambridge's second innings Jessop scored *46 out of 58 in twenty-five minutes* before being caught at long-off.

CHAPTER IX

The Turn of the Century (1900–6)

A Clamour for Reform—A Remarkable Game—Visit of the West Indies—The M.C.C. and the Press—Friction over a Tour—High Scoring—The South Africans Again—An Unsatisfactory Decision—An Interesting Debate—Australia's Great Team—Height and Width of the Stumps—The Philadelphians—A Most Extraordinary Match—C. B. Fry—Problems of Captaincy—Committee Meetings—The Match of the Season—R. O. Schwarz—"Jacker"—W. W. Armstrong—An Exciting Affair—N. A. Knox—Jessopian Innings—George Challenor

DURING the first weeks of the season the M.C.C. enclosed Lord's with a net about two feet six inches in height, with the idea of making the batsmen run out their hits, but the experiment met with no success and was given up. It was first arranged that when the ball went over the netting three runs should be scored, and that when it was stopped by the net two runs should be added to those already run. This method was modified after a few trials, with no better result. The plan penalized big hits over the ropes, and was generally voted clumsy. It certainly did not tire out the batsmen. It was the fieldsmen who complained of being overworked! I played for the M.C.C. *v.* Yorkshire in one of these games, and was fortunate enough to score 83 and 69, but my firm impression was that my 83 was worth about 65 to 70, and my 69 about 54 to 58. 1143 runs were made in this match, but under ordinary conditions about 150 runs fewer would probably have been scored. In another game 11 runs, including an overthrow, were scored for a late cut! C. J. Burnup was the bowler, and S. H. Wood the batsman.

About this period the scoring in fine weather was very high, due largely to the downright bad fielding of several county teams and to the ridiculously over-prepared wickets, of which those at the Oval and at Leyton[1] were glaring examples. As a result there

[1] The Leyton ground formed part of the Lyttelton estate, and was made under the superintendence of Mr R. Creed, F.R.I.B.A., at the cost of Lord Lyttelton, in 1883. A contemporary report said that the opening of the ground "gave unwonted loveliness to a district which but a short time since presented an appearance of the abomination of desolation."

was a clamour for reform in many quarters, and some went so far as to urge that for every maiden over sent down the fielding side should be credited with two runs. Imagine this on any sort of wicket against first-class bowling! Would it not have led to an attack directed entirely on the leg stump, outside it, with almost all the fieldsmen on the on side, thereby slowing down the game? A fine batting side against, say, Barnes and Hirst might well have been 25 to 30 runs down at the end of an hour. The idea was too ridiculous to deserve serious attention, but it showed to what extremes the 'reformers' in question were prepared to go. Their suggestion, if adopted, would have emptied every cricket ground in England.

The best match of the year was Gentlemen *v.* Players, and it was indeed a remarkable game, the Players, set 501 in the last innings, winning by two wickets. At half-past six, the time arranged for drawing stumps, the score stood at a tie, but Woods, the Gentlemen's Captain, decided to have another over, and he went on to bowl himself, Rhodes making the winning hit. Woods thereby broke the regulations, which are always, and very rightly so, strictly observed at Lord's, but many will say that in the circumstances he was justified. I am not sure myself—and what did the umpires, J. Wheeler and J. Phillips, have to say about it? Rules are made to be kept, otherwise confusion occurs; and if they are not going to be enforced trouble is bound to arise at some time or another.

On the second afternoon the Gentlemen were in such an apparently strong position that Woods gave his men instructions to get out in order to give the Players nearly half an hour at the end of the day, during which they lost a valuable wicket, that of Albert Ward. Next day truly magnificent batting by Hayward (111), J. T. Brown (163), and Abel (98) made victory possible. It was said of Abel that away from the over-marled Oval pitch he did not relish fast bowling, and the story goes that, being accused of flinching at Kortright in the Gentlemen *v.* Players match of 1898, he replied, "Well, I am the father of thirteen children, and there are plenty of other bowlers to make runs off besides Mr Kortright!" On this occasion, though Kortright was in the Gentlemen's Eleven, as well as Jessop, who was at that time really fast, there was no apprehension on his part.

Apart from its remarkable finish, this match will ever be memorable for R. E. Foster's two centuries (102, not out, and

136). In his first innings he was batting a little over two hours, and in his second an hour and three-quarters. Ten days previously he made 171 for Oxford *v.* Cambridge, and three years later he was to make 287 for England *v.* Australia at Sydney, both these scores being, at the time, the highest individual scores in these matches. Jessop, in *A Cricketer's Log*, calls him "the English Trumper," and he was indeed a glorious batsman, with every stroke. He was very quick on his feet, and his steel-like wrists he used to the full. He was also as great a fieldsman in the slips as there has ever been: I personally never saw him miss a catch. Foster was a brilliant forward at Association football, and a fine rackets player and golfer. Indeed, there was no game at which he did not excel. The Walkers, the Lytteltons, the Studds, the Steels, the Fords, the Ashtons, and the Gilligans, these are the famous cricketing families, but none were greater than the Fosters.

Eton *v.* Harrow was an umbrella-gnawing match, Harrow winning by one wicket. When A. Buxton, the last man, came in 7 runs were wanted to win.

The West Indies paid their first visit to England under the captaincy of my brother Aucher, but their matches did not count as first class. After a bad start they did fairly well, and L. Constantine, the father of the famous Constantine of to-day, C. A. Ollivierre, a brilliant player, who ran between wickets like a deer, and P. J. Cox were good batsmen, and S. Woods and W. J. Burton a pair of capital bowlers. The lessons they learned on the tour were absorbed, and at a later date they were to give us not only the 'younger' Constantine, but such batsmen as G. Challenor (to whom the M.C.C. Committee paid a great compliment by electing him a member, although he had not played the necessary number of qualifying matches required by Rule 10 of the Club, the M.C.C. in General Meeting acquiescing in this breach of the rules), Sir Harold Austin, G. Headley (the Bradman of the Caribbean), Martindale, John, Francis, the two Grants, Clarke, and many other first-class cricketers.

There was some friction this year between the M.C.C. and the Press, and Mr Pardon made this comment in his "Notes by the Editor" in *Wisden*:

> It was an ungracious and uncalled-for act to shift the Press representatives from the grand stand to the roof of the ground bowlers' house in the corner of the ground. Happily the protest in the newspapers was so loud and unanimous that the M.C.C. bowed

> before the storm, and at the Gentlemen *v.* Players match—immediately following the Oxford and Cambridge and Eton *v.* Harrow matches—the unhappy experiment was given up. I cannot see why the M.C.C. should be so reluctant to build a proper Press box, commanding an end-on view of the game. . . . The M.C.C. have spend thousands of pounds during the last few years to increase the accommodation for their members and the public, and they might surely do for the newspapers what has been done at Manchester, Leeds, and Nottingham. . . . It is hardly the thing for the first cricket club in the world thus to lag behind the counties in so simple a matter.

The M.C.C. immediately set to work and built a Press box at the north-west corner of the pavilion, giving an end-on view of the game, and the matter ended there.

During the winter of 1900–1 letters and cablegrams passed between the M.C.C. and Major B. Wardill, of the Melbourne Cricket Club, in regard to the visit of a team to Australia under the auspices of the M.C.C., but in the end nothing came of it. One cablegram sent by the M.C.C. was described by Wardill as "obscure," and was later followed by another from Wardill saying, "Propose to ask MacLaren to bring a side. Have you any objections?" The M.C.C. raised no objection, and at the General Meeting on May 7, 1902, the Annual Report merely stated that "it was found impossible for the M.C.C. to send a representative English team to Australia." MacLaren got together a pretty good side, but Yorkshire refused to allow Hirst and Rhodes to join it. Hirst had this summer acquired the deadly late swerve which was to make him one of the best of bowlers, and without the two Yorkshire cricketers MacLaren was sadly handicapped. To make matters worse for him, S. F. Barnes broke down during the third Test Match and did not play again during the tour. Yorkshire's reason for refusing permission was that a tour in Australia would wear out Hirst and Rhodes, and Yorkshire cricket would thereby suffer. I have never been able to understand why a tour in Australia should impair in any way the subsequent efficiency and stamina of any cricketer, and especially two such physically fit and strong men. Surely there are no hardships to be undergone when one begins with a five to six weeks' voyage on a luxurious liner and ends with another voyage of the same duration? Again, the lovely Australian climate, if occasionally a little too hot, is surely better for anyone's health than a winter in Briggate or Lascelles Hall? What many people seem to forget is that it is perfectly easy to rest your bowlers in Australia. Only one match is played a week, so that if a man is left out of a match he is ensured eight or nine days' complete rest. Naturally MacLaren resented Yorkshire's attitude, and a good deal of friction resulted, MacLaren thinking that he had been badly treated by Yorkshire, or, rather, by Lord Hawke, who was Yorkshire. It will be seen that two years later the M.C.C. decided to send a side, and both Hirst and Rhodes were in it.

> The 1901–2 venture was the last occasion upon which the sole selection of an English side rested entirely upon the caprice of the leader of the party. This unsatisfactory arrangement of such important affairs came to an end none too soon. Suggestions from those who were undertaking the financial risks of the tour as to the composition of the side about to visit them could no longer be tendered to an official body such as the M.C.C.[1]

The summer of 1901 was a season of tremendous scoring, superlatively good wickets and, in many cases, poor fielding contributing to this. Fry, G. Brann, who, however, played only ten innings, and Ranji averaged over 70, and twenty-four batsmen in all had averages of 40 and over. On the liquid marled pitches the many great batsmen were often completely masters of the many great bowlers, and only Rhodes and Hirst obtained their wickets at a fairly reasonable cost. In the circumstances Rhodes's 251 wickets was an astounding feat, though both he and Hirst had this advantage, that the wickets in Yorkshire were, generally speaking, nothing like so favourable to batsmen as those on many other grounds.

The Players put into the field one of the strongest sides that has ever represented them—Abel (Capt.), Carpenter, Tyldesley, Hayward, Braund, Storer, Lockwood, Hirst, J. Gunn, Trott, and Rhodes—the bowling being especially powerful, and they won the match by 221 runs. In reply to the Players' first innings of 394, to which Tyldesley contributed a brilliant 140, the Gentlemen at one time had 203 runs on the board with only one man out, and Fry and Ranji well set. At this point Lockwood, from the Nursery end, had Fry (126) brilliantly caught at slip by Braund—low down and very wide, with the right hand—and in an hour and a quarter the whole side were out for 245, Lockwood

[1] G. L. Jessop, *A Cricketer's Log*.

taking five wickets for 62 and Hirst four for 53. "As to the superlative quality of their bowling, there could not be two opinions," said *Wisden*. The Players made 256 for six wickets in their second innings, and declared, J. R. Mason taking five wickets for 72 runs in 42 overs. Mason was in some quarters underrated as a bowler. With his high action and accuracy, coupled with a clever slower ball by way of contrast to his normal medium pace, he was in reality a first-class bowler, who "kept knocking at the door," as Tom Emmett would have put it. Here he kept on over after over on a hot day in a wonderfully sustained effort.

On a somewhat worn pitch the Gentlemen could score no more than 184 in their second innings, Braund and Trott each taking four wickets. Jessop scored 35 out of 44 in seventeen minutes, but the batting was far too reckless. A little steadiness at the right moment, and the Gentlemen might well have drawn the match, for, with Jephson, Wells, and MacGregor at Nos. 8, 9, and 10, they were a formidable batting side. In an M.C.C. match earlier in the season against Leicestershire at Lord's Jessop made 169 out of 244 in an hour and three-quarters, and 49 out of 83 in thirty-five minutes. This wonderful cricketer was noted not only for his long-distance hitting, but also as is sometimes forgotten, for the consistency of his scoring: there has never been a batsman of such daring and original methods who could so often be relied on for runs.

The South Africans did not attract any marked attention as a team, but they were a pretty good side, with three outstanding cricketers in E. A. Halliwell, J. J. Kotze, and J. H. Sinclair. Halliwell was as great a wicket-keeper as has ever lived, standing up to the terrific fast bowling of Kotze, whose 'muzzle velocity' was equal to that of Kortright—some thought he exceeded it—and Sinclair was a fine all-rounder. Standing six feet four inches, he was a tremendous driver and a good medium-paced bowler, who made full use of his height and flighted the ball cleverly. George Lohmann had a high opinion of him, even if he did not quite come up to his expectations. G. A. Rowe, left-hander, and R. Graham, leg break, were two good bowlers, and if the South Africans could have commanded the services of G. C. B. Llewellyn they would have been a match for any county. Llewellyn was born in South Africa, but had a residential qualification for Hampshire, and played in only one match, in which he scored 4 and 88 and took thirteen wickets for 241 runs. He was a dashing batsman and a clever bowler, as well as a wonderful field at mid-off. He had a curious career, for he represented both South Africa and Hampshire, and was a reserve man for England at Birmingham in 1902. M. Bisset[1] was an admirable Captain both on and off the field. The M.C.C. defeated this side by 53 runs, Mead, in a sensational spell of bowling, turning the scale in favour of the Club when the South Africans looked like winning.

After heavy scoring the University Match was drawn. When Oxford's seventh wicket fell in their second innings forty minutes were left for play. At this point F. H. Hollins was apparently caught low down in the slips by E. R. Wilson,[2] who, being clearly under the impression that he had made the catch, threw the ball up. Hollins walked away to the pavilion. C. H. B. Marsham, the batsman at the other end, appealed, as he had a perfect right to do, but neither umpire, W. Hearn or J. Phillips, would give a decision, Hearn saying that the bowler, P. R. Johnson, had obstructed his view, and Phillips, the umpire at square leg, that W. P. Robertson, the wicket-keeper, who was standing back, had covered Wilson when he held the ball. It was a most unsatisfactory business that *both* umpires should have been unable to follow the ball. I do not like umpires who refrain from giving a decision on such grounds. It is their business to see. An umpire should not be a motionless figure standing rigidly at attention, with his eyes fixed to his front, as if on parade. A slight inclination of the head is all that is required.

After the ordinary business had been disposed of the 1901 Annual General Meeting of the M.C.C. was made special to consider a proposed alteration in the law of leg-before-wicket: "If with any part of his person (except the hand) which is between wicket and wicket he intercept a ball which would hit his wicket—Leg before Wicket."

On a ballot being taken, there were 259 votes in support of the change and 188 against it, but as no alteration in the Laws of Cricket can be carried by less than a two-thirds majority the proposal fell to the ground.

[1] Afterwards Sir Murray Bisset, Chief Justice, High Court of Southern Rhodesia.

[2] The brothers C. E. M. and E. R. Wilson had remarkable records in University Matches. C. E. M. made 115 in 1898, and E. R. 118 in 1901, while both were also good and very accurate bowlers, C. E. M. medium-paced and E. R. slow. Moreover, both were most able captains, with a profound knowledge of the history of cricket. Indeed, it is generally agreed that in any examination paper set on the game E. R. would probably romp away with an easy First, with C. E. M. *proxime accessit*. E. R. played for England *v.* Australia at Sydney in 1921.

There was a very keen debate, Alfred Lyttelton, R. A. H. Mitchell, and J. Shuter supporting the proposal and A. G. Steel and W. E. Denison, President of the M.C.C. in 1892 and a considerable figure in Nottinghamshire cricket, opposing it. It will be noted that the proposed alteration applied to both sides of the wicket. Lyttelton, with an able address and charming manner, urged that scoring was so high that too large a proportion of matches were unfinished, and he insisted that there should be "a bowler's territory, and that if a leg or any part of a batsman's person occupy that territory, and a ball hit a leg so occupying that territory which would have hit the wicket, then the batsman should be out." Shuter seconded Lyttelton. Denison, opposing the proposal, remarked that "a batsman's legs must be somewhere," and added, "There is no instance on record of the Marylebone Club endeavouring to pass into law any proposal to which there was a very strong and widespread objection." He then criticized the process by which the proposed law was brought forward. "It was proposed at a Cricket Sub-committee of the M.C.C., and was looked upon with doubt; as a matter of fact, they were divided, and made no recommendation on the point. It was then taken to a small meeting of the General Committee, at which it was adopted. The County Captains had voted unanimously against it, and, receiving their report from Lord Hawke, we naturally on the Cricket Sub-committee recommended to the General Committee that in view of the great weight of opinion against the proposal, it was not advisable to proceed with it any further at the present time. I do not know really what you keep the Cricket Sub-committee for if you are not going to take their advice." He then suggested that "to force upon a reluctant cricket world a measure to which so many eminent judges are entirely opposed cannot be anything but injurious to cricket, and, I think, disastrous to the reputation of the Marylebone Club as a cricket law-giver."

Thus ended one of the most interesting debates heard at Lord's, but the matter was not finished and done with until many years later.

At this distance of time it would seem that the M.C.C. Committee had not prepared the ground sufficiently. They did not pay sufficient attention to the views of the playing cricketers in this country—official consent from Australia, for example, had not been obtained—and to apply the proposed alteration to both sides of the wicket was far too drastic.

Some thirty years later the matter was far more ably handled, as the reader will see.

The splendid Australian team of 1902 won the rubber of Test Matches by two to one, the game at Lord's being utterly ruined by rain, only an hour and three-quarters' play being possible on the opening day. England won the toss, and lost Fry and Ranji without a run. Then MacLaren and Jackson took the score to 102. They had some luck, but their stroke play was very fine indeed. The Australians played two matches at Lord's against the M.C.C. They would have won the first had time allowed, and in the second, against a none too representative side, victory went to them by an innings and 34 runs. The most memorable feature of the first game was the magnificent batting of Trumper (105 and 86) and the bowling of W. G., who in the first innings had the following analysis:

O.	M.	R.	W.
19.5	5	29	5

Middlesex made a good fight, but in the end were defeated by six wickets on a pitch which had not quite recovered from rain. Trumble, bowling round the wicket, took twelve wickets for 149 runs, seven of them l.b.w. This was one of the greatest of Australian teams, with Trumble, Jones, Saunders, Armstrong, Howell, and Noble as bowlers, and the incomparable Trumper in glorious form. In a season of many sticky wickets he scored 2570 runs, with an average of between 48 and 49, making eleven centuries, the highest of them 128.

The Test Match at Birmingham was drawn—rain again—at Sheffield Australia won by 143 runs, and at Old Trafford by 3 runs. At the Oval England won by one wicket.

The games at Old Trafford and at the Oval were two of the most tremendous fights in all the long history of cricket, and those who saw them went through agonies of excitement. There was little or no difference between the sides, but the England team at Old Trafford was badly selected. Jessop, who had made 12 and 55 in the previous match at Sheffield, was dropped, as was Barnes, who had taken six wickets for 55 runs in Australia's first innings. Hirst was also passed over, Tate being played. Tate was a good bowler, but how he came to be preferred to Barnes or Hirst passes comprehension. And surely, if the weather was unsettled, Haigh would have been a preferable choice to Tate?

Altogether there was a complete muddle, and MacLaren and his selectors were clearly at variance. I have strayed from Lord's, but there was a strong feeling that but for mismanagement we should have won the rubber.

This has been called the Golden Age of cricket, but we, at any rate, did not on this occasion make anything like full use of the magnificent resources at our disposal.

Gentlemen *v.* Players followed immediately on the Test Match at Sheffield, and was something of an anticlimax. I have always held the view that there should be an interval of at least three days between such important fixtures. The weather for once was fine, and the wicket fast and inclined to be fiery. The Players won by an innings and 68 runs. Lockwood, just to show what a mistake had been made in leaving him out of the England Eleven at Sheffield, taking two wickets, those of MacLaren and Fry, in the first innings for 43 runs, and seven for 63 in the second innings. Both Braund and Lockwood had a great match, Braund scoring 141 and taking seven wickets for 91 runs, and Lockwood following up his splendid bowling with a century. Denton (93) hit brilliantly. There was only one side in it.

It was in this season that the length of the bowling crease was increased from six feet eight inches to eight feet eight inches. This gave the bowlers more manœuvring ground, and also widened the angle of delivery.

At their meeting at Lord's on December 8, 1902, the Captains of the first-class counties proposed that the stumps should be increased in width from eight to nine inches, and at the Annual General Meeting on May 6 following the proposal was debated, A. G. Steel and Lord Harris urging the alteration and W. E. Denison opposing it. On a vote being taken, the numbers were: For the proposal, 215; against, 199. The proposition was therefore lost, the necessary two-thirds majority being lacking.

Denzil Onslow proposed an amendment, conditional on the proposition being carried, that an inch should also be added to the height of the stumps, which is interesting in view of what was to happen many years later. The majority of the counties were in favour of the original proposal, but not all, and opposition came from Australia, South Africa, and America, but it was becoming obvious that many good judges were in favour of changes in the playing of the game, and that in the end they would probably gain the day, though not, perhaps, on exactly the lines they were advocating. The l.b.w. reformers went too far in urging the extension of "the bowler's territory," as Alfred Lyttelton so picturesquely put it, though I have heard it said that Don Bradman is not averse to the idea, but many of the sponsors of a wider wicket were to live to see the stumps not only widened, but heightened.

Some of the nicest people in the world live in and around Philadelphia, and the cricketers from that pleasant and attractive city have always been very welcome in this country. In 1903 they were without G. S. Patterson, one of their best batsmen, but this was undoubtedly a better side than that of 1897. They met a strong bowling side at Lord's, for the Club bowlers were J. T. Hearne, W. Mead, and A. E. Trott, and it was an uncommonly sticky wicket. The Philadelphians made 65 and 93, and the M.C.C. 104 and 55 for five wickets, of which I contributed 30, not out. I was missed at second slip low down off King when I had made 17, and had that catch been held there might well have been a desperate finish.

This was another very wet summer, but luckily the weather kept fine for the fortnight during which Gentlemen *v.* Players, Oxford and Cambridge, and Eton *v.* Harrow were played. Oxford, ably captained by W. Findlay, beat Cambridge by 268 runs. W. H. B. Evans, of Oxford, and E. M. Dowson, of Cambridge, were the best cricketers in the two elevens. Evans came of fine cricketing stock, and his style was easy and natural. He did not often play forward, but he was quick on his feet, and his off-drive was modelled on the lines of the best Malvern batsmen. He was also a fast-medium right-handed bowler, of moods, perhaps, but with a quick off-break. As he was a first-rate short slip as well, he looked all over a potential England cricketer, but he met with a tragic end, being killed flying with Colonel Cody.

Dowson too could claim a cricketing ancestry, for his father played for Surrey. He got into the Harrow Eleven in his first summer term, and I do not think it is an exaggeration to say that he was the best bowler of his age who has ever appeared, and the smallest boy, except, perhaps, A. N. Hornby, who has played at Lord's in this match, being at the time barely five feet in height. He was as accurate as an Alfred Shaw, an Attewell, or a J. T. Hearne, with his slow left-hand bowling. Subsequently he lost his bowling to a great extent, but developed into a tip-top batsman, with fine driving-power. His fielding, however, was not his strong point, and he gave the impression of a certain lassitude.

The most remarkable match at Lord's in 1903 was Gentlemen *v.* Players. The Gentlemen followed on 293 in arrears, but Fry and MacLaren put on 309 runs in just under three hours. Neville Cardus, in his *English Cricket*,[1] wrote, "Never has such batsmanship been seen as this for opulence and prerogative. It occurred a year after the Coronation of Edward VII; and it was indeed Coronation cricket." Here is the full score:

GENTLEMEN *v.* PLAYERS

***Played at Lord's, July* 6, 7, *and* 8, 1903**

Result: Drawn

PLAYERS

First Innings		*Second Innings*	
T. Hayward (Capt.), b. Dowson	51	b. Dowson	19
L. C. Braund, c. MacLaren, b. Dowson	69	not out	22
J. T. Tyldesley, run out	6	not out	13
D. Denton, c. Ranjitsinhji, b. Bosanquet	53		
A. E. Knight, b. Dowson	139		
J. Gunn, c. Warner, b. Brearley	28		
E. Arnold, b. Brearley	1		
A. E. Trott, b. Brearley	0		
S. F. Barnes, c. Evans, b. Brearley	56		
D. Hunter, b. Dowson	17		
S. Hargreave, not out	22		
Byes 16, leg byes 13, wide 1, no-balls 6	36	No-ball	1
Total	478	Total (1 wkt.)	55

GENTLEMEN

C. B. Fry, b. Hargreave	5	not out	232[2]
P. F. Warner, c. Hunter, b. Hargreave	51	c. Hunter, b. Hargreave	27
K. S. Ranjitsinhji, c. Tyldesley, b. Braund	9	c. Hunter, b. Gunn	60
C. J. Burnup, l.b.w., b. Braund	11		
A. C. MacLaren (Capt.), c. and b. Braund	9	not out	168
E. M. Dowson, c. Denton, b. Braund	29		
B. J. T. Bosanquet, c. Trott, b. Hargreave	26		
W. H. B. Evans, c. sub., b. Trott	21		
H. Martyn, c. Knight, b. Trott	7		
H. Hesketh-Prichard, not out	1		
W. Brearley, b. Trott	0		
Byes 13, leg byes 3	16	Byes 8, leg byes 2, no-balls 3	13
Total	185	Total (2 wkts. dec.)	500

[1] Collins, 1945.

[2] The highest score in Gentlemen *v.* Players matches at Lord's.

BOWLING ANALYSIS

GENTLEMEN

First Innings	O.	M.	R.	W.	*Second Innings*	O.	M.	R.	W.
Brearley	32	7	93	4	Brearley	4	0	16	0
Hesketh-Prichard	34	11	91	0	Hesketh-Prichard	5	2	9	0
Evans	24	6	52	0	Evans	8	2	17	0
Bosanquet	17	2	80	1					
Burnup	4	0	18	0					
Dowson	35.2	4	97	4	Dowson	6	1	12	1
Ranjitsinhji	2	0	11	0					

PLAYERS

	O.	M.	R.	W.		O.	M.	R.	W.
Barnes	1	1	0	0					
Hargreave	25	7	59	3	Hargreave	46	12	96	1
Braund	26	6	67	4	Braund	26	4	107	0
Gunn	5	0	26	0	Gunn	18	4	68	1
Trott	4	1	17	3	Trott	20	2	120	0
					Arnold	22	2	74	0
					Denton	4	0	22	0

Umpires: J. Phillips and V. A. Titchmarsh

It has been said that Charles Fry was a 'made' batsman. This is not correct, for he was a natural games-player mentally and physically. It is true that he brought a fine intellect to a close study of the methods and technique of batting, and this led him to remodel his style closer to perfection. He not only mastered the theory of every stroke, but was also an artist in their execution. If there is anything about batting that Charles Fry does not know it is still to be discovered. He is the great canonist on batsmanship. The hardest tests in batting are to play fast bowling on a fiery wicket and spin bowling on a sticky one. On such wickets Fry was as likely to score runs as any player I knew, for he could reduce the margin of error to a minimum. Ranji, in conversation with me a few years before his death in 1933, told me that he considered Fry the best of all batsmen, because of his ability to play every kind of bowling on every kind of wicket. In this he was like Jack Hobbs, of whom it may fairly be said that no greater batsman on all wickets has ever represented England.

MacLaren was "the grand manner personified. I have seen him all hauteur though bowled first ball," says Cardus, and this was one of his most masterly and dominating innings. The Players were extremely unfortunate in losing Barnes after he had bowled only one over in the match. Probably this was due to the extra strain involved in making 56 runs, and his absence was naturally a terrible handicap to his side, especially as the wicket had worn a little.

I spent the winter of 1902–3 in New Zealand and Australia.

Lord Hawke was to have captained the side, but at almost the last moment he was unable to do so, owing to the illness of his mother, and he did me the honour of inviting me to take his place. However, we were everywhere known as Lord Hawke's team, and wore his colours, so famous in almost every quarter of the globe. When we were in Melbourne a big dinner was given to us, and in the course of a speech Major Wardill gave a very clear indication that the Melbourne Cricket Club would like me to bring out the next side to Australia. He also wrote me a letter to this effect, but to all these suggestions I replied, "Ask the M.C.C. They are the proper people to send out a team." The Melbourne Cricket Club then urged me to use my influence to persuade the M.C.C. to send a side, and on my return to England I approached a prominent member of the M.C.C. Committee, with the result that F. S. Jackson was asked to act as captain. Jackson could not see his way to do so, and on June 4, 1903, I was summoned to the Committee Room and asked to undertake the captaincy. I pleaded for time for consideration, for I had never played for England in a Test Match, and that caused me furiously to think. After about ten days or a fortnight I made up my mind to accept, being encouraged to do so by several members of the Committee, who were good enough to say that they did not think that I should be likely to "drop any bricks," that I had apparently got on well with the Australians, and that my captaincy would not imperil England's chances of victory. All this, of course, was flattering to my *amour propre*, but my selection aroused criticism in certain quarters, which was, in the circumstances, not unexpected, for I was fully conscious of my shortcomings. I could not, for instance, be compared to either Jackson or MacLaren as a cricketer, and the point was stressed, and rightly stressed, that I had never before led an England side. I think I was lucky in one respect, that in the three Middlesex matches at Lord's, in the absence of MacGregor, I had captained the side, and we beat Gloucestershire, Somerset, and Yorkshire in succession. It was during the Yorkshire match that I was summoned to the Presence! I can recall to this day how my heart beat and my knees shook when I was asked to captain the side! And thus it came about that I became the leader of the first team the M.C.C. ever sent abroad.

On my return from Australia in the spring of 1904 I was

honoured with a place on the M.C.C. Committee. Mr Rutter has told us that he and Mr Green "were disgusted with the supercilious manner in which they were received"—he was writing of the middle seventies—but that was not my experience. I did sense a feeling that one was a 'new boy,' and as such, should be seen and not heard, or at any rate not be too ready to express an opinion. But this is no bad thing. A new member of any committee should try to get the atmosphere and the hang of things, should listen and learn, and certainly not butt in on any subject on which he is not thoroughly conversant. The committee man who is over-anxious to hear his own voice is a nuisance, and will lose any influence which he might otherwise eventually gain. But if you do know your subject I have always found that you will be listened to with respect, provided that your views are put forward in an agreeable manner, without arrogance and without what may be called 'cocksuredness': that does not go down at all, and rightly so. Before I was a member of the Committee I had been in contact with Lord Harris, A. G. Steel, A. J. Webbe, and W. H. Patterson over the selection of the team for Australia, and nothing could have exceeded their courtesy and consideration. They certainly were not "supercilious."

I have been a member of the Committee and of the Cricket Sub-committee on and off for over forty years, and I cannot imagine any committee which would, speaking generally, do its work better. Here and there, no doubt, mistakes have been made in selection—it would be extraordinary if it were not so, considering the difficulties of selecting a team for a tour abroad extending over many months—and possibly there have been occasions when we did not look sufficiently far ahead, but such decisions as have been arrived at have never been due to any lack of honest painstaking. And to-day the Committee includes a larger number of members of varying ages and experience than was sometimes the case. It must always be remembered that the Committee and the Sub-committees have to deal with a large number of matters apart from the actual playing of the game—finance, property and works, refreshments, the library and pictures, the care and maintenance of the ground, insurance, and many legal and even, occasionally, international questions. This being so, it is most important to have on the Committee men who are versed in affairs, with a wide experience of the world and of men.

I always enjoy Committee Meetings which are conducted with dignity and good manners, and where the cut and thrust of debate is invariably kept within bounds. Only once in my experience was there anything like a 'breeze.' Lord Harris made a proposal which did not appeal to Lord Alverstone,[1] who had just come from presiding as Lord Chief Justice at a famous murder trial. He looked rather worn out, and when he was tired he had a habit of rubbing his face and forehead with his right hand. After a more than usually vigorous rub he replied, "I think I ought to say at once that I shall oppose that tooth and nail." For a few moments the atmosphere was glacial, with two strong men in opposite camps, but it soon passed, and at the end of the meeting I heard Lord Alverstone remark, "George was very testy to-day!" 'Testy' seems a favourite word in the legal profession, and years before I remember H. H. Asquith so describing Lord Russell of Killowen. Asquith was leading, Alfred Lyttelton was his junior, and I, who was at the time in Lyttelton's chambers, was supposed to be taking a note of the case. The L.C.J. was not in the best of tempers, and Asquith turned to Lyttelton and said, "Alfred, Charles is very testy to-day!" I nearly fell off my seat on hearing the L.C.J. referred to as "Charles"! I was recently told by a high legal luminary that the word is still in vogue, and is thought to be very appropriate in certain circumstances.

The M.C.C. team which had won the rubber in Australia by three matches to two met the Rest of England at Lord's, on May 9, 10, and 11, but the weather was bitterly cold, the light none too good, and rain prevented a ball being bowled on the second day. Except for the absence of Fry, the Rest were well represented, but inevitably the match was drawn. On a slow if not difficult wicket Perrin, Jackson, and Denton batted very well, and for the M.C.C. Tyldesley and Hirst showed their best form on a good wicket on the first day. We felt the cold after the warmth of the Antipodes, and were not at our best, but at the finish we were in a fairly strong position, being 87 runs ahead with only one wicket down in our second innings.

I often wonder what the reaction would have been had we lost the rubber. I fancy the M.C.C. would have been criticized, but as things turned out their position and prestige were strengthened, and since then our Dominions and Colonies look automatically

[1] Richard Everard Webster, Viscount Alverstone, Lord Chief Justice, 1900–13.

to the Club to undertake the responsibility of these tours, while the Imperial Cricket Conference forms a close link between the overseas cricketing countries and the M.C.C. More than forty years have passed since this first tour, and I cannot imagine the day will ever come when a representative England team will again go abroad except under the ægis of the M.C.C.

Gentlemen *v.* Players was emphatically the match of the 1904 season, and proved a great attraction, 12,335 paying for admission on the first day, 11,545 on the second, and 9322 on the third. The pitch on the first two days was on the lively side, the ball occasionally getting up dangerously, but on the third day it rolled out perfectly, and the Gentlemen, set 412 runs to make, won by two wickets within ten minutes of time, H. Hesketh-Prichard holding his bat straight while A. O. Jones went for the bowling. In the absence of Hirst, owing to an injury, the Players were without a genuine fast bowler, and Arnold had to play this rôle in the final innings. Tyldesley, one of the original choices, was unable to play at the last moment, because of a damaged rib, and on the morning of the match J. H. King, of Leicestershire, was called on, and, as so often happens, the substitute was a brilliant success, for King, an enterprising left-handed batsman, scored 104 and 109, not out, thus rivalling R. E. Foster's feat in 1900. Curiously Ranjitsinhji was the last choice for the Gentlemen and Hayward for the Players, and both came off with a vengeance, Ranji scoring 5 and 121 and Hayward 88 and 14. It seems strange, indeed, that Ranji won a place only when A. J. Turner was unable to accept the invitation sent him. Turner was a fine batsman, but he was not a Ranji, while Hayward had been in wonderful form. It was rumoured that some of the Committee held the opinion that Ranji did not shine on a fiery wicket, and the Lord's pitches this summer were pretty lively, but if so, this was a grave error of judgment, for if ever there was a batsman who was a master when the ball was flying about it was the great Indian. At the end of the season he was at the head of the averages, with an aggregate of 2077 runs and an average of 74·17, and Hayward averaged 54·65, with 3170 runs to his credit!

Lilley, the Players' Captain, kept wicket brilliantly, catching six and stumping one, and could he have foreseen how the wicket would improve on the last day he would no doubt have asked the Gentlemen to follow on. The totals of this glorious match were: Players 327 and 255, Gentlemen 171 and 412 for 8 wickets.

The South Africans were not given a Test Match, but they made such an excellent impression that three years later their ability was recognized. A match against an England Eleven was, however, arranged at Lord's, which the visitors won by 189 runs. The outstanding figure of the match was R. O. Schwarz, who scored 102 and 26 and took eight wickets for 106 runs, getting Ranjitsinhji out in each innings. Sinclair also bowled well, and Halliwell's wicket-keeping was superior to that of any other wicket-keeper of the day. It was no mean performance to defeat so easily a team which included, besides Ranji, MacGregor, King, J. T. Hearne, W. H. B. Evans, Rev. F. H. Gillingham, J. Gunn, Wass, G. L. Jessop, G. W. Beldam, and J. Vine.

The game with Middlesex ended in a tie. At one time, with S. J. Snooke and G. C. White together, the South Africans wanted only 11 runs to win with two wickets to fall. Snooke was l.b.w. to Trott with the score a tie. Kotze came in, and Trott imperilled the situation by bowling the first ball to leg, which, fortunately for Middlesex, Kotze missed. The next ball was Trott's famous fast yorker, and the middle stump disappeared in a cloud of dust.

I was one of the Selectors for the Test Matches in 1905, the other two being Lord Hawke (Chairman) and J. A. Dixon, while Jackson, who was appointed Captain, and A. C. MacLaren were co-opted to help us. Everything went well, and England won the rubber by two matches to nil. We were victorious at Trent Bridge and at Old Trafford, the games at Lord's, Leeds, and the Oval being drawn. England had a very good side. The bowling was not so strong as in 1902, for there was no Lockwood in the team, but it was good without being exceptional, and Jackson, MacLaren, Fry, Tyldesley, Hirst, and Spooner formed the nucleus of the batting. Lilley kept wicket splendidly, but the fielding was not always up to the mark. The Selectors' task was really an easy one, our only trouble being the accidents and illnesses which deprived us from time to time of some otherwise certain choice. Our meetings were soon over, and I do not recall any difficulty arising which led to prolonged debate.

Tactful and diplomatic and a man of the world, Jackson was a highly successful captain, and he was a wonderful spinner of a coin. He not only won the toss in every Test Match, but also for the M.C.C. at Lord's and for C. I. Thornton's Eleven at Scarborough. No wonder Darling exclaimed, "What's the good of tossing with you, Jacker? I might just as well give you first innings!" Jackson was in great all-round form. He headed both batting and bowling averages in the Test Matches, scoring 492 runs, with an average of 70·28, and taking thirteen wickets for 15·46 runs each. Some suggested that he was a lucky batsman. The same was said of Field-Marshal Lord Roberts as a General, and the reply was, "Luck loves skill." "Jacker" was, of course, a great batsman, who possessed all the strokes, and he was essentially the man for a big occasion.

The Lord's match was spoilt by rain, there being no play on the third day. MacLaren, who had played one of his most masterly innings of 140 in the second innings of the first Test at Trent Bridge, was again at his best, scoring 56 and 79, but on a sticky wicket the Australians batted extraordinarily well, and, saving the follow-on in response to England's total of 282, extricated themselves from a difficult position. But then they are always at their best in a tight corner!

In their match against the Gentlemen of England at Lord's W. W. Armstrong played a magnificent innings of 248, not out. He hit two fives and thirty-eight fours, and his driving was so hard that, though H. C. McDonnell had three men in the deep, placed scarcely thirty yards from each other, he beat them time and again, the ball rebounding from the pavilion rails on one occasion almost back to the wicket. These drives rose to no high culminating-point, but the speed of their low trajectory was tremendous, and there is no more pleasant sound on a cricket field than the impact of leather on wood. Armstrong had a great season. He made 2002 runs, with an average of 48·82, and took 130 wickets for 17·60 runs each.

This Australian side was a most attractive one, and if, as a whole, it had lost something of its old characteristics of stubbornness and patience, it was from a spectator's point of view very good to watch. Neither Trumper, Hill, nor Noble came off in the Test Matches, but J. Darling, on his third visit to England, as Captain, played some fine innings, as did Duff.

For some reason A. O. Jones, who had done so much to win the match for the amateurs in the previous year, was not invited to play for the Gentlemen, but otherwise, except for the absence of MacLaren, the Gentlemen had about their best side, though the bowling was not suited by the slow state of the pitch on the first day, being almost entirely on the fast and medium side. The Players won the toss, and after a good start lost six wickets for 178, but Arnold (89) and Lilley (52) put on 103 runs in seventy minutes. On a pitch which was too slow to suit him Brearley bowled magnificently, taking seven wickets for 104 runs, keeping up his pace with indomitable energy. On the second day the wicket was much faster, but not quite easy, and the Gentlemen were all out for 185. Arnold, Lees, and Rhodes bowled very well, Rhodes having the distinction of clean bowling Jackson and Fry. Going in again with a lead of 171, the Players lost Bowley and Tyldesley for 19 runs, Brearley bowling them with consecutive balls. For the moment it looked as if Brearley, with his tail in the air, might run through the side, so finely was he bowling, but Hayward (123, not out), nearly always at his best in this match, and Hayes (73) gave a superb display, and next day Hirst hit hard. Lilley, the Players' Captain, declared, leaving the Gentlemen 465 runs to win. With the score at 13, Fry was clean bowled by Lees with a very good ball, but the second wicket did not fall until the score had reached 202, when Spooner, who had scored 81, a beautiful innings, if a little uneven in the latter part, was caught at the wicket. At the tea interval only three wickets were down, and the Gentlemen should have saved the match, but the bowlers now gained the upper hand, and at a quarter to seven the Players had won by 149 runs. The Players' bowling was maintained at a very high standard. It was my good fortune to have a long look at it in both innings.

The University Match was one of the most exciting in all its long history. When the sixth wicket fell in their second innings Cambridge were 24 runs behind. W. H. B. Evans, from the Pavilion end, was bowling very well, but soon after H. C. McDonnell joined L. G. Colbeck, Evans wrenched the heel of his left boot loose and had to stop bowling. He retired to the pavilion to be reshod, but was not the same bowler afterwards. McDonnell and Colbeck added 143 runs by brilliant cricket. McDonnell (60) played gallantly and aggressively; Colbeck off-drove splendidly, and over and over again cut fast balls on the wicket in a most remarkable innings of 107. Oxford, set 164 to win, had twenty-five minutes' batting at the end of the day, and, altering the order, lost three wickets for 15 runs. K. M. Carlisle, the Oxford Captain, was probably right in theory to do so, but in practice it did not come off. No fair critic can blame him for the course he adopted.

On the third morning, on a somewhat fiery wicket, G. G. Napier and A. F. Morcom bowled splendidly, a great catch by McDonnell at third slip, off Napier, got rid of Evans, the best batsman in the Oxford Eleven, and Cambridge won by 40 runs.

J. E. Raphael scored 99 for Oxford in his first innings. Had he made one more run he would have equalled W. Yardley's feat of scoring two hundreds in a University Match; E. L. Wright (95) was also unlucky not to get a century. The match will always be remembered as Colbeck's match, but it was Napier and Morcom who clinched matters by their bowling.

In his chapter on this University Match in the Badminton Library *Cricket* E. R. Wilson wrote, "The result of the match shows the importance of having a kit inspection."

The first two or three weeks of the season of 1906 were bitterly cold, with a persistent north-east wind, but after that the weather was gloriously fine and warm, and cricket flourished. Gentlemen *v.* Players at Lord's, celebrating, as it did, the Centenary of the present ground, was by common consent the match of the season, and large crowds flocked to see it. Jackson had closed his splendid career at the end of the previous summer, but, yielding to pressure, captained the amateurs. Both sides were at practically full strength, except that Hirst, who was enjoying the best season of his career—he scored 2385 runs and took 208 wickets—declined the M.C.C.'s invitation "*for the reason that he felt obliged to save himself for Yorkshire matches*" (*Wisden*). It is the custom, and has been for many a long day, for the counties to give up their men for this historic fixture, and here Yorkshire were thinking parochially, with their eyes fixed on the county championship, which, as it turned out, they did not win, being second to Kent.

The match will always be memorable for the splendid fast bowling of Fielder and Lees for the Players and N. A. Knox and W. Brearley for the Gentlemen. In the first innings of the Gentlemen Fielder, from the Nursery end, took all ten wickets for 90 runs—a feat never performed before (or since) in a Gentlemen *v.* Players match at Lord's—while Lees, putting on a lot of extra pace in the second innings—he was naturally a fast-medium bowler—took six wickets for 92 runs. But if the Gentlemen had to withstand a speedy attack it was nothing to what the Players had to face. Knox, from the Pavilion end, bowled at a speed which equalled, and at times surpassed, even that of Kortright or Kotze, while Brearley, at the other end, kept up a fine pace, if not equal to that of Knox. Of the forty wickets that fell the fast bowlers claimed thirty-eight, one batsman, Hayward, being run out. The wicket-keeping of Martyn and Lilley was magnificent, Martyn, for a time at any rate, standing up to the 6 foot 1 inch Knox, who, with his fair hair ruffled by the breeze, his long, bounding run, and his high action, was terrific. Hayward (54 and 34), always a magnificent player of fast bowling, Denton (48), Hayes (55), J. Gunn (42), and Lees (51) batted very well against this dynamic attack, but Knox was always dominating the situation. His analysis was

O.	M.	R.	W.
44.1	3	183	12

Brearley's figures were

O.	M.	R.	W.
45.4	7	147	6

For the Gentlemen Spooner played a glorious second innings of 114, his first hundred at Lord's since his 198 for Marlborough *v.* Rugby in 1899, but it should be remembered that the South African War cut some years off his cricket. Jackson (40), H. K. Foster (67), Bosanquet (56), and Jessop (73, not out) came off in one or other innings, Jessop making his runs in an hour, out of 92. The totals of this splendid match were Gentlemen 167 and 321, Players 199 and 244, the Gentlemen winning by 45 runs.

Cambridge won the University Match by 94 runs. The game began in a sensational manner, M. W. Payne making the first *45 runs in twenty minutes*, hitting N. R. Udal for *34 runs in two overs*. He was eventually caught at slip after making *64 out of 73 in under forty minutes*—a Jessopian or Lyons-like innings if ever there was one! R. A. Young played a very sound innings of 150, and Cambridge's first-innings total of 360 gave them a lead of 173. Eventually they set Oxford 422 runs to win. The ninth wicket fell at 237, but E. L. Wright, always a very good and determined batsman, especially in this match, batted extremely well for 79, and W. J. H. Curwen and E. G. Martin added no fewer than 90 runs for the last wicket. Cambridge had plenty of batting, and Napier, Morcom, and May were three good bowlers—all of them on the fast side, May definitely so—but Oxford, for whom Udal bowled both pluckily and successfully, in spite of the very disconcerting treatment he received from Payne, fought gallantly. Payne caught six men at the wicket and stumped one, and his first innings will never be forgotten.

Another good match was Eton *v.* Harrow, which Eton won by four wickets. No doubt the ornithologists were keenly interested in the Harrow side, which included not only a Bird, a Falcon, and a Crake, but a Griffin as well! One of this feathered tribe was destined to make history a year later.

The West Indies were here this year, and the M.C.C. beat them by six wickets, largely due to the splendid bowling of A. E. Vogler, the South African—for a time on the M.C.C. staff—who took nine wickets in the second innings for 44 runs. George Challenor, only eighteen years of age, showed great promise, which was more than fulfilled in later years.

CHAPTER X

The Close of an Era (1907–14)

An Unpleasant Match—Antagonism against the M.C.C.—Googly Bowlers—"The Croucher"—A 'Long' Innings—Captaincy and Selection Problems—Fowler's Match—P. R. Le Couteur—"The Golden Age"—A Great Gentlemen *v.* Players Game—The Triangular Tournament—H. W. Taylor—The Lytteltons—A Grand Gentlemen's Side—Centenary Match

THE Lancashire and Middlesex match at Lord's in 1907 ended abruptly and unpleasantly. On the first day Lancashire scored 57 for one wicket when rain put a stop to play. On the following morning the wicket was under water, and it was not until late in the afternoon that the umpires, Flowers and Marlow, decided to pull up the stumps. The crowd had grown exasperated at the long wait, and one or two of them walked on the wicket, and eventually MacLaren, the Lancashire Captain, refused to continue the match, declaring that the pitch had been deliberately torn up by the public. There was one heel-mark just where a half-volley would have pitched at the Pavilion end, and next day, after the roller had been put on, it had disappeared. The Middlesex President, R. D. Walker, was most indignant, and nine out of ten people thought that MacLaren had acted unwisely in taking so drastic a course of action. I do not believe he followed the dictates of his own reasoning, but allowed himself to be influenced by people who, for some reason or other, had little friendly feeling for Lord's.

At this period there was some antagonism against the M.C.C. It began, apparently, when Lord Hawke refused to allow Hirst and Rhodes to go to Australia with MacLaren's side during the winter of 1901–2, and when the M.C.C. undertook to send a team to Australia two years later the doings of that team were more than usually closely followed. As has already been said, I think MacLaren was harshly treated, and a sense of irritation remained, especially in Lancashire, for some time, and it is possible that Fry was influenced in the attitude he adopted on the occasion of Gentlemen *v.* Players in 1908 by the fact that

R. E. Foster had been preferred to him as Captain of England in 1907, and that he thought the time had come to protest. Foster, incidentally, was a very good captain, and a quite exceptional batsman and slip fielder. Anyway, there was a definite feeling in some quarters against Lord's, and it was rumoured that a proposal was on foot to form an M.C.C. of the North. This went no further than rumour, and after a short time nothing more was heard of it. In later years the M.C.C. invited MacLaren to captain their side to New Zealand and Australia, and that great cricketer not only batted magnificently at a time of life when most cricketers have put aside their bats, but captained the side both on and off the field with great ability.

I think it is important to mention these matters, so that posterity should realize that the Augustan Age of cricket had its troubles too! I fear that I myself was something of a bone of contention, but it never upset me, and it certainly did not interfere in any degree with my friendship with MacLaren, Fry, and Ranji. MacLaren was a man of great personal attraction and good looks, and his remark that he "always felt that he would get half a dozen if he came in at the wrong door at Lord's" was attributable to a sense of humour which he possessed in a marked degree. Of Fry I need say no more than that he remains to this day one of my greatest and most intimate friends, whose writings and sayings on cricket I study very carefully and whose brain I envy. Ranji was a most able and attractive man of fine character. Much kindness and hospitality did I receive from him, and I treasure some letters which he wrote me.

Under the captaincy of P. W. Sherwell the South Africans visited England this summer, and although it was not their good fortune to win a Test Match, they proved themselves a very fine side. They played 31 matches, won 21, and lost only 4; and not since the days of the earlier Australian elevens have any bowlers been more talked about than Schwarz, Vogler, Faulkner, and White. People flocked to see them bowl, their novel methods affording the greatest interest. Three Test Matches were arranged —at Lord's, Leeds, and the Oval—England winning at Leeds on a sticky wicket by 53 runs and the games at Lord's and the Oval being drawn, that at Lord's decidedly in England's favour.

On the sticky wickets which were so prevalent the South African googly bowlers were very good indeed, but on hard and true wickets they were not so effective; and it seems to be generally conceded that bowling of this type, though always difficult on any wicket if combined with a good length, is seen at its best when the turf is false or on matting wickets. The tour of the South Africans in Australia in 1910–11 bore out this theory, the googly meeting with but scant success on the cast-iron pitches at Sydney, Melbourne, and Adelaide. Vogler, at this period, was the best of these four remarkable bowlers, though Schwarz beat him on figures. Schwarz was not, strictly speaking, a googly bowler, as he broke only from the off, but he kept such a capital length and got so much spin on the ball that he thoroughly deserved his success. I have never met a bowler who put so much spin on the ball, which described what one may call a parabola in the air, coming off the pitch at an extraordinary pace and in a manner quite different from the normal off-break. Even on the best wickets he could turn the ball six or eight inches, and on sticky wickets he often broke a foot and more. Vogler had rather a hesitating run up to the wicket, but got into an easy stride in the last few steps. His variation of pace and flight was well concealed, he bowled a beautiful leg-break, and a googly which had, perhaps, more of top-spin on it than unadulterated googly. He could bowl for long periods at a time, and a dangerous ball of his was a slow yorker which seemed "more to quiver than to swing in the air," as R. E. Foster described it. He clean bowled Fry with this ball both at Leeds and at the Oval in the Test Matches.

Faulkner, on his day, was, perhaps, the most difficult of all, and in the match at Leeds he took six wickets for 17 runs, when his bowling was said to be "like playing Briggs in the air and Tom Richardson off the pitch." A few years later Faulkner could claim comparison as an all-rounder with any cricketer in the world, and Clem Hill told me that no one had ever batted better in Australia than Faulkner did. In addition to his batting and bowling, Faulkner was a great slip. White was much like Faulkner, only more uncertain. On his day he might go through a side, as he made the ball come very quickly off the ground. Apart from the googly bowlers, Sherwell could also command the services of Sinclair, Nourse, S. J. Snooke, and Kotze, though on the soft wickets the last had few opportunities. It may well be said that a side so rich in bowlers has never been on tour. The googly is better known and better understood now, but, bowled with length, it will always be a power in cricket, and the game owes a great debt to the South Africans for raising a new method of attack to a very high standard indeed.

The South African batting was sound, if not great, and the fielding was admirable, while Sherwell was a beautiful stumper, with no fuss whatever about his method, which in its quiet efficiency reminded one of MacGregor and Pilling. He was certainly one of the great wicket-keepers, and in the taking of googly bowling has had no equal. He seemed never to make a mistake as to which way the ball would turn.

The Selection Committee this year were Lord Hawke, H. K. Foster, and C. H. B. Marsham, and they chose R. E. Foster as Captain.

The first Test Match at Lord's will always be memorable for a great innings of 93 by Jessop, who scored his runs in an hour and a quarter. Jessop was in some ways the greatest genius that cricket has produced. He was the essence of unorthodoxy—it was said of him that he had reduced rustic batting to a science—but few batsmen watched the ball more closely, and he made use of every ounce of weight in his body. Bending low over his bat—he was called "the Croucher"—he used to drive the ball into the long field, or sweep it round to square leg, and if the ball was at all short he could cut magnificently.

In this match Kotze bowled on the short side to him, and his analysis suffered terribly. It was in this wonderful cut of his that Jessop was superior to all other hitters. Thornton, Bonnor, Lyons, Trott, Hammond, F. T. Mann, Jim Smith, drove, possibly, a longer ball, but none of them could cut like Jessop, whose ability to score with this stroke, added to his power in the drive, made it so difficult to place the field. In this innings at Lord's he received but sixty-three balls!

Jessop was sometimes omitted from the England Eleven. To do so was surely a mistake. His very presence was an asset, in that it paralysed the initiative of the opposing Captain. Jessop had only to be an hour at the wicket, or in a low-scoring match for half an hour, to alter entirely the aspect of any game. He could dominate or obliterate the time factor in cricket. His contemporaries thought his name not quite enough, and with a suggestion both of the mighty and the classic nicknamed him "Jessopus."

Bad light at various times on the first two days and a blank third day caused the Gentlemen *v.* Players match to be drawn, the Gentlemen with eight wickets in hand wanting 216 runs to win. The batting of Hayward (146, not out) in the Players' first innings, the bowling of W. Brearley and G. G. Napier, and the slip fielding of A. O. Jones made the game memorable. This was Hayward's fourth century in this match, and that great batsman has seldom played more finely; Brearley and Napier obtained nineteen of the twenty wickets that fell, one man, Arnold, being run out; and Jones brought off five superb catches. The full bowling figures of Brearley and Napier are worthy of record:

First Innings	O.	M.	R.	W.	*Second Innings*	O.	M.	R.	W.
Brearley	35.1	7	103	7	Brearley	19.1	1	74	3
Napier	31	12	72	3	Napier	22	8	39	6

There never was a greater 'striver' than Brearley: you just could not tire him out. Pace was combined with accuracy, an off-break, and the ball that went with his arm. He was a great and lion-hearted bowler. Napier used his height, made the ball run away, kept a length, and occasionally sent down an off-break. *Wisden* wrote of him, "He kept a length worthy of Alfred Shaw and Attewell at their best." Few bowlers have ever made such a successful début in Gentlemen *v.* Players at Lord's.[1] The totals of this match were Players 278 and 138, Gentlemen 160 and 41 for two wickets.

Eton *v.* Harrow was a great match, Harrow winning by 79 runs with a quarter of an hour to spare, it having been arranged to draw stumps at 7.30 on the second day. The game was rendered historic by the double century (100, not out, and 131) of M. C. Bird, the Harrow Captain. On a splendid wicket he used his great driving-power to the full and played fine forcing cricket. He also obtained five wickets, and captained his side admirably. When Bird made his second hundred his father, George Bird, was sitting in the pavilion next to H. G. Tylecote, whose private school M. C. Bird had adorned, and the two shook hands with joy, not unmixed with tears, murmuring, "Owner and Trainer, Owner and Trainer."

At the beginning of the season of 1908 I performed a feat which, I believe, has never before or since been accomplished, for I went in at Lord's on a Tuesday evening at six o'clock and was not out

[1] Incidentally, this was also Hobbs's first appearance in a Gentlemen *v.* Players match at Lord's.

on the following Saturday evening! This sounds impossible, but is a fact, and what actually happened was this. Playing for the M.C.C. against Yorkshire, I went in first in the second innings on Tuesday night, and was not out 7 at the drawing of stumps; next morning I carried my bat through the innings for 64, out of a total of 95, the match being over before luncheon. On the Thursday I again played for the M.C.C., this time against Kent. There was only twenty minutes' cricket on the first day owing to rain, when the M.C.C. scored 17 for the loss of one wicket, myself not out 4. It rained all the Friday, and on the Saturday cricket was possible only after lunch; again I carried my bat through the innings, and again for 64, out of a total this time of 124.

The next match at Lord's, M.C.C. *v.* Hampshire, began on the following Monday. Hampshire went in first and made 180. Just before six o'clock I had scored 52, and there was a good deal of excitement round the ground as to whether I should be again not out at the end of the day, but at this point Newman clean bowled me. The M.C.C. eventually won by nine wickets, having only 47 to get to win, of which I had made 23, not out. So that between Tuesday, May 12, and Tuesday, May 19, I was dismissed only once. I give the rain full credit!

I had the honour of captaining the Gentlemen this year, but, as *Wisden* put it, "the fact of P. F. Warner being made Captain of the Gentlemen in preference to Fry or Ranjitsinhji gave rise to a good deal of ill-feeling." When a fortnight before the match Lord Harris came up to me in the pavilion and told me that I had been chosen Captain I was naturally very pleased, but I ventured to say that I thought "the Committee were looking for trouble." "What do you mean?" he asked, and I answered that others who were senior to me might object. When the team was published in the Press my name was at the top of the list, but without the word captain in brackets after it, which is the usual custom. This was corrected in some newspapers, but before play began Fry had protested to Sir Francis Lacey, saying that it was nothing personal as regards myself, but that he felt that Ranjitsinhji had been gravely slighted. I happened to enter the Secretary's office in order to tell Sir Francis that the Gentlemen had won the toss when this was taking place, and the air was distinctly sultry. The whole thing was unpleasant and embarrassing. Now, as I have said earlier, Charles Fry has been a great and valued friend of mine since we were boys, and my regard for him was not affected in the slightest degree by this affair, but at the time it did not lead to a happy atmosphere, and the best match of the year suffered.

I, of course, had no say in the choice of captain, and as Ranji had been in India for the English cricket seasons of 1905, 1906, and 1907 there was some reason for not selecting him to lead the side. Fry was senior to me, but I had by this time taken two M.C.C. teams abroad, and was a member of the Committee. Personally I never can understand all this not playing under So-and-so. It is childish. What about the Royal Navy? Did not retired Admirals serve as Captains and Commanders in the War? There's an example for us.[1] Incidentally, the Players won the match by seven wickets.

A year later I was invited to captain the M.C.C. at Lord's against the Australians. A day or two before the match Lacey asked me to come and see him in his office. I had a pretty shrewd idea what it was all about, and I at once said, "If it is the captaincy you are worrying over, let me say straight off that I will willingly field long leg at both ends under Fry." And so Fry was Captain, led the side admirably, and we won the match by three wickets. Examine Fry's record as a Captain, and he will be found to have been extremely successful. He won the rubber of Test Matches in 1912 against both the Australians and the South Africans, and led the Gentlemen to victory in 1911 and 1914. He had the inestimable gift of making his men believe in themselves, with the result that they played if anything above their normal form, and he was at all times most pleasant and agreeable. I always enjoyed playing under him.

The Australians, under M. A. Noble, lost the first Test Match at Birmingham by ten wickets, but the Selectors—Lord Hawke (Chairman), C. B. Fry, and H. D. G. Leveson-Gower—made several changes in the England Eleven for the second game at Lord's. The Chairman was not well and was at Aix when the selections were made, and Fry was kept away from the deliberations owing to being a witness in a lawsuit. The responsibility for what was done therefore rested with Leveson-Gower and MacLaren, the Captain. Blythe, who had bowled finely in the

[1] W. G. on many occasions played under Lord Harris, A. N. Hornby, and A. G. Steel, to all of whom he was senior, and Fry himself played under R. E. Foster in Test Matches against the South Africans in the previous season (1907), and he was some six years senior in both age and cricketing experience.

first Test was ill, and King, of Leicestershire, took his place, Rhodes being apparently forgotten. Hayward, wko was lame, in defiance of medical opinion, came in for Fry, Jessop was dropped for G. Gunn, and there was no fast bowler in the side, although Brearley was at the top of his form at this period of the season. Barnes, the best bowler in England, was, it seemed, not considered. The result of all these changes was that England went into the field with Hirst, A. E. Relf, Haigh, and King to bowl on a *hard* wicket.

England lost by nine wickets. There had been a good deal of rain on the Saturday before the match began on Monday, June 14, but the glass was going up, and Noble, judging that the pitch would improve, on winning the toss, sent England in to bat. His judgment turned out to be perfect. England made 269 and 121, Australia 350 and 41 for one wicket. Armstrong's bowling settled the match. In the second innings, keeping a beautiful length, he took six wickets for 35 runs, clean bowling Gunn, King, Hirst, and Relf, catching and bowling Hobbs, and having Tyldesley stumped. V. S. Ransford (143, not out), for Australia, batted very well, but had he been caught at slip by MacLaren when only 12 the game might well have taken a different course.

The Australians won the rubber, but England had cruel luck at Leeds, for Jessop, when the game had been in progress for an hour, strained the muscles of his back so badly that he played no more cricket during the season. Truly the stars in their courses fought against MacLaren!

In the final match, at the Oval, Buckenham, the Essex fast bowler—and a very good one too—though included in the list of those from whom the team was to be selected, was left out on the morning of the match, in fine weather with a rising glass and on an Oval wicket. S. H. Pardon, the editor of *Wisden*, wrote, "The idea of letting England go into the field in fine weather, on a typical Oval wicket, with no fast bowler, touched the confines of lunacy"; and *Bailey's Magazine* went so far as to say that the Selection Committee had "betrayed England to Australia." There can be no doubt that a mistake was made in asking MacLaren to be Captain, for that once grand cricketer was now a long way past his best both as a batsman and a fieldsman, and he did not get on with his Selectors or they with him. England was not so strong all round as in 1899, 1902, and 1905, but the

Selectors did not make the best use of the material at their disposal.

The Players, with an especially powerful bowling side, defeated the Gentlemen by 200 runs. The wicket was never easy, and in this respect the Gentlemen had the worst of the luck. D. W. Carr, a great googly bowler, who began life as a medium-paced orthodox bowler, bowled very well, but the feature of the match was the superb bowling of Barnes, who took eight wickets for 55 runs, and, in a lesser degree, of Hirst. On a very difficult wicket Barnes, with his tremendous spin, tore pieces out of the turf. I have never played finer bowling.

Eton *v.* Harrow ended in a draw, there being no play on the second day, Eton, with three wickets in hand, wanting 53 runs to win. They were 43 runs behind at the half-way stage of the match—a useful lead on a sticky wicket—but R. St L. Fowler bowled very well, taking seven wickets for 33 runs in Harrow's second innings—a cloud, little bigger than a man's hand, which was to burst next year over Harrow like an atomic bomb!

In the history of cricket there has been nothing more sensational than the Eton *v.* Harrow match of 1910. Eton followed on, and when the *ninth wicket fell in their second innings they were only 4 runs ahead.* When all seemed over Manners and Lister Kaye put on 50 runs for the last Eton wicket in twenty-five minutes, but many people left the ground while Lister Kaye was making his way to the wicket.

One of the best descriptions of the closing stages of the game is given by the late Lieutenant-Colonel C. P. Foley, in his book *Autumn Foliage*:[1]

> I was going to spend that Saturday to Monday at Coombe with General Sir Arthur Paget, and, not being in the least anxious to see an overwhelming Harrow victory, I left the ground and called in at White's Club to pick up my bag. Providentially, as it turned out, my hair wanted cutting. Half-way through the operation Lord Brackley looked in and said, "Harrow have lost four wickets for 21 runs," and a few minutes later, "Harrow have lost six wickets for 21 runs." That was enough. I sprang from the chair with my hair half cut and standing on end, and we rushed together into the street, jumped into a taxi, and said, "Lord's! Double fare if you do it in fifteen minutes." We got there in 14 minutes 21⅗ seconds (I carry a stop-watch), paid the man, and advanced on the pavilion at a pace which is called in the French Army *le pas gymnastique*. The

[1] Methuen, 1935.

THOMAS LORD

From an oil painting (*c.* 1810) by George Morland.

By courtesy of the Committee of the M.C.C.

N. FELIX

From a self-portrait in watercolour.

ALFRED MYNN
From an oil painting (*c.* 1850) by W. Bromley.

GEORGE PARR

From a watercolour drawing (*c.* 1850) by C. J. Basébé.

ENTRANCE TO THE FIRST LORD'S

From a sketch in the Ashbridge Collection, Marylebone Public Library.

By courtesy of the Borough Librarian

CROWD LINING UP AT LORD'S FOR AN UNOFFICIAL TEST MATCH, 1945

Photo Sport and General

GEORGE OSBALDESTON

From an engraving by Roffe, after a drawing by Woodhouse.

By courtesy of the Rischgitz Art Studios

BENJAMIN AISLABIE

From an engraving (*c.* 1840) by Henry E. Dawe in the Ashbridge Collection, Marylebone Public Library.

By courtesy of the Borough Librarian

ENGLAND ELEVEN *v.* AUSTRALIA AT LORD'S, 1884

Left to right—Back row: C. K. Pullin (Umpire), E. Peate, A. P. Lucas, A. Lyttelton, A. Shrewsbury, F. H. Farrands (Umpire). *Middle row:* A. G. Steel, Lord Harris (Capt.), W. G. Grace, W. W. Read, G. Ulyett. *Front row:* S. Christopherson, R. G. Barlow.

By courtesy of the Committee of the M.C.C.

MARTIN BLADEN, SEVENTH BARON HAWKE

Photo "Gravure'

THE HON. SIR STANLEY JACKSON

P.C., G.C.S.I., G.C.I.E.

Photo Vandyck

ENGLAND ELEVEN *v.* AUSTRALIA AT LORD'S, 1896

Left to right—Back row: A. A. Lilley, J. T. Hearne, W. Gunn, T. Hayward. *Middle row:* T. Richardson, F. S. Jackson, W. G. Grace (Capt.), G. A. Lohmann, A. E. Stoddart. *Front row:* J. T. Brown, R. Abel.

By courtesy of the Committee of the M.C.C.

W. G. GRACE IN 1876

By courtesy of the Committee of the M.C.C.

VICTOR TRUMPER

By courtesy of the Committee of the M.C.C.

AUSTRALIAN TEAM, 1921

Left to right—Back row: W. Bardsley, J. S. Ryder, H. L. Hendry, J. M. Gregory, E. R. Mayne, T. J. E. Andrews, S. Smith (Manager). *Middle row:* A. A. Mailey, E. A. Macdonald, H. L. Collins, W. W. Armstrong (Capt.), C. G. Macartney, H. Carter, J. M. Taylor. *Front row:* C. E. Pellew, W. A. Oldfield.

By courtesy of the Committee of the M.C.C.

ENGLAND ELEVEN *v.* AUSTRALIA AT LORD'S, 1926

Left to right—Back row: R. Kilner, H. Larwood, M. W. Tate, F. E. Woolley, F. Root, H. Sutcliffe. *Front row:* H. Strudwick, A. P. F. Chapman, A. W. Carr (Capt.), J. B. Hobbs, E. Hendren.

By courtesy of the Committee of the M.C.C.

M.C.C. AUSTRALIAN TEAM, 1932–33

Left to right—Back row: G. Duckworth, T. B. Mitchell, Nawab of Pataudi, M. Leyland, H. Larwood, E. Paynter, W. Ferguson (Scorer). *Middle row:* P. F. Warner (Manager), L. Ames, H. Verity, W. Voce, W. E. Bowes, F. R. Brown, M. W. Tate, R. C. N. Palairet (Manager). *Front row:* H. Sutcliffe, R. E. S. Wyatt, D. R. Jardine (Capt.), G. O. Allen, W. R. Hammond.

By courtesy of the Committee of the M.C.C.

AUSTRALIAN TEAM, 1934

Left to right—Back row: W. Ferguson (Scorer), C. V. Grimmett, W. A. Brown, H. I. Ebeling, H. Bushby (Manager), W. J. O'Reilly, T. W. Wall, L. O'B. Fleetwood-Smith, W. C. Bull (Treasurer). *Middle row:* E. H. Bromley, A. G. Chipperfield, D. G. Bradman, W. M. Woodfull (Capt.), A. Kippax, L. S. Darling, W. H. Ponsford. *Front row:* B. A. Barnett, S. J. McCabe, W. A. Oldfield.

By courtesy of the Committee of the M.C.C.

R. AIRD, M.C.

Photo Frederic Robinson

COLONEL R. S. RAIT KERR, C.B.E., D.S.O., M.C.

By courtesy of the Committee of the M.C.C.

WALTER HAMMOND:
THE COVER DRIVE
Photo Sport and General

DON BRADMAN:
THE STRAIGHT DRIVE
Photo Sport and General

shallow steps leading into the pavilion at Lord's form a right-angle. Round this angle I sprang three steps at a time, carrying my umbrella at the trail. A dejected Harrovian, wearing a dark-blue rosette, and evidently unable to bear the agony of the match any longer, was leaving the pavilion with bowed head. I was swinging my umbrella to give me impetus, and its point caught the unfortunate man in the lower part of his waistcoat, and rebounded from one of its buttons out of my hand and over the side rails of the pavilion. The impact was terrific, and the unlucky individual, doubling up, sank like a wounded buffalo on to his knees, without, as far as I recollect, uttering a sound. I sprang over the body without apology, and, shouting out instructions to George Bean, the Sussex pro, who was the gate attendant, to look after my umbrella, dashed into the pavilion and up the many steps to its very summit, where I hoped to find a vacant seat.

I arrived there at the moment that Jameson was lying on the ground badly cut over, and was told that he had been batting forty minutes for no runs. As he has always been such an exceptionally quick scorer, this is worthy of record. With the total at 29, Fowler yorked Straker for 1 (29-8-1). The excitement then reached its climax. I do not think I ever saw or heard anything like it. The roars from the Harrow stand whenever a run was made were heard in the Zoological Gardens. Graham hit a 3, and then Fowler bowled Jameson. He had scored 2 and was ninth man out, and it was a thousand pities that he did not set up a record by carrying his bat through the innings for 0! (32-9-2) Alexander came in, looking horribly confident. The score crept up slowly. By now the cheering had swollen into such a volume of sound that its overtones included Paddington Station as well as the Zoological Gardens in its perimeter. Thirteen priceless runs were sneaked or stolen by the indomitable last pair. How I loathed both of them! And just as things began to look really desperate Alexander edged one to Holland in the slips off Steel, and Eton had won by 9 runs!

Needless to say the scene in front of the pavilion baffles description. I believe, though I do not vouch for it, that Lord Manners, the father of John Manners, who, gallant in his youth as in his manhood, had played such a conspicuous part in the victory, left the ground in despair at lunch-time and retired to his room with strict orders that he was not to be disturbed. It is further said that the butler knocked twice at his door with the object of telling him what his son had done, and so forth, and that he was told to "Go away" on both occasions. If it is true that the prospect of a Harrow victory was too much for Lord Manners, his regrets that he failed to see the finish must indeed have been poignant. Sir Ian Malcolm, in his recollections of Mr A. J. Balfour says, "I can never forget the magnificent finish of the Eton and Harrow match in Fowler's year, when at the close of play A. J. B., Walter Forbes, Alfred Lyttelton, and two of his brothers all leapt on to the green bench upon which we had been sitting in the pavilion and waved their hats and cheered Eton in an abandonment of enthusiasm." It has always been called "Fowler's match." As he made top score in both innings—namely, 21 and 64—and took twelve wickets, such a designation is entirely justified. His analysis for the last innings was 10 overs, 2 maidens, 23 runs, 8 wickets.

Here is the full score of a game which is a typical instance of the saying that no match is lost until the last ball has been bowled:

ETON *v.* HARROW

Played at Lord's, July 8 and 9, 1910

Result: Eton won by 9 runs

First Innings		*Second Innings*	
HARROW			
T. O. Jameson, c. Lubbock, b. Fowler	5	b. Fowler	2
T. B. Wilson, b. Kaye	53	b. Fowler	0
G. W. V. Hopley, b. Fowler	35	b. Fowler	8
T. L. G. Turnbull, l.b.w., b. Fowler	2	c. Boswell, b. Fowler	0
G. F. Earle (Capt.), c. Wigan, b. Steel	20	c. Wigan, b. Fowler	13
W. T. Monckton,[1] c. Lubbock, b. Stock	20	b. Fowler	0
J. M. Hillyard, st. Lubbock, b. Fowler	62	c. Kaye, b. Fowler	0
C. H. B. Blount, c. Holland, b. Steel	4	c. and b. Steel	5
A. C. Straker, c. Holland, b. Steel	2	b. Fowler	1
O. B. Graham, c. and b. Steel	6	not out	7
Hon. R. H. L. G. Alexander,[1] not out	2	c. Holland, b. Steel	8
Byes 18, leg byes 2, no-ball 1	21	Bye	1
Total	232	Total	45
ETON			
R. H. Lubbock, l.b.w., b. Earle	9	c. Straker, b. Hillyard	9
C. W. Tufnell, b. Hillyard	5	l.b.w., b. Alexander	7
W. T. Birchenough, c. Hopley, b. Graham	5	c. Turnbull, b. Jameson	22
W. T. Holland, c. Hopley, b. Hillyard	2	st. Monckton, b. Alexander	5
R. St L. Fowler (Capt.), c. Graham, b. Jameson	21	c. Earle, b. Hillyard	64
A. I. Steel,[1] b. Graham	0	c. Hopley, b. Hillyard	6
D. G. Wigan, c. Turnbull, b. Jameson	8	b. Graham	16
A. B. Stock, l.b.w., b. Alexander	2	l.b.w., b. Earle	0
Hon. J. N. Manners, c. Graham, b. Alexander	4	not out	40
K. Lister Kaye, c. Straker, b. Alexander	0	c. Jameson, b. Earle	13
W. G. K. Boswell, not out	0	b. Earle	32
Byes 10, wide 1	11	Byes 2, wides 3	5
Total	67	Total	219

[1] The Hon. R. H. L. G. Alexander is now the famous Field-Marshal, and W. Monckton, Sir Walter Monckton, K.C. A. I. Steel was a son of A. G. Steel.

BOWLING ANALYSIS

Eton

First Innings	O.	M.	R.	W.	Second Innings	O.	M.	R.	W.
Fowler	37.3	9	90	4	Fowler	10	2	23	8
Steel	31	11	69	4	Steel	6.4	1	12	2
Kaye	12	5	23	1	Kaye	3	0	9	0
Stock	7	2	12	1					
Boswell	8	4	17	0					

Harrow

	O.	M.	R.	W.		O.	M.	R.	W.
Earle	12	9	4	1	Earle	17.3	3	57	3
Hillyard	19	9	38	2	Hillyard	23	7	65	3
Graham	9	7	3	2	Graham	8	12	33	1
Jameson	4	1	4	2	Jameson	9	1	26	1
Alexander	4.1	1	7	3	Alexander	14	4	33	2
					Wilson	2	2	0	0

Umpires: J. Moss and J. P. Whiteside

W. D. Eggar, a science master at Eton, composed the following lines to celebrate the occasion. They appeared in a small volume of verse, *A Song of Lord's and Poems for the Mag*.

ETON *v*. HARROW

(*July* 8, 9, 1910)

If so be you chance to call
"Heads," and straightway tails shall fall,
Do not make a fruitless fuss,
Do not say, "'Twas ever thus";
Exercise some self-control,
Cultivate a steadfast soul.

If your safest drop a catch,
Do not say, "There goes the match."
If so be one ball in six
Beat the bat and beat the sticks,
Still proceed your best to bowl,
Still possess your patient soul.

If, when now your turn is nigh,
Clouds and darkness fill the sky
Ere the hour of six have struck,
Say not sadly, "Just our luck!"
Strive to keep your wicket whole,
Set your teeth, O steadfast soul.

If they make you follow-on,
Do not say, "All hope is gone";
What though sky and fortune frown,
We may slowly wear them down.
Sure 'twill mitigate the pain
Just to put them in again.

Samuel Johnson late, like you,
Found his fame, his Boswell too,
"Manners makyth man," God wot!
Manners maketh "forty not."
Put them in? Why, man alive,
Put them in for fifty-five!

Birds may 'scape the Fowler's snare;
Just as well no Bird is there.
Harrow's turn to scrape for runs,
Less like birds than furry ones.
Joy we all the same to feel
Foemen worthy of our Steel.

Swift reward for patient pluck;
Not to every man such luck.
One who cursed remains to bless—
Eton, mayst thou still possess,
When still deeper waters roll,
Thy "unconquerable soul."

W. D. E.

By half-past three on the second day the Gentlemen *v.* Players match was over, the Players winning by ten wickets. The Gentlemen were fairly strong in bowling, with F. R. Foster the star, but it was the weakest Gentlemen's batting side I have played on. We were, of course, immensely weaker in this respect than in the days of Jackson, MacLaren, and Ranji, and Fry played practically no first-class cricket this year. It was none too good a wicket, and Hirst, Fielder, and Smith, of Surrey, were too much for us. In the first innings Smith took five wickets for 18 runs. He was a very clever slow-to-medium bowler, who could turn the ball both ways.

Oxford beat Cambridge by an innings and 126 runs, P. R. Le Couteur achieving the greatest all-round performance in the history of the match by scoring 160 and taking eleven wickets for 66 runs. He was a first-class leg-break bowler, with an occasional googly, though rather more of a top-spinner than a genuine googly. Moreover, he kept a length. As a batsman he was no stylist, but a sound back-player and a very good hooker of short-pitched balls, of which on this occasion he received an undue proportion. The ground was drenched by heavy rain, and play was impossible before ten minutes to four on the first day, and then the turf was hardly fit for cricket. This was before the days of covering the bowlers' ends of the pitch, and it was very difficult indeed to stand. The pitch was very slow and dead easy, and of that pace which limits a good-length ball to a very restricted area. Oxford won the toss, and the game began sensationally, A. G. Cowie, fast right-hand, from the Pavilion end, sending down two wides and then taking a couple of wickets. But he could not keep his feet, and went off after two overs. Cambridge missed several catches, Le Couteur being let off at 42, 89, 114, and 157, and C. V. L. Hooman, who played an attractive innings of 60, at 37. On the second day the wicket was faster and sticky, and Le Couteur took every advantage of it. On the form of the season there was little difference between the two sides, but the Cambridge bowlers, generally speaking, could not accommodate themselves to the sodden turf, and there were also the missed catches.

At the Annual General Meeting of the M.C.C. Law LIV was altered, power being given to declare the innings closed at any time on the second day of a three-day match.

The period between 1895 and 1910 is often talked of as the Golden Age of English cricket, or the Augustan Age, and the England Eleven at Lord's in 1902 is thought by many to have been the best that has ever represented us. On pure results, however, we were far from successful during this period, losing the rubber in Australia in 1897–98 and 1901–2, and in England in 1899, 1902, and 1909. The England Eleven of 1902 certainly bristled with illustrious names—Ranji, Fry, MacLaren, Jackson, Jessop, Hirst, Rhodes, Lockwood, Braund, Lilley, and J. T. Tyldesley—and there are those who contend that no English side since then could look at it. While in no way lacking in admiration for this great side, I hold the view that the M.C.C. Australian teams of 1911–12, 1928–29, and 1932–33 would, were such a match possible, make them gallop all the way, and possibly defeat them. The England Eleven in England in 1912 was also a fine side, as was that of 1926, though the latter fell just short of greatness: it would have attained that had Hammond been available. Unfortunately he was very ill that summer and played no cricket.

The 1911–12 team possessed not only an outstanding opening pair of batsmen in Hobbs and Rhodes, but an incomparable pair of bowlers in Barnes and Foster. Australian opinion is almost unanimous that they were the best pair of bowlers England has ever sent to Australia, and they were ably backed up by Douglas. In a letter which I received recently from an Australian were these words: "I believe the 1911–12 side to be the best England has sent down under." I am not sure of this, as Chapman's 1928–29 M.C.C. team was tremendously powerful in batting, with Sutcliffe now Hobbs's partner—the greatest first Test Match pair England has ever had—and Hammond (in tremendous form), Jardine, Woolley, Hendren, and Chapman in support, magnificent fielding and wicket-keeping (Duckworth), and Tate, Larwood, White, Geary, and Hammond to bowl. It may be that in Barnes and Foster the 1911–12 side held the trump cards, but I would not like to lay odds on it.

Jardine's 1932–33 side too was a powerful combination. It lacked an opening pair in any way comparable to Hobbs and Rhodes or Hobbs and Sutcliffe, but it could bat down to the last man, and I have not seen better bowling *all round* than that of Larwood, Voce, Verity, Allen, and Hammond on good wickets. Moreover, only one catch was missed until the fifth and final Test, which, curiously enough, was almost exactly what happened in the case of Chapman's Eleven. These sides *won four of the Test Matches* on each tour—a tremendous feat in Australia. It is surely, therefore, not a false appreciation to rank them as at least the equals of the 1902 Eleven.

In certain quarters there has been a tendency to belittle our cricket between the two wars, but I do not subscribe to that view. This depreciation was no doubt due to the fact that the standard of play was very low immediately after the First German War. Certain false doctrines in the art of batting had sprung up, such as an inclination to 'sit in the block-hole,' to move the feet backward before gauging the length of the ball, and to rely on 'safety first.' The good-length ball which pitched on the stumps and swung away did not encourage the forcing forward stroke, but this type of ball—always a difficult one—did not last beyond a few overs, unless there was a wind to help it. Again, the inswinger was more securely met by a back or half back stroke unless the ball was well up, and then it could be driven hard and with safety on the on side through or over the heads of the various short legs, not altogether to their liking. This super-defensive style concentrated for the most part on on-side strokes, and was terribly dull to watch, but it soon disappeared in face of the strongest condemnation, and all the time there were the great Hobbs, Woolley, Hendren, Hammond, and others to show the world the real art of batting.

The summer of 1911 was a glorious one, and the game flourished exceedingly, the fact that the M.C.C. were sending a side to Australia in the autumn stimulating interest. That team was very carefully chosen, and though neither Fry nor Spooner was able to accept the M.C.C.'s invitation, we had just about the best side we could get together. Fry was originally asked to be Captain. Eventually the choice fell on me. The younger generation was well represented by F. R. Foster, Woolley, Mead, J. W. Hearne, E. J. Smith, and Hitch, and our manager was T. Pawley. We were fortunate in him, for by his able administration and care for our every comfort he contributed in a marked degree to the happy results achieved. Owing to illness, I played in only the opening match of the tour, my place being taken by J. W. H. T. Douglas, who captained the team with great success.

There was a grand Gentlemen *v.* Players match, the Gentlemen winning by 130 runs. As this was one of the best elevens that has ever represented the amateurs I give the names in the order of going in: C. B. Fry (Capt.), R. H. Spooner, I. P. F. Campbell, P. F. Warner, J. W. H. T. Douglas, A. P. Day, G. L. Jessop, F. R. Foster, W. B. Burns, P. R. Le Couteur, K. L. Gibson (wicket-keeper). Brearley was unable to play, and Burns took his place. Douglas, Foster, and Le Couteur formed a strong and varied combination of bowlers, and the side could bat down to the last man. The Players too were a very powerful side, with Barnes, Hirst, Buckenham, Rhodes, Tarrant, and Iremonger to bowl and such batsmen as Hayward, Hobbs, Tyldesley, and Hardinge, in addition to Tarrant, Hirst, and Iremonger. The final scores were: Gentlemen 352 and 271 for nine wickets declared, Players 201 and 292 (Hobbs 154, not out). The cricket all round was of very high quality, and that so many runs were made against such high-class bowling on a wicket which was always on the lively side was convincing proof of the strength of the batting.

There was a good University Match, Le Couteur's bowling—

eleven wickets for 179 runs, eight for 99 in the second innings—winning the game for Oxford by 74 runs. In Oxford's first innings J. F. Ireland, the Cambridge Captain, performed the hat trick, but after one more over, for some unaccountable reason, he took himself off. Cambridge led by 14 runs in the first innings, and were in a strong position when Oxford lost five wickets in their second innings for 119. But a stand by H. Brougham (84) and H. S. Altham (47) and some useful tail-wagging left Cambridge 315 to win. D. C. Collins, who had scored 57 in his first innings, again batted admirably—50 this time—but Le Couteur, if his length was not always accurate, was generally on top. For Oxford R. H. Twining (71 and 44) and R. V. Bardsley (71) batted very well. There was some beautiful fielding on both sides, in which S. H. Savile, Bardsley, and Altham were conspicuously good. Both sides were strong in bowling, but it is doubtful if Cambridge made the best use of theirs.

Two Test Trial matches were played—one at Lord's, where England defeated the Rest by ten wickets—and these, with the Gentlemen *v.* Players matches, helped materially in the selection of the team for Australia.

What was called an All Indian team, under the captaincy of the Maharajah of Patiala, played against a strong M.C.C. side, and were defeated by an innings and 168 runs, the bowling of J. T. Hearne and Tarrant being too good for their batsmen, with the exception of Major K. M. Mistri, who played a brilliant innings of 78, out of 106, in eighty minutes. The M.C.C. ran up the large total of 468, to which E. H. D. Sewell contributed 129, G. J. V. Weigall 103, and A. E. Lawton 75. Sewell, an all-round athlete of distinction, was a fine natural hitter, but somehow seldom did justice to his ability. When he got going, as he did on this occasion, he was very good to watch, for he hit cleanly and put tremendous power behind his drives.

Lord's was a busy place in 1912. This was the year of the Triangular Tournament, and there were three Test Matches—England *v.* Australia, England *v.* South Africa, and Australia *v.* South Africa, in addition to the M.C.C. Australian Team *v.* the Rest, Gentlemen *v.* Players, Oxford *v.* Cambridge, Eton *v.* Harrow, and the usual Middlesex and other fixtures.

The Triangular Tournament did not fulfil expectations, and this was due to three causes—first, the abominably wet summer;

secondly, the unrepresentative character of the Australian team, owing to a bitter dispute between the Australian Board of Control, which had recently been formed, and several of the leading Australian cricketers; and, finally, the fact that this year the South Africans fell far below the standard of the famous 1907 team.

As for the Australians, C. G. Macartney was very fine indeed. Having nearly every scoring stroke at his command, his neat and rapid footwork was a marked characteristic of his play. His aggressiveness lay rather in stepping back to make the ball shorter in length than in jumping out to drive. His dazzling cricket proved conclusively that a mistake had been made in choosing him for only one Test Match against the M.C.C. team in the previous winter. Another great player was W. Bardsley, the accomplished left-hander, who was even more successful than Macartney.

Kelleway was not attractive, but he was a wonderful defensive batsman, and of enormous value to his side. Few men have been harder to bowl out. The rest of the batting, on the almost continuous succession of wet wickets, was rather weak, but the bowling was good and the fielding extremely fine. Matthews brought off a double hat trick against South Africa at Old Trafford—an unprecedented feat in Test Matches.

Macartney did not bowl a great deal, but W. J. Whitty (left-hand medium) and G. R. Hazlitt (slow right) were good bowlers, and Emery had some great days. The last was potentially the most difficult googly bowler I have ever seen. He bowled at the pace of J. T. Hearne, varied by an occasional fast yorker, as fast as anything Knox or Mold ever sent down, and, being immensely strong in the forearm and wrist and possessing long and powerful fingers, used to impart tremendous spin to the ball. It can be imagined, therefore, that when he struck a length he was a match-winner, but he was uncertain, and after starting well fell off badly. Yet some overs he bowled at various times remain vividly in one's memory. He once accomplished a great feat at Melbourne, on a perfect wicket, for New South Wales *v.* Victoria—and Noble held a high opinion of his possibilities.

The South Africans were, as I have said, disappointing, losing five of their six Test Matches. S. J. Pegler and Faulkner had to do nearly all the bowling. Both were very good, but received little support, while the batsmen could not cope with Barnes in the Test Matches. A. D. Nourse was the best on figures, but the finest batting was shown by H. W. Taylor, whose success in subsequent years did not surprise those who had watched carefully his methods. Indeed, the M.C.C. team which visited South Africa in 1913–14 came back declaring that there were few finer players in the world than this young cricketer, who mastered even the great Barnes on the matting wickets, on which that splendid bowler used to make the ball turn very quickly and in addition get up. Like all the best modern batsmen, Taylor relied largely on back-play for defence.

England had a fine side, and did not lose a Test Match. Not once did the team bat on a good wicket, and their play under adverse conditions stood out conspicuously above that of their rivals. C. B. Fry was a keen and encouraging Captain, who got the best out of his men, and who managed his bowling well, except on one memorable occasion against Australia at Lord's, when he did not let Woolley bowl.[1]

A fine player this season was A. C. Johnston, of Hampshire, a batsman with a beautiful style and method, who played a remarkable innings of 89 on a drying wicket against Barnes in the Gentlemen *v.* Players match at Lord's. On his form this year he was good enough for England.

On my return from Australia the doctors told me I might attempt first-class cricket, and I began in great form, scoring three hundreds out of four innings in ten days. I had one of Gunn and Moore's very best bats, and six months on milk and soda had given me an eye like a hawk, but each innings was an effort, and before the end of June I was in bed, where I stayed, on and off, until October.

One of my hundreds—the last—was for the M.C.C. Australian Eleven *v.* the Rest of England at Lord's on May 23. Frankly, I prayed to do well in that match. Because of illness, as I have related, I had played but once for my team, in the opening match at Adelaide, so my coming in meant the leaving out of Mead, who played for the Rest. I scored 126 before giving my wicket away. I was dead beat, and my feelings may be imagined when,

[1] Fry has given an explanation of what at the time evoked some criticism. The wicket after rain played slowly and easily—even the great Barnes found the turf unresponsive—and the Captain, taking a long-term view, decided to hold Woolley in reserve for a later Test Match. Fry regards his tactics as justified, since Woolley in the subsequent Test Match at the Oval, on a very sticky pitch, took a total of ten wickets for 49 runs.

with my score at 97, I drove Dean past mid-off for four and saw the magic figures go up on the score-board. The crowd gave me a great welcome, and Tom Pawley wept with joy.

We won by an innings and 10 runs, scoring 509 to the Rest's 237 and 262. Hobbs, for once in a way, did not come off, but Woolley scored a grand 101, Rhodes 55, Douglas 41, Foster 43, and Smith 38.

Jessop, for the Rest, played marvellous innings of 88 and 55, in true Jessopian style, but the superb bowling of Barnes and Foster in both innings, and of Hitch in the second, rammed home the initial advantage of a big total.

Here is the score:

M.C.C. AUSTRALIAN XI *v.* THE REST

Played at Lord's, May 23, 24, and 25, 1912

Result: M.C.C. Australian XI won by an innings and 10 runs

M.C.C. AUSTRALIAN XI

W. Rhodes, c. Strudwick, b. Humphreys	55
J. B. Hobbs, c. Thompson, b. Dean	3
G. Gunn, c. Strudwick, b. Dean	36
P. F. Warner (Capt.), st. Strudwick, b. Day	126
J. W. Hearne, b. Humphreys	26
F. E. Woolley, b. Dean	101
J. W. H. T. Douglas, b. Dean	41
F. R. Foster, c. Strudwick, b. Brearley	43
E. J. Smith, b. Brearley	38
S. F. Barnes, l.b.w., b. Brearley	0
W. Hitch, not out	11
Byes 15, leg byes 6, no-balls 8	29
Total	509

THE REST

	First Innings		Second Innings	
E. Humphreys	l.b.w., b. Barnes	2	c. Foster, b. Hitch	58
G. J. Thompson	b. Barnes	6	c. Woolley, b. Barnes	11
R. H. Spooner	l.b.w., b. Foster	1	b. Barnes	60
C. B. Fry (Capt.)	b. Douglas	30	c. Barnes, b. Foster	46
C. P. Mead	st. Smith, b. Foster	4	b. Foster	2
A. P. Day	b. Hitch	52	c. Rhodes, b. Foster	12
G. L. Jessop	c. Barnes, b. Foster	88	c. and b. Hitch	55
H. Strudwick	b. Hitch	5	b. Hitch	5
D. W. Carr	b. Barnes	17	b. Hitch	0
H. Dean	not out	8	b. Hitch	0
W. Brearley	c. and b. Barnes	4	not out	3
	Byes 11, leg byes 7, no-balls 2	20	Byes 6, leg bye 1, no-balls 3	10
	Total	237	Total	262

BOWLING ANALYSIS

THE REST

	O.	M.	R.	W.
Brearley	37	0	173	3
Dean	39.5	11	118	4
Carr	25	3	91	0
Humphreys	11	1	40	2
Thompson	6	0	27	0
Day	5	0	31	1

M.C.C. Australian XI

First Innings	O.	M.	R.	W.	Second Innings	O.	M.	R.	W.
Foster	24	5	71	3	Foster	23	7	67	3
Barnes	21.3	11	38	4	Barnes	29	8	65	2
Douglas	8	2	44	1	Douglas	9	0	52	0
Hearne	4	0	30	0	Hearne	3	0	23	0
Hitch	6	1	34	2	Hitch	12.4	2	41	5
					Woolley	2	1	4	0

Umpires: W. A. J. West and G. Webb

The Universities were evenly matched, Cambridge winning by three wickets, thanks largely to the all-round cricket of E. L. Kidd, who made scores of 46 and 45, took eight wickets for 143 with his high-actioned leg-breaks, and fielded finely. He was also an extremely good Captain. The finish might have been even closer if G. E. V. Crutchley had been able to bat in Oxford's second innings. In the first innings, going in No. 6, he played in beautiful style for 99, not out, in spite of a temperature, but at the end of his innings he was found to be suffering from a severe attack of measles. It was a hard, keen match from start to finish, and there was nothing better in it than the splendid outfielding of Altham and Campbell on the last morning.

I had the honour of captaining the Gentlemen at Lord's in 1913. The professionals won by seven wickets, after a most interesting game, the chief features of which were the bowling of Barnes and Hobbs's 72, not out. Barnes had a regular glue-pot to bowl on in the second innings, and took seven wickets for 38 runs. He turned his leg-break at a great pace, and made it get up. Barnes had a lithe, springy run up to the crease, and with his tall, loosely built figure was the embodiment of hostile action.

I made 24, and this I consider one of the best innings I ever played in my life. I was out to a wonderful catch at the wicket by E. J. Smith, the Warwickshire and England stumper, who caught a fast, rising ball in front of his nose.

Alfred Lyttelton died on July 5, 1913. His style of batting was vigorous and very straight, most of his runs being made in front of the wicket. As a wicket-keeper he was a very sure catch, but he did not take the ball quite so near the wicket as Blackham and Pilling, the latter of whom Lyttelton himself thought was even better than Blackham. He was a great all-round athlete, the C. B. Fry of the eighties, excelling at Association football, rackets, and tennis. As Lord Curzon of Kedleston said in his eloquent appreciation of him in *The Times*, "No boyish hero was ever quite such a hero" as Alfred Lyttelton was at Eton. A few days after Lyttelton's death Mr Asquith, the Prime Minister, spoke of him in the House of Commons in these words: "He perhaps, of all men of this generation, came nearest to the mould and ideal of manhood which every English father would like to see his son aspire to, and if possible, attain. . . .

> "This was the happy warrior; this was he
> Whom every man in arms should wish to be."

All the Lytteltons that I have known possess great charm of manner, and Alfred had it in full measure, his happy personality, cheery manner, and smile radiating good-fellowship and affection.

A wonderful tribute was paid to his memory during the Oxford and Cambridge match at Lord's. At noon, the hour of the Memorial Service to him at St Margaret's, Westminster, the flags were lowered to half-mast, and for two minutes the players in the field stood to attention with their caps off, and every man and woman on the ground stood up. His appointment to the Colonial Secretaryship coincided with the departure of the M.C.C. team to Australia in September 1903, and I recall a leading article in *The Times* which commented on the new Cabinet appointments, saying that his appointment as Colonial Secretary should appeal to our kinsmen in Australia. He was the eighth and youngest son of the fourth Baron Lyttelton: seven of them were in the Eton Eleven. It was said of his father, a great scholar, that he would read Homer or Virgil during the progress of a match at Eton, but never at the time when his sons were at the wicket. The Lytteltons have a very long association with Lord's, going back to June 22, 1835, when the fourth Baron was elected to the M.C.C. Three Lytteltons have been Presidents of the Club, the fifth Lord Lyttelton, eighth Viscount Cobham, in 1886, Alfred in 1898, and the present Viscount Cobham in 1935. Alfred was the best cricketer, C. G. the second best. Alfred was of opinion that C. G. was the finest of them all, but that, perhaps, was modesty on his part. C. G. was a fine free hitter, a useful medium-paced bowler, and a good wicket-keeper; he played for the Gentlemen between 1861 and 1866, represented Cambridge at tennis, and could throw a cricket-ball over a hundred yards. He took a First in law, and a Second in the Classical Tripos.

Edward, whose fame rests chiefly on his innings of 113 for Middlesex *v.* the Australians, already referred to, was Captain of the famous Cambridge Eleven of 1878, and afterwards headmaster of Haileybury and Eton.

R. H. Lyttelton ("Bob") was a very well-known figure at Lord's. He wrote delightfully on cricket, was a very close follower of the game, and used to carry about with him a notebook in which he jotted down the all-round performances of cricketers. He considered that Braund's 31 and 34 and fifteen wickets for 71 runs for Somerset *v.* Yorkshire at Sheffield in June 1902 as great as any other. The match was played on a very difficult wicket, the scores being Somerset 86 and 106, Yorkshire 74 and 84. Nine of Braund's wickets were clean bowled, including F. S. Jackson twice.

In a letter Lord Cobham, the present Treasurer of the Club, wrote:

> Eleven Lytteltons played against Bromsgrove School at Hagley on August 26, 1867. The family side was made up of: the peer (my grandfather); his two brothers, Billy, who was Rector of Hagley, and Spencer; and his eight sons, the youngest of them, Alfred, being ten years old. Bromsgrove School had the help of two or three masters, and made 150. The family replied with 191, of which my father made 27, the younger Spencer 51, and Albert 46. Not one of the three members of the older generation troubled the scorer. Then Bromsgrove were bowled out by my father and N. G. for 51, and the family knocked off the 12 runs required, winning by ten wickets, "amidst the cheers of the numerous spectators and the congratulations of their backers and friends," as the local report puts it. The report starts: "This very peculiar event, which it is sad to reflect the History of the World can in all probability contain but once, has passed off with great success in the presence of a very large gathering from the neighbourhood."[1]

The Gentlemen's batting at the Oval in 1914, except for a beautiful innings of 71 by R. H. Spooner, had been disappointing, but at Lord's, in spite of Spooner's unavoidable absence, the batting was excellent, though it was Johnny Douglas's superb bowling that won the match for us by 134 runs. In the first innings of the Players, which extended over four hours and a half, he was off for only three-quarters of an hour, taking nine wickets

[1] Mr Stanley Christopherson, President of the M.C.C. from 1939 to 1945, tells me that his father and his *ten sons* played as a team in several matches, and were probably at their best at the end of the eighties.

for 105 runs. His analysis for the whole game was thirteen wickets for 172 runs.

The Players scored 256, which gave the Gentlemen a lead of 9 runs, and in our second innings we scored 275, A. H. Hornby, who, like his father, the famous A. N. ("Monkey") Hornby, the maker of Lancashire cricket, scorned to wear a hat, making 69 and S. G. Smith, who had contributed 52 in the first innings, 50. The Players were left with 285 to win, but Douglas and Foster had six of them—Hobbs, Tarrant, J. W. Hearne, Mead, G. Gunn, and Woolley—out for 28! Eventually the total reached 150. It was emphatically Douglas's match, and he was backed up by fine slip fielding by Foster and Fender, while H. G. Garnett kept wicket beautifully, his stumping of Hitch off a fast, swinging leg ball of Foster's being worthy of Blackham, Pilling, MacGregor, or Halliwell. This was a great Gentlemen's side, though it did lack Spooner, who was unwell: Fry (Capt.), Hornby, A. P. Day, Warner, Smith, Douglas, Foster, Jessop, Fender, Garnett, and Jacques. It was no mean feat to win against a Players' team which was composed of Hobbs (Capt.), Tarrant, J. W. Hearne, C. P. Mead, G. Gunn, Woolley, Humphreys, Hitch, Kennedy, Barnes, and Strudwick.

The most memorable event in the season of 1914 was the match to celebrate the centenary of the present Lord's ground between the M.C.C. team which had recently returned from a successful tour in South Africa and the Rest of England. The game, however, did not come up to expectations, for Barnes was prevented from playing for the M.C.C. team by a strained leg, and the weather favoured the Rest, who batted all the first day on a perfect wicket, while rain in the night made the pitch difficult for their opponents. Hitch took altogether twelve wickets for 93 runs. He was a great personality on the cricket field, who bowled with all his heart and soul, and his very long hopping run up to the crease, if condemned by the purists, was the delight of the Oval crowd. It looked so venomous! He was also a magnificent fieldsman at short leg and a batsman who possessed a rather better defence than he was usually credited with, but whose real value to his side was his powerful driving. Here is the score of this match:[1]

[1] There was a great dinner on the second evening of the match at the Hotel Cecil, with Lord Hawke presiding. W. G. was given an enormous ovation when he rose to reply to the toast of "The County Cricket Club."

M.C.C. SOUTH AFRICAN TEAM *v.* REST OF ENGLAND

Played at Lord's, June 22, 23, *and* 24, 1914

Result: Rest of England won by an innings and 189 *runs*

REST OF ENGLAND

E. Humphreys, b. Woolley	111
F. A. Tarrant, b. Relf	28
G. Gunn, b. Woolley	38
S. G. Smith, b. Douglas	78
C. B. Fry (Capt.), b. Booth	70
A. P. Day, c. Bird, b. Rhodes	79
G. H. Hirst, run out	15
F. T. Mann, c. Smith, b. Booth	3
W. Hitch, b. Woolley	28
A. Dolphin, not out	4
G. Geary, c. and b. Relf	0
Byes 3, leg byes 7, no-balls 3	13
Total	467

M.C.C. SOUTH AFRICAN TEAM

First Innings		*Second Innings*	
J. B. Hobbs, b. Hitch	6	c. Fry, b. Hitch	16
W. Rhodes, c. Dolphin, b. Hitch	0	c. Hirst, b. Smith	52
J. W. Hearne, c. Dolphin, b. Geary	1	c. Dolphin, b. Hitch	26
C. P. Mead, c. Gunn, b. Hitch	21	c. Dolphin, b. Geary	9
J. W. H. T. Douglas (Capt.), l.b.w., b. Day	16	c. Dolphin, b. Smith	14
F. E. Woolley, b. Hitch	9	b. Hitch	12
Hon. L. H. Tennyson, c. Fry, b. Hitch	1	c. Geary, b. Smith	29
A. E. Relf, b. Hirst	5	c. Geary, b. Smith	5
M. C. Bird, c. Humphreys, b. Hitch	15	c. Smith, b. Hitch	1
M. W. Booth, not out	16	b. Hitch	0
E. J. Smith, b. Hitch	0	not out	1
Leg byes	4	Byes 14, leg byes 3, no-balls 2	19
Total	94	Total	184

BOWLING ANALYSIS

M.C.C. South African Team

	O.	M.	R.	W.
Douglas	25	2	87	1
Booth	37	8	106	2
Relf	32.3	11	67	2
Hearne	11	0	64	0
Woolley	26	2	93	3
Rhodes	16	5	37	1

Rest of England

First Innings

	O.	M.	R.	W.
Hitch	14.5	4	42	7
Geary	7	3	20	1
Tarrant	6	3	4	0
Day	7	4	8	1
Hirst	8	2	16	1

Second Innings

	O.	M.	R.	W.
Hitch	31.3	13	51	5
Geary	24	11	36	1
Day	10	4	16	0
Hirst	13	4	22	0
Humphreys	1	0	1	0
Smith	17	7	39	4

Umpires: J. Moss and W. A. J. West

CHAPTER XI

The First German War

Military Necessity—Charity Games—England and the Dominions —Death of A. E. Stoddart, Victor Trumper, and W. G. Grace—The Greatest of All Cricketers—Post-war Experiment—The A.I.F.

DURING the First German War Lord's was used for military purposes. Accommodation was found for units of the Territorial Artillery, the A.S.C. (Transport), the R.A.M.C., wireless instruction, and military cooking classes, while 2 Grove End Road was lent as H.Q. to the Royal Volunteer Battalion (London Regiment).

When the R.A.M.C. left the War Office used the buildings and practice ground as a training centre for Royal Artillery cadets. In the pavilion the staff and some members occupied spare time in making hay nets for horses, and some 18,000 of these were sent to Woolwich.

Only Service matches were played at Lord's, but the M.C.C. continued to send sides against the Public Schools. At the start of the War the playing of cricket was thought almost unseemly, but it was gradually realized that any ban on cricket had become illogical, and in 1917 two charity matches were arranged—one an English Army Eleven *v.* an Australian Army Eleven and the other the Navy and Army *v.* Australian and South African Forces. The English Army and the Navy and Army lost both these games against the Dominion forces. The matches proved a great success, and the gates and subscriptions so satisfactory that £1320 was raised for St Dunstan's and Lady Lansdowne's Officers' Family Fund. In 1918 more charity matches were arranged, two England *v.* the Dominions games being played at Lord's. Large crowds watched the cricket, and the second match was honoured by the presence of His Majesty the King and H.R.H. the Duke of Connaught.

Another match, which proved a big attraction, was the Hon. F. S. Jackson's Eleven against my own side, though Jackson himself was unable to play. Jackson's team seemed the stronger in bowling, but they were beaten by an innings, Hobbs, to the delight of all, making a very fine 86.

A charming account of the first of the two matches against the Dominions, played on the 29th of June, 1918, appeared in *The Spectator*, under the initials E. B. I am permitted to quote the following:

Hot sunshine poured down upon ten thousand spectators, as on the ideal gala day at Lord's; there was a crowd in the pavilion, and a scramble for lunch and tea at the buffet outside, the scene of such scuffles for many happy years. There was the right sprinkling of muslin frocks and gay parasols, and of knowing urchins in grey flannels and club colours who instruct fathers and uncles in the points of the game. And when that dramatic moment arrived, and the file of white figures came from the pavilion to take up their respective positions in the field, followed by two famous bats who were to make, or not make, their century each, the usual cheers broke out, and when they had subsided there was the usual hush as the expectant crowd settled down to that enjoyment which is not less intense because so decorous.

Incidentally, it may be remarked that the decorum, in the circumstances, was somewhat of a surprise. The match being one between England and the Dominions, the latter consisting chiefly of Australians, it was to be expected that colonial exuberance would have triumphed handsomely over etiquette. But decorum had its way. There were no long-drawn 'coo-ees,' no partisan shouts, no caustic pleasantries such as one associates with the friendly critics from overseas. When Docker flashed dramatically into the game with his lightning balls that caused one after another of England's famous bats to stand like "Ole Bill," asking, "Where did that one go?" the Dominions gave no more than their share of hand-clapping. The men from overseas in khaki, or the pathetic blue of the hospitals, looked on, smiled satirically or encouragingly from under their slouch hats, commented in low voices, and when England was all out for 98 lounged off with the rest of the crowd.

There was little in the game itself to dispel the illusion that we were not at war. England had out a 'star' team, but it did not scintillate more than any two teams brought together for a county match. The Dominions' team was almost an unknown quantity, save for such names as Macartney and Kelleway; but a Dominions team, in the nature of things, is always, save to the inner ring of experts, an unknown quantity.

The Dominions went in first, and as Kelleway and Macartney made their stand memory went back to the famous fights between the Mother Country and Australia when "Plum" Warner—there he is now, out in the field against his old rival Macartney, wearing the famous Harlequin cap—took out his team and brought back the

'Ashes.' The Dominions game was full of interest, though not, perhaps, in any way startling. In the absence of Fender, the brunt of the bowling fell to Kirk, who in the stress of his work as a 'Sergeant Instructor' has not lost his form with the ball. He kept up his reputation and took seven wickets, and the Dominions were out for 166. It was when England, with its galaxy of favourites—even the etiquette of Lord's could not suppress obvious pride in the names as the list was read: Fry and Warner, Gillingham, affectionately dubbed "the Parson," Hardinge and Humphreys and Hendren—took the bat that the surprise came.

Valiant efforts were made by England, but with little result. "The Parson" had mighty intentions, as witness those three great sweeps round to leg which were meant for boundaries, and succeeded only in missing the ball and sending the batsman swirling round like a teetotum. But he secured only six runs in the total. Fry, taking his catastrophes smilingly, as might have been anticipated, contrived to better this by four. It was "Plum" Warner who made the stand, imperturbable as ever, who scored off Macartney with comparative ease, and even received Docker's lightning with such equanimity that we began to think it was playable after all. McIver, wary and painstaking, ably supported him, and put 17 on to the score. It was when Warner was joined by a slim youth whose name was strange to the outer ring, but who, asserted an excited voice from the back benches, "got 203 for his school the other day," that it looked as if England might make a big stand. But Stevens, the newcomer, who quickly won our admiration, though he made a brilliant innings, could not contrive also to make it long, and fell to Barbour for 18. The 'tail' was slaughtered quickly and painlessly, and England was all out for 98. It was the day of the Dominions, but yet no one 'coo-eed.'

There were moments, as has been said, when it was possible to forget that it was war cricket, but the moments were few. The reminders to the contrary were numerous, and many of them too obvious. There was the hospital blue in the pavilion, in those reserved balconies, and sprinkled among the crowd in all directions. Khaki was prevalent, and that in only too many cases marked with the blue band. Special constables, wearing the star of long service, patrolled the green. A band played, thus accentuating the fact that the match was for charity—for whoever heard of a Test Match at Lord's being accompanied by a band! It was provided, no doubt, with the best intentions, but in truth we somewhat resented it. When "Plum" was facing Docker it seemed sacrilege to hear *The Merry Widow* waltz on a band.

Only one scoring-board was working. The other, shuttered and eyeless, was a mute reminder of happier days. And even the working one seemed out of practice, and the unwonted sight was witnessed of spectators trespassing on the green to study figures that seemed to have no connexion with those on the match-cards.

But in truth it was only necessary to glance down the scoring-card to know that England was at war. Only one name, and that the "Parson," had not a naval or military prefix. Kelleway is a lieutenant; so also is the redoubtable Docker; Hardinge is a sergeant-major; Humphreys an A.B.; Yeoman, who carried his bat for 22, is a Staff Q.M.S. Privates, gunners, corporals, sergeants, lieutenants, captains, majors, commanders—such is the list of players for a game at Lord's in the summer of 1918.

As we read it we seem to see beyond the smooth turf, and the group of white figures, and the still crowds where the 'great game' is being played, to those fields in France and Flanders, in Italy and in Mesopotamia, and the spaces of the seas where the greater and ghastly game is being played in which many of these men have played and will play again, and in which many also who wielded bat or ball at Lord's have played their last ball and closed a noble innings.

The cricket world sustained in 1915 the loss of three outstanding cricketers. In April Andrew Ernest Stoddart died, the saddest of deaths. It is remarkable that he did not take up the game until twenty-two years of age. He played for the Hampstead Club, for whom in 1886 he scored 485 runs against the Stoics, at that time the largest individual score known in cricket. He became the most prominent batsman on the Middlesex side. He had every stroke at his command, and was a great player on every sort of wicket. He was also a brilliant field and a useful change bowler. Coming back after retirement to play in J. T. Hearne's benefit match in 1900, he made his highest score in first-class cricket—221 against Somerset. Stoddart was also a great Rugby player, and one of the few who have represented England both at cricket and football.

On June 28 Victor Trumper died at Sydney. Before the advent of Macartney and Bradman no more brilliant batsman had ever appeared for Australia. On his first visit in 1899 he made a great century of 135, not out, in the Test Match at Lord's, and of this *Wisden* wrote, "His innings at Lord's was sufficient to prove that Australia had found a world's batsman. Nothing could have been better." He was impervious to the state of the weather or the condition of the ground. When orthodox batting was of no avail he could in a flash improvise the most daring and dazzling strokes.

On a hard wicket the way he hooked good-length balls was amazing. He was followed to the grave by thousands, who regarded him as a national hero. Never robust, he died at the early age of thirty-seven.

On October 23 cricket suffered its hardest blow in the death of William Gilbert Grace, the greatest of all cricketers, and the maker of modern cricket. No book on Lord's would be complete without an extended reference to this transcendent player, for, as Lord Harris wrote after the Champion's death, "the Gloucestershire matches took him to all the great cricketing counties; but I think he would have said that his home in first-class cricket was Lord's."

W. G. Grace was the Leviathan of cricket, and with his huge bearded figure, massive shoulders and arms, he looked it. His family history has been given in many books, and it is sufficient to say that he was born at Downend, near Bristol, on July 18, 1848, his father being a country doctor, a profession he himself followed. Looking at the well-known picture *The Doctor*, by Luke Fildes, R.A., I always think that if the artist had taken W. G. as the model for the bearded figure sitting by the child it would have been very suitable, as Dr Grace worked among the poorer classes in Bristol, where, in the winter-time, carrying a black bag, he was a well-known figure.

W. G. created, almost at the start of his career, an entirely new standard of aggregates, averages, centuries, and all-round play: *he made and popularized cricket.* His first century in first-class cricket, in 1866, was 224, not out, for England against Surrey at the Oval. This was an extraordinary achievement for a boy, and one that set a standard often to be repeated and excelled. In 1871 he scored 2739 runs, with an average of 78·25. Five years later he made 2622 runs, with an average of 62, with the highest score of his career—344, for the M.C.C. *v.* Kent at Canterbury—followed by 177 against Nottinghamshire and 318, not out, against Yorkshire—in all, 839 runs in three consecutive innings, once not out. In that month he scored 1278 runs, with an average of 127·8. This was the pinnacle of his success, along with consecutive scores in Gentlemen *v.* Players in the six games of 1871 to 1873 of 217, 77, 112, 117, 163, 158, and 70. He also scored 109 and 215 in 1870, 110 in 1874, 152 in 1875, and 169 in 1876.[1] With no Test

[1] Including Gentlemen *v.* Players at the Oval. He made seven centuries for the Gentlemen at Lord's, four at the Oval, one at Brighton, one at Prince's, one at Scarborough, and one at Hastings.

Matches in those days, these were the most important fixtures. During his career he made 54,896 runs in first-class cricket. It is well to record this, as the modern generation, with some scepticism as to former players, often inquire if there were ever such run-getters as Hobbs, Bradman, and Hammond. This demands an answer, but the conditions were so different that no real comparison is possible. It must be remembered, too, that W.G. did an immense amount of bowling. In the six Gentlemen *v.* Players matches of 1875 and 1876, including those away from Lord's, he took fifty-nine wickets, and from 1865 to 1891 2429 wickets, a larger number than any professional. After that year he did less bowling, but as far on as 1902, at Lord's for the M.C.C. *v.* the Australians, he had an analysis of five wickets for 29 runs. In his whole career in first-class cricket he obtained 2864 wickets for 17·99 runs each. As he was also a very fine fieldsman, with a huge pair of hands, he towered over his colleagues.

It is now over fifty years ago since, in 1895, he had such a remarkable season, scoring 1000 runs in May and his hundredth century (288) against Somerset. His actual thousandth run was scored at Lord's on May 30 in an innings of 169, against Middlesex, in the course of which he hit a ball through the committee-room window. His best innings that season was also at Lord's, in Gentlemen *v.* Players. On a fiery and faulty wicket he and A. E. Stoddart opened with a partnership of 151 (W. G. 118 and Stoddart 71). With the exception of Sir T. C. O'Brien (21), there was no other double-figure score, and W. G.'s defence against the fast bowling of Richardson and Mold was masterly. His next year (1896) was nearly as remarkable, with mammoth scores of 301 and 243, not out, against Sussex. He was still a formidable player until 1899, when, after playing in the first Test Match against the Australians at Trent Bridge, he finally stood down from the England side. In 1898, as we have seen, the M.C.C. arranged the Gentlemen *v.* Players match on his fiftieth birthday. There was a memorable scene at the close. In the final innings, owing to lameness and a bruised hand, he went in No. 9, and with C. J. Kortright, the last batsman, 75 runs were added before Kortright was caught at cover-point five minutes before time. The crowd gathered in front of the pavilion, and the Champion and Kortright came on to the dressing-room balcony to acknowledge the cheering. He still went on playing, mostly for London County, the management of which he had undertaken, and increased his centuries to 126, until he finally passed out of first-class cricket with a solitary appearance in 1908. His last century in first-class cricket, at the age of fifty-six, was 166 against the M.C.C. for London County in 1904. It was, and remains, the longest of all careers (1864–1908). He was a most loyal member of the M.C.C., and always wore the cap. As a cricketer he was for long *pars magna* of Lord's, where he scored 12,690 runs and took 654 wickets, scoring nineteen centuries for the Club.

The modern generation often ask what sort of a player W. G. really was, and would he have played with success googly and swing bowling? To the first question I can describe him only when past his prime. Looking at him, you noticed very long and slanting eyes, as he stood at the wicket, with his left shoulder pointing down the pitch and with both eyes on the bowler. His judgment seemed instinctive and instantaneous as to where the ball would pitch. The bat, wielded with consummate ease, was put against the ball with the body following into the stroke with a perfect adjustment of weight. The technique was hardly attractive, as a masterly efficiency rather overshadowed style. Always, however, there was the impression of power. At Lord's in 1902, when fifty-four, in the second innings of the M.C.C. *v.* Lancashire match, he hit Hallows out of the ground over the Grand Stand into a garden. Three years later he hit J. N. Crawford out of the Oval. He kept up his superb cutting, both late and square, and he was very good on the on side. He seldom left an off ball alone, and when he scored his hundredth century, for Gloucestershire *v.* Somerset at Bristol, the wicket-keeper, the Rev. A. P. Wickham, said that only five balls passed his bat.

To the second question a conversation with the late A. C. M. Croome, that vivid correspondent of *The Times*, supplies some sort of answer. Croome instanced as showing the genius of W. G. that at the end of the eighties he altered his style. Owing to his medical work he played comparatively few innings from 1879 to 1881, and this was followed by a marked increase in weight. This bothered him, and he changed his play, dropping strokes that required quick foot movement and practising and perfecting others, more especially the pull stroke. This ability to readjust his play and accommodate himself to other methods, with his run-getting unimpaired, makes one believe that he would have mastered both googly and swing bowling, for he 'murdered' fast bowlers on fiery wickets at the start of his career. I once ventured to ask him which type of bowling he liked least, and he replied, "I didn't care what they bowled if I was in form, but the faster they bowled the better I liked them!"

As to his bowling, originally medium pace, he later adopted a slower delivery, the ball being bowled with a round-arm action which has been described as like that of Grimmett. If he did not actually make the ball swing, he bowled a ball which E. H. D. Sewell has aptly described as having "a sort of drift," and its flight was very deceptive.

One of the best-known men in England, he held a position which he maintained with dignity. He could enjoy a joke or a bit of chaff, but he was not to be adventured on by any ill-timed familiarities. His figure demanded respect, and he knew how to ensure it. As a captain he was a martinet in face of slackness, but he had a warm heart, especially for young players. He knew all about wickets and about the game, and he could keep a grip on it and on any side he led. He did not bother much about theory, as he had an unanalytical mind, nor did he display any special finesse in leadership. His captaincy was sound and efficient on accepted lines, and if a game was falling flat he was the first to spur it on to more action. He liked to warm his bowlers up with several overs, and if bowling well he would 'bowl them out.' He did, however, overdo this when C. L. Townsend, in his seventeenth year and still a schoolboy, was bowled for seventy-one overs in his first innings in county cricket. Perhaps in kindness of heart he wanted the son of one of his oldest friends to take as many wickets as possible. Short spells of 'shock' tactics would not have appealed to one whom no exertion or length of effort could tire. He was a generous-minded man, and when he was the best-known player in the world was always ready to play in a benefit match to ensure its success. This was very marked in his early career, and he kept it up until 1900, when in September of that year he played in a North *v.* South match at Lord's for the benefit of Philip Need, the dressing-room attendant at Lord's, and scored 126 and 13.

It is a proud memory to me to recall that more than once I had the honour of going in first with him. I remember an occasion in the 1920's when a cricketer who had recently played for England *v.* Australia asked me in the dressing-room at Lord's, "Was W. G. really a great batsman?" It was said at the time by those present that when I had recovered from a dead faint

I dealt with him properly! So many of the present generation seem to forget that there were great men before Agamemnon!

He died at Eltham, Kent. He disliked the Zeppelin raids, and when, during his last illness, H. D. G. Leveson-Gower called on him, at Mrs Grace's request, and asked him, "How can you mind the Zepps, W.G., you who have played all the fastest bowlers of your time?" he simply replied, "Ah, but I could see those beggars. I can't see these."

As a former Bishop of Hereford said of him, "Had Grace been born in ancient Greece the *Iliad* would have been a different book. Had he lived in the Middle Ages he would have been a Crusader and would now have been lying with his legs crossed in some ancient abbey, having founded a great family. As he was born when the world was older he was the best known of all Englishmen and the King of that English game least spoilt by any form of vice." In July 1923 gates were erected at the members' entrance to Lord's, with the following inscription:

TO THE
MEMORY OF

WILLIAM GILBERT
GRACE
THE GREAT CRICKETER
1848–1915

THESE GATES WERE
ERECTED BY THE M.C.C.
AND OTHER FRIENDS
AND ADMIRERS

There was much discussion in committee as to the exact wording of the Memorial, and opinions were invited. Some sent in suggestions in English, others in Latin, and a few even in Greek —but the question was finally solved by Sir Stanley Jackson, who said, "Why not simply 'the great Cricketer'?" There the inscription stands, governed by the all-important word 'the'; there, like the image to Horatius, it stands plain for all folks to see.

One should, I think, mention two deaths in 1917. On December 3 died the Rev. Sir Emilius Bayley-Laurie, Bart. His great score of 152 in the Eton and Harrow match of 1841 stood as a record for sixty-three years. At the time of his death, being in his ninety-fifth year, he was the oldest cricketer alive, having outlived all his contemporaries. It is startling to find that when he played for Kent in the side were Mynn, Felix, Pilch, Wenman, and Hillyer. His life, like that of Jenner-Fust and Ponsonby-Fane, spanned, indeed, whole periods of cricket history. His father, Sir John Bayley, Bart., was President of the M.C.C. in 1844. He himself lived near Lord's for many years, being Vicar of St John's, Paddington, from 1867 to 1888.

On November 10 died G. H. S. Trott. No Australian Captain was more popular in England, and good judges thought him as great as any Australian Captain. By his pleasant character he won the regard of cricketers wherever he played. He was always generous in defeat, and when he lost the rubber at the Oval in 1896 was the first to praise the great bowling of J. T. Hearne and Peel. His great innings in the Test Match at Lord's that year was a fine fighting effort, for Tom Richardson was bowling at lightning pace on a very fast wicket.

After the First German War English cricket had to be rebuilt, and a great mistake was made when county matches were limited to two days. The experiment, which was sponsored by Lancashire, was rather hastily decided on, and was a complete failure. The longer hours of play exhausted the players, and there could have been no worse preparation for Test Match cricket. The M.C.C. had no part in the scheme, and the University Match and Gentlemen *v.* Players were of the usual duration. The Australian Imperial Forces team toured the country, playing three-day matches, and were seen at Lord's on three occasions—*v.* the M.C.C., *v.* the Gentlemen of England, and *v.* Middlesex. They defeated a fairly strong M.C.C. team by ten wickets, drew with Middlesex in a big-scoring game, and were beaten by an innings and 133 runs by the Gentlemen, J. W. H. T. Douglas, J. C. White, M. Falcon, C. S. Marriott, and A. J. Evans bowling extremely well on a good wicket, and the Rev. F. H. (now Canon) Gillingham heading the Gentlemen's total of 402, in which there were nine double-figure scores, with a dashing innings of 83. The A.I.F. had some fine players in H. L. Collins, W. A. Oldfield, J. M. Gregory, C. E. Kelleway, J. M. Taylor, and C. E. Pellew, who were to form the nucleus of the subsequent powerful Australian Test Match teams.

The summer was a gloriously fine one, and great crowds flocked to the matches: I remember seeing 20,000 people at the Oval on a Monday morning at the Surrey *v.* Kent match *before the game began.*

Oxford beat Cambridge by 45 runs, after a most interesting game,[1] and Gentlemen *v.* Players was drawn. D. J. Knight (71 and 124) and Hobbs (113 in his second innings) carried off the honours for batting,[2] but perhaps the best thing was the splendid bowling of Douglas, who in the Players' first innings took eight wickets for 49 runs.

At the Annual General Meeting of the M.C.C. Admiral Viscount Jellicoe, Admiral Sir David Beatty, Field-Marshal Viscount French, and Field-Marshal Sir Douglas Haig were made Honorary Members of the Club as a mark of appreciation of their services to the country.

[1] It was in this match that Miles Howell scored 170.

[2] At the Oval Hobbs also made a century: only W. G. had previously accomplished this feat.

CHAPTER XII

Between the Wars—I

(1920–30)

Growing Interest—My Last Big Match—"Disheartening" Cricket—A Fine Australian Eleven—Hours of Play—Perfect Fielders—Recovery begun—The World's Best Fieldsman—The South Africans Again—Death of Sydney Pardon—Hobbs's Year—Selection Committees—The Turn of the Tide—Pace Bowling—The New Zealanders—Oxford and Cambridge Centenary—Leary Constantine—Exciting Cricket—*Embarras de richesse*—A Great Australian Team—Don Bradman—Duleep—Bad Tactics

THE interest in cricket in 1920 was greater than at any other period in its history. People flocked to the best county matches, and where in previous years seven or eight thousand spectators had been considered a good gate, we now found twenty, twenty-five, and even thirty thousand at Lord's. At the Oval it was much the same, and at Old Trafford in the Yorkshire *v.* Lancashire match all records were broken. "Never has there been a more dismal failure than the crusade against cricket after the Armistice. The people who had clamoured for drastic alterations in the game, and argued that cricket, as we had known it, would lack its old charm and attraction, found themselves utterly routed, and all through the season they preserved a discreet silence," wrote *Wisden*. Some newspapers were confident even that baseball would supersede cricket as the national game!

Naturally after four blank seasons and the ravages of war the quality of the play was far below that of 1914, and some of the county elevens were very weak, but the fact that the game held all its old attraction was most satisfactory. Oxford and Cambridge, however, had surprisingly good sides, so good, indeed, that five University players appeared for the Gentlemen—H. Ashton, Chapman, Wood, Stevens, and Bettington, but the Varsity Match was ruined by bad weather, although four days were allotted to it, Oxford scoring 193 and Cambridge 161. The Players defeated the Gentlemen by seven wickets. Rain on the second afternoon hit the Gentlemen hard, Woolley on a drying wicket taking five wickets for 20 runs.

The best match of the season at Lord's was the last—that between Middlesex and Surrey—and the crowd was so great that on the first day (Saturday) people were sitting two deep in front of the pavilion, the gates having to be closed early in the afternoon, and on the second day also. Middlesex had won eight matches in succession in August—and what matches they were, Kent being beaten by 5 runs at Canterbury and Yorkshire by 4 runs at Bradford! The position when the Surrey match began was this: to win the championship Middlesex had to defeat Surrey—a draw or a loss would have given Lancashire first place. The game was played on a fast wicket and in lovely weather, and was one long crescendo of excitement. The story of the match has often been told, and it will be sufficient here to state that at twenty-two minutes past six—stumps were to be drawn at seven o'clock—Stevens clean bowled Strudwick with a beautiful-length googly, which came like lightning off the pitch, and Middlesex had won by 55 runs.

It was my last match for Middlesex—my last big match at Lord's—and I should be less than human if I should ever forget it. Indeed, I can even now, after six-and-twenty years, recall every phase, every ball, every moment, of it, and the wonderful and affectionate reception the crowd gave me is the most treasured memory of my cricketing life. At one moment Surrey looked like winning, but a glorious catch in the deep field, near the screen, by Hendren changed the situation. It was a fine side of which I was in command—well-disciplined, keen, enthusiastic, and with a loyalty to its captain which has certainly never been surpassed. I had loved Lord's ever since I first saw it, and the gods were indeed good to me in decreeing that my last first-class match there should end so happily for me. I hope no one will accuse me of being boastful or arrogant—I have had too many failures in my time, including a pair of spectacles twice at Lord's, to be that—but there are some things of which one may, perhaps, be allowed to write exactly as one feels—and this is one of them. To lead the great county for which I had had the privilege of playing since 1894, under the captaincy of men like A. J. Webbe, A. E. Stoddart, and G. MacGregor, to the top of the tree in the last stage of my cricketing life was an experience which no lapse of time, no future happening, can ever eradicate from my memory.

In September the M.C.C. sent a side to Australia under

J. W. H. T. Douglas, though they were reluctant to do so, saying with good reason that we had not recovered from the War. Australia, however, were most anxious that a team should be sent, stressing the fact that they had had no side since 1911–12. In the circumstances the M.C.C. assented, and though we failed to win a single Test Match, cricket in Australia undoubtedly benefited greatly, and huge crowds watched the matches.

The summer of 1921 was beautifully fine and warm, but a sad one from an English point of view. In regard to it S. H. Pardon wrote:

> During all the years I have edited *Wisden* there has never been a season so disheartening as that of 1921. England was not merely beaten, but overwhelmed. . . . We had no Test Match bowlers of the pre-War standard, and our fielding, compared with the brilliant work of the Australians, was very second-rate. At Lord's the contrast was humiliating. Never before was an England side so slow and slovenly.

While admitting the great superiority of the Australians, it should not be forgotten that fortune dealt hardly with us, for our best two batsmen at that time—Hobbs and J. W. Hearne—were absent through injury or illness. It was like taking Bardsley and Macartney away from the Australian Eleven.

The Selection Committee—H. K. Foster, J. Daniell, and R. H. Spooner—were faced, therefore, with a very difficult task, and the fact that thirty players appeared for England in the Test Matches looked as if they "lacked a settled policy and were inclined to snatch at straws," as Pardon put it. In the first Test at Trent Bridge we were beaten by ten wickets, and never before has England had such a tail to their batting.

But amid all the shortcomings and disappointments Woolley's two glorious innings of 95 and 93 at Lord's will be remembered, and the Hon. L. H. Tennyson, after an early escape, played very well, but the fielding was poor, almost slovenly, and the bowling lacked length. Some improvement was shown at Leeds, though we were easily beaten, where we batted one short in both innings, Hobbs, after fielding for an hour or so, being seized with appendicitis and having to be operated on immediately. We had little the worse of the games at Old Trafford and the Oval, but we did not win, and this meant that we had lost eight Test Matches in succession. This was no fault of Douglas, the England

Captain, the Australians being by far the stronger side, but for the Leeds Test the Selectors appointed Tennyson captain, and Douglas worked loyally under the new leader, giving, as always, of his best and bravest. Tennyson was a good, lion-hearted, and encouraging captain, and his innings of 63 and 36 at Leeds were splendidly plucky efforts, as his right hand had been severely cut when fielding.

The Australian Eleven was probably as fine a side as ever came to England. Their two fast bowlers—J. M. Gregory and E. A. Macdonald—were of the highest class, both men of great stamina and stature. A. A. Mailey was the best googly bowler of his day, and W. W. Armstrong turned the ball slightly from leg and could "pitch her on a sixpence." The bowlers were backed up by beautiful fielding—fast and accurate—and W. A. Oldfield and H. Carter were two fine wicket-keepers.

Warren Bardsley and C. G. Macartney were the two outstanding batsmen, but the whole side could get runs. This splendid all-round team were a tremendous attraction, and of the Test Match at Lord's *Wisden* wrote: "The arrangements for dealing with the crowd proved inadequate, many ticket-holders being greatly delayed and inconvenienced in getting through the gate. The M.C.C. came in for some sharp criticism and were compelled to put forward an explanation." Perhaps they had not taken sufficient note of the greatly increased numbers of spectators in the previous summer.

There was some friction with the Australians over the hours of play in matches other than Test Matches. In their fixture with Surrey at the Oval early in May the Australians had insisted that the hours of play should be 12 to 6, in spite of Daylight Saving, and Surrey, under protest, gave way. They took the same line in the match against the M.C.C. at Lord's, and the M.C.C., like Surrey, agreed. The match had been advertised in the newspapers, and it was stated that stumps would be drawn at 6.30, a notice to this effect appearing on the score-cards. Consequently the M.C.C. had to issue an apology to the public. To draw stumps at 6 o'clock—5 by the sun—on a beautifully fine afternoon on a Saturday seemed absurd, and though there was a good deal of coming and going between the Australian dressing-room and the Committee Room by Mr Sidney Smith, the Australian manager, the Committee held a special meeting, and in the end bowed to the Australians. It was not wise or tactful to force the M.C.C. to issue an apology to the public, and the general opinion was that the M.C.C. should have insisted on the normal hours of play at Lord's being kept. When the fixture-list was drawn up no mention was made of any departure from the usual hours, and the Australian attitude came as something like a bolt from the blue. The Headquarters of cricket should not have been treated in so cavalier a manner. In Australia England always adheres to the Australian hours of play. In England Australia should do the same. This sort of thing does not happen nowadays, every detail being carefully arranged before a tour begins.

Middlesex, under the able captaincy of F. T. Mann, won the championship for the second year in succession. In their last game of the season, again at Lord's and once more against Surrey, they had but to draw the match and the championship was theirs, but, set 322 to win, the runs were obtained with the loss of only four wickets, Twining making 135 and J. W. Hearne 106. More than once Middlesex seemed to be beaten, but some fine bowling by Haig in Surrey's second innings caused a collapse, and splendid batting did the rest. So the members of the M.C.C. rejoiced again in the success of their tenants.

As for University cricket, Cambridge were a good side, and beat Oxford by an innings. So strong was their batting that M. D. Lyon was No. 7 or 8 in the order of going in. The fielding was magnificent, and in C. H. Gibson and C. S. Marriott they had two first-class bowlers. Gilbert Ashton was an admirable captain, and his brother Hubert the best batsman in the Eleven, while Claude was a superb fieldsman and a dangerous, quick-scoring run-getter. Then there was A. P. F. Chapman, great in the field and full of runs, while C. A. Fiddian-Green was another batsman of distinction and A. G. Doggart a useful all-rounder.

The fielding of the Ashtons, Chapman, and others earned the Cambridge Eleven a well-deserved reputation. More perfect fielding would be hard to imagine. Oxford had three outstanding cricketers in D. R. Jardine, R. H. Bettington, and G. T. S. Stevens, though Bettington and Stevens were not quite the bowlers they had been in the previous year.

In 1922 Cambridge, under the captaincy of Hubert Ashton, had another fine eleven, and again won the Varsity Match by an innings, the scores being Cambridge 403 for four wickets, innings declared closed, Oxford 222 and 81. Ashton declared the innings closed although he needed only ten runs to rival W. Yardley's feat of getting two hundreds in the University Match (subsequently achieved by H. J. Enthoven and A. T. Ratcliffe, both Cambridge men), and Chapman, who had been very disappointing in the trial matches, found his best form and scored a brilliant 102, not out. W. W. Hill-Wood made 81 and A. G. Doggart 71. Oxford were greatly handicapped by the absence through an injury to his knee of Jardine, far and away their best batsman, and, further, Stevens, the Captain, was far from fit. F. B. R. Browne, G. O. Allen, and P. A. Wright bowled exceptionally well, and the Cambridge fielding was of the highest class, with H. Ashton making three splendid catches at short leg. Ashton soon afterwards went to Burma, and, except on very rare occasions, was lost to cricket. Had he been able to continue playing he would probably have been Captain of England; many held the opinion that he might well have been chosen to play in the Test Matches against Australia in 1921.

English cricket began to recover this year. There was some superb batting in the Gentlemen *v.* Players, the fielding of Chapman, Carr, A. E. R. Gilligan, and H. Ashton was brilliant, while G. M. Louden bowled very well. Chapman followed up his hundred in the University Match with a splendid innings of 160, thus equalling R. E. Foster's record in 1900, and Carr's powerful driving left the deep fieldsmen standing. Hobbs, recovered from his operation, was almost at his best, but we still needed a great bowler.

In 1923 two Test Trial matches were arranged—North *v.* South at Old Trafford and England *v.* the Rest at Lord's. The Selectors —H. D. G. Leveson-Gower (Chairman), J. Daniell, L. H. W. Troughton, and J. Sharp—took the greatest pains, and improvement was manifest, although far too many catches were dropped by the England side, as was also the case by the Players in the Gentlemen *v.* Players, in which M. D. Lyon played a magnificent innings of 120, marred only by a chance to short leg. The bowling was now clearly of better class, with Tate, now a great bowler, R. Kilner, Arthur Gilligan, Louden, Fender, Stevens, and Parkin, while Woolley could get most people out on a sticky wicket. In the Trial at Lord's Tate took five wickets in a quarter of an hour without having a run hit from him, four clean bowled and the other l.b.w.

The Annual Report of the M.C.C. referred to the death of Mr R. D. Walker, "their old friend and colleague, the last of the Walkers, of Southgate, who have done so much for English cricket," and a former Trustee of the Club. It also stated that increased accommodation for the general public was engaging the attention of the Committee.

The West Indies, under the captaincy of H. B. G. Austin,[1] paid us a visit that season, but no Test Matches were arranged. George Challenor batted superbly. As *Wisden* put it, "He had everything—style, hitting-power, and strength of defence." He made eight hundreds, six of them against first-class sides, and the critics placed him very high.

Francis, John, and Constantine were three fine fast bowlers, and Browne, right-hand medium, and Pascall, left-hand slow, an uncle of Constantine, also bowled well. The fielding was amazingly good and keen, with Constantine glorious at cover-point, or, indeed, in any position, and even then the finest fieldsman in the world. The West Indies' best performance was at Scarborough, when they ran Leveson-Gower's strong Eleven to four wickets. Leveson-Gower's Eleven had to make only 28 runs in the last innings, and half the side did not think it worth while to change into flannels. But Francis and John had six men out for 19!

The University Match was a rather tragic affair. Oxford won in two days by an innings and 227 runs, the most overwhelming victory in the whole series, but they were unduly favoured by fortune. They won the toss on a beautiful wicket, and within half an hour of the start Allen (who had been bowling finely throughout the season) strained a muscle in his side, and was practically useless for the rest of the innings. To make matters worse, there was a terrific thunderstorm during the night, and next day Cambridge batted on a sticky wicket. Bettington, the Oxford Captain, and Stevens bowled superbly on the damaged pitch. From the pavilion they looked extraordinarily difficult to play, and Cambridge had no chance.

The summer of 1924 was one of the wettest on record, but it had some compensations, for there was a spell of fine weather between June 12 and July 17 which enabled the first three Test

[1] Afterwards Sir Harold Austin, Speaker of the House of Assembly, Barbados.

Matches against the South Africans, Gentlemen *v.* Players, England *v.* the Rest, and Oxford *v.* Cambridge to be played under pleasant conditions, and our cricket continued to improve. The South Africans were not up to the standard of the Australians, but our batting and fielding were extremely good, and Tate had developed into a great bowler. The change bowling, however, was a weak point, but up to the end of June A. E. R. Gilligan, who captained the England Eleven, and Tate had shown themselves a formidable pair of opening bowlers. Unfortunately Gilligan was never the same cricketer again after receiving a very severe blow over the heart while batting in Gentlemen *v.* Players at the Oval. After the end of the season we find in *The Cricketer* the following remark: "We have every hope that Tate will emulate the doings in Australia of those great bowlers Lohmann, Barnes, and F. R. Foster." It is a matter of cricket history how superbly Tate bowled on the 1924–25 tour.

The South Africans, under the captaincy of H. W. Taylor, were frankly disappointing, and were no match for England, who won the first three Tests, the other two being drawn owing to rain, the game at Old Trafford being limited to two hours and three-quarters on the opening day. Their batting was fairly strong, as totals of 390, 342, and 323 in the Test Matches proved: it was their bowling which failed. E. P. Nupen, a 'terror' on the then matting wickets in his own country, was handicapped by a strained back, but before this he had not been a great success.

The Players beat the Gentlemen at Lord's by an innings and 231 runs, Hobbs (118) and R. Kilner (113) batting very well, and some critics thought that there had rarely been a stronger Players' side—Hobbs, Sutcliffe, J. W. Hearne, Woolley, Hendren, E. Tyldesley, R. Kilner, Tate, Duckworth, Freeman, and Howell.

Under the captaincy of T. C. Lowry, Cambridge were a fairly good side, if not of the same excellence as the Elevens of 1921 and 1922, and they won the University Match by nine wickets, but there was not all that difference between the two teams. Cambridge had the better bowling, with Wright back in his form of 1922, a useful fast bowler (and a fine slip fieldsman) in W. R. Shirley, and R. J. O. Meyer and H. M. Austin. N. B. Sherwell, a brother of the Captain of the famous South African team of 1907, was a superb wicket-keeper, and the fielding was very smart and keen. Lowry was the best batsman, full of daring, power, and originality, and H. J. Enthoven's 104 was characterized by quickness of foot and certainty in punishing the loose ball. There were no fewer than three Australians in the Eleven—J. E. F. Mann, H. M. Austin, and A. H. White—and Lowry himself was a New Zealander.

F. T. Mann only just failed to equal Albert Trott's record. In the Middlesex *v.* Yorkshire match he hit four sixes into the pavilion. Two from consecutive balls landed on the top balcony, one hitting the wall at the back high up.

No fewer than four members of the Cambridge Eleven of 1925—K. S. Duleepsinhji, E. W. Dawson, H. J. Enthoven, and N. B. Sherwell—found places in the Gentlemen's Eleven at Lord's, a rare distinction which recalled the days of Edward and Alfred Lyttelton, A. G. Steel, and A. P. Lucas, of the famous Cambridge Eleven of 1878. The game was drawn after some heavy scoring, Stevens making 75, run out, and 129 for the amateurs, and A. W. Carr 82, while for the professionals Hobbs was at his best in a great innings of 140, Sutcliffe made 50, run out, Holmes 92, and R. Kilner 59. Curiously enough, Tate did not get a wicket in either innings.

In the University Match Enthoven made 129, Duleepsinhji, a freshman from Cheltenham and a nephew of the great Ranji, scored 75, and L. G. Crawley, a player of natural ability and tremendous driving-power, 98. Cambridge, under the captaincy of C. T. Bennett, were, according to *Wisden*, "a very good team—probably the best sent up to Lord's by either university since the War." Oxford, with J. L. Guise as Captain, had plenty of batting, but were short of bowling. E. R. T. Holmes, a freshman from Malvern, made a good impression with his fine in-front-of-the-wicket strokes, as did G. B. Legge—alas, no more, one of the gallant few to whom so many owe so much.

Sydney Pardon, for thirty-five years the famous editor of *Wisden*, died on November 20, 1925. He had a very sound outlook on all cricket matters, and wrote with a charm peculiar to himself; he could say a great deal in a few words. His views were always balanced, one might almost say judicial. A most interesting and many-sided talker, his knowledge of cricket, racing, music, and the drama was complete, and made him a rare companion.

This year (1925) was Hobbs's. He made 3024 runs, with an average of 70·32, and scored sixteen centuries, including a beautiful 140 for the Players at Lord's. On August 17 he equalled W. G.'s great record of 126 hundreds, and on the following day surpassed it, in the match between Surrey and Somerset at Taunton. During my time Hobbs, taking him all in all, was the best of the great English batsmen. From about 1910 to 1927 he was, indeed, the finest batsman in the world. He won many matches for England, and was always at his best on the big occasion. His style was the essence of ease, and he excelled on every sort of wicket and against every type of bowling. If W. G. was the Champion Hobbs was the Master. A charming, extremely modest character, to hear him talk one would think that he had never made a run in his life.

At a Meeting of the Board of Control at Lord's on February 24, 1926, I was appointed Chairman of the Selection Committee, the other members being P. Perrin and A. E. R. Gilligan. We were instructed by the Board to co-opt two professionals, one from the North and one from the South, and subsequently were unanimous in selecting Rhodes and Hobbs. This was the first occasion on which professionals had served on a Selection Committee, and both these fine players were of the greatest help. The captaincy was given to A. W. Carr, who had led Nottinghamshire with much distinction, and, as is the invariable custom, he was added to the Committee. Naturally he had a big say in the choice of the team. We were kept pretty busy, for we had to choose the Elevens not only for the Tests, but also for the Trial matches—England *v.* the Rest, North of England *v.* the Australians, and South of England *v.* the Australians. Our task in selecting teams for the Tests was simplified by these Trial matches, which enabled us to gauge the form of the players in a higher class of cricket than the majority of county matches afford, and we were therefore in a happier position than our predecessors in 1921. The Trials were successful financially, and on the first day of England *v.* the Rest at Lord's 26,623 people paid gate, the takings of the match being something over £3400. There was, of course, a good deal of correspondence and telephoning, and it was the Chairman's duty to make the arrangements for hotel accommodation and railway travelling for the team. And here Lord's afforded us every facility and lightened our labours considerably.

The first Test, at Trent Bridge, was completely ruined by rain, only fifty minutes' play being possible, during which Hobbs and

Sutcliffe scored 32. The second, at Lord's, was drawn. Carr declared England's innings closed at 475 for three wickets. This gave us a lead of 92 runs, and Carr was criticized for his action, but he knew that neither Bardsley nor Taylor would have been able to bat owing to injuries to their hands, and a couple of quick wickets would have put Australia in an anxious position. The first wicket went for nothing, but Collins batted nearly two and a half hours for 24, while Macartney played a glorious innings of 133, not out. At the end of the match Australia's second-innings score was 194 for five wickets. Towards Australia's first-innings total of 383 Bardsley contributed 193, not out, carrying his bat through the innings. This great left-hander, who may well be compared with Clem Hill, was a batsman so good that it was truly said that England had never beaten Australia until Bardsley was out. Bardsley, like Fry and Ranji, was a great believer in net practice. For England Hobbs (119) and Sutcliffe (82) put on 182 for the opening partnership, Woolley made 87, Hendren 127, not out, and Chapman 50, not out, the Australian bowling being completely mastered.

There was very nearly "an unpleasant incident." Early on the second morning of the match it was found that the *middle of the pitch* was very wet. At first 'foul play' was suspected, but on inquiry it was proved that through some carelessness the hose-pipe had been connected with the water-supply. If the escape of water had affected either end the umpires would have been faced with a very awkward problem.

The third and fourth Tests were also drawn, and the fifth at the Oval ended in a glorious win for England by 289 runs. *England had won only one Test Match against Australia out of the previous nineteen*, and I am not likely to forget Sunday, August 8, when the Selection Committee met for the last time to choose the team for the vital game. The prestige of English cricket seemed to depend on our decisions, some of them bristling with difficulties. For instance, Carr, the Captain, had been suffering from a severe attack of tonsilitis, and, with the greatest regret, we came to the conclusion that he should stand down, the leadership being given to Chapman. Happily all went well, and at five minutes past six on the afternoon of August 18 Geary bowled down Mailey's wicket, and after many long years of waiting and disappointment English cricket had come into its own again.

The magnificent batting of Hobbs (100) and Sutcliffe (161) on for the most part a difficult wicket has never been surpassed even by that famous pair of opening batsmen, and the bowling of Rhodes, 'recalled to the colours' at the age of forty-eight, Tate, and Larwood was of a high standard, and was backed up by perfect fielding and catching. The Australians were an extremely powerful batting side, with Woodfull, Macartney, and Bardsley outstanding, but Gregory was not the bowler he had been, and on Mailey and Grimmett fell a tremendous lot of work.

Gentlemen *v.* Players at Lord's followed immediately on the Test at Leeds, with a consequent reaction. There was some heavy run-getting, the Players making 579 and 97 for one wicket, and the Gentlemen 542. Hobbs (163) and Sutcliffe (107) put on 263 for the opening partnership of the Players, and E. Tyldesley, going in first wicket down, scored 131. For the Gentlemen Chapman (108), Jardine (85, run out), and Wyatt (75) were in great form, while Enthoven did the hat-trick, dismissing Kilner, splendidly caught in the deep field by Jardine, Geary, stumped, and Strudwick, caught at the wicket by W. B. Franklin, who kept superbly.

One of the vivid memories of this season is Allen's bowling for Middlesex against the Australians. He obtained the last four wickets for 11 runs (his full analysis was five for 63), in each case sending a stump somersaulting, and in Australia's second innings he again ripped a stump out of the ground. This must surely be a record, and one had to wait ten years for anything like it—for Gentlemen *v.* Players at Lord's in 1936, when Farnes three times in succession sent a stump catapulting head-high to drop at the feet of W. H. Levett, who was standing back a dozen yards, the batsmen in this case being Gimblett, Hammond, and Hardstaff. Farnes's pace that afternoon was terrific.

In the University Match R. G. H. Lowe accomplished the hat-trick, taking the last three wickets in Oxford's first innings with successive balls. Lowe, a medium-paced right-hander, had an analysis for the match of eight wickets for 54 runs, and he and H. J. Enthoven, his Captain, who scored 51 and 23 and took six wickets for 79 runs, were chiefly responsible for a Cambridge victory by 34 runs. It was one of the most interesting of Varsity Matches. The weather was rather unkind, and the pitch was consequently not favourable to batsmen, the highest individual score being 52 by J. S. Stephenson, of Oxford. Cambridge totalled 178 and 191, Oxford 162 and 173.

The summer of 1927 was fine up to almost the end of June, but then the weather broke up so completely that it was probably one of the worst in the history of cricket. The New Zealanders, under the captaincy of T. C. Lowry, paid us their first visit as cricketers, and of twenty-six first-class matches won seven, lost five, and drew fourteen. Their batting was attractive, with C. S. Dempster, R. C. Blunt, Lowry, J. E. Mills, M. L. Page, and C. C. Dacre the stars. Dempster eventually attained greatness, but the bowling generally was weak, with W. E. Merritt and Blunt, of the googly type, exceptions. K. C. James was a brilliant wicket-keeper. The fielding was not up to first-class standards, many catches being missed. They played twice at Lord's—against the M.C.C. and against Middlesex—drawing with a strong amateur side of the Club in a heavy-scoring game in which Allen, with innings of 38 and 104, not out, and ten wickets for 156 runs, greatly distinguished himself. The King honoured the county game with his presence on the first day, and Middlesex won by three wickets, after a very good match.

Hammond, now completely recovered from his illness, had a great season, scoring 2969 runs, with an average of 69.04, and Jardine made 1002 runs in fourteen innings, heading the first-class averages with 91·09. Here were obviously two England batsmen. The Selectors—H. D. G. Leveson-Gower, J. W. H. T. Douglas, and A. W. Carr—made excellent choices, and their work contributed greatly to building up the fine team that was destined to achieve such notable triumphs in Australia eighteen months later.

Gentlemen *v.* Players at Lord's was spoiled by the weather. Not a ball was bowled on the first day, and on the third no cricket was possible until late in the afternoon. The Gentlemen made 276, Jardine scoring a magnificent 123, and the Players 132 for two wickets. Hobbs was unable to play, and the famous Yorkshire pair, Sutcliffe and Holmes, put on 107 for the first wicket. In this match Hammond made his first appearance for the Players at Lord's.

Cambridge would have been an even better eleven this year had not Duleepsinhji—who began the season with scores of 101, against Yorkshire, and 254, not out, against Middlesex—been subsequently laid low with such a severe attack of pneumonia that at one time his life was despaired of. A beautiful batsman, with all the suppleness and quickness of his countrymen, no one has ever played googly bowlers like Freeman, Robins, and others with such complete mastery. The University Match was won by Cambridge, who were a strong batting side, by 116 runs. A. K. Judd played a good innings of 124, but the honours of the match went to E. R. T. Holmes, the Oxford Captain, whose 113 in the second innings was marked by superb driving on both sides of the wicket.

On July 6 the Centenary of the Oxford and Cambridge Match was celebrated by a dinner at the Savoy Hotel under the chairmanship of Lord Harris. There were gathered together Old Blues of every generation, from E. F. S. Tylecote, Captain of Oxford in 1871 and 1872, to E. R. T. Holmes and E. W. Dawson, the Captains of 1927. It was a great occasion, but unfortunately time was called before the orators had got any farther in their reminiscences than the middle seventies. One would have liked to have heard some reference to the moderns, and particularly to Holmes's great innings, but that was the only flaw in an evening during which old friendships were renewed, happy memories recalled, and former battles refought. Lord Harris could not fail to talk well on cricket, and said he regarded himself as "the connecting-link in University cricket, as he had known one or more of the players in every match from the first in 1827."

The West Indies, under the captaincy of R. K. Nunes, were given Test Match honours in 1928, but they were beaten by an innings at Lord's, Old Trafford, and the Oval, and their general record was not good. George Challenor, at the age of forty, was not the splendid batsman he had shown himself to be in 1923, and the slip-fielding and wicket-keeping left much to be desired. The strength of the team lay in the fast bowlers—Constantine, Griffith, and Francis—and the scores of catches dropped off them must have been most discouraging. Nunes went so far as to say that had he possessed a Chapman and a Hammond in the slips the England totals in the three Test Matches would have been halved.

Although he failed as a batsman in the Tests, Constantine was the outstanding personality in the Eleven, his fielding being brilliant in the extreme,[1] and during the Lord's Test Sutcliffe

[1] Constantine is generally admitted to have been the best of all fieldsmen. That at least is the opinion of Chapman, Hendren, and Hammond, and they ought to know!

told me that he had never played finer fast bowling than his, Griffith's, and Francis's. Against Middlesex Constantine covered himself with glory. It was his match with a vengeance, for he made scores of 86 and 103, and in the county's second innings took seven wickets in fourteen overs and three balls for 57 runs—the last six in six overs and three balls for 11 runs. Two of his strokes I shall remember to my dying day. The first was when he hit a good-length ball of Allen's over extra-cover's head far up into the Grand Stand, and the second when he played back to Hearne with such tremendous force that the ball, after striking the pavilion rails, ricochetted among the seats, scattering the members of the M.C.C. and of Middlesex, and bringing destruction to woodwork and paint. On its ferocious passage from the bat Hearne very pluckily put one of his hands in the way of the ball, and was so badly hurt that he played no more cricket that season.

Although the Players beat the Gentlemen easily by nine wickets, scoring 423 and 112 for one wicket to the amateurs' 200 and 333, it was a fine game to watch, full of most excellent cricket. For various reasons, Hobbs, Sutcliffe, Geary, and Larwood were not able to play, which left the professionals rather short of bowling, but they were still a powerful batting side, with Hammond and Leyland at Nos. 6 and 7, and Tate, at this period a dangerous hard-hitter, at No. 8. Jardine (86 and 40, run out), Wyatt (70), Chapman (59), and A. M Crawley (53) were in form for the amateurs, but, except for Jardine, they could do little in their first innings against Freeman's splendid bowling. One of my keenest memories is Duckworth's wicket-keeping and some overs from Hammond (at the Pavilion end), who looked for a while like another Barnes. Neither side possessed a fast bowler, which made the batsmen's task easier, but there was some very fine fielding, and W. B. Franklin was almost as good as Duckworth as a wicket-keeper. Wyatt was knocking loudly at the door of international cricket—he had done very well in South Africa during the previous winter with the M.C.C. team—and Jardine was, as he had been in 1927, clearly an England batsman. Two other fine cricketers in the Gentlemen's team were M. D. Lyon and A. M. Crawley, both of them attractive, stylish, and punishing batsmen, who were always a pleasure to watch. One could easily have picked two England sides this year so far as batting went.

The University Match will live long in the minds of those who saw it, the finish being most exciting, so exciting that the headmaster of Eton broke into verse in the columns of *The Times*. When the last Oxford man—E. T. Benson, the wicket-keeper—joined C. K. Hill-Wood twenty minutes remained for play, and with seven minutes to go Hill-Wood offered a sharp chance high up to short leg, who was standing very close in, off Robins. The catch was missed, and the two batsmen held the fort until seven o'clock, by which time I had nearly gnawed the handle off my umbrella. Cambridge totalled 292 (Killick 74, Robins 53, Duleepsinhji 52, and Seabrook, the Cambridge Captain, 44) and 329 for seven wickets declared (Robins 101, not out, Seabrook 83), and Oxford 287 (Garland-Wells 64, not out, Kingsley 53, N. M. Ford 40) and 227 for nine wickets (Garland-Wells 70). Hill-Wood (20, not out) kept up his end for an hour and forty minutes, and also bowled well in Cambridge's first innings. Robins was a little lucky in the 80's, but, forcing the game with a view to a declaration, in an hour and three-quarters he made 101 in that quick-footed, wristy manner which was to be a feature of his cricket at Lord's in after-years. I thought, however, that on the whole Garland-Wells showed the best batting. His on-driving reminded me of F. S. Jackson.

In the same week as this thrilling University Match Eton *v.* Harrow was played, Eton winning by 28 runs a quarter of an hour before time. I. Akers-Douglas, of Eton, played a brilliant second innings of 158. Harrow went for the runs—they were set 308 to make in three hours and a half—and failed gloriously. As the headmaster of Eton put it in "Lord's, 1928," already referred to:

> Harrow's glorious hours begin,
> Harrow batsmen hurrying in,
> One and all with the will to win.
> Cheers and counter-cheers rend the air!
> Harrow's down with her colours flying,
> Great in doing and great in dying.
> Eton's home with a head to spare!

In September the M.C.C. sent a team to Australia under the captaincy of Chapman. Lord Harris was Chairman of the Selection Committee appointed to choose the side, and the others were Leveson-Gower, Douglas, Carr, A. E. R. Gilligan, and myself. At a later date Hobbs, on the suggestion of the Chairman, joined us in our deliberations. The side was very carefully chosen, and we made no strategical mistakes. We suffered from an *embarras de richesse* so far as batting was concerned, so much so, indeed, that even the great Woolley did not find a place, and a wail went up from one end of Kent to another, and even farther afield. The left-handed batsmen were Mead and Leyland, and so strong was the batting that they played in only one Test Match, Mead in the first, when he scored 8 and 72, and Leyland in the last, when he covered himself with glory with innings of 137 and 53, not out. So fine a batsman as E. Tyldesley could find a place only in the last Test.

England won the rubber by four matches to one, losing only the last Test. It was a very happy tour in every respect, Chapman being a splendid and inspiring captain, and he and the whole team were immensely popular. F. C. Toone, the Secretary of the Yorkshire C.C.C., was the perfect manager—his third visit to Australia—and on his return to England he was knighted, but, alas, lived but a short while to enjoy the honour which had been bestowed on him. It was a great pity that this splendid side did not play a match with the Rest of England, as the 1903–4 and 1911–12 teams had done.

The South Africans did not win a Test Match in 1929, but they ran us pretty hard at Lord's, Leeds, the Oval, and Birmingham, and they might have achieved victory but for a succession of accidents and illnesses which cost them at various times some of their best men. At Lord's, for instance, they were deprived of their best batsman, H. W. Taylor, and two of their best bowlers, Quinn and Vincent, and at Leeds of Taylor and of Cameron, their splendid wicket-keeper and batsman. We won the third Test at Leeds by five wickets, but it was by no means the easy victory it might appear on paper, for, set 184 to get, five men were out for 85, and Larwood would probably have been unable to bat because of a strained tendon. Woolley pulled us through, with Tate to help him, but early in their partnership there was a very confident appeal for l.b.w. against Tate.

The Players won at Lord's by seven wickets, the scores being Gentlemen 138 and 310, Players 253 and 196 for three. The Gentlemen had plenty of bowling, with Allen, Haig, Robins, White, and Fender, but there was not much solidity about their batting after Nos. 4 or 5. Freeman obtained thirteen wickets in the match for 144 runs, eight of them in the first innings for 41.

Killick, Wyatt, and Carr batted well, but they were not adequately supported, while Hendren, Hammond, and Woolley scored most of the runs for the Players. Both wicket-keepers—Duckworth and E. T. Benson, of the Oxford Eleven—were very good.

The University Match was drawn—Oxford 246 and 202 for three wickets, Cambridge 377 and 220 for four declared. E. T. Killick, B. H. Valentine, G. C. Grant (a West Indian), M. J. Turnbull, and E. D. Blundell, of the Cambridge Eleven, were subsequently international players, while the best-known cricketer on the Oxford side was the Nawab of Pataudi, who scored 106 and 84. He was to surpass even this great performance in the University Match of 1931, and to score a century against Australia in his first Test Match at Sydney in 1932. A. M. Crawley (33 and 83), of Oxford, was another batsman of high class, with great power in his many strokes. For Cambridge J. T. Morgan, who had been out of form, rose to the big occasion with a brilliant innings, after six wickets had fallen for 147 runs. A left-hander, he scored 149 out of 208 in three hours and a half. Blundell, a New Zealander, was the best of rather a moderate lot of bowlers. A strongly built man, he kept a very steady length at a fast-medium pace. A. T. Barber and M. J. Turnbull were the rival leaders, and both subsequently captained their county teams—Yorkshire and Glamorgan.

The Selection Committee in 1930 was composed of H. D. G. Leveson-Gower, F. T. Mann, and J. C. White, and in view of the fact that the English team had won four of the five Test Matches in Australia during the winter of 1928–29 general confidence was felt that we would retain the Ashes. Close observers, however, had not forgotten that the Australians had pressed Chapman's men hard in the last three Tests—I recall Hobbs emphasizing this to me—and, although hopeful, they were not guilty of wishful thinking. They realized that there were some extremely capable young batsmen among the visitors, that the old hands, like Woodfull and Ponsford, were more reliable than ever, that Oldfield was the best wicket-keeper in the world, and that the bowling, if not great, possessed variety—and *Grimmett.* In the sequel Australia won at Lord's and the Oval, and England at Trent Bridge, the games at Leeds and Old Trafford being drawn. Our bowlers were not good enough on the perfect wickets to prevent the Australians making such huge totals as 335, 729 for six wickets, 566, 345, and 695. It was not our batting which lost us the rubber, for, although Hobbs, now in his forty-eighth year, Woolley, and Hammond were rather disappointing, we were defeated both at Lord's and the Oval after we had made over 400 runs in the first innings.

The trouble was that Larwood was terribly expensive, his four wickets in Test Matches costing 73 runs each, while Tate's fifteen were obtained at an average of 38·26. As a side we seemed to deteriorate from match to match, while our opponents, on the other hand, went from strength to strength.

And so we lost the Ashes to a fine side, which always seemed to be on top of us after the first Test. The batting of the Australians was very strong indeed. Bradman I will leave for the moment, but the part that Woodfull played must not be forgotten. He was the man whose unwearying defence wore down the bowling at the beginning of an innings, except in the first Test, in which he was twice dismissed for single figures, and which Australia lost. The other great batsmen were Ponsford, Kippax, McCabe, and Jackson. Ponsford was quick on his feet, and played the spin bowling as well as anyone except Bradman. The manner in which he dealt with Larwood at the Oval was masterly. Kippax was a lovely batsman. He had wrists, cut beautifully, and he played well off his legs. McCabe, the youngest member of the team, foreshadowed his future great doings, and was already the finest straight driver in the eleven. Jackson was not too fit, but it was obvious that he was naturally a tip-top batsman. Some thought him the successor of Victor Trumper, but death carried him off at the early age of twenty-three.

Fairfax was the best all-rounder, and Richardson a fine hitter and fieldsman. Grimmett was a great bowler—far better than in 1926. He was the mainstay of the attack, and was not always blessed by fortune. Like C. T. B. Turner ("the Terror"), of the Australian teams of 1888, 1890, and 1893, it was a pleasure to see him bowl, for he so obviously delighted in every ball. Fairfax, Hornibrook (left-hand), Wall, and McCabe all bowled steadily and well, and better than their figures would indicate. The attack had the great merit of accuracy, with the result that the placing of the field was a comparatively easy matter. They followed the old Australian tradition of bowling to the field. Fairfax had a fine action, and with his great height made the ball rise quickly off the pitch. The fielding was good without being outstanding, and Oldfield was a great wicket-keeper, who never appealed unless the batsman was out, or very nearly so.

For the second Test at Lord's Allen, Duleepsinhji, and White took the places of Sutcliffe, Larwood, and R. Tyldesley, Woolley going in first with Hobbs. It was a magnificent match of splendid cricket, but our bowling was completely collared, and although we made totals of 425 and 375 we were beaten by seven wickets. "Duleep," in his first Test against Australia, scored 173 and 48 under the delighted eye of his uncle; and when England seemed likely to be beaten in an innings Chapman (121)—a glorious innings after a shaky start: he was missed before he had made a run—and Allen (57) put on 125 for the sixth wicket—a very gallant effort. Chapman hit four sixes off Grimmett—huge on-drives into the stands. Bradman scored 254, Woodfull 155, Ponsford 81, and Kippax 83. The third wicket did not fall until the score was 585! Australia's total was 729 for six wickets declared. They were set 72 runs to win, but three wickets fell in twenty minutes for 22 runs. Ponsford was bowled, Bradman magnificently caught low down at backward point by Chapman from a hard cut, and Kippax caught at the wicket. Robins was spinning the ball tremendously, and Tate was dead on the spot. For a moment it looked as if there might be a hard finish. Robins got past even Woodfull's cast-iron defence three balls in succession, and off his bowling the Australian Captain was missed when only 1 at mid-on—a difficult catch low down on the right side, to get to which the fieldsman had to move quickly. The crowd were on the tiptoe of excitement, but McCabe batted well, and after sending down seven almost perfect overs Robins lost his length for a couple of overs, and the Australians were on the road to victory. The four-day Test Match, against Australia at any rate, had come to stay. Over 110,000 spectators watched this splendid match.

I now come to Bradman. At the end of the tour he published a book—*Don Bradman's Book*[1]—and was good enough to ask me to write an Introduction. Here is what I said then:

> As for Bradman's own performances, they were unique in the annals of cricket. In all matches he scored 3170 runs, with an average of 99·06. He made eleven three-figure innings—six of these over 200—and in the Test Matches his scores were 8, 131, 254, 334

[1] Hutchinson, 1930.

(a world's record), 14, and 232—974 runs, with an average of 139·14. These great innings followed on two seasons' unbroken success in Australia, and it is no exaggeration to say that not even W. G.—at Bradman's age—had attained so world-wide a reputation.

What were the secrets of his triumphal march through England? First, immense natural skill. Secondly, an idealism which urged him to learn everything he possibly could, and to profit by the lessons learnt. Thirdly, tremendous concentration of mind. Fourthly, physical strength. Fifthly, extreme fitness; and lastly, a cool, calm temperament. As to the actual technique of his play, he was blessed with a wonderful eye, steel-like wrists, and small and beautifully neat feet, which a Genée or a Pavlova might have envied, and which made him quite exceptionally quick in moving back or forward to the ball, every stroke fully developed, except, possibly, the straight drive, and, above all, an amazingly strong defence—which, as he says in his chapter on batting, is the keynote of all successful batsmanship in first-class cricket. His hooking of anything the least short was masterful to a degree; he missed nothing on his pads; he off-drove brilliantly; but, above all, the cut, both late and square, was his chief glory. I have seldom seen finer or safer cutting—for he was always right on top of the ball.

Again, he watched the ball very closely and played all his strokes with his nose exactly over the ball—the "smell her, sir, smell her," of the renowned Yorkshireman Tom Emmett—and his extreme quickness of foot enabled him almost to dictate the length to the bowler—at least, so it appeared in the Test Matches at Lord's and at Headingley. Another noticeable feature of his batting was his placing of the ball, and the absolute certainty with which he hit a full pitch for 4. He seldom played forward, though he was often yards down the pitch to a slow bowler, and he scarcely ever lifted a ball off the ground. His drives clung to the turf, and how clean and powerful they were; and I cannot agree that his eschewing the high drive was a weakness in his play, though so highly do I rate Bradman's cricket that I am sure he could play any stroke on which he cared to concentrate.

So much for his batting—but he was also a long field of the very highest class, quick to start, a fast runner, and the possessor of a return so swift as an arrow from a bow, and full pitch into the wicket-keeper's hands. Australia have had many fine deep fields, but never a finer, judging him on his form here, and those who were at the Test Match at Headingley will never forget the manner in which he threw down Hobbs's wicket, at Oldfield's end, from deep mid-off. Never have I seen anyone move forward faster to a ball, pick it up more quickly, or throw it in harder.

What is his future? Is he destined to break his own records?

Will he one day play an innings of 600 or 700, and put the aggregates of Grace and Hobbs, and their number of centuries, in the shade? Remember, he is only twenty-two, and, given good health, he should have at least twenty more years of cricket before him. He seems certain to plague, and at the same time delight, England's bowlers for many future seasons—indeed, boys yet unborn are destined to suffer at his hands. Personally, I believe him to be possessed not only of the skill, but of the ambition, the physique, and the temperament to accomplish these feats. A batsman, as a general rule, does not attain to his best until he is thirty-four or thirty-five, and by the time Bradman reaches that age he will have had immense experience to build on to his natural skill. Have I praised him too highly? I don't think so, if one remembers his youth, and the fact that it was his first visit to England, and our varying wickets.

Do people realize his astonishing figures? Take the Test Matches. In these the Australians scored 1743 runs from the bat, of which Bradman contributed no less than 974. Again, he invariably made a huge proportion of the runs scored while he was in—namely, 131 out of 255 at Trent Bridge; 254 out of 423 at Lord's; 334 out of 506 at Headingley; and 232 out of 411 at the Oval. One may also add that *v.* Worcestershire, at Worcester, he scored 236 out of 413; *v.* Surrey, at the Oval, 252 out of 363; and *v.* Kent, at Canterbury, 205 out of 302.

Bradman looked every inch a cricketer. He was scrupulously neat and smart in his turn-out, and he played the game with rare zest and enjoyment. Short in height, though long in the leg, and with very broad shoulders, he is, from a cricket point of view, finely and compactly built, and one was particularly struck by the fit of his cricket boots on his small feet; and I think that he should present his boots to the Australian nation, to be placed in the pavilion at Sydney, there to be kept in a glass case for future generations to gaze on, and to inspire them to something like his own nimbleness of foot!

There is no need to stress here Bradman's performances since 1930. All the world knows them, but I may add that he has made fifteen centuries for Australia against England, two of them over 300 and four of them over 200. He has also scored four centuries for Australia against South Africa, one of them 299, not out, and one century (223) against the West Indies.

Gentlemen *v.* Players at Lord's was rendered memorable by the performance of Duleepsinhji, who, batting magnificently, scored two separate hundreds (125 and 103, not out), thus rivalling R. E. Foster and J. H. King. The match was interrupted by rain, the

Gentlemen scoring 292 and 197 for four wickets declared, and the Players 263 (Sutcliffe 80, Leyland 44, Hobbs 35) and 38 for three wickets. J. H. Parsons (57), R. E. S. Wyatt (44 and 26), and Allen (40, not out), gave best support to "Duleep." Parsons also made five catches, four of them in different positions in the field, one in the deep field and another at mid-on being particularly good. One of the best features of the match was the fine bowling of Robins and Peebles, who on the soft turf on the third day made the ball 'talk,' while Leyland came out as an all-rounder by taking nine wickets for 130 runs. Bowling left-hand, slow, for the most part over the wicket, he spun the ball into the batsman, often making it break a foot.

The Test Trial at Lord's—England *v.* the Rest—was also spoilt by rain, there being no play on the third day, England—375 (Hendren 101, Hobbs 80, Hammond 79, Larwood 47)—leading on the first innings by 237. Duleepsinhji, Wyatt, Leyland, and White, of the Rest team, subsequently played in the Test Matches. Jardine also figured among the Rest, but he was seldom seen on the cricket field this summer, and was not invited to play in any of the Tests.

Oxonians do not like to recall the University Match of 1930. They had an exceptionally good batting side, and an absolutely first-class bowler in Peebles, but they never became a team, and by casual and poor fielding and wicket-keeping, and by bad tactics, presented the match to Cambridge, being beaten by 205 runs. They held a lead on the first innings of 26 runs—314 to 288—and had down three Cambridge wickets for 66 runs. Then Killick and Carris were both missed at the wicket.

Set 307 runs to win in two hours and twenty minutes, Oxford most unwisely altered their batting order. How could they reasonably have expected to get the runs in the time on a crumbling wicket? Moore, the usual No. 1, was put in lower down, and Kingsley went in first with Crawley. The third wicket fell at 78, and Oxford were all out a quarter of an hour before time, the last seven wickets falling for 23 runs in an hour.

It would be ungenerous not to pay a warm tribute to Cambridge, who took every advantage of their opponents' mistakes and gained a notable victory. Several men contributed materially to the result, but the downfall of Oxford was in the main due to Killick, who played two splendid innings of 75 and 136. Peebles was the man Cambridge had to fear, and Killick, who had had many hours of practice against his bowling at the Faulkner School, and knew all his devices by heart, took charge of one end. I should imagine that Peebles, who sent down 81 overs in the match (and obtained thirteen wickets) bowled at least three-quarters of them to Killick. Brown and Hazlerigg were the best of the Cambridge bowlers. Both spun the ball—Brown from the leg and Hazlerigg from the off—and they were backed up by keen and sure fielding, Ratcliffe and Kemp-Welch, at short-leg, and Hazlerigg, at slip, making fine catches in the second innings. The contrast between the two teams in the field was very marked.

CHAPTER XIII

Between the Wars—II

(1931–39)

Selection Troubles—The New Zealanders—Record University Scores—Lord Harris—The Indians—"Body Line"—An Unhappy Season—The West Indians—The Australians Again—Verity's Great Bowling—A Great Australian Captain—Gentleman's Agreement—The South Africans—'Leather-jackets'—A Bad Decision—New L.B.W. Rule—Brighter Cricket—The Indians Again—More Problems of Selection—The 150th Anniversary—Anniversary Matches—"Patsy's" Retirement—A New Captain—Hammond's Wonderful Innings—The Largest Crowd—A "Thriller"—Death of Lord Hawke—Interminable Test—The West Indians Again—Len Hutton and Denis Compton

At the end of April 1931 the Board of Control appointed me Chairman of the Selection Committee, the other two members being P. Perrin and T. A. Higson. We were to hold office for two seasons—1931 and 1932—and our eyes were fixed on September 1932, when the M.C.C. would be sending a side to Australia. Our ideas and selections invariably had this period in view.

The New Zealanders were in England this summer, and originally only one Test Match was arranged, but after the excellent form they showed in this match at Lord's two more Tests were added, at the Oval and at Old Trafford.

We chose D. R. Jardine to captain England. He had had a fine record as a batsman for Winchester, Oxford, and Surrey. Further, he had distinguished himself in Australia with Chapman's 1928–29 M.C.C. side, and over and over again in Gentlemen *v.* Players, both at Lord's and the Oval, he had been a very prominent figure. He was also a good field near the wicket, being a particularly safe catch at backward point. And above all he was a keen student and a close and intelligent observer, versed in the tactics and strategy of the game. The majority of modern captains know little of cricket other than that of their own period; Jardine was a notable exception. He had a genius for taking pains, he was always helpful in debate, and I have no hesitation in saying that this Committee was the best on which I have ever served.

The New Zealanders rather surprised us in the Lord's match, although we held a lead of 230 runs on the first innings, Ames (137) and Allen (122) putting on 246 runs in two hours and three-quarters after seven wickets had fallen for 190. Both batted extremely well, and Woolley made a very good 80. In their second innings New Zealand scored 469 for nine wickets, declared. Dempster (120), Page (104), and Blunt (96) collared the bowling. England were set 240 to make in two hours and twenty minutes, and scored 146 (Hammond 46, run out) for five wickets. Our bowling did not come up to expectations. Voce, though he bowled well in both innings, did not obtain a wicket, the googly bowlers Robins and Peebles were expensive, and Allen was more of an all-rounder than a stock fast bowler.

The New Zealanders played altogether thirty-two first-class matches, won six, lost three, and drew twenty-three, the large number of unfinished games being due to the abominable weather. Apart from the Test Match at Lord's, their best performance—also at Lord's—was a victory by an innings and 122 runs over an M.C.C. team which included Chapman, Jardine, Jupp, Robins, White, A. M. Crawley, Allom, Turnbull, and J. W. Hearne. The M.C.C. had the worst of the wicket, but the bowling of Merritt (seven for 28) and Cromb (six for 46), backed up by fine fielding, was really good, and only Jardine (62, not out, and 19) offered any resistance. In their second innings the M.C.C. were dismissed for 48. Lowry was a most excellent Captain, and insisted on the most rigid application of the two-minute rule between the fall of wickets. Dempster, a fine batsman, had a good seconder in Blunt. Vivian, only eighteen, was a promising left-handed batsman and bowler, while Mills, another left-hander, Lowry himself, Page, and Weir all got runs. James kept wicket very finely, and the fielding showed a marked improvement on that of the previous tour. Merritt bowled too many loose balls, but at times he was an effective googly bowler. On the whole Cromb was the best of the bowlers—fast-medium, with accuracy of length and pace off the ground. He could keep an end going admirably.

Some of the best cricket seen this season was in the University Match, when Pataudi and Owen-Smith were batting to the bowling of Brown, Farnes, and Hazlerigg. Brown was bowling his leg-breaks of almost medium pace uncommonly well, Farnes, with his arm in the sky, had plenty of pace and devil, and Hazlerigg kept a length and flighted his off-breaks; but the batting was of the highest quality, Pataudi very sound and full of strokes and Owen-Smith very quick on his feet and making some lovely drives and square-cuts. It was a memorable match, for A. T. Ratcliffe, in Cambridge's first innings, scored a splendid 201—a record individual score in the University Match, which he was destined to hold for only twenty-four hours, for on the following day Pataudi beat it. Ratcliffe was the last choice—indeed, he gained his blue only because J. G. W. Davies had sprained his ankle a day or two before. Cambridge were the stronger bowling side, but thanks to Pataudi's and Owen-Smith's superb batting and some good bowling by R. S. G. Scott and E. M. Wellings, Oxford won by eight wickets, the scores being Oxford 453 for eight wickets declared (Pataudi 238, not out, Owen-Smith 78, A. Melville 47), and 55 for two wickets, Cambridge 385 (Ratcliffe 201, G. D. Kemp-Welch, the Captain, 87) and 122. The Oxford Captain, D. N. Moore, was unable to play because of a serious illness. In the early part of the season he had batted very well, and had proved himself an admirable captain. He built up a side which played together in real combination, so different from the eleven of the previous year. Melville, who was later to captain Sussex and South Africa, led Oxford in Moore's absence, and did so very well.

Gentlemen *v.* Players was spoilt by the weather, there being no play on the opening day, and none after lunch on the third day. The wicket favoured the bowlers throughout, and it was a small-scoring match: Gentlemen 131 (Jardine 49) and 166 (Robins 48, Duleep 37); Players 88 and 33 for no wicket. Verity, Mitchell, of Derbyshire, and Bowes, Brown, Robins, and C. S. Marriott were the successful bowlers. Brown obtained two wickets in eight overs, and bowled magnificently, repeatedly beating Sutcliffe, who admitted that he had never previously met a bowler who made him feel so silly—a generous compliment from a great player. The fielding on both sides was very fine indeed, and the wicket-keeping of W. H. V. Levett and Ames—both of Kent—could not have been bettered.

Lord Harris died at Belmont, his seat in Kent, on March 24, 1932, at the age of eighty-one.

George Robert Canning, fourth Baron Harris, was born at

Government House, Trinidad, on February 3, 1851, his father being Governor of the island from 1846 to 1853, and his mother a daughter of the Venerable Archdeacon Cummins, of Trinidad. My father, who was a prominent figure in the island, was a great friend of the Governor, who confided in him that he was very much attached to Miss Cummins, and was anxious to marry her —but "I find it very difficult in my position to see as much of her as I should like." My father said, "Well, as for that, my garden is always at your disposal." And there it was that he proposed to her.

Lord Harris won almost every distinction the cricket field has to offer. He was Captain of Eton, Kent, the Gentlemen, and England, and was President, Trustee, and Treasurer of the M.C.C. and Chairman of various committees at Lord's for innumerable years. He loved Lord's and everything to do with it, and in his book *A Few Short Runs* he writes, "My whole life has pivoted on Lord's." He was interested in every aspect and avenue of the game—the actual playing of it; the Laws—one dare not talk of *Rules* of cricket in his presence: he would interrupt with "Laws, not Rules, please"; the organizing and financial sides; and the general welfare of the professional cricketer. He was also an admirable Chairman of a committee, and never better than when presiding over the selection of a team for Australia. I had close experience of this on more than one occasion. He was deferential to the opinions of others, did not force his own views, and was fair and balanced. He inspired confidence. He was very fond of adjourning a meeting for lunch or tea when general agreement seemed unlikely: "It helps us to adjust our ideas" —and it was nearly always so.

Occasionally a little 'testy,' some thought that it was as well to "agree with him while one was in the way with him," but he was ready to listen to the other side, and if convinced of the soundness of an argument would modify or change his views. I have heard it said that he was a little *difficile* to play under, being apt to be somewhat cantankerous and abrupt in his manner, but on the only two occasions on which I played with him—once for the M.C.C. *v.* Eton, in 1894, when we went in first together, C. M. Wells being the Captain of the M.C.C. Eleven, and a second time, when he played under my captaincy against Westminster in 1918—no one could have been more agreeable and pleasant. On both occasions he scored a few runs in good style, and at Vincent Square made a very good left-handed catch at backward point off P. G. H. Fender's bowling.

Cricket owes him a special debt for the strong attitude he took up against the unfair bowling prevalent in the eighties. He declined to allow Kent to arrange fixtures with Lancashire because of Crossland's action, and refused to play for Gentlemen *v.* Players at Lord's if Crossland was included in the Players' Eleven. A. N. Hornby, the Lancashire Captain, and Lancashire generally, were pretty angry with him, but they came to see that he was right, and when, on returning from his term of office as Governor of Bombay, he played for Kent at Old Trafford he was given a tremendous reception.

G. J. V. Weigall, who was playing for Kent on that occasion, has described the scene in graphic language:

> He went in first wicket down, and as he came down the pavilion steps the ground and pavilion rose to him and cheered him all the way to the wickets. Mold was the bowler, and the first ball he snicked between the wicket and his legs for four. The second, a superb break-back, knocked his middle stump flying yards, and as he walked back to the pavilion, cap in hand, the crowd applauded as if he had made a century. He had the reception of an Emperor.

The beautiful Memorial to him at Lord's, a source of constant admiration to all, and especially to visitors from our Dominions and Colonies, was unveiled by Lord Hailsham, the President of the M.C.C., in May 1934, a tribute to all he did for cricket and the M.C.C. On his eightieth birthday, at the request of the Editor of *The Times*, he sent the following message:

> Sir,
>
> I appreciate, I assure you, the suggestion that I might like to send a message of goodwill to all my cricketing friends on my eightieth birthday, and I gladly, in the words of Rip Van Winkle, greet them and "their wives and families, and may they live long and prosper."
>
> Only there is something a bit ominous about the suggestion. Does it convey a hint that it is time I said farewell to cricket? If so, I have no intention of complying with it. Cricket has been too good a friend to me for nearly seventy years for me to part with it one moment before I have to. I cannot remember a time when it did not convey its friendly welcome. In school at Eton the tapping of the bats in Sixpenny assured me of happy hours to come, and reminded me of happy hours in the past. I have been fairly busy for most of my life, but never so busy that the thoughts of cricket

and my companions were not an inspiration to get on with the work that I might the sooner enjoy its invigorating capacity.

And my message includes youth, and I advise them to get all the cricket they can. They will never regret it: I might apply to it Mr Jorrocks's commendation of hunting: "It's the image of war without its guilt, and 25 per cent. of its danger." And in my message to youth I will repeat what I said to the half-holiday cricketer: "You do well to love it, for it is more free from anything sordid, anything dishonourable, than any game in the world. To play it keenly, honourably, generously, self-sacrificingly, is a moral lesson in itself, and the classroom is God's air and sunshine. Foster it, my brothers, so that it may attract all who can find the time to play it; protect it from anything that would sully it, so that it may grow in favour with all men."

Thus, Mr Editor, thanks to your kindness, I have the opportunity of sending my greeting to all my friends round the world, both those I do not know, as well as those I do, for we are all comrades in the world of cricket.

Yours faithfully,

BELMONT, FAVERSHAM HARRIS

February 2, 1931

After Lord Harris's death I was privileged to see a diary which he had kept from his Eton days, and which covered not only his cricketing experiences, including his tour in Australia in 1878–79, but his term as Under-Secretary of State for War, his Governorship of Bombay, and his later days in the City. It is a great pity that he has had no biographer, for he touched life at many points —at Court, in the affairs of State, in the Yeomanry, in county affairs, in agriculture, and in the hunting field. As for cricket, did he not say in his letter to *The Times* that his life seemed to have been centred round it?

The Indians were here in 1932, and with the one Test Match at Lord's, two Test Trials, North *v.* South at Old Trafford, and England *v.* the Rest at Cardiff, as well as Gentlemen *v.* Players at Lord's, the Selectors were afforded plenty of opportunity to make the last four or five always difficult selections for the team for Australia. In spite of the fact that neither Duleepsinhji, through a sudden and severe illness which befell him in the middle of August, and which was to close his brilliant career, nor Robins, because of the claims of business, was able to accept the invitation of the M.C.C., we evolved a very good side, with Jardine, who had shown himself a fine captain, in command. Towards the end of July Lord Hawke, as Chairman of the M.C.C. Cricket Committee and Selection Sub-committee, joined the Selectors, and took the chair at the final meeting, which was held during the Test Trial at Cardiff. Thus those responsible for the final selections were Lord Hawke, Perrin, Higson, Jardine, and myself.

England won the Test at Lord's by 158 runs, after a keen struggle, the scores being England 259 and 275 for eight wickets declared, India 189 and 187. Jardine (79 and 85, not out) batted superbly on both occasions when runs were badly wanted, and Ames (65) and Paynter (54) were also seen to advantage. The bowling of Bowes, Voce, Brown, and Hammond was good, if it did not look to have quite the sting of that of our opponents, for whom Nissar, Amar Singh, and Jahangir Khan, with their accuracy and speed off the pitch, won the enthusiastic approval of the critics. Both sides fielded splendidly. Amar Singh was the only Indian to score over 50 runs, and his 51 in the second innings was a glorious display of driving.

The Indians played attractive cricket, the fielding attaining a high standard, the throwing in being hard and accurate, while Amar Singh and Nissar were two very good bowlers, and Wazir Ali, Nazir Ali, C. K. Nayudu, and Jeoomal fine batsmen. On his form on this tour, and again in 1936, Amar Singh would have been a strong candidate for a World Eleven. He bowled fast-medium, with a very loose arm and great pace off the ground, and could make the ball swing either way.

Gentlemen *v.* Players would probably have been won by the Gentlemen had not Hobbs been missed in the slips off Allen when the Players, with Sutcliffe, Woolley, Hammond, and Hendren out in their second innings, were only some 30 runs ahead. The scores were: Players 301 (Hammond 110) and 320 (Hobbs 161, not out[1]), Gentlemen 430 for eight declared (Pataudi 165, Duleep 132, Jardine 64).

Pataudi was a very neat and 'compact' batsman—sound, quick on his feet, and blessed with exceptional eyesight, as are so many of his race. He was always careful to play himself in, and then he would bring out his many strokes, the best of which were the cut and the off-drive, while few balls, indeed, on his legs escaped punishment. At this period he, Duleep, Jardine, and Wyatt had clearly established themselves as the four best amateur batsmen in the country. For the Gentlemen Allen stood out as a bowler,

[1] This was Hobbs's seventh century for the Players at Lord's.

taking eight wickets in the match for 168 runs, and bowling 63.2 overs. Larwood, going on at the Nursery end at 410, sent back Jardine, Allen, Chapman, and Brown in four overs for 5 runs.

Cambridge won the toss for the seventh year in succession, and scored 431 (D. R. Wilcox 157, A. Ratcliffe 124), to which Oxford replied with 368 (B. W. Hone 167, Owen-Smith 67). Hone's was the innings of an experienced batsman. He was an Australian, and had played for South Australia. Owen-Smith was a delight to watch, with his nimble feet, supple wrists, and that touch of genius which marked his cricket and Rugby football, not to mention his boxing.

In their second innings Cambridge made 163 for nine wickets, and honours were even. Farnes was clearly the best bowler on the two sides—he stood out by himself—and Barlow and Legard bowled steadily and well for Oxford. The bowling, as a whole, however, was not up to the mark, and on the first day before lunch there were too many full-pitches and long-hops. The fielding, especially that of Oxford, was good, and both wicket-keepers—Oldfield and Comber—were excellent. There was only one Etonian (Hazlerigg) and no Harrovian or Rugbeian in the two Elevens. Oxford had three representatives from South Africa—Melville, Owen-Smith, and Van der Bijl—as well as the Australian Hone.

The match will always be memorable for the fact that Ratcliffe, having made 201 in 1931, joined W. Yardley, H. J. Enthoven, and the Nawab of Pataudi in the select band of those who have scored two separate hundreds in the University Match.

Australia, 1932–33

Perhaps I may be permitted to depart for a moment from Lord's, and from a description of the main matches there, in order to say something of the M.C.C. tour in Australia of 1932–33, and of the repercussions therefrom, which were felt very clearly at Headquarters.

As all the cricket world knows, the M.C.C. team returned victorious, winning four of the five Test Matches. Jardine, the Captain, had many admirable qualities, and was as good a tactician and strategist as any captain I have ever seen. He planned and thought and never spared himself, and set a fine example of physical fitness. He was absolutely unselfish, and would never ask anyone to do anything which he would not do himself. Especially was he a master in the art of changing his bowling and in keeping his bowlers fresh. As for "Body Line," as the Australians called it, he himself thought that this type of bowling was legitimate and within the rules. It should be noted, however, that the Body Line field was not set for every batsman. It was always set for Woodfull, Ponsford, Bradman, Fingleton, and Richardson, but not, at any rate to the same extent, for the others, and when Grimmett, for instance, was in there were as many as five men in the slips, while to O'Reilly, Iremonger, and Wall bowl-at-the-wicket was the order of the day. Voce also bowled to a closely packed leg-side field, but he was a far better bowler with an orthodox field and keeping a length, as he himself came to recognize later in his career. Bowes too wasted his abilities in trying to bowl Body Line, as he also realized. Allen never bowled Body Line, and, as *Wisden* put it, "enjoyed many successes. Surely, with his extra pace, Larwood could have done as well as Allen, and so prevented the bitter feeling?"

Much confusion has been caused by a very large number of people who thought that Body Line was another term for Leg Theory, a form of bowling which has been in use in this country and in Australia for at least sixty years. Body Line is absolutely and entirely different from Leg Theory, and this fact was not at first generally recognized over here.

This Body Line bowling was first seen in England in 1910, when W. B. Burns, who for a few overs was extremely fast, bowled it for Worcestershire against Middlesex at Lord's. He, like Larwood, placed seven men on the leg side, six of them in the short-leg area, but this form of attack met with instant disapproval and was not persisted in. I thought then that this method of bowling seemed against the interest and the spirit of cricket. From that view I have never wavered, and somewhere about 1927 or 1928 I criticized Macdonald, the great Australian fast bowler, for adopting these tactics, as I did Bowes in the Surrey *v.* Yorkshire match at the Oval, in the columns of *The Morning Post* of August 22, 1932. My objection to Body Line, therefore, dates back to a period when Jardine was at a preparatory school, and when many of the M.C.C. Australian team of 1932–33 were in their perambulators.

Cables continued to flow throughout the summer of 1933 between England and Australia on the Body Line controversy, and a special committee, with Lord Hailsham as Chairman, was appointed, before which I, among others, gave evidence.

As I have said, the question was not understood in this country. Very few people here had seen Body Line in full blast, and I was of the opinion that if let loose in England the pavilion critics would condemn it, and that in a short while spectators would begin to leave the ground. That I was correct in holding these views was later proved by the happenings in certain matches. However, some people, who had never seen Body Line, held that I "had got the wrong perspective."

This was not a happy season. Larwood's interviews in the Press and Jardine's book did not help matters, and a section of the Press seemed determined to make trouble. Larwood might well have said, "Save me from my friends"—and he had some pretty bad ones! The cricket world was indeed upside-down. Nerves were frayed, and people known for their courtesy had some strange lapses. I felt particularly sorry for Larwood, and here I think that the Nottinghamshire Committee might possibly have done more to guide him and to keep him from being 'stunted' by certain newspapers.

The West Indies won only five of their thirty matches, drew sixteen, and lost nine, and in so fine a summer they should have done better. They were unlucky in losing a good all-rounder in F. R. Martin, who strained a leg muscle so severely that he took part in but five games, and an even greater handicap was that Constantine, because of a Lancashire League engagement, was available for only one of the three Tests. The West Indies had, however, two exceptionally fine cricketers—G. Headley and E. A. Martindale. Headley's reputation had preceded him, and he lived up to it, scoring 2320 runs, with an average of 66·28. Like Bradman, he was short in height, and, like the Australian champion, neatly and compactly built. His defence was very strong, and he was a remarkably fine cutter and hooker. He did not often drive straight, playing many strokes off his back leg. He must be reckoned among the world's great batsmen. Martindale obtained 103 wickets at a cost of 20·98 runs each. With the loose, free arm so characteristic of West Indies' fast bowlers, he kept up a great pace. Grant was a clever and enthusiastic captain, and inspired the team by his own admirable example. He was a magnificent fieldsman at backward point or short leg, and a useful and determined batsman. The team left behind them a fine impression of keenness, combined with modesty and unfailing good temper.

The Players beat the Gentlemen by ten wickets. Winning the toss, they lost five wickets for 91 runs, and then Ames (82) and James Langridge (71) added 147, but before he had scored double figures Ames was missed at slip, and this mistake altered the whole run of the game. The Gentlemen had to bat on a difficult wicket, and only Jardine (59) offered much resistance. His first half-dozen runs occupied him an hour. In the next hour he made 53 out of 78. It was a splendid innings. Following on 166 behind, the Gentlemen made 177. M. J. Turnbull scored 72, an innings almost to be compared with Jardine's, while Owen-Smith made a fine 37; but on the last morning Hammond made two superb slip catches off Clark, and the last four wickets fell for 25 runs.

The University Match was drawn, but it produced a thrilling finish. Cambridge held a first-innings lead of 45, and on Oxford going in again they lost six wickets for 32 runs. At this point V. G. J. Jenkins joined F. G. H. Chalk, and, batting finely on a lively wicket, they stayed together for ninety minutes, at which point time was called. The weather was most unkind, and on the first two days play was cut short. The full scores were Oxford 164 and 79 for six wickets, Cambridge 209. Oxford fielded well, indeed, and Cambridge were one of the best fielding sides I have seen. Jahangir Khan, medium right, and R. S. Grant, slow right, bowled Leg Theory, with six or seven fieldsmen on the on side, of good length and direction, to which no possible exception could be taken, but Farnes, with a packed leg field, often dropped the ball short, and with his great pace more than one of the Oxford batsmen received nasty blows. P. C. Oldfield, the Oxford wicket-keeper, was bowled off his jaw, and Townsend hit his wicket after being struck on the neck by a rising ball. The match served to educate those who hitherto had not understood the difference between Leg Theory and Body Line, and the Cambridge tactics certainly did not meet with general approval.

The Australians were due in this country at the end of April 1934, and every one was hoping that the hatchet had been buried with the last of the M.C.C. cables, dated December 14, 1933. The M.C.C. had passed the following resolution: "That any form of bowling which is obviously a direct attack by the bowler upon the batsman would be an offence against the spirit of the game," and on November 23, 1933, at a joint meeting of the Board of

Control and the Advisory County Cricket Committee, at which fourteen of the seventeen county captains were present, and the remaining three represented, this resolution was accepted, and an understanding arrived at to the effect that the county captains would not permit or countenance such form of bowling.

The Australian cricketers were warmly welcomed, but shortly before their arrival a discordant note was struck, and the day after the conclusion of the Test Match at Trent Bridge it was obvious that trouble was brewing. I believe that Larwood was only too ready to play for England, but on June 17 came an outburst by him in the Press. Obviously by so acting he "put himself outside the pale of playing for England," as *Wisden* put it.

The Selection Committee for the Test Matches was Sir Stanley Jackson (Chairman), P. Perrin, and T. A. Higson. The Body Line trouble deprived them of the services of Jardine, Larwood, and Voce, and as Jardine was a fine captain and batsman, and Larwood our best bowler, and Voce one of our best bowlers, they were heavily handicapped. The Australians won the first and fifth games and England won the second, the third and fourth being drawn, the fourth greatly in favour of the Australians. Wyatt was to have led England in the first Test, but in the Test Trial at Lord's he received a severe blow on the thumb and was forced to stand down, C. F. Walters taking his place.

At Lord's Wyatt was able to play, and we won the toss. Walters played a beautiful innings of 82, but four wickets were down for 130, and five for 182. Then Ames (120) joined Leyland (109) and put on 129, and the total was 440. As Leyland came through the Long Room Gerry Weigall said to me, "Here comes the cross-batted village greener! Where's Woolley?" A gross slander, which should have involved the utterer in heavy damages, but the "village greener" batted magnificently, and Ames was at his best and most attractive. At the end of the second day Australia's score was 192 for two wickets.

During the week-end it rained heavily, and at ten minutes to six on the Monday the match was over, England winning by an innings and 38 runs, her first victory in a Test Match at Lord's against Australia since 1896, when Lohmann and Richardson swept the Australians off their feet.

The wicket was sticky, and Verity, from the Pavilion end, seized his opportunity, taking in all fifteen wickets for 104 runs, thus excelling Rhodes's feat at Melbourne in 1904 of fifteen wickets for 124 runs. There is this to be said, however, that, whereas at Melbourne Rhodes was badly supported in the field, Verity was backed up by the safest catching, with Hammond, in the slips, and Hendren, at silly point, at their best. That Verity bowled grandly there is no question. He kept a length, and, not being exactly slow through the air, the batsmen could not get at him. To Bradman he placed a deep mid-off and a deep mid-on, and with malice aforethought, no man in the out-field, with the idea of tempting Bradman to have a go at the wrong ball. Whether the great Don thought to himself, "I am not going to allow anyone to bowl to me without a long field," I cannot, of course, say, but he took the bait, had a wild swipe at a good-length turning ball, and up she went, with Ames, the wicket-keeper, and Hammond, at slip, in full cry. Eventually Ames made the catch, Bradman retired for 13, and I can see now the look Woodfull gave him as he walked past him to the pavilion. It must be said that, with the notable exception of Woodfull, whose 43 was a masterly innings, the Australians were all at sea on the false turf, but that they had the cruellest of luck in the weather must be admitted. It was a case of the toss meaning the match. Here are Verity's analyses in full:

First Innings				*Second Innings*			
O.	M.	R.	W.	O.	M.	R.	W.
36	15	61	7	22.3	8	43	8

Selection Committees sometimes are blessed with luck. This year's Committee were certainly not so favoured. The Body Line trouble deprived them of three indispensable cricketers, and when they gambled the wheel of fortune looked the other way. They deserved sympathy, not criticism.

One of the keenest disappointments of the Selectors was the failure of Hammond, who in eight innings scored but 162 runs, with a highest score of 43. It is only right to point out that he was troubled with a strained back, but who would have imagined that this magnificent batsman, who had done such great things in Australia, would achieve so little?

During the whole tour the Australians lost only one match—against England at Lord's, when rain played into their opponents' hands—Woodfull captaining the side with sound judgment. At the end of the season he announced his retirement from first-class cricket. He made many friends, not only on but also off the field, and always played the game according to its best traditions.

For the first time since 1914 the Gentlemen beat the Players at Lord's by seven wickets. Hendren, the Players' Captain, declared the second innings closed, and the amateurs had to make 232 runs in two hours and fifty minutes. They did so with half an hour to spare, Wyatt and Walters putting on 160 runs in eighty minutes, and thus getting well ahead of the clock. Even Verity could not keep the runs down. The scores were Players 263 (Leyland 80, Ames 76) and 245 for five wickets declared (A. Mitchell, of Yorkshire, 120, Sutcliffe 65), Gentlemen 277 (J. H. Human 66, G. O. Allen 63) and 232 for five wickets (Wyatt 104, not out, Walters 79).

In the Middlesex *v.* Australians match H. J. Enthoven accomplished the hat-trick and Bradman scored *160 out of 225 in just over two hours*—an amazing innings, which made even the most fervent admirers of W. G. admit that another champion had arisen. Robert Lyttelton told me next day that his absolute limit was one glass of port after dinner, but "last night I had to have another in honour of that innings."

The M.C.C. Committee, supported by the Advisory C.C.C. and the county captains, had endeavoured to settle the bowling controversy by what may be called a "gentleman's agreement," but the events of 1934 obviously called for a definite decision as to what exactly constituted direct attack, and in March 1935 the M.C.C. issued the following instructions:

I. During the cricket season of 1934 there was evidence that cases of the bowler making a "direct attack" upon the batsmen occurred. The M.C.C. Committee have defined a "direct attack" as "persistent and systematic bowling of fast short-pitched balls at the batsman standing clear of his wicket."

II. The M.C.C. Committee have always considered this type of bowling to be unfair, and that it must be eliminated from the game. Umpires are the sole judges of fair and unfair play (*vide* Law 43), and are therefore empowered to deal with "direct attack."

III. If in the opinion of the umpire at the bowler's end unfair bowling of this type takes place he shall adopt the following procedure:

(*a*) As soon as he decides that such bowling is becoming persistent he shall forthwith 'caution' the bowler.

(*b*) If this caution is ineffective he shall inform the captain of the fielding side and the other umpire of what has occurred.

(*c*) Should the above prove ineffective the umpire at the bowler's end shall:

(1) At the first repetition call "dead ball," and the over shall be regarded as completed.

(2) Request the captain of the fielding side to take the bowler off forthwith.

(3) Report the occurrence to the captain of the batting side as soon as an interval of play takes place.

(4) At the end of the day make a report to the Secretary of the M.C.C., and also to the Secretary of the County Club to which the offending bowler belongs.

IV. A bowler who has been taken off as above shall not bowl again during the same innings.

V. Umpires should note that they will be strongly supported by the M.C.C. Committee in any action which they may take under Law 43 to prevent this type of bowling from being practised. The Advisory C.C.C. on November 21, 1934, confirmed the recommendation of the M.C.C. Committee "that the County Committees and the County Captains shall take all steps in their power to eliminate from the game the type of bowling as now defined—*i.e.*, direct attack."

VI. Umpires appointed to stand in first- and second-class county matches are reminded that it is their duty to report forthwith to the Secretary of the M.C.C. any case on or off the field of a captain or a player criticizing or showing resentment to the decision of an umpire. The umpires are, however, required to give notice to the captains during the match that it is their intention to make such a report.

We heard no more of "direct attack," these very clear instructions putting an end to a controversy which had disrupted the cricket world and impaired the good relations between England and Australia.

The South Africans, under the captaincy of H. F. Wade, were our visitors this year, and for the second Test James Langridge, Mitchell, of Derbyshire, and Farrimond, of Lancashire, replaced Iddon, Robins, and Bowes, who had been in the England Eleven at Trent Bridge, Ames playing as a batsman and Farrimond as wicket-keeper. The choice of this team involved the longest Selection Committee meeting of my experience. It began at 11 o'clock in the morning, and did not end until seven. The point at issue was whether Robins or Mitchell should play. The Selectors were unanimous in urging the claims of Robins, and Wyatt, for his part, was emphatic in supporting Mitchell. We pointed out that Robins was one of the best all-round cricketers in England, but 1935 was the year of the 'leather-jacket'—the larva of the daddy-long-legs, as it was officially described—which had descended on Lord's and caused it to look like the sand on the seashore, and Wyatt was cast-iron in his opinion that Mitchell would win the match for us on the 'leather-jacket' wicket. Now the Captain has a casting vote, and great weight must obviously be given to his views. No argument, no comparison of previous performances, could convince him, and in the end, physically and mentally exhausted, we gave way. None of us can escape responsibility: it was a Committee decision. Dearly were we to pay for it, and to this day I curse myself! There was a difference of only 30 runs on the first innings—South Africa 228, England 198. Cameron played a glorious innings of 90, out of 126. He hit three sixes, his driving being magnificent, while his cutting brought him many runs.

South Africa made 278 for seven wickets in their second innings and declared the innings closed, Bruce Mitchell going in first and scoring 164, not out. He was batting for five and a half hours, without a mistake of any sort. Six wickets were down for 177 runs, but Langton played an invaluable innings of 44. H. F. Wade, the South African Captain, left England four and three-quarter hours in which to make 309 runs. 151 was all we could score, Balaskas and Langton each taking four wickets, Balaskas's analysis for the match being 59 overs, 16 maidens, 103 runs, 9 wickets. In both innings South Africa's fielding and wicket-keeping (Cameron) were up to the highest standard. We were fairly and squarely beaten, and the crowd gave the winners an enthusiastic reception, gathering in front of the pavilion and cheering for a quarter of an hour. The South Africans had travelled a long way since the first English team—Major Wharton's—had visited them in 1888 and Castens' side of 1894 had come to England. And of all places to achieve their first Test Match victory in this country Lord's was clearly indicated.

Here is the score:

ENGLAND *v.* SOUTH AFRICA

Played at Lord's, June 29 and July 1 and 2, 1935

Result: South Africa won by 157 runs

SOUTH AFRICA

First Innings		*Second Innings*	
B. Mitchell, l.b.w., b. Nichols	30	not out	164
I. J. Siedle, b. Mitchell	6	c. Farrimond, b. Mitchell	13
E. A. Rowan, c. Farrimond, b. Verity	40	l.b.w., b. Nichols	44
A. D. Nourse, b. Verity	3	b. Verity	2
H. F. Wade (Capt.), c. Hammond, b. Langridge	23	b. Verity	0
H. B. Cameron, b. Nichols	90	c. Ames, b. Mitchell	3
E. L. Dalton, c. and b. Langridge	19	c. Wyatt, b. Verity	0
X. Balaskas, b. Verity	4		
A. B. Langton, c. Holmes, b. Hammond	4	c. and b. Hammond	44
R. J. Crisp, not out	4		
A. J. Bell, b. Hammond	0		
Bye 1, leg bye 1, wide 1, no-balls 2	5	Byes 3, leg byes 5	8
Total	228	Total (7 wkts. dec.)	278

ENGLAND

R. E. S. Wyatt (Capt.), c. Nourse, b. Dalton	53	b. Balaskas	16
H. Sutcliffe, l.b.w., b. Bell	3	l.b.w., b. Langton	38
M. Leyland, b. Balaskas	18	b. Crisp	4
W. R. Hammond, b. Dalton	27	c. Cameron, b. Langton	27
L. E. G. Ames, b. Balaskas	5	l.b.w., b. Langton	8
E. R. T. Holmes, c. Bell, b. Balaskas	10	b. Langton	8
J. Langridge, c. Mitchell, b. Balaskas	27	l.b.w., b. Balaskas	17
W. Farrimond, b. Balaskas	13	b. Crisp	13
M. S. Nichols, c. Cameron, b. Langton	10	not out	7
H. Verity, l.b.w., b. Langton	17	c. Langton, b. Balaskas	8
T. B. Mitchell, not out	5	st. Cameron, b. Balaskas	1
Byes 4, leg byes 5, wide 1	10	Leg byes	4
	198		151

BOWLING ANALYSIS

ENGLAND

First Innings	O.	M.	R.	W.	*Second Innings*	O.	M.	R.	W.
Nichols	21	5	47	2	Nichols	18	4	64	1
Wyatt	4	2	9	0	Wyatt	4	2	2	0
Hammond	5.3	3	8	2	Hammond	14.4	4	26	1
Mitchell	20	3	71	1	Mitchell	33	5	93	2
Verity	28	10	61	3	Verity	38	16	56	3
Langridge	13	3	27	2	Langridge	10	4	19	0
					Holmes	4	2	10	0

SOUTH AFRICA

	O.	M.	R.	W.		O.	M.	R.	W.
Crisp	8	1	32	0	Crisp	15	4	30	2
Bell	6	0	16	1	Bell	12	3	21	0
Langton	21.3	3	58	2	Langton	11	3	31	4
Balaskas	32	8	49	5	Balaskas	27	8	54	4
Dalton	13	1	33	2	Mitchell	2	0	11	0

Umpires: E. J. Smith and F. Walden

Mr W. H. Brookes, the editor of *Wisden*, could not make up his mind as to the quality of the Selectors' work. He thought that we "made more than one unfortunate mistake," and then added: "No one could have done very much better than our Selectors did." I think that we did make one definite mistake—in playing Mitchell at Lord's. But injuries deprived us at various times of such players as Leyland, Clark, Copson, Hollies, and Allen. I felt, however, that the critics had treated us very fairly. There was some rather loose criticism at one period about Hammond, who eventually headed the batting averages in the five Tests, with an average of 64·83, who fielded splendidly, and who proved a useful bowler, but that was all. My experience has been that criticism, if constructive, is helpful, and is certainly not resented.

Whether the South Africans were a better side than P. W. Sherwell's famous team of 1907 is open to question, but they had a better record, winning seventeen and losing only two of their thirty-one first-class games, as against the seventeen wins and four defeats in twenty-seven matches of their predecessors. Until August 13 they did not know defeat. Sherwell's team was stronger in bowling, with Vogler, Schwarz, Faulkner, White, Kotze, and Sinclair, but Wade's team was a better batting side. Not, perhaps, quite so good in the field, it had in Cameron a wicket-keeper in the same class as Sherwell, which is the highest praise. The South Africans were very fortunate in their captain, who managed his bowling admirably, fielded splendidly near the wicket, and played some useful defensive innings, particularly in the Tests at Leeds and Old Trafford.

Mitchell was their best batsman, very sound and reliable, if at times over-cautious. He was the mainstay in the Test Matches, and his 164, not out, at Lord's was a great innings. He was also a fine slip fieldsman and a useful leg-break bowler. Viljoen, Siedle, Nourse, Dalton, Rowan (very quick on his feet), and Cameron formed a strong group of batsmen, and in the Tests at Lord's and the Oval Langton played innings of great value. They were a difficult side to get out. Bell, Vincent, Crisp, and Langton were the chief bowlers, very little being seen of Balaskas after his splendid bowling at Lord's. Bell was fast-medium, swung the ball, and made haste off the ground; Vincent, slow to medium left, with accuracy of length; Crisp, fast right; Langton, very tall, medium right, who swung the new ball, and when the shine had worn off changed his pace cleverly, always with length and spin.

Cameron fairly won a place among the great wicket-keepers in the history of the game. Both as a catcher and a stumper it is not overpraising him to say that he was magnificent. His death shortly after his return to South Africa came as a great shock, and was a tremendous loss to the game. Like Ames, he was worth two men to any side. Apart from his wicket-keeping, his beautiful hitting remains an abiding memory.

Gentlemen *v.* Players was finished in two days, the professionals winning by nine wickets. The amateurs were without Walters, because of illness, Allen, and Robins. Only Wyatt and Brown, of the amateur batsmen, did themselves justice. Smith, W. Barber, and Leyland, were the successful batsmen for the Players. Smith, an attractive left-hander, drove well on the off side and hooked well. He was after runs, as were Barber and Hardstaff. Hammond bowled and fielded excellently. H. D. Read had by no means a good action, but he bowled very fast, and was physically well equipped. J. C. Clay, bowling slow right round the wicket, with the easiest of actions and a dead-sure length, imparted considerable spin to the ball, and with his high action often deceived the batsman in the flight.

Cambridge won the University Match by 195 runs, with scores of 302 and 223 to 221 and 109. G. W. Parker, the Cambridge Captain, played a great part in this victory, scoring 76 and 14, taking a wicket, and making two grand catches at backward point. He also captained the side with excellent judgment.

During the summer of 1935 a trial was given in first-class cricket to the new l.b.w. rule, by which a batsman could be given out if the ball pitched outside the off stump and would, in the umpires' opinion, have hit the wicket, the batsman's leg or legs being in front of the stumps at the moment of impact. In this experiment the South Africans willingly co-operated. The M.C.C. Committee had taken great care to ascertain the various views on the subject, and on three different afternoons leading cricketers, both amateur and professional, and umpires were called into conference. Some of them regarded the proposal with misgivings, Sutcliffe, for instance, anticipating for himself the most lugubrious future. It was suggested that he was grossly underrating his abilities, which turned out to be true, and he was one of the earliest converts, to be followed by almost every one. This experiment has now been universally adopted not only here, but in our Dominions and Colonies. R. H. Lyttelton and F. G. J. Ford, who for years had urged an alteration, were naturally very pleased, and their persistent advocacy deserved to be rewarded. Some people suggested that the law should apply to both sides of the wicket, but, without entering into an argument, this may be said: a batsman must have his legs somewhere!

Coinciding with the change in the l.b.w. law, cricket brightened. A new school of class players began to emerge, as aggressive as they were skilled. About the same time C. B. Fry began to write his articles in the *Evening Standard*, to which he brought the 'pep' of an American newspaper columnist to give sparkle to his knowledge as an outstanding cricketer and his erudition as an Oxford scholar. His column soon became a great feature, and rekindled in many an interest in big cricket which had been dying. Not only were batsmen like Hammond, Leyland, Ames, Walters, Barnett, Wellard, Hardstaff, and later Compton and Edrich, able to play innings of great dash and enterprise, but Fry was there to make them live again most vividly for readers of the "Final Night." His picturesque language, rich allusion, and caustic humour were equalled only by his penetrating comment and sound judgment of play and players.

The Indians were here in 1936, and the Selection Committee were busy with three Test Matches, a Trial Match at Lord's, and a tour in Australia in the offing. England won the first Test, at Lord's, in which rain caused several delays, by nine wickets. Allen, on winning the toss, sent India in to bat, and a total of 147 gave them a lead of 13 runs on the first innings. India scored 93 in their second innings (Allen five for 43), and England were left with 107 to win. Before a run had been made Mitchell was caught off his glove at backward point from a ball which got up straight, and in view of what had gone before the position was momentarily one of some anxiety. Turnbull joined Gimblett, and for a time it was a grim struggle. Amar Singh was bowling in his best form, and off him each batsman was missed from difficult chances. Turnbull showed sound defence, however, and when Nissar came on for a second spell Gimblett hit four successive balls to the ring, and the match was won. England were without Hammond, who had recently undergone an operation for the removal of his tonsils, and in his absence the batting and slip-fielding suffered. Allen led the side with spirit and judgment, and made good use of his bowlers at both ends. He forced considerable pace out of a wicket which was slow—a difficult thing for a fast bowler to do—and his reward was ten wickets for 78. In both innings he got his side out of a difficulty, but the finest bowling was that of Amar Singh, who took six wickets for 35 runs in the first innings.

The M.C.C. had selected Allen to lead the side in Australia. Until this season he had had, except in a few matches for Middlesex, little experience of captaincy, but he had shown himself a capable leader, full of ideas and bursting with energy, and his bowling in the Test Matches had been very successful; also he had behind him an excellent all-round record during the 1932–33 tour in Australia. Moreover, his family connexion with Australia was in his favour for an enterprise which was to be one of goodwill.

It was a difficult side to choose. Sutcliffe, at the age of forty-two, was not the batsman he had been, we could not lure Walters from his tent, and a partner for the dashing C. J. Barnett was somewhat of a problem. Eventually Wyatt and A. Fagg were decided on—the former sound and experienced, and Fagg one of the young school. Wyatt had been out of form until the beginning of August, when he came with a rush, but he was very brittle, and, most unfortunately, he was hit on the left arm very early in the tour, a bone being fractured, and so missed the first three Test Matches. Fagg, far from lucky in the games in which he took part, fell ill, had to be sent home, and eventually developed rheumatic fever. There were other injuries and accidents, the most serious being that to Robins, who broke the second finger of his right hand at fielding practice during the first week of the tour, with the result that he could not spin the ball. Allen could well say that Fate fought against him.

To my mind it was a grave mistake to leave out Paynter. He was a left-hander, he could bat anywhere in the order—No. 1, 5, or 7—his splendidly plucky cricket had been one of the features of the 1932–33 tour, and he was a great fieldsman. Moreover, he had had a great season, scoring 2016 runs, with an average of 45·81. The side was also overloaded with fast bowlers—Allen, Farnes, Voce, and Copson, who, though he bowled successfully in other matches, did not play in a single Test. A medium-paced bowler of stamina and determination, like J. W. A. Stephenson, would have fitted better into the framework of the side, and his superb fielding would have been an inspiring asset. His remarkable bowling in Gentlemen *v.* Players did not receive sufficient consideration. Those responsible for the selection of the team were Sir Stanley Jackson (Chairman), Lord Cobham, H. D. G. Leveson-Gower, representing the M.C.C., Allen, Perrin, Higson, and myself. I was then, and still am, convinced that we were guilty of serious strategical errors, and that a closer examination of individual skill and experience, and *cricket history*, would have made just the difference between victory and defeat.

"Gentlemen *v.* Players at Lord's," wrote *Wisden*, "will long be remembered for its stirring finish. G. O. Allen, who led the Gentlemen, declared his innings closed at five o'clock on the third day, and set the Players 132 to get in roughly seventy-five minutes, including the extra half-hour. By six o'clock the Players had four men out for 33 runs." Eventually the Players scored 63 for five wickets, and the match was drawn, there having been no play on the first day. Farnes bowled at a tremendous pace, and when he tired Allen was equally fast, the stumps being uprooted in each instance. It was great bowling, but the outstanding performance was that of Stephenson, who in the Players' first innings obtained nine wickets in succession. As he also claimed the first wicket—Barnett's—in the second innings he actually obtained ten wickets in a row. One has to go back to the match of 1914, when J. W. H. T. Douglas took nine wickets in the Players' first innings, for a similar performance.

Cambridge, winning the toss for the ninth time in eleven years, won the University Match by eight wickets, not that winning the toss on this occasion gave any undue advantage to them. Oxford were handicapped by the absence of R. C. M. Kimpton, the Australian, an original and enterprising player, owing to an accident, although his substitute, J. W. Seamer, played a good second innings of 43 and fielded well. The scores were Cambridge 432 for nine wickets declared and 17 for two, Oxford 209 and 239. Cambridge were a good batting side, with unusual ability at Nos. 7, 8, 9, and 10, and only bowling of high class could have kept their total within reasonable limits on a perfect wicket. The Cambridge bowling was considerably stronger than that of Oxford, Jahangir Khan sending down 65 overs, 27 maidens, for 83 runs and six wickets. He maintained a most accurate length and was quick off the wicket. J. M. Brocklebank, slow-medium leg-break, a nephew of Sir Stanley Jackson, also realized the cardinal virtue of length, and obtained ten wickets for 139 runs.

The year 1937 was the one hundred and fiftieth anniversary of the foundation of the M.C.C., and to celebrate this historic event two matches were arranged—North *v.* South and the M.C.C. Australian Eleven *v.* the Rest of England. On May 25 *The Times* published a special number of twenty-four pages. This number was profusely illustrated in a beautiful binding, and contained a message from the President of the M.C.C., Colonel the Hon. J. J. Astor.

Later, on July 15, during Gentlemen *v.* Players, there was a dinner at the Savoy, at which Colonel Astor presided. The Duke of Gloucester was present, and read a message which the King was graciously pleased to send. It was a great event in the history of the Club, but the speeches were not worthy of the occasion, and a frightful *faux pas* was committed when the names of Lord Harris and of W. G. were not even mentioned—and they the only two men to whom permanent memorials have been erected at Lord's. To Allen, who had done so well in Australia, earning praise from the critics for his captaincy on the field and for his tact and general attitude off it, putting the cricketing relations between the two countries back on its old happy footing, was entrusted the reply to the toast of "Cricket," which had been proposed by Sir Stanley Jackson. We were all looking forward to hearing from him something of the inside story of his interesting and exciting tour, but he confined his remarks almost entirely to the preparation of wickets, and never said a word about the tour, or about Bradman, his opposite number, whose wonderful batting had won the rubber for Australia after England had been victorious in the first two Test Matches, or about the great hospitality of the most hospitable people in the world.

As I have said, to celebrate the occasion two representative matches were played at Lord's. The outstanding feature of the North *v.* South match was Hammond's batting. He drove superbly, and gave an object-lesson in the art of playing the slow bowling of Verity and Hollies, and was equally at home with the faster deliveries of Voce and A. V. Pope. There was a very keen fight in the second game. The Rest at one period looked like winning, but Allen captained his side extremely well, and good catching did the rest. Worthington carried his bat for 156 in the Australian Eleven's first innings. Gover, for the Rest, has never bowled better. At one period in the M.C.C.'s second innings he obtained *five successive wickets in fourteen balls for 5 runs.*

Here are the scores of these two Anniversary matches:

NORTH *v.* SOUTH

Played at Lord's, May 22, 24, *and* 25, 1937

Result: The South won by six wickets

NORTH

First Innings		*Second Innings*	
E. Paynter, b. Gover	3	b. Robins	51
L. Hutton, c. Robins, b. Langridge	102	b. Farnes	15
J. Hardstaff, c. Ames, b. Robins	71	c. Robins, b. Farnes	4
M. Leyland, c. Barnett, b. Todd	31	c. Ames, b. Farnes	5
R. E. S. Wyatt (Capt.), c. Ames, b. Gover	23	l.b.w., b. Farnes	49
H. E. Dollery, b. Farnes	11	b. Farnes	4
C. R. Maxwell, b. Farnes	5	b. Gover	30
A. V. Pope, c. Compton, b. Robins	15	b. Robins	10
H. Verity, st. Ames, b. Robins	2	not out	4
W. Voce, not out	0	c. Ames, b. Gover	1
E. Hollies, l.b.w., b. Robins	0	b. Gover	0
Byes 5, leg bye 1, no-balls 2	8	Byes 6, leg byes 2, no-balls 3	11
Total	271	Total	184

SOUTH

First Innings		*Second Innings*	
C. J. Barnett, c. Hollies, b. Verity	22	c. Maxwell, b. Hollies	22
H. Gimblett, b. Hollies	20	c. Maxwell, b. Voce	10
W. R. Hammond, c. Voce, b. Pope	86	not out	100
L. Ames, st. Maxwell, b. Hollies	24	b. Verity	2
L. J. Todd, c. Maxwell, b. Verity	3	b. Verity	5
D. Compton, b. Verity	70	not out	14
W. J. Edrich, c. Dollery, b. Voce	19		
J. Langridge, l.b.w., b. Pope	0		
R. W. V. Robins (Capt.), l.b.w., b. Verity	38		
A. Gover, not out	1		
K. Farnes, c. Verity, b. Hollies	0		
Byes 9, leg byes 7, no-ball 1	17	Leg byes	5
Total	300	Total (4 wkts.)	158

BOWLING ANALYSIS

SOUTH

First Innings	O.	M.	R.	W.	*Second Innings*	O.	M.	R.	W.
Gover	20	6	49	2	Gover	15	5	40	3
Farnes	21	6	35	2	Farnes	17	8	43	5
Todd	15	4	48	1	Todd	5	0	28	0
Hammond	10	4	17	0					
Langridge	15	4	37	1	Langridge	5	1	7	0
Robins	16	2	54	4	Robins	13	4	47	2
Compton	5	0	23	0	Barnett	3	1	8	0

NORTH

	O.	M.	R.	W.		O.	M.	R.	W.
Voce	19	3	43	1	Voce	10	1	43	1
Pope	22	4	59	2	Pope	11	2	24	0
Hollies	23.2	3	73	3	Hollies	10	0	47	1
Wyatt	2	1	5	0					
Verity	24	5	66	4	Verity	14	4	23	2
Hutton	6	0	37	0	Hutton	2.2	0	16	0

Umpires: F. Chester and F. Walden

M.C.C. AUSTRALIAN ELEVEN *v.* THE REST

Played at Lord's, May 26, 27, *and* 28, 1937

Result: M.C.C. Australian Eleven won by 69 *runs*

M.C.C. AUSTRALIAN ELEVEN

First Innings		*Second Innings*	
C. J. Barnett, c. Langridge, b. Gover	12	b. Gover	7
T. S. Worthington, not out	156	c. Todd, b. Gover	12
W. R. Hammond, c. Jones, b. Stephenson	47	c. Hutton, b. Todd	45
M. Leyland, c. and b. Stephenson	25	c. Holmes, b. Todd	28
R. E. S. Wyatt, c. Maxwell, b. Stephenson	0	b. Gover	42
J. Hardstaff, l.b.w., b. Gover	2	c. sub., b. Gover	24
L. Ames, c. Jones, b. Gover	45	c. Holmes, b. Gover	4
H. Verity, c. Dollery, b. Jones	17	b. Gover	0
R. W. V. Robins, c. Paynter, b. Langridge	58	not out	3
G. O. Allen (Capt.), b. Langridge	0	l.b.w., b. Gover	0
K. Farnes, b. Stephenson	5	b. Stephenson	1
Byes 3, leg byes 4, no-balls 2	9	Byes 5, leg byes 2	7
Total	376	Total	173

THE REST

L. Hutton, c. Hammond, b. Robins	18	c. Allen, b. Verity	50
J. Parks, l.b.w., b. Allen	2	b. Farnes	64
E. Paynter, c. Worthington, b. Farnes	1	c. Farnes, b. Verity	21
H. E. Dollery, b. Robins	15	c. Worthington, b. Wyatt	41
L. J. Todd, c. Ames, b. Allen	24	c. Ames, b. Verity	3
E. R. T. Holmes (Capt.), b. Verity	11	c. Hammond, b. Wyatt	8
J. Langridge, c. Hammond, b. Farnes	80	not out	22
C. R. Maxwell, b. Allen	4	c. Hammond, b. Allen	17
J. W. A. Stephenson, not out	68	b. Allen	1
A. Gover, b. Hammond	1	b. Allen	7
E. C. Jones, absent, hurt	0	absent, hurt	0
Bye 1, leg byes 4, wide 1, no-balls 5	11	Bye 1, leg byes 7, no-balls 3	11
Total	235	Total	245

BOWLING ANALYSIS

THE REST

First Innings	O.	M.	R.	W.	*Second Innings*	O.	M.	R.	W.
Gover	27	3	76	3	Gover	14	1	44	7
Todd	9	2	50	0	Todd	11	2	46	2
Stephenson	25.4	3	90	4	Stephenson	12.2	1	63	1
Langridge	20	4	68	2	Langridge	3	0	13	0
Jones	9	0	46	1					
Hutton	5	0	24	0					
Parks	7	1	13	0					

M.C.C. AUSTRALIAN ELEVEN

	O.	M.	R.	W.		O.	M.	R.	W.
Farnes	20	3	54	2	Farnes	16	4	30	1
Allen	16	2	50	3	Allen	15	2	65	3
Hammond	7.3	2	18	1	Hammond	9	0	31	0
Robins	16	0	58	2	Robins	8	1	40	0
Verity	9	4	13	1	Verity	18	5	55	3
Leyland	3	0	15	0					
Wyatt	6	1	12	0	Wyatt	8	1	13	2
Worthington	2	0	4	0					

Umpires: W. Reeves and F. Walden

Allen played very little cricket during this season, and Robins captained England in the three Tests against New Zealand. The first, at Lord's, was drawn. England had a very powerful batting side, with Ames and Robins at Nos. 7 and 8, and, winning the toss, scored 424. Hammond hit a six and fourteen fours in a masterly innings of 140, Hardstaff made some glorious strokes in his 114, while Paynter scored a good 74.

The Players defeated the Gentlemen by eight wickets, the match being decided on the stroke of time on the second day, but there was scarcely a dull moment. The pitch always gave the bowlers some help, the scores being Gentlemen 165 and 184, Players 229 and 121 for two. Hammond captained the professionals, made 68, and took four wickets for 67 runs. There were only three individual scores of 50—by Hammond, Mitchell-Innes (50), and Kimpton (59). F. R. Brown had a good match, scoring 47 in the second innings and taking four wickets for 78 runs. Both wicket-keepers (Ames and Maxwell) were in form, Ames having six catches and two stumpings to his credit, and Maxwell two catches and one stumping. The two West Countrymen, Goddard and Wellard, bowled admirably, and Farnes, as so often in this game, was at his best, with five wickets for 65 runs in the Players' first innings. For the first time for a dozen years there were four University cricketers in the Gentlemen's team—N. S. Mitchell-Innes, R. C. M. Kimpton, and D. H. Macindoe, of Oxford, and N. W. D. Yardley, of Cambridge.

Oxford gained their first victory over Cambridge since 1931, winning by seven wickets, though Cambridge again won the toss. Macindoe and Darwall-Smith bowled well at the start, making their fast-medium deliveries rise and swing. Four wickets were down for 45, but Yardley batted beautifully, and Cameron watched the ball carefully and cut nicely. Yardley was eventually caught at the wicket by Matthews, who made no fewer than five catches, for a splendid innings of 101. Oxford headed the Cambridge total of 253 by 14 runs, J. N. Grover (121) and Dixon (61) putting on 139 after four wickets had gone for 56. Dixon was freely 'cursed' by Cantabs for his rocklike defence, but his cool head saved the situation at a time of crisis. The advocates of brighter cricket, in their zeal, forgot the tactical situation. Dixon did not, and his innings had a marked influence on the result. Grover batted finely. He was missed in the deep when 49, but this was the only chance in a splendidly free innings, during which he hit one six—a magnificent on-drive into the stand on the right of the pavilion—and twelve fours. P. A. Gibb's 87 in Cambridge's second innings was a most able display, and had he not been run out the finish might well have been closer.

Oxford wanted 160 to win, and when Dixon, Mitchell-Innes, and Grover were out for 74 there was a buzz of excitement round the ground. But Kimpton (52, not out) and M. R. Barton (74, not out) soon put the result beyond doubt by some brilliant stroke-play. Kimpton, a most original and daring batsman, made his last 45 runs in twenty-eight minutes, and Barton batted in a very pleasing style. Oxford were a well-balanced side, cleverly captained by A. P. Singleton, and Macindoe and Darwall-Smith were clearly the best bowlers in the match.

At the age of forty-eight "Patsy" Hendren was almost as great a batsman as ever, but retired at the end of this summer, having been appointed coach at Harrow. When he came out to bat against Surrey at Lord's in his last championship game he was given a vociferously affectionate welcome, the crowd singing "For he's a jolly good fellow" and cheering for several minutes. He replied with a splendid innings of 103. There has been no more popular cricketer. He was a great favourite wherever he played, whether it was in this country or in our Dominions and Colonies, and he thoroughly deserved his immense popularity. An Irishman, he had a ready but never an unkind wit, and he was a rare mimic.

Middlesex for some years had relied on J. W. Hearne and Hendren for the majority of their runs,[1] and when they left the field of action we were fortunate indeed to find such successors as Compton and Edrich. "Young Jack" was a splendid all-round cricketer, and a man of sterling worth, liked, admired, and respected by all. In spite of his poor health and many an accident, his record was outstanding. He was a great cricketer, and would have been a greater had he been physically stronger. Before he was twenty-one he had made a century for England against Australia at Melbourne, and on his day he could make his leg-break positively 'buzz.'

In the spring of 1938 the Board of Control increased the Selection Committee from three to four, substituting Sellers for

[1] In all first-class cricket Hendren scored 57,610 runs, with an average of 50·81, and J. W. Hearne 37,250 runs, with an average of 41·02.

Higson and including Turnbull. Perhaps the White Rose thought that it was time that they had a representative—there is still a certain rivalry between the houses of York and Lancaster—but many, and myself among them, regretted the passing over of Higson.

The question of the captaincy gave us much thought. Since Jardine's reign England had had three Captains—Wyatt, Allen, and Robins—and now Hammond, who in the previous autumn had announced his intention of playing in future as an amateur, was another candidate, and a strong one, with an outstanding record, being an automatic choice for any England Eleven, and with previous experience as Captain of Gloucestershire.

The Test Trial was spoilt by the weather, for the first two days were very cold, with a thirty-mile-an-hour wind from the west, which meant hard work for the bowlers at the Nursery end. The fielding was much below the standard expected, but the cold and the wind had much to do with this. Wright, of Kent, was the find of the match. Bowling leg-breaks, with an occasional googly, at medium pace, he kept a length for the most part, but he experienced cruel luck, four catches and one chance of stumping being missed off him. He looked the sort of bowler who might turn a game in a few overs. Pollard, of Lancashire, a persevering and accurate fast-medium bowler, obtained the wickets—all clean bowled—of Hardstaff, Ames, and Brown in four balls. The scores were The Rest 298 (Paynter 79) and 188 for three wickets (Fishlock 109, not out), England 377 (Hammond 107, Edrich 80). Hammond was rather lucky, for he was missed four times and was in trouble with Wright, a feather in that bowler's cap, for there is no finer player of 'twisty stuff' than Walter.

A few days later the Selectors chose Hammond to captain England in the first Test. With Voce unable to play at this period of the season because of a strain, and Allen and Bowes also *hors de combat*, our bowling was a problem, but we felt that we had a powerful batting side, even though Leyland was suffering from a badly strained shoulder and did not run into form until the beginning of July. Wright, on his form in the Trial, had fairly won a place, Farnes was the fast bowler, Verity the left-hander, with Sinfield to supply accuracy of length, plus Hammond and Edrich, a tearaway, whirlwind bowler, fast for a few overs, in support.

For the second Test only one change was made in the England

Eleven, Wellard replacing Sinfield. We won the toss, and lost three wickets for 31 runs. McCormick, bowling very fast, with a beautiful action, made the ball swing in to the batsmen and rise awkwardly. He had Hutton and Barnett caught at short leg, and Edrich was bowled in trying to hook. At this point Hammond was joined by Paynter, and they put on 222 runs in just over three hours. Hammond was at his best, cool and unruffled and masterly both in defence and stroke play. He was never once beaten by O'Reilly, or any other bowler, and he drove Fleetwood-Smith hard and often, one extraordinarily powerful stroke hitting the boundary near the screen and ricochetting along the rails, to be picked up behind extra-cover. Paynter once again proved his worth in a masterly innings of 99, in which he hit a six and thirteen fours. At the drawing of stumps the score was 409 for five wickets (Hammond 210, not out). Curiously enough he made 70 runs before lunch, 70 between lunch and tea, and 70 between tea and six-thirty. As he came through the pavilion gate the members of the M.C.C. rose to him. Ames batted very well, but just before the end he called his partner for a short run, and Hammond pulled a muscle in his leg.

On the second day the cricket was watched by the biggest crowd ever seen at Lord's, 33,800 being the official estimate. Hammond was very lame, but he made 30 more runs before being clean bowled by a good-length off-break of McCormick's. It would be hard to imagine a finer innings on a good wicket than his 240. He was batting six hours, hit thirty-two fours, and did not give the semblance of a chance, unless a red-hot drive which split the finger of the bowler, Chipperfield, and went flying to the ring can be so called. Just before he was out he received a very nasty blow on the left elbow, and this, combined with the strained muscle, prevented him from bowling in the match. Ames was ninth out for a splendid innings of 83, and England's total was 494. Australia made a strong reply. Fingleton was out at 69, caught at slip by Hammond off Wright, and Bradman (18), cheered all the way to the wickets, played on to Verity just after the hundred had gone up. McCabe's magnificent hooking and square-cutting looked ominous for England, but after making 38 out of 51 he was out to a great catch, off Farnes, by Verity, at backward point, who held a very hard cut low down with his left hand as he fell over. Hassett made an attractive 56, but was l.b.w. to Wellard, and Wellard also bowled Badcock in the same over. Barnett was in with Brown (140, not out) at the close. Brown batted in a most polished style, but the bowlers, and particularly Farnes, seemed unable to keep the ball off his pads, and of this he took full advantage : anything on his leg stump meant runs. He also cut square effectively.

The huge fire escape in the east corner of the ground, on which was placed the television apparatus, brought the wonders of modern science before every one's eyes. What would Grace and Murdoch, Spofforth and Palmer, Trumper and Ranji, have thought of it? Perhaps from the Elysian Fields they did view the wizardry of this marvellous invention, and their shades, perhaps, were in the pavilion itself, from which they had so often emerged to give pleasure to thousands.

There was one moment on the third day when England had an opportunity of making Australia follow on. This was when seven Australian wickets had fallen for 308 runs. O'Reilly was the next batsman, and when he had made 11 he was missed at long on by Paynter off Verity. It was not an easy catch, but, misjudging the flight of the ball against the dark background of the pavilion, which makes almost every deep-field catch at the Nursery end a matter of some difficulty, Paynter moved forward, and when the ball came to him it was above his head. O'Reilly then made two huge pulled drives for six in succession off Verity, taking 16 runs off the over. Farnes, coming on at the Pavilion end, bowled O'Reilly, and had McCormick caught at short leg off the next ball, and Fleetwood-Smith came in to save the hat-trick. He was missed first ball by Compton at third slip. Rain then fell, and there was a delay of three hours. When play was resumed the Australian innings closed for 422, Brown carrying his bat for a splendid innings of 206. He hit a five and twenty-two fours, and held his bat dead straight throughout his whole innings. The rain turned an easy wicket into one soft on the top and hard underneath, and when England went in again with a lead of 72 McCormick made the ball fly very nastily. At the end of the day Barnett and Hutton were out, Edrich and Verity playing out time, and the score was 28 for two. Some people were not sorry that Compton had missed Fleetwood-Smith, for had the catch been held we should have had another half an hour's batting on a most unpleasant wicket, with the tails of McCormick and O'Reilly up in the air.

The fourth and last day was a 'thriller.' McCormick bowled

at a great pace, and half the side were out for 76, including Hammond, who was more or less a cripple and had to have a runner. At this critical point, and with the wicket still helping the bowler. Compton joined Paynter and proceeded to play an innings which Bradman afterwards described as one of the best in this series of Test Matches. He and Paynter carried the score to 128, when Paynter (43) ran himself out, and Ames was caught at slip after a very fast ball had broken a finger (146–7–6), and the time just after luncheon. In the hour of great need, however, Compton batted superbly. He met the fast, rising balls of McCormick coolly, drove grandly on either side of the wicket, and hooked any short-pitched deliveries of McCormick with the utmost certainty, invariably keeping the ball on the ground, after the manner of Bradman. Wellard made some big hits, including an on-drive for six into the balcony of the Grand Stand. He scored an invaluable 38, and Hammond declared with the total at 242 for eight (Compton 76, not out, 56 of which came from fours). He received almost as great a reception as Hammond on the first day, and he deserved it, for at a time of stress and strain he had batted with the judgment, skill, and nerve of one who had played in a score of Test Matches, and he was only just twenty years of age. In Australia's second innings Paynter kept wicket instead of Ames, and though he had not kept wicket since he was a boy in knickerbockers, he did his job well, handing on a chance off Verity to Hutton at second slip and making a catch standing back to Edrich.

I always think that there were two events which prevented England winning the rubber this season—the first this breaking of Ames's finger, and the second the Middlesex *v.* Yorkshire match at Lord's on July 16 and 18, during which Hutton, Leyland, and Gibb were so badly injured that they were unable to play at Leeds. Australia were set 315 runs to win in two hours and three-quarters. Fingleton, Brown, and McCabe were out for 111. However, the Don was there, and he and Hassett (42) made the game safe. Had Ames been keeping wicket a chance of stumping Hassett, off Wright, might have been snapped up. Edrich, bowling very fast down wind from the Pavilion end, obtained two wickets, but when time was called the score was 204 for six (Bradman 102, not out—just another Don innings!). It was Bradman's fourteenth hundred against England, and in scoring it he passed the highest individual aggregate in the series—the 3636 runs made by Jack Hobbs.

The feature of the Gentlemen *v.* Players match was H. T. Bartlett's first innings of 175, not out, out of 256. He started badly, and, indeed, he looked like being out almost any ball during the first twenty minutes he was at the wickets, the bowlers just failing to find the edge of his bat. Then suddenly he made a glorious off-drive to the ring, and from that moment he was the complete master. His on-driving brought him four sixes, two of them pitching high up in the Mound Stand, off P. Smith, and one, off Nichols, bowling at the Pavilion end, landing on the highest part of the turret at the western end of the Grand Stand. He hit five fours in one over off Nichols, and two sixes and two fours in the next over off Smith. In all he hit four sixes and twenty-four fours during the two hours and three-quarters that he was batting. A left-hander, with an immense range and power of stroke, he used his wrists as well as his shoulders in driving, and with apparently little effort the ball flew from his bat. Such hitting had not been seen at Lord's for many a long day. Yardley (88) and Hammond (46) put on 120 for the third wicket. Hutton (52), Woolley (41), and Paynter (36) batted well, but no one mastered the splendid bowling of Farnes, whose analysis was 21.3 overs, 6 maidens, 43 runs, 8 wickets, Hammond adopting quite different methods from those of Woolley, the Players' Captain, in using his bowlers in short spells. The Players' total was 218, and the Gentlemen, going in again, had scored 172 for eight wickets when the innings was declared closed. The Players were left 366 to get to win. Edrich made a splendid 78, and he and Compton (45) added 79 for the fifth wicket. Farnes again bowled well, as did Stephenson and R. J. O. Meyer, and the Gentlemen won by 133 runs.

In captaining the Gentlemen, after having been Captain of the Players at Lord's in previous years, Hammond enjoyed unique personal distinction and led the side splendidly. Few will forget the reception Woolley, whose last season it was in first-class cricket, met with on going in to bat. All the way to the wicket the crowd and the Gentlemen's Eleven cheered him, and he made a superb gesture. Standing as if on parade, with his bat at the order, he raised his cap with a rare dignity. His 41 runs were so beautifully made that a visitor from the Malay States remarked to me that "it was worth coming all the way to see that innings."

The University Match was drawn, the scores being Cambridge 425, Oxford 317 and 126 for six wickets. It was a keen struggle, however, and but for rain on the third day Cambridge might have won. Oxford were the better bowling and fielding side, but the Cambridge batting, with two such experienced cricketers as Yardley, the Captain, and Gibb, and a fine hitter in M. A. C. P. Kaye at No. 10, looked rather the stronger. E. J. H. Dixon (73) and J. M. Lomas (94) gave Oxford a good start, the score being 156 before the second wicket fell. Gibb's 122 was a splendid innings. He had an old head on young shoulders, his defence was cast-iron, and the latter half of his innings was full of good strokes. He was clearly a first-class batsman, with the right temperament for a big occasion. Yardley made 61 very good runs, and J. R. Thompson (79), a freshman from Tonbridge, batted in an attractive manner. It did not seem likely at one time that Cambridge would have much of a first-innings lead, but Kaye scored a brilliant 55, not out, by hard, straight driving, hitting a six and nine fours, and the last wicket added 51 in twenty minutes. On the last day Oxford found themselves 108 runs behind with one wicket down. It rained heavily, and play was impossible until late in the afternoon. The pitch naturally helped the bowlers, and if no more rain fell three hours and a half remained for cricket. The fifth wicket fell at 69, but J. N. Grover (35), the Oxford Captain, and P. M. Whitehouse (26, not out) put on 45, and, bad light intervening, Oxford saved the game. They had had the worst of the wicket and the light, and deserved credit for warding off defeat.

Martin Bladen, seventh Baron Hawke, died on October 10, 1938. Wherever the game of cricket is played his name is known. Captain of Yorkshire during the county's most famous days, he was also a great figure at Lord's.

He holds, with Mr Stanley Christopherson, an M.C.C. record, for they are the only men who have been Presidents in consecutive years. Lord Hawke was President in 1914 and throughout the First German War; Mr Christopherson held the Presidency from 1939 to 1945.

Lord Hawke was an ideal leader of a touring team. He thought first of others and last of himself. He kept his teams in order, but his affectionate nature and charm of manner endeared him to all, and the influence of a man of his high character on a tour overseas cannot be over-emphasized.

Prominent as he was in the councils of the Club, his name, to most people, is primarily connected with Yorkshire cricket: he was the maker of modern Yorkshire efficiency and discipline. When he took over the side in the early eighties he had a somewhat unruly element to handle, but his firmness and tact, allied with fairness, created a great eleven, which, in turn, gave him both loyalty and devotion. His contribution to the game was great, especially in raising the standard of professional conduct and comfort, together with provision after retirement, but he sometimes dwelt too much in the past, and was not sufficiently receptive of new ideas when conditions were changing. For one who had travelled so far and done so much for Dominion and Colonial cricket, it was curious that he was not always anxious to welcome Australian teams. He was fearful of the demands on his Yorkshiremen: he loved Yorkshire too well. It may be that on occasions he made speeches which were carelessly phrased and which did not convey his exact meaning, but this is a small point and does not detract from his services to cricket.

Lord Hawke's colours—light blue, dark blue, and yellow—a combination of those of Eton and the Quidnuncs—were known the world over—in Australia, New Zealand, South Africa, India, the West Indies, the United States, Canada, and the Argentine; he was the Odysseus of cricket. It was the ambition of many a young cricketer to win his colours, and those who were fortunate enough to gain his approval were lucky indeed, for a tour with him was a delightful experience from first to last—and, I may add, an education. To wear his colours was a distinction, and to some it seemed a pity that towards the end of his life he bestowed them on men who had never had the privilege of going on any of his famous tours. Somehow these colours lost something of their lustre in the minds of many who held them in high regard. In recent years his dinners at his house in London, where he was wont to gather round him his old colleagues, live in memory. He was the perfect host, and as we sat at dinner we could see a portrait of his famous ancestor, Hawke, of Quiberon Bay, the first Baron, whom he greatly resembled.

The M.C.C. tour in South Africa in the winter of 1938–39 was a great success, and the captaincy of Walter Hammond earned high praise. Of him Louis Duffus, the able correspondent of *The Cricketer* in South Africa, wrote:

He maintained rigid discipline, set his field shrewdly, and was for ever besetting the batsmen with new strategies. Indeed, he introduced new methods to South African cricket by his policy of continually changing his attack and using his bowlers in short spells. He was an exemplary Captain.

Hammond also batted very finely, and his fielding in the slips was as splendid as ever. We had so powerful a batting side, in spite of the absence of Compton, who was playing football for the Arsenal, and Hardstaff, that Yardley played in only one Test, and Bartlett never once! The wickets were preposterously perfect, absolutely 'plumb,' and with no life in them, even easier than the easiest of Australian wickets, and the batting averages on both sides were fantastically high. England led by one match in the series after four had been played. The fifth, at Durban, was to have been played to a finish. It never ended, although it lasted *ten days*: the eighth was a blank owing to rain. Think of it—ten week-days and two Sundays!

The tour went without a hitch of any sort in a country brimful of interest, inhabited by charming people, with a delightful climate. Who can forget the wonderful sunsets, "an' the silence, the shine and the size of the 'igh inexpressible skies"?

After serving on the Selection Committee for several years I thought it time that I should make way for a younger man, and Perrin was appointed Chairman in my place, with Sellers, Turnbull, and Flight-Lieutenant A. J. Holmes, the Sussex Captain, who had been a highly successful manager of the team in South Africa, to help him.

The last fortnight of the cricket season coincided with the closing phases of international tension, and led to the cancellation of several matches. We were lucky to have enjoyed almost a complete season's cricket, as for weeks, in the words of John Bright at the time of the Crimean War, "the angel of Death had been abroad throughout the land. You might almost hear the beating of his wings."

The West Indies were our visitors, and, dealing with the Test Matches, which were limited to three days each, England won the only game (at Lord's) which was finished, but it may be said that, while the West Indies improved, England fell away, and I think that a mistake was made in changing the England team which played at Lord's. That team consisted of, in the batting order, Hutton, Gimblett, Paynter, Hammond (Capt.), Compton, Hardstaff, Wood, Verity, Wright, Copson, and Bowes, and it acquitted itself splendidly, bowling with more life and accuracy than any England side for several seasons past, fielding finely, and scoring 404 for the loss of only five wickets in the first innings, eventually winning by eight wickets.

The first day of the first Test at Lord's was sunless, with a bitterly cold north wind. The wicket was of an easy pace which never really suited either the fast or the slow bowlers, the latter of whom could find no bite in the turf. The West Indies batted first, Grant and J. Stollmeyer opening to Bowes and Copson (Pavilion end). A neat catch low down with the left hand at forward short-leg, standing very close in, dismissed the West Indies Captain at 29, and then followed a long stand. At lunch-time the score was 95 for one (Headley 28, Stollmeyer 44) and it was not until 147 that a wicket fell, Stollmeyer being clean bowled at this point by Bowes, now at the Pavilion end.

Headley is a beautiful late- and square-cutter, hooks finely, and is very quick on his feet, though he uses his quickness of foot almost entirely in going back towards the stumps. He plays the large majority of his strokes off his back foot, and in this innings, at any rate, seldom used his feet to go forward. We did not see from him on this occasion the orthodox off-drive as played by Bradman, Hammond, Compton, and Hutton, among the moderns, or by L. Palairet, Jackson, and Spooner, of the past. Headley plays the ball very late, and his powerful and supple wrists impart pace to his back-stroke.

On the second day there was a rise in temperature of several degrees as compared with the Saturday, but it was a day spoiled by much bad light, play being twice interrupted—for a quarter of an hour at one period and for fifty minutes at another. The wicket played easily.

After a hard fight for a considerable time the game swung in favour of England, who by scoring 404 for five wickets put themselves in a strong position, but two catches were dropped at critical points. The turning-point of the day's play was when Compton joined Hutton, with three wickets—those of Gimblett, Paynter, and Hammond—down for 147 runs.

One could not but sympathize with our visitors, who deserved a larger share of fortune's favour, for they had bowled finely and with delightful keenness and enthusiasm, and had fielded splendidly. Constantine was not at his best as a bowler, but both Hylton and Martindale were in fine form, and Cameron—a much improved bowler since his Cambridge days—went on at the Pavilion end at 49 and did not rest until the score was 184. He kept an excellent length, and sent down 26 overs for only 66 runs and three wickets. He bowled Gimblett with his second ball, and had Paynter caught at the wicket and Hammond at short extra-cover by Grant, who set a great example to his team. The West Indies' bowlers bowled at the wickets and made the batsmen play, and until well after lunch they were on top. It was a rare struggle for runs.

Hutton (196) played a magnificent innings. His defence was perfect, and after tea he produced a great variety of strokes. He cut, he off-drove, he was strong off his legs, and two or three times he jumped out and drove the fast bowlers over their heads. Perhaps the best stroke of all was an exquisite off-drive from the ball before he was out.

Compton admittedly was lucky at the start, but very soon he was making strokes all round the wicket with that bat of his which seems to drive better than any bat that was ever made!

England are fortunate indeed in the possession of two such superb players, and Herbert Sutcliffe had been a thousand times right when four years earlier he had said that Yorkshire had a lad who would go in first for England for many a long day.

At three minutes to six on the third day England had won by eight wickets. The weather was fine and warm—a real summer's day. The wicket remained good, and the cricket was interesting from start to finish.

Headley was the first cricketer to score a century in each innings in a Test Match at Lord's. Other batsmen to perform the feat in Test cricket are Bardsley, Hammond, Russell, and Sutcliffe. His second innings was far better than his first. He played as befits a batsman who is placed by many in the same class as Bradman and Hammond. Always he carried his side on his shoulders. C. B. Fry discovered that Headley's second Christian name is Adolph. It should have been Atlas!

Gentlemen *v.* Players was a most disappointing game, and lacked the spirit of energetic endeavour and high skill of the previous year. The pitch, for the most part, was soft on top and hard underneath, and one or two of the Gentlemen were obviously not in love with the fast bowling of Bowes, Copson, and G. H. Pope. Gentlemen *v.* Players is a game of long and high tradition, and one expects much from it. That this was not forthcoming was obvious, and criticism was rife. The Players were a fine side (captained by Paynter), even if their catching in the second innings was not up to standard, and those two great batsmen Hutton and Compton, ably seconded by Dollery and Gimblett, were delightful to watch, their stroke-play being magnificent. There was some untidy bowling by the Gentlemen, but Farnes, with his great height and fine action, looked as good as ever, and Stephenson also bowled well. Wyatt received a nasty blow on an already injured left thumb in the first innings, and in the second his right thumb was the target of a fast riser, and he retired hurt. True to his reputation, he had stood up unflinchingly to a heavy bombardment. Stephenson too could not bat in the Gentlemen's second innings, because of a severe blow on his left arm. The weather was abominable, very cold, with frequent showers. The scores were Players 270 (Dollery 70, Compton 58, Gimblett 52) and 202 for four wickets declared (Hutton 86, Compton 70), Gentlemen 158 for seven wickets declared (Wyatt 35) and 154 (Bartlett 60). Bartlett made some tremendous drives, but he was missed four times. Winning the toss gave the Players a big advantage.

Oxford *v.* Cambridge, on the contrary, was a magnificent game, Oxford winning by 45 runs with only twenty-five minutes to spare. Moreover, the cricket was of good class, and must have disturbed certain critics who for some time had been decrying University cricket, writing of it in almost contemptuous terms. The fielding on both sides was splendid, and there was some fine batting. It was a hard, punishing game, and Oxford owed a great deal to the steady and persevering bowling of G. Evans, D. H. Macindoe, and S. Pether, and to the cool and capable captaincy of E. J. H. Dixon. P. J. Dickinson (100) played a very good innings, while the ninth and tenth wickets put on 95 and 40 runs. No University Eleven had ever before made so many as 384 runs in the fourth innings of this match. Cambridge were beaten, but there was not an Oxford man who did not salute them for a very gallant effort. For Oxford Dixon (75), Lomas (91), R. B. Proud (87), R. Sale (65), G. Evans (59), and J. Stanning (38 and 39, not out) all batted admirably, and the successful batsmen for Cambridge, besides Dickinson, were B. D. Carris (44 and 36), F. G. Mann

(57), A. H. Broadhurst (34 and 45), and J. Webster (60). The full scores were Oxford 313 and 273 for three wickets declared, Cambridge 157 and 384.

After many long years of waiting and disappointment—they had not won since 1908—Harrow beat Eton by eight wickets. The result meant much to Harrow, and, incidentally, did no harm to Eton. Harrow were a capital side, well captained by A. O. L. Lithgow, who finished the match with three splendid drives. Both elevens made some fine strokes, and the cricket was good to watch. There was tremendous enthusiasm at the finish. *Forty Years On* was sung, and the Harrow Eleven and Hendren, their coach, were called on to the pavilion balcony, while the crowd below roared and a few top-hats were broken.

CHAPTER XIV

The Second German War

Distinguished Visitors—One-day Matches—Glorious Finishes—The R.A.A.F.—Unofficial Tests—A Most Thrilling Match—Walter Hammond—The Second Army—The C.M.F. Team—Attendances Extraordinary—Umpires and Umpiring—Lord's under Fire—Heavy Losses

When the Second German War broke out Colonel Rait Kerr and Mr R. Aird left Lord's to take up military duties, and I was appointed Deputy Assistant Secretary, with Mr Findlay coming up once a week to guide my footsteps. I have known and loved Lord's for the best part of my life, but I was to see it from a new angle, for the Secretary's duties are concerned not solely with cricket. Lord's is an estate, and all sorts of matters outside the game demand attention. The practice ground was requisitioned and the buildings occupied by the R.A.F. at the end of June 1941, but we were able to use the playing area, the pavilion, and the stands for cricket. And here I should like to pay tribute to the consideration, help, and courtesy experienced at all times from the R.A.F. authorities.

It was realized by the Government, and by the Services, that cricket provided a healthy and restful antidote to war strain, and every year we had a good programme of matches. In addition I had the feeling that if Goebbels had been able to broadcast that the War had stopped cricket at Lord's it would have been valuable propaganda for the Germans. Clubs of all kinds—the Royal Navy, the Army, the R.A.F., the Police, and all branches of the Civil Defence services—put elevens in the field, and the Universities, except in 1940, and the Public Schools, with the exception of Eton and Harrow, played as usual in August, though not in 1944, when the risk of flying bombs was thought by headmasters too great a responsibility. And we had a new match, the Dartmouth cadets playing the Air Force cadets.

His Royal Highness the Duke of Gloucester honoured us with his presence on one occasion, and lunched with the President in his box.

Cabinet Ministers, prominent sailors, soldiers, and airmen, together with distinguished Allied officers, including a Russian General, at different times watched the games, and in May 1944 Mr Curtin, Australia's Prime Minister, came twice to Lord's. We also had the pleasure of welcoming Dr H. V. Evatt, the Australian Minister for External Affairs, while the Prime Minister of Queensland and the High Commissioners of our Dominions were frequent visitors.

A remark of Mr Curtin's in a speech will be long remembered: "Australians will always fight for those twenty-two yards. Lord's and its traditions belong to Australia just as much as to England."

Nearly all the games were one-day matches, the public took to these, and cricket enjoyed a boom. The number of close finishes was a great attraction, as the side batting first generally left its opponents enough time, if enterprising cricket was played, to make the runs necessary for victory, and time after time a thrilling finish was seen. The most exciting, though typical of many, was the finish to the British Empire Eleven *v.* the Buccaneers match, played on May 30, 1942. Just on seven o'clock C. B. Clarke bowled the last ball to Lambert, the Gloucestershire player, with two runs needed for victory. Lambert jumped out and made a fierce drive. As it rose one saw the ball clearly against the screen, and it seemed a certain six, but L. B. Thompson, running from long on some thirty yards to his left, brought off a splendid catch. A glorious finish, and as fine a deep-field catch as was ever seen at Lord's!

On the 23rd of July in the same year the match between Sussex Home Guard and Surrey Home Guard was abandoned because of the tragic death at the wicket of Andrew Ducat. He had made 29 when he played a ball to mid-on. The ball was returned to the bowler, who had started to deliver the next ball when Ducat collapsed at the wicket and was found to be dead when carried to the pavilion. Such an event had never happened at Lord's before, and the sudden tragic passing of this very popular Surrey cricketer and famous footballer, apparently full of health and vigour, was a severe shock to those present.

The match on August 3 and 4, 1942—Middlesex and Essex *v.* Kent and Surrey—saw another great finish, and on the first day (August Bank Holiday) there was a crowd of 22,000. Middlesex and Essex were left with 190 to win in 100 minutes. Edrich and D. Compton put on 68 runs in 35 minutes, but with five minutes left for play 25 runs were required, when L. Compton joined his brother. By brilliant hitting, D. Compton scoring boundary after boundary, 20 runs were added, and then D. Compton took the last over, with 4 runs to win. In a gallant attempt to hit a boundary he was stumped, and the match was drawn.

On June 12, 1943, there was another great match, between the Army and the Civil Defence. The Army declared their innings closed at 252 for eight wickets, and the Civil Defence won by six wickets, H. Gimblett scoring 124 in an hour and forty minutes by fearless hitting. He made one remarkable stroke. The wicket was pitched rather away from the middle, some fifteen yards up towards the Grand Stand, and he hooked a ball from Nichols, the Essex bowler, full pitch into the middle of the Mound Stand. Some newspapers asserted the carry to be 150 yards. It was scarcely that, but certainly near 130 yards, and, though longer drives have been made at Lord's, this must be a record hook stroke. It was a great match, and 505 runs were scored in the day!

Another great finish this year was on August 2 and 3—England *v.* the Dominions. The latter collapsed in their first innings, being out for 115, D. Compton taking six wickets for 15 runs, and were left to make 360. C. S. Dempster scored 113, a most attractive innings, but the Dominions lost by 8 runs, a wonderful catch dismissing Constantine when he had made 21. He hit a ball that actually cleared the pavilion rails, but L. Compton, leaning back against the rails, caught it one-handed behind his head. As he was standing within the boundary Constantine was fairly out, though there were protests from spectators sitting in the front of the pavilion who had overlooked the law. Constantine never hesitated, and walked back quite satisfied to the pavilion. When 14 runs were wanted, with two wickets in hand and Sismey well set, Robins, with a species of *léger de main*, which Mr Winston Churchill, in one of his books, says every great commander should possess, called on Robertson. Sismey made a couple of twos off him on the on side, was then very finely caught low down at mid-on by A. V. Bedser, and off the last ball of the over Bailey caught Roper, a well-judged catch at extra-cover, and England had won!

There were fewer Australian soldiers in the European theatre of war, than in the First German War, but the Royal Australian Air Force had some fine cricketers, and they frequently played in Service matches at Lord's. Generally captained by L. Hassett, a member of the 1938 Australian side, a neat and attractive batsman, they had a particularly fine player in K. Miller. Tall and well built, he had strokes all round the wicket; he could also bowl a fast ball and make it lift. Carmody and Stanford were both high-class batsmen, and Pepper, Pettiford, and Cristofani all-rounders. Cristofani, in a match against the R.A.F. at Lord's in 1944, took seven wickets for 39 runs, his top-spinner puzzling the batsmen. There were two fast bowlers in Roper and Williams, and a slow left-hander in Ellis, who bowled over the wicket. Sismey's wicket-keeping was a feature of the R.A.A.F.'s cricket, and he was also a capable defensive batsman. Against this combination two single-day matches against England were played in 1944. England won the first by six wickets and the second by 33 runs. In the second match Hammond played a great innings of 105, but Miller, with 85, suffered little if at all by comparison. It was clear that he was more than a batsman of mere promise.

These matches led in 1945, after a readjustment of fixtures, to the playing of five non-official Tests between England and Australia, three of them at Lord's.

Before the first unofficial Test the following cables passed between Mr Curtin,[1] Prime Minister of Australia, and Mr S. Christopherson, President of the M.C.C.:

16*th May*, 1945

Although my illness precludes me from attending official duties at present, I cannot forbear tendering my warmest good wishes to English cricket in the coming season, and particularly to all those gracious people who will assemble at Lord's, where tradition so richly nourishes and perpetuates our great game. I would be glad if my greetings could be extended to the ladies and gentlemen whom it was my privilege to meet under your guidance in May last year, and would be particularly grateful if you would convey to Sir Pelham Warner and respective captains my sincere good wishes for the reopening of a series which I hope will never again be interrupted.

Personal regards,

JOHN CURTIN

To the Prime Minister, Canberra

Your cablegram greatly appreciated by myself, Sir Pelham, both teams, and all at Lord's. M.C.C. hope always to maintain the great traditions of a game which means so much to both England and Australia. We and those who had the privilege of meeting you last

---

[1] The Right Hon. John Curtin died at Canberra on July 5, 1945.

May have the happiest recollections of your visit to Lord's. We warmly reciprocate your wish that never again will the matches be interrupted. We all wish you a rapid recovery.

STANLEY CHRISTOPHERSON
President M.C.C.

The first of the unofficial Tests, at Lord's on May 19, 21, and 22, 1945, was won by Australia by six wickets, after an exciting finish. The attendance on the three days was just over 70,000. England scored 267 and 294, and Australia, scoring 455 runs, had 107 to make for victory, but only seventy minutes in which to make them. They were made just on seven o'clock, amid great excitement, after two run outs, Pepper making 54, not out. He forced the pace in splendid style, hitting one tremendous six to long-on. The fielding of the England side was magnificent, but it was clear that our bowling was neither so good nor so varied as the Australian attack, and in the last innings Gover and Stephenson bowled unchanged. Possibly Wright might have been used when Pepper was hitting at nearly every ball.

In the third match, at Lord's on July 14, 16, and 17, Australia won again, by four wickets, though England was dogged by misfortune. Hutton scored 104 and 69, and held the side together in the first innings in a total of 254. Places were given to the Etonian the Hon. L. R. White, the Reptonian D. B. Carr, and J. G. Dewes, who had made over 1000 runs for Cambridge. None of these quite realized expectations, though Dewes batted soundly for 27 in England's first innings.

Australia were dismissed for 194, Pollard having a fine analysis of six for 75. The England side had to take the field after the first day without Hammond, who was seized with lumbago and took no further part in the match, while Washbrook, because of a badly damaged thumb, went in very late in the second innings, and batted practically with one hand. The Australians were left to make 225, and though they won, had Miller been caught at deep square leg with his score at 38, victory might have rested with the England side. Miller went on to make 71, not out. It was a fine game, but the loss of Hammond and the injury to Washbrook, two of the best three batsmen on the English side, were tremendous handicaps.[1]

[1] Neither G. Pope nor W. E. Phillipson was able to accept the invitation sent him, the former because of a League engagement and the latter owing to a strain.

The fourth unofficial Test was played at Lord's on August 6, 7, and 8. The gates were remarkable. On the first day 30,236 paid for admission, the gates being closed at a quarter to twelve; on the second day 30,937, the gates being closed at five minutes past twelve; and on the third day 23,860 paid for admission. The total for the three days of 85,033 is a record for a three-day match at Lord's. Field-Marshal Montgomery was at Lord's for a few hours one afternoon. As his car entered the Members' Gate he was at once recognized, and on his way to the Committee Room he was cheered to the echo, the pavilion standing up to welcome him. A heavy-scoring game ended in a draw, Australia making 388 and 140 for four wickets and England 468 for seven wickets declared. Rain at the start and bad light at the end of the second day somewhat curtailed play. The chief scorers were Miller 118 and 35, not out, Sismey 59, Pepper 57, Washbrook 112, Hammond 83, Edrich 73, not out, and Hutton 69.

At Sheffield, on June 23, 25, and 26, England won by 41 runs, and at Old Trafford, on August 20, 21, and 22, by six wickets, after two very keenly contested games. The scores at Sheffield were England 286 (Hammond 100, one of the best innings he has ever played; Washbrook 63) and 190 (Hutton 46, Hammond 38, Griffith 35), Australia 147 (Carmody 42) and 288 (Workman 63, Whitington 61). At Old Trafford, where 72,463 paid gate, England scored 243 (Hutton 64, Hammond 57) and 141 for four wickets (Edrich 42, not out, Robertson 37, Hutton 29), while Australia's score was 173 (Miller 77, not out) and 210 (Cristofani 110, not out). The result of these five games was thus: England two wins, Australia two wins, and one game drawn.

These games showed our batting strength, but we were in need of new bowlers, particularly a fast bowler, a slow left-hander, which we have hitherto never lacked, and a medium-paced bowler who can spin and flight the ball.

There was a great match this year on August 25, 27, and 28, between England and the Dominions. On the morning of the match Hassett, who was to have captained the Dominions, was ill and could not play, and the side elected as Captain the West Indian player L. Constantine—a well-deserved tribute to a great all-round cricketer. In a match in which 1241 runs were scored England lost by 45 runs when set to make 357. The turning-point of the match was the dismissal of Phillipson in the last innings. He went in No. 9, and was batting with great confidence when he was thrown out from deep mid-on by Constantine. It was a very near thing, perhaps the fraction of a second, and but for it there might have been a desperate finish. The tone and pace of the match were set in the opening innings by the New Zealander M. P. Donnelly, a great left-hander, who scored a splendid 133. In the Dominions' second innings K. Miller played perhaps his best innings at Lord's, scoring 185. One of his drives hit the pavilion guttering above the dressing-room, and must have given a severe shock to the B.B.C. commentators. For England Hammond, batting as only he can, made a century in each innings—121 and 102. In his second innings one of his sixes went through the door of the Long Room like a bullet, and bounced up against one of the display cases, without, miraculously, breaking the glass—a mighty blow! There was almost a riot of hitting, sixteen sixes being scored in the match, a record for Lord's, and the crowd had a feast of brilliant stroke-play.

It was cricket *in excelsis*. A *joie de vivre* in the batting sparkled through a game which fulfilled any known axiom as to how cricket should be played. With an ever-added momentum, the match moved from thrill to thrill, and gripped the spectators from start to finish. If this match was advanced as an argument for three-day Test Matches it could stand up to any objection or criticism. Many thought it one of the finest matches ever played at Lord's. D. V. Wright, who had bowled with little luck in the unofficial Tests, took ten wickets for 195 runs. He seems on the border of greatness, and perhaps with more flight and change of pace he will cross it. These qualities have marked many great bowlers—to name only four, Spofforth, Lockwood, Lohmann, and O'Reilly.

The Dominions team was made up of eight Australians, one South African (Fell), one New Zealander (Donnelly), and one West Indian (Constantine). I cannot recall such splendid hitting on any ground in the world. Under all this heavy punishment the bowlers never wilted, and the fielding remained at a high standard. When England looked like being easily beaten Davies and Griffith, by most attractive cricket, added runs fast, but it was Constantine's magnificent pick-up and return which turned the scale. That glorious fieldsman, with his long arms and catlike activity, is a bad man to run to: never attempt a run in his vicinity unless it is certain that the ball has passed him!

Here is the full score of this great match:

ENGLAND *v.* THE DOMINIONS

Played at Lord's, August 25, 27, and 28, 1945
Result: The Dominions won by 45 runs

THE DOMINIONS

First Innings		*Second Innings*	
D. R. Fell, c. Griffith, b. Wright	12	b. Davies	28
H. S. Craig, c. Davies, b. Phillipson	56	c. Hammond, b. Davies	32
J. Pettiford, b. Davies	1	b. Wright	6
K. R. Miller, l.b.w., b. Hollies	26	c. Langridge, b. Wright	185
M. P. Donnelly, c. and b. Hollies	133	b. Wright	29
L. N. Constantine (Capt.), c. Hollies, b. Wright	5	c. Fishlock, b. Hollies	40
C. G. Pepper, c. Hammond, b. Wright	51	c. Robertson, b. Hollies	1
D. R. Cristofani, l.b.w., b. Edrich	6	b. Wright	5
R. G. Williams, l.b.w., b. Wright	11	c. Hammond, b. Wright	0
R. S. Ellis, b. Wright	0	st. Griffith, b. Hollies	0
C. D. Bremner, not out	1	not out	0
Leg byes 3, wides 2	5	Bye 1, leg byes 8, no-ball 1	10
Total	307	Total	336

ENGLAND

L. B. Fishlock, c. Pettiford, b. Ellis	12	run out	7
J. D. Robertson, l.b.w., b. Constantine	4	c. Fell, b. Pettiford	5
James Langridge, l.b.w., b. Cristofani	28	b. Pepper	15
W. E. Phillipson, b. Pepper	0	run out	14
S. C. Griffith, b. Williams	15	c. Pepper, b. Pettiford	36
W. R. Hammond (Capt.), st. Bremner, b. Pepper	121	st. Bremner, b. Cristofani	102
H. Gimblett, c. Pettiford, b. Cristofani	11	b. Pepper	30
W. J. Edrich, c. Pepper, b. Cristofani	78	c. Pepper, b. Ellis	31
J. G. W. Davies, b. Pepper	1	b. Pepper	56
D. V. P. Wright, l.b.w., b. Pepper	0	b. Cristofani	0
E. Hollies, not out	0	not out	0
Byes 7, leg byes 6, wides 2, no-balls 2	17	Byes 6, leg byes 5, no-balls 4	15
Total	287	Total	311

BOWLING ANALYSIS

England

First Innings	O.	M.	R.	W.	*Second Innings*	O.	M.	R.	W.
Phillipson	16	2	40	1	Phillipson	2	1	1	0
Edrich	9	1	19	1	Edrich	3	0	13	0
Wright	30	2	90	5	Wright	30.1	6	105	5
Davies	22	9	43	1	Davies	13	3	35	2
Hollies	20.2	3	86	2	Hollies	29	8	115	3
Langridge	6	1	24	0	Langridge	8	0	57	0

The Dominions

	O.	M.	R.	W.		O.	M.	R.	W.
Miller	1	0	2	0	Miller	5	0	28	0
Ellis	4	3	4	1	Ellis	20	4	54	1
Williams	22	4	49	1	Williams	2	0	11	0
Cristofani	23.3	4	82	3	Cristofani	21.3	1	64	2
Constantine	15	2	53	1	Constantine	6	0	27	0
Pettiford	5	0	23	0	Pettiford	14	3	45	2
Pepper	18	3	57	4	Pepper	33	13	67	3

Umpires: A. Fowler and G. Beet

In 1942 R. C. Robertson-Glasgow wrote the following tribute to Walter Hammond in *Wisden*:

> His colossal achievements command the respect of every sort of cricketer.
>
> Figures must largely fill a sketch of so great a batsman, but I should like future generations of cricketers to think of him as something more than a wonderful maker of runs. For, as an all-rounder, he is the greatest cricketer of this generation, not merely in centuries, in the taking of wickets, and in the making of catches, but in his attitude to the game, which he, while drawing from its fame, has enriched with a grace, a simplicity, and a nobility that may never be seen again.

Hammond is a glorious cricketer, with a striking personality. Success does not spoil him in the least. On the contrary, as his fame grows the more modest he becomes, and he is understanding and sympathetic to those who have failed. On a committee he is sound, knows his mind, and gives good reasons for a point of view. I admire his cricket beyond measure. Everything he does is graceful, with a tremendous sense of power. There is majesty about his batting, he makes the most difficult catches look easy, and his bowling action is perfect in rhythm, swing, and delivery. Walter Hammond is *a very great cricketer*—one of the Immortals.[1]

Two laws of cricket are rarely put in operation—obstructing the field and handling the ball—but the latter law was enforced in the match R.A.A.F. *v.* the South of England on June 30, 1945. G. O. Allen played a ball from Roper, and it trickled and lay dead at the stumps, which it actually touched. Allen picked the ball up and returned it to the bowler. Roper, perhaps because he thought the bails were disturbed, or perhaps involuntarily, appealed, and Allen was given out. The umpire had no option. As he reached the pavilion Allen was asked to return, but quite rightly declined. Research into history shows that this law had not been invoked at Lord's for nearly ninety years, the last occasion being in 1857, when Grundy, playing for the M.C.C. *v.* Kent, was so given out, the score-book reading, "J. Grundy, handled ball, b. Willsher, 15."

There were two other matches of particular interest, General

[1] In all first-class cricket up to the end of the season of 1945 Hammond has scored 47,637 runs, with an average of 55. In Test cricket, not including the unofficial Tests in 1945, he has played 125 innings and scored 6883 runs, made 101 catches, and taken 83 wickets. The unofficial Tests were first-class matches, but do not count in the official records of England *v.* Australia.

Dempsey's Second Army meeting a side got together by myself and the Central Mediterranean Force opposing a Lord's Eleven. The match against the Second Army was originally intended to be a two-day fixture, but the second day was a blank owing to rain, and two one-day matches were arranged. Both games were drawn. The Second Army showed remarkably good form after a few days' hard practice in the nets, R. Sale, A. W. Allen, P. G. T. Kingsley, M. M. Walford, and L. Compton batting extremely well. They were captained by the Rev. J. W. J. Steele, the Hampshire cricketer, Chaplain to the Brigade of Guards. General Dempsey, a fine cricketer at Shrewsbury, could not be persuaded to take the field, but he honoured the first match with his presence, together with some of his Corps and Divisional Commanders. The then C.I.G.S., Lord Alanbrooke, was also present, and altogether it was quite an occasion. The Second Army flag flew from the top-gallants of the pavilion, and this flag was presented to the M.C.C. by General Dempsey, together with a plaque of oak on which in enamel were the Army, Corps, and Divisional signs.

Field-Marshal Alexander, hearing of the match, intimated that the C.M.F. would be not unwilling to throw down the gauntlet, and on August 23 and 24 the famous C.M.F. flag was in its turn hoisted at Lord's. Before the game began the President of the M.C.C. sent the following telegram to the Field-Marshal: "The M.C.C. are proud to welcome to Lord's the cricketing representatives of an Army whose peer the world has seldom seen." The Field-Marshal was immersed in more important affairs, and was unable to be present, and what a match he missed, the Lord's Eleven winning by one wicket! The C.M.F. were a good side, including the Hon. A. G. Hazlerigg (Capt.), who played an excellent first innings of 45, D. N. Moore, T. F. Smailes, W. E. Merritt, A. W. Wellard, and H. E. Dollery; while the Lord's Eleven included F. R. Brown (Capt.), M. P. Donnelly, R. J. O. Meyer, A. W. H. Mallett, T. E. Bailey, E. D. R. Eagar, D. B. Carr, and G. A. Wheatley, the Oxford Captain. One of the features of the match was the wicket-keeping of G. A. Wheatley and A. J. M. McIntyre, of Surrey. We were disappointed not to see Field-Marshal Alexander, who, like General Dempsey, gave his flag and a plaque to the M.C.C., so that in future members of the Club will be able to gaze with admiration and pride on the emblems of two of the most famous Armies in British military history.

These matches and the unofficial Tests doubled the gate money, as the following figures of attendance during the War show:

1940[1] ..	53,330
1941 ..	89,611
1942 ..	125,562
1943 ..	232,390
1944 ..	167,429
1945 ..	413,856

The drop in 1944 was due to flying bombs. The total paying attendance during the War was 1,082,178, and £23,000 was raised for war charities. So great were the crowds[2] for the unofficial Tests that more than once the gates had to be closed at noon.

Any comment on war-time cricket at Lord's would be incomplete without mentioning the names of A. Fowler and G. Beet, who, umpiring in match after match, became an institution; and here I would like to dwell on the general excellence of umpiring. It has been very good for many years, and never more so than to-day. To take an example from my own personal experience. In all the many hundreds of innings I have played at Lord's I have only once known of a wrong decision, and that was in my favour! The match was Middlesex *v.* Nottinghamshire in 1897, and when I had made but a single I was 'plumb' out l.b.w. to Attewell. The ball pitched on the middle and leg stumps, came quickly off the pitch, kept low, and hit me just above the ankle. The umpire judged me not out, and I am almost ashamed to confess that I subsequently made 176! If I may go farther afield than Lord's, on only two occasions have I been the victim of a wrong decision. The first occasion was at Taunton in 1900, when I hit the ball and was given out l.b.w., but as the bells in the church hard by were ringing for a wedding at the time the umpire —a very good one—had every excuse. The second was in a far country, when I was given run out when almost past the bowler's crease. I remember short leg laughing as I passed him on my way to the pavilion, and saying, "Bad luck! You were almost

[1] The figure for 1939 was 330,616.

[2] In 1940 and 1941 all officers and men in uniform were admitted free, and the charge to the public was only 6*d.* In 1942 and 1943 the Services, as well as the general public, were charged 6*d.* In 1944 and 1945 the gate was raised to 1*s.* At all times officers in uniform in the British and Allied forces were given the *entrée* to the pavilion.

in the stand!" Think of it—only three wrong decisions in a playing career in first-class cricket which extended from 1894 to 1920!

In a recent conversation with Walter Hammond he told me that his experience was much the same, that, in fact, he found it difficult to recall an occasion on which a wrong decision had been given, whether in his favour or against him. In earlier days this high standard of umpiring did not always prevail, and there were occasionally rather unpleasant incidents, but the selection of umpires is now very carefully made. And it is hard work indeed —both mentally and physically—for the hours are long, and every second of them umpires have to have their eyes 'skinned' and their attention riveted on every ball.

To these umpires cricket owes a great debt of gratitude, for nothing spoils a match more than a lack of confidence in the umpiring. I am glad, indeed, to pay a tribute to a fine body of men.

Anxiety must have been felt all over the Empire for the safety of Lord's in the Blitzes. Though Lord's received the scars of war, happily it escaped any major disaster, though it is true that all round and outside the ground itself, and, indeed, at its very gates, there was heavy damage. The first bomb was in Wellington Road on September 16, 1940. On October 16 of the same year an oil bomb fell on the ground some thirty yards to the left of the bowling screen. Out of this, when it burst, came a photograph of a young German officer with "With Compliments" written across it.

On November 1 Lord's had a lucky escape when a high-explosive bomb wrecked the Synagogue and a corner of the flats opposite the Grace gates.

On December 9 another high-explosive bomb, weighing 1000 lb., fell just short of the stand in the north-east corner of the ground, digging an enormous crater, which the groundsmen filled up so well that no trace of it remains to-day.

Houses belonging to the M.C.C. adjoining the ground were severely damaged at different times, and No. 6 Grove End Road was completely destroyed. In an incendiary raid the Secretary's house, the Grand Stand, and the roof of the pavilion were set on fire, and a hole in the ceiling of the Long Room still remains as a witness to this visitation. The Lord's Fire Fighting Squad, aided by the R.A.F. and the N.F.S., did splendid work on these occasions. No. 6 Elm Tree Road was wiped out by an incendiary bomb in March 1945.

When the flying-bomb attacks began many fell in and around Regent's Park. Lord's had a narrow escape when such a bomb demolished the wing of a block of flats at the corner of Grove End Road, and on the other side of the road broke the windows of the Roman Catholic Church, built in 1836, which appears in all the early prints of Lord's. Had this bomb burst a hundred yards nearer the pavilion might have been seriously damaged. As it was, the roof of the tennis court suffered severely. On July 29, 1944, during the Army *v.* R.A.F. match, a flying bomb looked like landing on the practice ground, but fell some two hundred yards short, in Albert Road. The players and umpires lay on the ground, and spectators were to be seen in curious postures in the pavilion and round the ground. Characteristically, perhaps, the first ball bowled when the game was resumed was hooked by J. D. Robertson for six, amid tremendous cheers.

The figure of Father Time on the Grand Stand, as we have seen, was dislodged during the War, but not strictly by enemy action. A balloon in a gale got loose from its moorings, and the cables, becoming entangled with the figure, wrenched it from its setting, and it slid down into the seats in front of the Grand Stand.

The cricket world suffered many losses during the War. Of those who fell in action Hedley Verity, Maurice Turnbull, and Kenneth Farnes, who was killed in a flying accident, were well-known figures at Lord's. Verity's death recalled that of Colin Blythe, another great left-hander, in the First German War. His feat in the Test Match at Lord's against Australia, when he took fifteen wickets for 104 runs, has already been mentioned. Death also removed F. G. J. Ford in 1940 and J. T. Hearne in 1944. Francis Ford, 6 feet 3 inches in height, was a great left-handed batsman. He was not a good starter, but once set was a most attractive player and a very fast scorer. He played many brilliant innings for Middlesex, and batted extremely well in the Gentlemen and Players match of 1897.

J. T. Hearne was essentially a Lord's cricketer, where he took more wickets than any other bowler. His beautiful method was a model for all time, his rhythm in action, lovely swing, and control of pace and length being as near perfection as any bowling could be.

Another professional identified with Lord's, G. J. Thompson, died in 1943. His all-round play had much to do with the promotion of Northamptonshire to the first-class counties, and he was an outstanding player for many years. In the following year died two well-known Kent players—W. M. Bradley, the fast bowler, and G. J. V. Weigall. "Gerry" had hosts of friends in the pavilion, where his odd metaphors and pungent criticisms were a delight to a large circle. Voluble and pleasantly dogmatic, he accompanied his words by dramatic action with any weapon at hand, and he will be sadly missed. If his exuberant theories seemed at times a little wild there was a vein of common sense and much knowledge behind them, and many of his dictums had a touch both of originality and genius.

Australia too had grievous losses of players who had made their mark at Lord's. In 1940 died W. P. Howell, a fine medium-paced bowler, M. A. Noble, one of her greatest all-rounders and a fine captain, and in 1943 T. W. Garrett and Ernest Jones. Garrett was a member of the 1878, 1882, and 1886 sides, and took part in the famous M.C.C. match at Lord's in 1878 which established the greatness of Australian cricket. When I went to Australia in the winter of 1932–33 I had many talks with him. He was then seventy-four years of age. With all the mellowness of age, I found him a delightful companion, and his reminiscences of the great matches in which he played were fascinating. Ernest Jones was the fastest bowler who ever came from Australia, at times as fast as Kortright. He seldom failed at Lord's, where his bowling often rocked the defences of the opposing side.

In 1944 died C. T. B. Turner, the "Terror." His performances in England challenge comparison with any other Australian bowler. Medium to fast, W. G. thought it a toss-up between him and Spofforth for first place among Australian bowlers.

It is a curious fact that though Australia has had few great left-handed bowlers—indeed, J. J. Ferris alone is in a class with the long list of English left-handers—she has always had a great succession of left-handed batsmen, and one of these, Clement Hill, died in 1945. Clem Hill, the pride and joy of Adelaide, was a great artist: with his flashing blade, he was almost a left-handed Trumper. Most judges would say that he was the most attractive of all the Australian left-handed batsmen; he was as efficient as any in defence, and had a greater brilliancy in attack. He was something of a combination of Bardsley and our own Woolley, and there is no higher praise than this.

Two great personalities at Lord's passed away during the War —A. J. Webbe and Sir Kynaston Studd. Webbe died on February 19, 1941, at the age of eighty-six. He was three years in the Harrow Eleven—Captain in 1874—and four years in the Oxford Eleven—Captain in 1877 and 1878. He first appeared for Middlesex in 1875, and followed his great friend I. D. Walker as Captain in 1885. He succeeded R. D. Walker as President of the County Club in 1922, retiring in 1937. His membership of the M.C.C. Committee began in 1886, and at the time of his death he was a Trustee of the Club. I do not think I am exaggerating when I say that to know "Webbie" was to love him. He possessed charming manners, he had the kindest of hearts, and he was a veritable champion in pleading the cause of anyone who was in trouble. The great gift of sympathy was his in full measure, and if at times some thought that he allowed his heart to govern his head, well, we all know what Tennyson wrote of kind hearts. He was my friend for nearly forty-seven years, and a truer and more loyal friend there could not be.

On the death of Sir Kynaston Studd on January 14, 1944, *The Times* asked me to write an obituary notice, and I reproduce it below:

> Sir Kynaston Studd was a man of such fine character that no one who met him could fail to be influenced by him. One felt instinctively that here was an individual of no ordinary mould, with great charm of manner and possessed of a most generous heart. I have often heard tell of his many acts of kindness, and one who knew him intimately told me that if ever there was a saint on this earth it was he. His courage was amazing and the admiration of all. In recent years he had met with more than one very painful accident, but he never complained and was always cheerful and happy. As recently as last Monday he attended a committee meeting of the M.C.C., of which he had been a member since 1878. He loved Lord's, and almost always sat in the right-hand corner of the committee room. I was fond of persuading him to talk of his Cambridge days, and particularly of the game at Fenner's against the Australians in 1882, when he and his brother, G. B., put on 106 for the first wicket in the second innings of Cambridge. The match, which Cambridge won by six wickets, was a triumph for the Studd family, G. B. scoring

42 and 48, J. E. K. 6 and 66, and C. T. 118 and 17, not out, and taking eight wickets.

But I need not dwell further upon his cricket, except to say that the Studd family ranks with the Graces, Lytteltons, Steels, Fosters, and Ashtons as the greatest cricketing families. When he was Lord Mayor of London Sir Kynaston Studd gave a great dinner in honour of cricket, and of all the excellent speeches on that memorable evening, his, in reply to the toast of his health, was the finest. It was delivered with rare charm and was so modest in tone. He described himself as "a very ordinary person," and I cannot imagine that there was ever a better man in the best sense of that expression.

At the Memorial Service to him Canon F. H. Gillingham gave the address, and no one who was present will ever forget it, for the Canon is one of the best preachers in England.

A. C. MacLaren died on November 17, 1944, within a few days of his seventy-third birthday. He captained England against Australia on twenty-two occasions, and with his fine features, beautiful eyes, and commanding personality looked every inch a leader. He will always remain one of the great figures in a great era in English and Australian cricket.

I ceased to be Deputy Secretary at Lord's in September 1945, hoping that I had done something for the game I have always loved and for the place where I have spent so many happy hours on and off the field. I took immense pride in working for the great Club, and my work was made very much easier by the help and loyalty of the staff.[1]

Lieutenant-Colonel H. A. Henson, the Secretary of the Gloucestershire C.C.C., who had recently been invalided out of the Army, joined me in January 1944, and remained until we both departed twenty months later. With his white hair, soldierly carriage, and suavity of manner, he soon became a well-known figure. He was a very hard worker, who, delighted at finding himself at Lord's, at all times gave me wholehearted support and took a great deal of work off my shoulders. His energy was amazing, and his knowledge of how best to utilize the space available often eased the problem of accommodation for spectators.

Colonel Rait Kerr, when his duties brought him nearer the vicinity of Lord's, was often in and out, and in the midst of all

[1] For the work of the staff see Appendix VI, pp. 284–285.

his very important Staff work found time to give his attention to many matters. He can draw up an important memoranda or write minutes literally in a few minutes.

And, finally, from the President of the Club, Mr Christopherson, and from the Committee I received every encouragement, courtesy, and kindness. At one time they were inclined to think that I was too optimistic and too ambitious in regard to the list of matches, but as good sides followed one another and the crowds grew in size their enthusiasm blended with mine. The President, though often very far indeed from well, was a great supporter of these matches, and on Saturdays was always at Lord's before play began. He followed the games with almost as much keenness as in the days when he used to bowl for England and for Kent. My work was made all the more pleasant by the fact that one was working not only for the Club, but under extraordinarily nice people. No human institution is perfect, but it would, in my opinion, be impossible to find nicer men than those who constitute the government of Lord's. To them I tender my most grateful thanks.

APPENDIX I

A Diary of Main Events

1787. Formation of the M.C.C. The first Lord's (Dorset Square).

1792. First century scored at Dorset Square.

1805. First match between Eton and Harrow.

1806. First match between Gentlemen and Players.

1811. The second Lord's, North Bank, St John's Wood.

1814. The present Lord's opened.

1816. E. H. Budd scores the first century.

1820. W. Ward scores 278.

1822. B. Aislabie elected Hon. Secretary.

1825. Pavilion and all records destroyed by fire.
C. J. Barnett first President.

1827. Round-arm bowling introduced.
First Oxford and Cambridge match.

1832. Death of Thomas Lord.

1837. Jubilee match.

1838. First stone of the tennis court laid.

1842. R. Kynaston elected Hon. Secretary.

1848. Lord's drained for first time.

1854. Last of the old Schools' week.

1855. First match between Rugby and Marlborough.

1858. A. Baillie elected Hon. Secretary.

1863. R. A. Fitzgerald elected Hon. Secretary.

1864. Lease relinquished by J. H. Dark to the M.C.C.

1866. Purchase of freehold for £18,333.
Over-arm bowling legalized.

1868. New Tavern erected.
Comforts of the Press considered for the first time.
Position of Secretary ceased to be honorary.

1871. Turnstiles first used.

1873. Ground relevelled.

1876. H. Perkins appointed Secretary.

1877. Middlesex begin playing their matches at Lord's.

1884. First Test Match between England and Australia.

1887. Centenary of the M.C.C.
Henderson's Nursery purchased.

1888. One hundred Life Members at £100 each elected, and entrance fee raised from £1 to £5.

1889. Five balls to the over legalized.

1890. Present pavilion built.

1891. Site of the Clergy Orphan School secured.

1893. First match between Cheltenham and Haileybury.

1895. Follow-on law altered.

1898. F. E. Lacey appointed Secretary.

1899. Mound Stand built on site of tennis court.

Albert Trott hits a ball over pavilion.

1900. Follow-on law again altered.

Six-ball over introduced.

Two hundred Life Members elected at £200 each, in order to pay for Mound Stand.

1901. Proposal to alter l.b.w. law rejected.

1902. Proposal to widen width of wicket by one inch rejected.

Bowling crease increased in length by two feet.

Easter cricket classes established.

1903. M.C.C. send their first team abroad to Australia.

1907. First Test Match between England and South Africa.

1910. Power given to declare innings closed at any time on second day of three-day match.

Permission given to cover bowler's run-up to the wicket *and 3 feet 6 inches, not more*, in front of popping-crease.

1914. First match between Tonbridge and Clifton.

1926. W. Findlay appointed Secretary.

1927. First match between Beaumont and Oratory.

1928. First Test Match between England and West Indies.

1931. First Test Match between England and New Zealand.

Stumps heightened and widened by one inch—to 28 inches and 9 inches.

Maximum rolling of pitch between innings reduced from ten to seven minutes.

1932. First Test Match between England and India.

1935. Trial given to new l.b.w. proposal.

1936. Colonel R. S. Rait Kerr appointed Secretary.

1937. 150th anniversary of M.C.C.

L.b.w. law altered after two years of experimental trial.

APPENDIX II

The Long Room Pictures

By Viscount Ullswater, P.C., G.C.B.

The pavilion at Lord's, built in 1890 in order to accommodate the largely increased number of members of the Club, contains a very striking feature in its Long Room. The room is over a hundred feet long, and occupies the whole of the ground floor between the two towers. During a match it is the rendezvous of members, who can obtain a fine view of the whole field from the windows, exchange their criticisms and prophecies, partake of such refreshment as may be required to invigorate their enthusiasm or dispel their depression, renew old or make new acquaintance-ships, and study the tape records of the progress of matches in other places. During the intervals the collection of pictures on the walls of the Long Room, as well as those in other parts of the building, affords much interest and some amusement to the connoisseurs and amateurs of the game. When Sir Spencer Ponsonby-Fane started the collection, about 1864, he found that the pictorial property of the Club was limited to two pictures only, both by Francis Hayman, R.A., but both of considerable historical interest. It was a labour of love to Sir Spencer to look out for cricketing pictures, portraits, or prints as they came up for sale at the auction-rooms or in the dealers' showrooms, and as he was able to persuade the Committee to become the owners of many of them the Club soon became possessed of a most interesting and valuable collection, to which the generosity of private donors has added a large number. To Sir Spencer's industry and research the Club is indebted, also for the portraits of former Presidents which hang in the Committee Room at the south end of the building—but that is another story. The pictures in the Long Room may be divided into portraits and landscapes, with only one or two 'subject' pictures as well.

Prominent among the portraits is that of the foremost champion of the game, Dr W. G. Grace. It was painted by Archibald Stuart-Wortley, the well-known painter of sporting subjects, and was subscribed for by some three to four hundred members, and presented by them to the Club. It depicts W. G. at the wicket in the centre of Lord's ground, standing ready to play the ball, in the correct position, his right foot behind the popping-crease, left foot slightly advanced, with toes off the ground, his left shoulder well forward and head slightly turned to the bowler.

His browned, brawny arms (sleeves turned up above the elbow), his massive frame and powerful shoulders, look like the embodiment of strength and drive. Woe betide a loose ball! If on the leg side it will infallibly fly to the boundary just below the old tennis-court and clock, which are depicted in the distance, especially as there seems to be no fielder (or even an umpire) shown in the picture who could intercept a fourer. It has been critically observed that the clock appears to point to 2.30, an hour at which there was never any play in W. G.'s time at Lord's. But this is hyper-criticism! The champion is wearing brown boots, a sign that the fashion of the pipe-clayed boot or shoe had not then come in. A fair criticism of the picture is that the boundary appears rather too distant, the stretch of green from the wicket to the tennis-court, where the Mound Stand now raises its ugly height, being excessive. For an artistic production the colouring is rather gaudy—the grass is very, very green, the red-and-yellow cap (the M.C.C. colours) very bright, the clothes very white, and the arms very brown—but as a likeness of the "Old Man," as he came to be familiarly called, "in his habit as he lived," it is incontestably a most satisfying presentment.

The picture of Lord Harris is by Arthur Hacker, R.A. There is no special cricket feature in this portrait. It is a pleasant, genial portrait. One would not guess that from 1868 to 1926 Lord Harris had played the game of cricket. The picture represents him leaning back in rather a *négligé* attitude, showing a considerable expanse of white waistcoat, in the armhole of which his thumb is temporarily resting, ready to talk of "short runs" and long hits, or of the past and present doings of the Club and its financial prosperity.

His immediate predecessor as Treasurer, Sir Spencer Ponsonby-Fane, is represented in a portrait painted for the Club by W. W. Ouless, R.A., in the Diamond Jubilee year. It is a good but not striking likeness. Sir Spencer had a very mobile mouth, often on one side, which gave him a whimsical, playful expression, but the artist has not caught this side of his physiognomy—perhaps he thought the mouth out of drawing. The light colour of the grey suit, too, is so accentuated as to distract the eye from its proper target—namely, the face of the sitter. "Spencer," though only a name to modern cricketers, was a very familiar figure at Lord's for over seventy years. Elected in 1840, he was appointed Treasurer in 1879, and from that time until his death in 1915 devoted time, energy, forethought, and care to the interests of cricket in general and of the M.C.C. in particular. But cricket was not his only occupation. He was an officer of the Lord Chamberlain's Department, and was constantly in attendance upon the sovereign at official functions. He was also a keen amateur actor, and was one of the founders of the Old Stagers, who during the Canterbury Week provided theatrical entertainments in the evenings for those who had been playing or watching cricket during the day.

A later addition to the portraits is one by Francis Dodd, R.A., of A. J. Webbe, a figure well known at Lord's from the time when he first played as a Harrow boy until 1900, when he retired from first-class cricket. Middlesex owes a great deal to him for past services, and it was only fitting that this portrait, presented by members of the Middlesex C.C.C., should find a place on the walls of Lord's, with which he was for so many years closely associated. It is a good likeness and a pleasing portrait. He sits facing the spectator, in a blue suit, his flannels finally laid aside, the embodiment of friendliness and bonhomie.

Besides the portraits referred to, there is a miscellaneous collection of portraits of famous cricketers: Beldham, who played for England in 1787, and was well known as "Silver Billy," from the very light colour of his hair; Alfred Mynn, of Kent fame, a demon bowler and a hard hitter to boot; Benjamin Aislabie, who played his last match in 1841, being then sixty-seven years of age, and served as Honorary Secretary of the Club from 1822 to 1842; George Parr, of Nottinghamshire, for many years reckoned as the best batsman in England; John Wisden, of Sussex, successful with bat and ball; the Hon. Robert Grimston, a great patron of the game, and President of the Club in 1883, whose heart was in Harrow cricket, and so deeply engaged therein that he often found it difficult to watch the Eton *v.* Harrow match when fate was adverse to his favourite school; V. E. Walker, of Harrow and Middlesex, who played for the Gentlemen when he was only nineteen—a first-rate lob bowler and field; R. A. H. Mitchell, of Eton, commonly known as "Mike," who was to Eton what Bob Grimston was to Harrow—a painstaking coach, and often an agonized spectator at the crucial school match; Colonel Henry C. Lowther, who played much for the M.C.C. early in the nineteenth century, but whose title to fame rests less on his performances in the cricket-field than in the House of Commons, where he sat for fifty years without making a speech.

But in addition to the above-mentioned portraits of well-known performers with bat and ball there are several pictures of interest and merit, of which only a few can be selected for attention. There is a delightful picture attributed to Gainsborough, and said to represent the Prince of Wales who became George IV. It was presented to the Club by Mr H. Smith Turberville, and depicts a youth with long and fair hair in a picturesque blue coat, yellow waistcoat and breeches, and black shoes, leaning upon a curved bat. He is placed in a landscape which, though beautiful to look at, seems hardly suitable for cricket, as there is a substantial tree in proximity to the wicket (three stumps with a stick across), and immediately adjacent thereto a big stub or two, with a group of vegetation not usually found on a well-conducted cricket-pitch. Gainsborough, or whoever the painter, was evidently more inclined for artistic effect than accurate realism. The colouring, however, is soft and harmonious, the composition agreeable, and the effect satisfactory. This charming picture has been reproduced in colour, and copies are available to a purchaser.

Tossing for Innings, by R. James (about 1850), is an extremely pleasing picture, perhaps the most delightful picture of the collection. It represents four ragged boys on a common. One has just tossed a bat up in the air and is watching it; so are two of the others, while the fourth is occupied in piling together the coats which the boys have taken off in order to make a rustic wicket. The composition is altogether attractive. It tells its little story of youthful and bucolic enthusiasm with simplicity and charm.

Portrait of a Boy, attributed to Hoppner, will also arrest the attention of the picture-lover. It represents a youth in a yellow waistcoat and brown breeches, with a ruffle round his throat, holding a bat over his right shoulder. It is evidently well painted, but the general effect is somewhat marred by the addition of a big dog in the foreground, who seems as much out of place in the cricket-field as he would be on a racecourse.

Lewis Cage is a copy by Mrs Hughes D'Aeth of a picture by Francis Cotes, painted in 1768. Cotes was a fine portrait-painter in his day, and his pictures are still much admired, though it must be confessed that the crude colour of this one is disappointing. The subject represented is a small full-length of a youth, in green jacket and breeches, with black buckled shoes, his left stocking slipping down his leg and exposing a bare knee. The left hand rests on his hip, and his right holds a bat, in the transitional stage of development from the curved to the straight form, with much wood in it. The artist's name and date are on the bat. Again a big dog appears, but what is more interesting is a representation of the wicket then in use. It consists of two crutched sticks about a foot high, with a long cross-stick laid over the crutches. This was one of the early forms of wicket. An earlier form was in the nature of a hoop, under which was the popping-hole, into which, while the run was being made, it was the endeavour of the fielding side to hole the ball. It is possible that this idea was derived from the game of golf, a more ancient pastime than cricket. At all events, it was from this term that 'popping-crease' is derived. It is believed that the popping-hole was discontinued in about 1775, and that the third stump then took its place.

One of the figures which should be noted is a curious and remarkable one. It represents a gentleman in a dancing-master attitude, with left leg far advanced, wearing a tightly buttoned double-breasted blue swallow-tail coat, big white choker, dark khaki breeches, and white stockings, a dress not conducive to much freedom of action. His feet are of abnormal, even ridiculous length, and he wields a bat which, looking like Hercules' club, is of gigantic proportions, and would never pass any known gauge.

The series of landscapes, each of which has a cricket match depicted in the foreground, represents the game in the stage of its development between 1745 and 1800. As a game for boys it had been known since the reign of Elizabeth, but it was not until the middle of the eighteenth century that it became fashionable. It was, in its early stages, a combination of stool-ball, cat and dog, and rounders. Horace Walpole mentions it in 1736, and Lord Chesterfield refers to it in 1740. The earliest laws of cricket were drawn up in 1774, and these pictures are extraordinarily interesting as showing the stage of development reached by the game at about that period. From that point of view the picture give us a record of the nature of the wickets used and the dresses worn. The poet Huddesford, in apostrophizing Whitsuntide, invites that season to bring with it cricket "in slippers red and drawers white." We should now consider that costume somewhat eccentric, but the poem was written in 1791, and it is evident from the M.C.C. pictures that a dress something like the poet's fancy costume was worn. The players in this group of pictures are shown to be wearing loose white shirts, tight white or black breeches, and white silk stockings. Red slippers or shoes appear in one picture, and red or black caps, like jockey caps, are worn by the respective sides. In some of the pictures the players are wearing pig-tailed wigs, and the umpires always appear in their best clothes, generally also with three-cornered hats. The scorers, too, also in full dress, are often introduced 'notching' the runs on sticks, and sometimes appear to occupy prominent and somewhat 'unhealthy' places on the ground. This is probably due to artists' fancy, who would not omit the opportunity of showing the picturesque dresses and gaining credit for a complete realization of the scene.

It is interesting to observe that in almost all these pictures the wickets are depicted as two upright forked sticks, generally erect, but sometimes sloping backward, with a cross-stick resting on the top. In *Cricket at Hampton Wick* (in reality Moulsey Hurst) the three-stump wicket is shown. This picture was attributed to R. Wilson, R.A., who died in 1782, and must therefore have been painted before the latter date, but it is doubtful if the attribution is correct. The presence of the third stump, however, would seem to date the picture about 1775 to 1780. In all these pictures the old curved bat is in use, and some examples of this instrument are to be seen in the collection of articles preserved in the pavilion, which it would not be boastful to describe as a museum. The best of these pictures is undoubtedly that of *A Cricket Match*, by F. Hayman, R.A. It is of good, uniform quality throughout, and, apart from its historical interest, is a most pleasing bit of landscape painting.

The general effect produced upon the spectator of these ancient records is that the essentials have been very slightly modified, and that in all important elements—the function of the wicket, the disposition of the field, and the position of the umpires—the game is very much the same as it was 190 years ago. If any of these old gentlemen could return to Lord's in the year of grace he would know perfectly well what was going on, and would be quite at home if called upon to take his place in a team. Some of the later landscapes show the players wearing black top hats, white yachting caps, and sometimes straw hats, and are, therefore, interesting as exhibiting the evolution of dress in the cricket-field. Pads do not seem to appear until about 1845, and it remains for us to conjecture whether they were due to faster bowling or more sensitive shins.

The last picture worthy of attention of visitors is one which, although not introducing any form of cricket, represents tennis in an early stage of development, but combines it with many other motifs. The artist is unknown, and the date, although appearing upon the picture, is not quite clear. It was probably 1534. The distance, a coast-line with steep, rocky mountains, is most delicately and minutely painted in pale blue, reminiscent of Flemish or German medieval art. The middle distance is occupied by a magnificent castle, with gardens, pools, orchards, parks, and a maze, and the foreground represents the walls and bastions of a noble fortress, in the centre of which a game of tennis is in progress. Some of the onlookers are seated along the wall inside the court, a very dangerous spot, while one is peeping through the grille and watching the progress of the game. A remarkable feature is that several of the consecutive incidents in the story of David and Bathsheba are shown as occurring simultaneously. High up on the right hand David observes Bathsheba at her ablutions. In the distance on the left the messenger is seen delivering the King's message to the lady in her bath. In the left foreground Bathsheba and her lady-in-waiting are shown approaching, and in the right-hand corner David, accompanied by two priests in scarlet and black, said to be Luther and Melanchthon, is handing to a messenger his royal orders to Joab, instructing him "to set Uriah in the forefront of the hottest battle, and retire from him that he may be smitten and die." The costumes are of the sixteenth century, and are German or Dutch. The delicate minuteness of the painting, its mellowed colours, and the interest of the incidents cannot fail to commend themselves to even the most careless observer. The club is indebted to Mr J. J. Freeman for this very valuable contribution to the Long Room pictures.

The portrait of Sir F. E. Lacey[1] is a good likeness, though the face is rather pale, but the general *ensemble* depicts very well an industrious Secretary working at his desk. Among more recent acquisitions is a picture of the Test Match England *v.* Australia, at Lord's, in 1938 by Charles Cundall, R.A., R.W.S. The picture is good in detail, bringing in successfully the various buildings and stands surrounding the ground. The pavilion itself seems somewhat dwarfed. The green of the turf is not quite satisfactory, having a rather pale tinge, while the players seem more indicated than painted. A portrait of Benjamin Aislabie mounted on a horse in hunting kit is a pleasant picture, if the horse is somewhat stiff and the pink coat rather killed by the red brick wall in the stableyard. A water-colour sketch of Lambert reading a newspaper is a clever portrait, with light but artistic touch.

From Sir Jeremiah Colman's collection was recently purchased a picture attributed to Paul Sandby, R.A., painted by the gouache method, honey and gum being added to the pigments. It is an early picture, two stumps only being used in the match in progress. It has been suggested that the scene is on the Yorkshire wolds at sunset. Perhaps owing to some fading of the colouring, the first impression is of a match played upon the ice, an idea dispelled by the foliage on the trees. It is a picture entirely *sui generis*, and to be fully appreciated would be best hung apart from any other distraction.

Of all the paintings at Lord's none gives a better picture of a match than one by W. J. Bowden, dated 1852. The scene may possibly be Daniel Day's ground at Itchen, near Southampton. To the right of the picture there is a crowd of spectators in mid-Victorian costumes which is a pleasing medley of colour, and

[1] I am indebted to an artistic cricketing friend for these remarks on Sir Francis Lacey's portrait and other pictures.

the players and umpires are well depicted. Apparently one of the sides is a naval team, for the white ensign is flying in a corner of the ground.

Outside the Long Room, on the stairs on the left side leading to the dressing-rooms, has been assembled a collection of portraits by Nicholas Wanostrocht (N. Felix). The earliest, dated 1847, is of the Right Hon. Sir Spencer Ponsonby-Fane batting. There are three of Felix himself, one of Felix with Alfred Mynn, also Alfred Mynn, William Mynn, W. Dorrington, Daniel Day, and William Clarke. Two sketches of Brighton and a print of the All England Eleven, one of Felix's best-known compositions, all show what a veritable artist Felix was, both in portraiture and landscape.

A rearrangement of all the pictures, prints, and photographs at Lord's is now *sub judice*, and a few in the Long Room may be moved to other parts of the pavilion.

In the Long Room—that historical picture-gallery of the game—you may meet men who have seen and done things—Viceroys, Governor-Generals, Prime Ministers, Cabinet Ministers, members of Bench and Bar, sailors, soldiers, and airmen, with famous Bishops and Church dignitaries (especially during the Varsity, Eton *v.* Harrow, and Test Matches), and great Civil Servants, diplomats, famous captains of industry—men of varying views and interests and ideas, but all united in a common bond and love of cricket.

The whole atmosphere is easy and pleasant, and for that the Secretaries have been largely responsible, a tradition fully maintained by those now in office—Colonel Rait Kerr and R. Aird.

And in these days, when cricket has become the interest of the whole of the British Empire and Commonwealth, and, indeed, of almost half the world, whither should cricketers turn for guidance but to the Club which has grown up with the game, which has fostered it, and which has always endeavoured to preserve its finest traditions?

APPENDIX III

Presidents of the M.C.C.

It may be that the M.C.C. had Presidents from its earliest days, but no list can be regarded as authentic before 1825. The Presidency of the M.C.C. was well described by Viscount Chelsea (later fifth Earl of Cadogan), who was President himself in 1873, as "the Woolsack of cricket."

For some time it was the custom for the President to be elected by the members, generally on the recommendation of the Committee, but on October 3, 1840, Colonel Lowther proposed, and Mr Kynaston seconded, that Rule IX of the Club should be as follows: "The President of each year shall nominate his successor at the Anniversary Dinner." This was considered by the Committee on May 17, 1841, when, only five being present, the meeting was adjourned. The resolution was passed, however, in committee on the 24th of May. The second Earl of Craven, in 1841, was the last President to be elected, and when he was absent at the next Anniversary Dinner without naming his successor "it was agreed by the members present that a President should be chosen at a future meeting of the Committee." The only subsequent occasion on which the Presidency has been filled on the Committee's recommendation was in 1879, when "Lord Fitzhardinge, the retiring President, nominated Mr Nicholson as his successor, and in so doing said it gave him great pleasure to adopt the recommendation of the Committee, who thought it a fitting compliment to his liberality."

It was customary for the retiring President to name his successor at the Anniversary Dinner, but in 1899 Alfred Lyttelton unwittingly broke the rule by nominating Lord Justice A. L. Smith at the Annual General Meeting. The rule of the Club (XIII (*a*)) runs as follows: "The President shall vacate office at the Anniversary Dinner[1] succeeding his nomination, and shall then nominate his successor. If he omits to do so, or if the office of President be at any time vacated by death,[2] resignation, or otherwise, the Committee shall forthwith nominate a fresh President." There are only two instances of the position being held twice by the same person (except during the First and Second German Wars, when Lord Hawke and Mr Christopherson held office

[1] In recent years I have known the President nominated at the Annual General Meeting more often than at the Anniversary Dinner.

[2] The Hon. Robert Grimston is the only President who has died during his term of office.

throughout hostilities), the second Earl of Verulam holding the Presidency in 1837 (as fourth Viscount Grimston) and 1867, and the eighth Duke of Beaufort in 1853 (when Marquess of Worcester) and 1877.

The Presidency is a closely guarded secret. Not more than, perhaps, two or three men know beforehand the name of the new President, and on a few occasions the secret has been closely locked in the retiring President's breast.

The following is a list of the Presidents and Trustees of the M.C.C. from earliest recorded times to the end of 1945:

Presidents

1825. C. J. Barnett
1826. Lord Frederick Beauclerk, D.D.
1827. H. Kingscote
1828. A. F. Greville
1829. J. Barnard
1830. Hon. G. Ponsonby
1831. W. Deedes
1832. H. Howard
1833. H. Jenner
1834. Hon. A. H. Ashley
1835. Lord Charles Russell
1836. Fourth Baron Suffield
1837. Fourth Viscount Grimston
1838. Second Marquess of Exeter
1839. Sixth Earl of Chesterfield
1840. First Earl of Verulam
1841. Second Earl of Craven
1842. Earl of March
1843. Second Earl of Ducie
1844. Sir John Bayley, second Bart.
1845. T. Chamberlayne
1846. Fourth Earl of Winterton
1847. Twelfth Earl of Strathmore
1848. Second Earl of Leicester
1849. Sixth Earl of Darnley
1850. Lord Guernsey
1851. Seventh Earl of Stamford
1852. Viscount Dupplin
1853. Marquess of Worcester
1854. Earl Vane
1855. Earl of Uxbridge
1856. Viscount Milton
1857. Sir F. H. Hervey-Bathurst, third Bart.
1858. Lord Garlies
1859. Ninth Earl of Coventry
1860. Second Baron Skelmersdale
1861. Fifth Earl Spencer
1862. Fourth Earl of Sefton
1863. Fifth Baron Suffield
1864. First Earl of Dudley
1865. First Baron Ebury
1866. Seventh Earl of Sandwich
1867. Second Earl of Verulam
1868. Second Baron Methuen
1869. Fifth Marquess of Lansdowne
1870. J. H. Scourfield
1871. Fifth Earl of Clarendon
1872. Eighth Viscount Downe
1873. Viscount Chelsea
1874. Marquess of Hamilton
1875. Sir Charles Legard, eleventh Bart.
1876. Second Lord Londesborough
1877. Eighth Duke of Beaufort
1878. Second Lord Fitzhardinge
1879. W. Nicholson

1880. Sir William Hart-Dyke, seventh Bart.
1881. Lord George Hamilton
1882. Second Baron Belper
1883. Hon. Robert Grimston
1884. Fifth Earl Winterton
1885. Third Baron Wenlock
1886. Fifth Baron Lyttelton
1887. Hon. Edward Chandos Leigh
1888. Sixth Duke of Buccleuch
1889. Sir Henry James
1890. Twenty-second Baron Willougby de Eresby
1891. V. E. Walker
1892. W. E. Denison
1893. Sixth Earl of Dartmouth
1894. Seventh Earl of Jersey
1895. Fourth Baron Harris
1896. Fourteenth Earl of Pembroke
1897. Third Earl of Lichfield
1898. Hon. Alfred Lyttelton
1899. Sir Archibald L. Smith
1900. Hon. Ivo Bligh
1901. Fourth Earl Howe
1902. A. G. Steel
1903. First Baron Alverstone
1904. Marquess of Granby
1905. C. E. Green
1906. W. H. Long
1907. First Baron Loreburn
1908. Third Earl Cawdor
1909. Tenth Earl of Chesterfield
1910. Second Earl of Londesborough
1911. First Baron Desborough
1912. Ninth Duke of Devonshire
1913. Earl of Dalkeith
1914–18. Seventh Baron Hawke
1919. First Lord Forster
1920. Fourth Earl of Ellesmere
1921. Hon. Sir Stanley Jackson
1922. First Viscount Chelmsford
1923. First Viscount Ullswater
1924. First Baron Ernle
1925. Admiral of the Fleet Sir John de Robeck, Bart.
1926. Third Viscount Hampden
1927. Third Baron Leconfield
1928. Fifth Earl of Lucan
1929. Field - Marshal Baron Plumer
1930. Sir Kynaston Studd, first Bart.
1931. First Viscount Bridgeman
1932. Viscount Lewisham
1933. First Viscount Hailsham
1934. Second Earl of Cromer
1935. Ninth Viscount Cobham
1936. Sixth Baron Somers
1937. Colonel Hon. J. J. Astor
1938. First Earl Baldwin of Bewdley
1939–45. S. Christopherson

Trustees

First Earl of Dudley
Fourth Earl of Sefton
Hon. F. Ponsonby (sixth Earl of Bessborough)
R. J. P. Broughton
} Original Trustees, appointed 1864

W. Nicholson
First Earl of Londesborough
V. E. Walker
Sixth Duke of Buccleuch
Sir Spencer Ponsonby-Fane
Fourth Baron Harris
First Baron Alverstone
R. D. Walker
Third Earl of Lichfield

Sixth Earl of Dartmouth	Sir Francis Lacey
Seventh Baron Hawke	Seventh Duke of Buccleuch
Ninth Duke of Rutland	Hon. Sir Stanley Jackson
A. J. Webbe	Seventh Earl of Dartmouth
Fourth Earl Howe	Sir Kynaston Studd, first Bart.

APPENDIX IV

Secretaries of the M.C.C.

I HAVE already tried to convey to the reader something of the character and personality of the Club's first Secretary, Benjamin Aislabie.[1] He was succeeded by Roger Kynaston in 1842, after acting as Honorary Secretary for twenty years. Kynaston had the welfare of the professionals at heart, but was said to be "somewhat fussy, and on occasions there was dissent with the staff." He held office at a difficult period, and probably had a good deal to put up with.

Alfred Baillie succeeded Kynaston in 1858, but his appointment was never intended to be permanent, and in 1863, his health being very poor, he resigned. Happily for the M.C.C. a good man was forthcoming for the post in Robert Allan Fitzgerald. At first he was the Honorary Secretary, but the volume of work connected with the position increased so rapidly that on January 1, 1868, he became the first paid Secretary of the Club.

To the great regret of all Fitzgerald's indifferent health caused him to resign in 1876. The M.C.C.'s Annual Report of 1877 said that he had filled his office "to the great advantage of the Club for a period of thirteen years, during which time the number of members increased from 650 to 2080, a result mainly attributable to the zeal, ability, and popularity of the Secretary."

Fitzgerald was a good cricketer, being a forceful batsman. On one occasion he hit a ball over the old tennis-court into the St John's Wood Road.

As early as 1867 he captained a team in Paris, and in 1872 took what was to all intents and purposes an M.C.C. team for a tour in America and Canada. An amusing account of this tour was written by him in *Wickets in the West*.[2] Fitzgerald died on October 28, 1881, at the early age of forty-seven. It is interesting to recall that the familiar red-and-yellow colours of the M.C.C. were adopted during his Secretaryship.[3]

Fitzgerald's place was taken by Henry Perkins in 1876. Called to the Bar in 1858, he was well known on the Norfolk circuit, and it was against the advice of his legal friends that he threw up his profession to become Secretary of the M.C.C. Perkins made a success of his position, but he was somewhat unorthodox, and it is stated, with what truth I do not know, that when he

[1] See p. 39. [2] London, 1873.

[3] There is no record of why the original colours—sky blue—were changed.

handed over to Sir Francis Lacey he said, "Don't take any notice of the —— Committee!"—a piece of undisciplined advice which was about the last thing that would have appealed to Sir Francis.

"Perkino," as he was known to everybody, was a small, slightly built man with a great shaggy beard, almost invariably dressed in a grey suit with a tail coat, and he had a habit of rubbing his hands together. A very friendly person, he could be a little fierce when he liked, as on one occasion when some one questioned a dictum of his he replied, "Do you think I am going to be told the law by a silly beggar like you? Get out of the room!"

If ever there was a character it was he! He became something of an institution. The Secretaryship of the M.C.C. in his time was nothing like so big an affair as to-day. Seventy years ago there were only 2188 members; to-day they number 7000. And there were no Boards of Control, Advisory C.C.C., Imperial Conferences, or the organization and selection of teams to visit our Dominions and Colonies. There was enough work to do, no doubt, but the sphere, influence, and ramifications of the M.C.C. were small compared to those of modern times. Perkins was a clever and capable man who did not suffer fools gladly, but he occasionally did things which would not now be tolerated. My own memories of him are very happy.

Sir Francis Lacey, like Perkins, was a barrister, and he soon showed that he possessed remarkable powers of organization. He combined a fine brain with great industry. He was full of ideas, and the Club owes much to him. During his reign many reforms were introduced. Sub-committees were formed, the Refreshment Department was placed on a better monetary footing, the Easter classes for boys owe their origin to him, and the year after he took office the Mound Stand was built. In every way the Club's influence was extended and the ground improved.

It is, I hope, not indiscreet at this distance of time to say that when Sir Francis came to Lord's certain things needed tightening up, and tightened up they were. Reformers are very often a target for criticism, but the benefit of his efficient rule is apparent to-day. He found the finances of the Club not too well balanced, but by strict economy, which, of course, had its critics, he put the affairs of the Club on a sound basis, and his work in this connexion cannot be over-estimated. Some thought that his manner in the Secretary's office was at times a little cold and official, and, perhaps, over-rigid in interpretation of rules and regulations, but he was a delightful host, with a sense of humour and a charming smile. He was a great Secretary and a man of high character and integrity.

Sir Francis was a very good batsman. He was a rare stroke-player, and hit the ball uncommonly hard. In 1887 he made 323, not out, for Hampshire against Norfolk at Southampton. Captain of Sherborne, he was a contemporary of the Studds in the Cambridge Eleven of 1882.

W. Findlay is the only Secretary of the M.C.C. who had had previous experience of the secretaryship of a cricket club. He came from the Oval in 1920 to be Assistant Secretary to Sir Francis. His industry was equal to that of his predecessor: he never spared himself. He held all the threads in his hands, and the Club were fortunate indeed to have so courteous and charming a man at the wheel. Did not Field-Marshal Lord Plumer, who was President in 1929, say of him, "If Findlay had been a soldier I should like to have had him on my Staff"? This great compliment shows how fortunate the Club were to have had his services: he worked himself to a standstill. He realized fully the importance of cricket as an imperial asset, and his charm of manner made him very popular with the members, the officials of the various counties, and with Dominion and Colonial visitors. He radiated a most pleasant atmosphere.

Captain of Eton and Oxford, he was a fine wicket-keeper, and for a time of great service to Lancashire. On leaving he received presentations from the Imperial Cricket Conference, the first-class counties, the minor counties, and the staff at Lord's.

Findlay was succeeded by Colonel R. S. Rait Kerr, D.S.O., M.C. He was in the Rugby Eleven of 1908 and 1909, and in the former year carried his bat through Rugby's second innings against Marlborough for 54; he also headed the school batting averages that season, with an aggregate of 419 runs and an average of 34·92. Going into the Army, he made many runs in India, and for I Z. and Free Foresters in this country.

My great-grandfather, General Sir Charles Shipley, was a Sapper, and I have always been brought up to regard the R.E. with veneration: they have been called the brains of the Army, and with considerable reason. It is no disparagement to former holders of the office to say that Rait Kerr is the ablest Secretary the M.C.C. have ever possessed. His industry is like unto that of the ant and the bee combined. He is absolutely tireless, and he thinks of everything. He has what may be called a 'Greats' brain, and a man who has gained a First in Lit. Hum. can hold, and distinguish himself in, almost any position. Rait Kerr is well versed in the history of the game, his knowledge of its literature is comprehensive, and he knows a great deal about paintings, prints, engravings, and lithographs. No previous Secretary has interested himself so much in the Long Room and in the Library, which is now the finest of its type in the world. He is a master of memoranda and drafting of minutes, and you cannot stump him on the laws of cricket. In the years which lie ahead he will be a tower of strength.

The following is a list of the Secretaries of the M.C.C., with their periods of office:

SECRETARIES

B. Aislabie	1822–42
R. Kynaston	1842–58
A. Baillie	1858–63
R. A. Fitzgerald	1863–76
H. Perkins	1876–97[1]
Sir Francis Lacey	1898–1926
W. Findlay	1926–36
Colonel R. S. Rait Kerr	1936 to date

The question is often asked, "By what right do the M.C.C. govern cricket?" and the answer is, "By no right at all, for there is no 'constitution' or legal instrument, but by long-established custom and with the ready acceptance and consent of cricketers the world over."

The present arrangement works admirably, and I do not think anybody desires a change. The M.C.C. are always willing to give sympathetic consideration to any suggestions, and, generally, the policy of the Club is to advise, guide, and direct—but not to dictate. They reign, but do not rule.

The counties and the Board of Control look to the M.C.C. for a lead, and the M.C.C.'s lead has always been followed. The M.C.C. make the laws of cricket, and these laws have been revised by them from time to time, in several instances additions being made only for Australia and New Zealand, such as eight balls to the over and the 200-runs law for the follow-on.

In 1904 an important step was taken, with the approval of the counties. The M.C.C. formed the Advisory County Cricket Committee to consider cases arising out of county and other cricket.

This Advisory County Cricket Committee consists of a representative of each of the seventeen first-class counties, three members representing and appointed by the Minor Counties' Cricket Association, and at least one member of the M.C.C. The Chairman of this Committee is the President of the M.C.C.,

[1] J. A. Murdoch was Assistant Secretary from 1878 to his death in 1907, W. Findlay from 1919 to 1926, and R. Aird from 1926 to the present time. A. Cornwall Legh was Clerk to the Committee from 1907 to 1926.

or some other member of the M.C.C. Committee nominated by him, or, in default of such nomination, by the Committee of the M.C.C.

All resolutions passed by this Committee must be submitted to the M.C.C. Committee for confirmation. Their confirmation is essential to the passing of any resolution.

At the request of the counties the M.C.C. in 1898 formed the "Board of Control of 'Test' Matches at Home." This Board consists of the President of the M.C.C. (Chairman), five of its Club Committee, and one representative from each of the ten first-class counties at the top of the previous season's list. Recently the other seven first-class counties have been allowed to attend the meeting of the Board, but they are not entitled to vote. Here, again, any resolution must be confirmed by the M.C.C. Committee. The Board appoint the Test Match Selectors of the England Eleven in England.

Ever mindful of the growth of the game throughout the Empire, the M.C.C. realized the importance of having every interest represented, and thus the largest clubs outside England were invited to form governing bodies and to send delegates to an Imperial Cricket Conference, which holds usually, in time of peace, one meeting a year. The governing bodies of cricket in countries within the Empire to which cricket teams are sent, or which send teams to England, are entitled to have two representatives at the Imperial Cricket Conference.

The M.C.C. have well been described as the mother and the trustee of cricket. The sun never sets on their influence.

Until 1903 cricket tours abroad were the result of private enterprise, but it was felt, especially in regard to Australia, that the tours had assumed such scope and importance that they should be controlled and conducted by some responsible body. The M.C.C. accepted this responsibility, and from that date onward all official tours to various parts of the Empire have been under the control of the M.C.C.[1]

For more than forty years the M.C.C. have sent teams not only to Australia and South Africa, but to India, New Zealand, West Indies, the United States of America, Canada, South America, Holland, and Denmark. The Club's interest in, and care of, the game is therefore world-wide.

[1] The earlier tours to Australia involved financial loss to the M.C.C., but the tour of 1924–25 enabled the M.C.C. to restore the Foreign Tours Fund, which had been exhausted by advances, and since then each of the first-class counties and the Minor Counties Association have received, on an average, £400 after each tour. Our tours to Australia and Australia's to England have brought considerable monetary benefit to our counties. Indeed, they look to these tours for a very large proportion of the sinews of war.

The oldest M.C.C. membership list in existence is for the year 1832, and contains 202 names. The continual growth of the Club is shown by following figures:

Year	Members
1850	562
1870	1265
1890	3666
1910	5219
1920	5568
1930	5724
1945	7174

It will be observed that the increase during the period 1910–30 was only just over 500, but a Special General Meeting of the Club, held on May 2, 1934, authorized 800 additional members to be elected that year over and above the 200 sanctioned under Rules VII and IX. At that meeting the limit of the number of members was increased to 7000. In 1936 and subsequent years the Committee have been empowered to elect 300 new members in each year, instead of 200.

APPENDIX V

Test Selection Committees

1899. Lord Hawke,[1] W. G. Grace, H. W. Bainbridge.
1902. Lord Hawke, H. W. Bainbridge, G. MacGregor.
1905. Lord Hawke, J. A. Dixon, P. F. Warner.
1907. Lord Hawke, H. K. Foster, C. H. B. Marsham.
1909. Lord Hawke, C. B. Fry, H. D. G. Leveson-Gower.
1912. J. Shuter, C. B. Fry, H. K. Foster.
1921. H. K. Foster, R. H. Spooner, J. Daniell.
1924. H. D. G. Leveson-Gower, J. Sharp, J. Daniell.
1926. P. F. Warner, P. A. Perrin, A. E. R. Gilligan.
1928. H. D. G. Leveson-Gower, J. W. H. T. Douglas, A. W. Carr.
1929. H. D. G. Leveson-Gower, J. C. White, N. Haig.
1930. H. D. G. Leveson-Gower, J. C. White, F. T. Mann.
1931. P. F. Warner, P. A. Perrin, T. A. Higson.
1932. P. F. Warner, P. A. Perrin, T. A. Higson.
1933. Lord Hawke, P. A. Perrin, T. A. Higson.
1934. Sir Stanley Jackson, P. A. Perrin, T. A. Higson.
1935. P. F. Warner, P. A. Perrin, T. A. Higson.
1936. P. F. Warner, P. A. Perrin, T. A. Higson.
1937. Sir Pelham Warner, P. A. Perrin, T. A. Higson. (E. R. T. Holmes was later co-opted as an additional member.)
1938. Sir Pelham Warner, P. A. Perrin, A. B. Sellers, M. J. Turnbull.
1939. P. A. Perrin, A. B. Sellers, M. J. Turnbull, Flight-Lieutenant A. J. Holmes.

[1] The name of the Chairman of the Committee is placed first in each case.

APPENDIX VI

The Staff

DURING the Second German War, as Deputy Secretary, I had the opportunity of getting to know the members of the staff better than I had ever done before. For six years I enjoyed their help and loyalty, and I cannot adequately thank them for their co-operation and support.

The Chief Clerk, James Cannon, retired at the end of 1944, after sixty-five years' devoted service, and the announcement of his retirement did not pass unnoticed even in such far-distant places as Bagdad, Basra, and Calcutta. When he first came to Lord's Cannon picked up tennis-balls and held the heads of the horses of members who had ridden on to the ground, and he ended the trusted servant of the Secretary, the Committee, and the members. Findlay has told me that Cannon never failed to put his finger on any point which might by chance have been overlooked in preparation for a Test Match. In addition to his purely M.C.C. duties, he kept an eye on the affairs of Middlesex. Both clubs owe him a debt of gratitude, and on his leaving the M.C.C. Committee voted him a pension, a subscription list was opened, and the Middlesex C.C.C. made a substantial donation.

Mrs Belsham has a complete knowledge of the workings and ramifications of the Secretary's office, with every detail and happening at her finger-tips, and also discretion and tact beyond praise.

The getting up of teams—sometimes both teams—was an important part of my work, and here Mrs Brookhouse, and later Miss Manley, two of the lady secretaries, were invaluable. Miss Manley knows telephone numbers by heart, and is that *rara avis*, a lover of the telephone! In selecting teams during the Second German War one naturally depended on the help of Commanding Officers, and I managed to draft a letter so persuasive that it often brought tears to their eyes, and, what was more important, consent! But for their goodwill we should never have been able to get together the almost invariably good sides which took the field.

During the War we had perforce to work with a greatly depleted staff, but this served only to increase their zeal and enthusiasm. I should like to pay a special tribute to C. Wray and the staff of the Ticket Office—the 'engine-room' of Lord's—where an enormous amount of work is done in connexion with finance, members' subscriptions, passes and tickets, candidates, etc., etc. Few members know of, and therefore appreciate, the work done by this office. And then there is the Cricket Office, under the efficient and hard-working A. J. Howes, which deals with M.C.C. fixtures, the Easter classes for boys, umpires, etc. The Works Department, under A. Midy, a Chesterfield in manners; the Printing Office, under W. H. Holland, a former Royal Marine, with the efficiency of that famous Corps all over him; and the Ground Staff, with H. Gladwell[1] at their head, who, as mentioned elsewhere, came to Lord's as far back as 1896, were all very important cogs in the machine. Another who must be mentioned is J. O'Shea, the admirable and courteous dressing-room attendant during the summer, and a member of the Works Department during the winter, when he specializes as a sign-painter. His service in the R.A.M.C. during the First German War has helped to make him something of an expert in looking after the sprains and strains which sometimes afflict cricketers. These men formed a band of brothers, and though there was, of course, a healthy rivalry between departments, all combined to make the wheels run smoothly.

All in all, the staff at Lord's make up a magnificent team—a team with which I shall always regard it as an honour—and pleasure—to have been associated.

[1] A. Martin, the Head Groundsman, served in the Metropolitan Police throughout the War.

APPENDIX VII

The Ground Staff

THE Ground Staff at Lord's play, or used to play, a very important part. Lord himself started his career as a practice bowler, and Dark, who took over the lease, as a ball-boy. Among the earliest bowlers were William Caldecourt, who also umpired, John Bayley, and John Sparks. The staff was gradually increased, and at one period as many as sixty professionals were employed. Some of the best-known cricketers in the country were engaged, more particularly from the county of Nottinghamshire, and a M.C.C. Eleven at full strength differed little from an England side. Prominent among the Nottinghamshire players was Alfred Shaw, whom the Secretary (R. A. Fitzgerald) engaged after seeing him take thirteen wickets for 63 runs in a Colts match.

As Shaw became, perhaps, one of the most famous right-hand slow-to-medium bowlers in the history of England cricket his success was a triumph for Fitzgerald's judgment. Shaw was the high priest of length, and in his career bowled 24,700 overs for 24,107 runs: of these overs 16,450, or just under two-thirds, were maidens. He took 2051 wickets. Perfect length, flight, with subtle change of pace, with just enough break to beat the bat, formed a technique which baffled the greatest batsmen of the day.

His association with Fred Morley, of Nottinghamshire, was famous, Morley, fast left-hand, being an admirable foil to him. In 1887 Shaw retired to take up an appointment, mainly secretarial, with Lord Sheffield, and also as coach to the Sussex players. In 1894 the Sussex bowling was so weak that it was suggested that Shaw should be brought into the side, and after some reluctance he consented. At the time he was fifty-two years of age. He at once showed that his length was as perfect as ever, and against Nottinghamshire his analysis was 39 overs, 24 maidens, 34 runs, 7 wickets. For the whole season his record was 422 overs, 201 maidens, 516 runs, 41 wickets.

The corresponding match in the following year ended his career with a unique performance. On an icy day in May at Trent Bridge, so cold that Ranjitsinhji "kept his hands in his pockets and fielded the ball with his feet," and not a soul was to be seen outside the pavilion, Nottinghamshire scored 726. In this long innings Shaw sent down 100 overs and a ball, and in doing so sprained the sinews of his foot. In spite of this in the next match, against Lancashire, he bowled 58 overs unchanged. After a long rest he played against Middlesex, but was in such pain that he could hardly bowl, and after the match decided to retire.

Shaw's bowling will always be famous, and also his four tours to Australia, managed in conjunction with Shrewsbury. The last tour, owing to the presence of another touring side, led to heavy financial loss, though he was not well treated by what were known as Murdoch's men, who declined to play except on their own terms. At one time they demanded half the gate as personal emoluments. This led Shaw to state that his experience led him to "the strong opinion that the arrangement of visits of English teams to Australia should be in the hands of a representative body like the M.C.C."

A great Nottinghamshire player, James Grundy, was head bowler when Shaw joined the staff, and it may be that their influence secured for the M.C.C. the services of so many famous Nottinghamshire players. A famous quartette whose Christian names were William—Scotton, Barnes, Gunn, and Attewell—together with Fred Morley and Wilfrid Flowers, all played for England. Scotton was left-handed and a stonewaller, immortalized by *Punch*.

Barnes was a great all-rounder. As a batsman he had strong defence and great hitting-power, without any pretensions to style; he was a dangerous medium-fast bowler on a broken wicket. In 1887, at Lord's in Gentlemen *v.* Players, he took ten wickets for 58 runs, and in the Test Match of 1888 at the Oval seven wickets for 50 runs. For his county, the M.C.C., the Players, and England he was uniformly successful, and in Australia, which he visited three times, he twice headed the bowling averages. At Lord's in 1882, against Leicestershire, he scored 266 for the M.C.C., he and Midwinter putting on 473 runs in five and a half hours.

Gunn was one of the great professional batsmen who, in conjunction with Arthur Shrewsbury, challenged the supremacy in batting so long maintained by the amateurs. Standing six feet three inches, he had a long reach, and was essentially a player of the forward school, with a beautiful style. Unfortunately he was apt to curb his hitting-powers, and during his great score of 228 at Lord's in 1890, for the Players against the Australians, he was at the wickets for nine and a half hours. He was a magnificent outfield, a very fast runner, and a certain catch. He founded the business of Gunn and Moore, whose bats are known all over the Empire, and left the largest fortune of any professional cricketer —just over £60,000.

Attewell was the successor of Shaw in the Nottinghamshire Eleven, and his style was founded on the precepts of that great bowler—first, foremost, and always accuracy of length. As a length bowler he stood alone until the advent of J. T. Hearne.

Fred Morley, as already stated, was Alfred Shaw's companion-in-arms. He was the finest left-hand bowler of his day. An injury on a voyage to Australia, when his steamer was in collision with another, ended his career. He had two ribs broken, but the injury was not discovered by the doctors, and he actually bowled in several matches on arrival in Australia, with the result that his side was permanently damaged.

Wilfrid Flowers was below his Nottinghamshire contemporaries as a force in representative matches, but he was the first professional to score 1000 runs and take 100 wickets in a season (1883).

When Grundy retired in 1872 Tom Hearne became head bowler, the best Middlesex professional until the nineties, with the advent of J. T. Hearne and Albert Trott. Later came E. Hendren, J. W. Hearne, and H. Murrell. Tom Hearne was a fine bat and a useful bowler on the Lord's wicket, and in 1866, in his fortieth year, scored 122, not out, against the Gentlemen. Kent gave to the M.C.C. the three Hearnes, George, Walter, and Alec, F. Martin, Huish, Fielder, and Hubble, while from Sussex came G. Bean, H. Butt, G. Cox, and A. E. Relf; from Gloucestershire J. H. Board and H. Wrathall; from Essex W. Mead, T. M. Russell, H. Pickett, H. Carpenter, and J. Burns. Other famous professionals were L. C. Braund, of Somerset, G. C. B. Llewellyn, of Hampshire, G. J. Thompson, of Northamptonshire, and George Brown, P. Mead, and A. Kennedy, of Hampshire.

Many of the staff came from the then second-class counties, Derbyshire supplying William Mycroft (a very successful fast left-hander), Tom Mycroft (a wicket-keeper), G. Hay, and J. Platts, followed later by William Chatterton, William Storer (a batsman and wicket-keeper), and George Davidson. Leicestershire supplied Wheeler (a batsman), Parnham (slow left-hand), and Rylott (slow left-hand), followed by a redoubtable pair of bowlers, Pougher and Woodcock, the former one of the heroes of the M.C.C. *v.* Australia match in 1896, and the latter a really good fast bowler, J. H. King, a left-handed all-rounder, who scored a century in each innings in the Gentlemen *v.* Players match of 1904, and W. E. Astill in later years.

In 1903 arrived F. A. Tarrant from Australia, one of the greatest of all-round cricketers.

In more modern days other counties, such as Northamptonshire, Worcestershire, etc., being 'promoted,' the result has been that the Championship programme is now so long that a professional's time is fully taken up with county cricket *pure et simple*. The Staff consequently is greatly reduced, and to-day the M.C.C.

find it difficult to field a side comparable, at any rate in bowling, to those of the seventies, eighties, and nineties. The leading Middlesex professionals, D. Compton, Edrich, and Robertson, are on the Club's staff, but their *forte* at the moment is batting. We may hope that the county will again produce a J. T. Hearne, an Albert Trott, and a Tarrant.

APPENDIX VIII

School Cricket

The M.C.C. have always been keenly interested in school cricket. The first Eton *v.* Harrow match dates back to 1805[1] on the first Lord's ground, and between 1825 and 1854 there was a Triangular Tournament between Eton, Harrow, and Winchester. Rugby and Marlborough first met at Lord's in 1855; Cheltenham and Haileybury in 1893; Clifton and Tonbridge in 1914;[2] and Beaumont and Oratory in 1927. In 1913 the game between the Lord's Schools (Eton, Harrow, Rugby, Marlborough, Cheltenham, Haileybury, Clifton, Tonbridge, Beaumont, and Oratory) and the Rest was instituted, and in times of peace an Eleven representing all the schools meets the Army. During the Second German War what was called a Lord's Eleven, giving a wide area of selection, took the place of the Army. It was in this match in 1944 that R. W. V. Robins gave such an inspiring example of all-round cricket, playing innings of 43 and 127, taking 17 wickets for 131 runs, and fielding brilliantly. Boys could have had no better example of how cricket should be played than was shown by this great all-round cricketer. Lord's Eleven won by 72 runs.

The Easter cricket classes were started in 1902 by Sir Francis Lacey, and began with two nets and six boys. Just before the Second German War there were fifteen nets and 200 boys every day of the three weeks over which the classes extend. Even during the War we managed to have eight nets—some 100 boys daily—and when a land-mine exploded in the grounds of St John's Wood Church early on the morning of April 4, 1941, and shattered the arbours on the practice ground the boys were in the nets as usual. In wet weather coaching takes place under cover, the arbours, covered tea-gardens, and bars being made use of for this purpose.

Instruction is given in batting, bowling, fielding, and wicket-keeping, and the late W. Brearley, who died on January 30, 1937,

[1] Eton played Westminster on the first Lord's ground in 1799, the scores being Eton 47 and Westminster 13 for five wickets. It is reported that for this match the betting was 5 to 4 on Eton! The match was played again in 1800 (Eton 213, Westminster 54 and 31) and 1801 (Eton 99 and 81, Westminster 34 and 17). Samuel Britcher is quoted as saying that "this match [the 1801 game] was played for 500 guineas." Britcher's scores were printed by T. Craft.

[2] Tonbridge and Stowe met in 1940, and in the same year Marlborough played Haileybury, neither Clifton nor Rugby sending teams to Lord's. Charterhouse played Westminster from 1867 to 1871. Berkhamsted and Bishop's Stortford also played at Lord's during the Second German War.

was in charge of the bowling, and proved himself a most able and enthusiastic coach.

These classes have a most pleasant and happy atmosphere, and on fine afternoons, and, indeed, mornings—for cricket begins at ten and goes on until five—the practice ground is crowded with fathers and mothers, following keenly the progress of their sons. The coaching is conducted on sound lines. There is nothing stereotyped about it—an embryo Jessop is not forced to bat in the style of a Hammond—individuality and originality are given scope, it being borne in mind that no two men or boys bat exactly alike. None the less orthodoxy and certain principles are stressed. At one time there was criticism of the methods in vogue, and Lacey replied to this in a lucid article in *The Cricketer*. Whatever opinions were then expressed, he must be a captious critic indeed who to-day finds fault. These classes are doing much for cricket, and many a fine cricketer owes his skill to this early training. Lacey's successors—Findlay, Rait Kerr, and Aird—carried on the good work. Year by year competition for places in these classes grows. Lord's may well be called "the Caterham[1] of Cricket."

[1] Caterham, where the young Guardsmen are trained.

APPENDIX IX

Tennis and Rackets

At various times during its history Lord's has been used, on a few occasions, for other games or sports, such as running, baseball, lacrosse, hockey, and a balloon ascent (on September 13, 1837), and in August 1844 the Iowa Indians camped there and gave exhibitions of archery and dancing, plus "the Great Mystery Medicine Man." At one time also billiards professionals played matches on Mondays during the season. But Lord's is a cricket ground *par excellence*, and the only other game which has any real standing there is tennis, which dates back to 1839, though at one time a considerable amount of rackets was played. During the last twenty years and more, however, the rackets court, which is not one of the best in the world, has been very little in demand. The Public Schools Championship took place at Lord's in 1886, Harrow winning, but for well over fifty years Prince's, and now Queen's, has been the scene of these games. Squash rackets is a popular game, giving rare exercise, but tennis holds pride of place, and has always had a following at Lord's, the tennis prizes being established in 1867.

In 1872 the Tennis Sub-committee of the M.C.C. (Sir Spencer Ponsonby-Fane, J. M. Heathcote, E. Chandos Leigh, Sir William Hart-Dyke, and the Hon. C. G. Lyttelton) framed the laws of the game, and in 1896 the competition for the prizes, which had hitherto been limited to members of the M.C.C., was thrown open to all amateurs. The famous George Lambert was for many years the tennis master. He was at his best, perhaps, in the early seventies. C. G. and Alfred Lyttelton, G. G. and H. E. Crawley, R. D. Walker, Sir Edward Grey, J. M. Heathcote, are names that stand out during the last half of the nineteenth century, the games between Alfred Lyttelton and Grey crowding the dedans and galleries.

In the early part of this century, and between the two German Wars, great figures on the court were E. H. Miles, Major A. Cooper-Key, E. B. Noel, whose book on the game is a fine work, Captain J. B. Gribble, R. K. Price, Lord Aberdare, V. H. Pennell, W. M. Cazalet, E. M. Baerlein, L. Lees, R. H. Hill, W. D. Macpherson, E. A. C. Druce, and R. Aird. Between 1940 and 1945 the game, like others, naturally suffered, but there were always a few enthusiasts, and during the summer of 1945, it was clear that with the conclusion of hostilities the game would revive, an unofficial tournament during April drawing a considerable number of spectators. It is to be hoped that this beautiful game, with its long and notable history,[1] will never die out, but it is expensive to play, and there are few courts in England: all the more reason, therefore, why it should be supported at Lord's. On the walls round the dedans there are many interesting photographs and pictures of the great exponents of this game, including one of the immortal Frenchman Barré.

Here are the names of the holders of the Silver and Gold Rackets:

Silver Racket

M.C.C. Only

1867.	J. Marshall
1868.	G. B. Crawley
1869.	Hon. C. G. Lyttelton

Open Competition

1870–73.	Hon. C. G. Lyttelton
1874–75.	G. B. Crawley
1876–77.	R. D. Walker
1878–79.	Courtenay Boyle
1880–81.	Hon. A. Lyttelton
1882.	J. M. Heathcote
1883.	Hon. A. Lyttelton
1884–85.	J. M. Heathcote
1886.	B. N. Akroyd
1887.	J. M. Heathcote
1888.	A. J. Webbe
1889–91.	Sir Edward Grey
1892.	H. E. Crawley
1893–95.	Sir Edward Grey
1896.	Hon. A. Lyttelton
1897.	Sir Edward Grey
1898.	H. E. Crawley
1899–1904.	Sir Edward Grey
1905.	H. E. Crawley
1906.	Major A. Cooper-Key
1907.	E. H. Miles
1908.	E. B. Noel
1909.	W. M. Cazalet
1910.	Captain R. K. Price
1911–13.	Major A. Cooper-Key
1914 and 1919.	Captain R. K. Price
1920–21.	E. A. C. Druce
1922–23.	Hon. C. N. Bruce
1924.	E. A. C. Druce
1925.	R. H. Hill
1926–27.	Hon. C. N. Bruce
1930.	E. M. Baerlein
1931.	Lord Aberdare
1932.	W. D. Macpherson
1933–34.	R. Aird
1935–36.	Lord Aberdare
1937–38.	W. D. Macpherson
1939.	R. Aird

Gold Racket

M.C.C. Only

1867–69.	J. M. Heathcote

Open Competition

1870–81.	J. M. Heathcote
1882.	Hon. A. Lyttelton
1883.	J. M. Heathcote
1884–85.	Hon. A. Lyttelton
1886.	J. M. Heathcote
1887–95.	Hon. A. Lyttelton
1896.	Sir Edward Grey
1897–99.	E. H. Miles

[1] Those who know their Shakespeare will recall that tennis is mentioned in *Henry V*.

1900.	J. B. Gribble	1930.	Lord Aberdare
1901–6.	E. H. Miles	1931.	E. M. Baerlein
1907.	V. H. Pennell	1932–34.	Lord Aberdare
1908–13.	E. H. Miles	1935–36.	L. Lees
1914.	J. F. Marshall	1937.	Lord Aberdare
1919.	E. A. C. Druce	1938.	R. H. Hill
1920.	Captain R. K. Price	1939.	W. D. Macpherson
1921–29.	E. M. Baerlein		

APPENDIX X

The Refreshment Department

Before 1897 the catering was run by a tenant, who found the undertaking unsatisfactory. The M.C.C. then decided to take over the liability and to employ their own manager. For the first six years this resulted in a loss to the Club of approximately £600 a year, in spite of the fact that no rent or rates were paid, and that some of the tradesmen's accounts were paid by the Club.

In 1902 F. E. Lacey asked the Committee to allow him to supervise the running of the Department. At this time the business of the Department was confined to the summer months only, with the exception of the public bar, which was open for a few hours each day in the winter.

At this time, too, the plant and equipment of the Department were very inadequate, and neither the Club nor the Refreshment Department itself had the money to spend to bring it up to date.

In 1902 the present Manager, Mr G. Portman, came to supervise the catering for the big matches, and at the end of the season was asked to report and make suggestions for improving the plant and arrangements generally.

The improvements in plant and equipment came gradually, because, although after this the Club started to make small profits, the financial position allowed only a limited number of improvements to be carried out each year.

It was felt that the efficient running of the Department would be easier if a nucleus of the staff was retained all the year round, and the public bar and the saloon bar were to keep open in the winter. Later a bakery was built, in addition to a shop and a restaurant, and all these are working full-time to-day. Modern equipment for baking bread, making cakes, etc., is now installed, and also a large refrigerating plant, which is essential for keeping stocks not used owing to wet weather.

The difficulties of cricket catering and the financial risks involved are often not appreciated. Success depends almost entirely on fine weather on the big match days, as it is necessary to engage a large temporary staff and prepare a great deal of food for a particular day, and if that day is wet a very serious loss in money and food is the result.

By careful management and the experience gained over a period of forty-four years Mr Portman has achieved what at one time seemed impossible—the successful management of cricket catering. This is due in no small measure to his own personality and drive, and to his quite exceptional capacity for work on behalf of the Club. Mr Portman in his own line is a genius, and the Club owe much to him. On his completion of forty years' work at Lord's he was presented with a silver salver by the Committee.

The M.C.C. Refreshment Department to-day pays rent for its premises to the Club and has an efficient business operating all the year round. Plans for an enlargement of the members' luncheon room and for extra accommodation for the public have been approved and will be set on foot when conditions allow.

APPENDIX XI

M.C.C. Tours Abroad

To Australia

1903–4
P. F. Warner (Capt.)
R. E. Foster
B. J. T. Bosanquet
T. Hayward
A. A. Lilley
J. T. Tyldesley
W. Rhodes
G. H. Hirst
E. Arnold
A. E. Relf
A. E. Knight
L. C. Braund
H. Strudwick
A. Fielder
(Manager: J. A. Murdoch)

1907–8
A. O. Jones (Capt.)
K. L. Hutchings
F. L. Fane
J. N. Crawford
R. A. Young
G. Gunn
J. Hardstaff
W. Rhodes
J. B. Hobbs
L. C. Braund
S. F. Barnes
E. G. Hayes
A. Fielder
C. Blythe
J. Humphries
(Manager: Col. Philip Trevor)

1911–12
P. F. Warner (Capt.)[1]
J. W. H. T. Douglas
F. R. Foster
W. Rhodes
S. F. Barnes
J. B. Hobbs
G. Gunn
H. Strudwick
S. P. Kinneir
J. Iremonger
J. Vine
F. E. Woolley
C. P. Mead
E. J. Smith
J. W. Hearne
W. Hitch
(Manager: T. Pawley)

1920–21
J. W. H. T. Douglas (Capt.)
P. G. H. Fender
E. R. Wilson
J. B. Hobbs
H. Strudwick
W. Hitch
J. W. Hearne
E. Hendren
F. E. Woolley
H. Makepeace
C. H. Parkin
W. Rhodes
A. Dolphin
A. Waddington
H. Howell
A. C. Russell
(Manager: F. C. Toone)

1924–25
A. E. R. Gilligan (Capt.)
J. L. Bryan

[1] Douglas captained in the Test Matches, Warner being ill.

A. P. F. Chapman
J. W. H. T. Douglas
J. B. Hobbs
H. Sutcliffe
E. Hendren
A. Sandham
F. E. Woolley
J. W. Hearne
W. Whysall
R. Kilner
M. W. Tate
R. Tyldesley
A. P. Freeman
H. Strudwick
H. Howell
(Manager: F. C. Toone)

1928–29

A. P. F. Chapman (Capt.)
J. C. White
D. R. Jardine
J. B. Hobbs
H. Sutcliffe
W. R. Hammond
E. Hendren
E. Tyldesley
C. P. Mead
M. Leyland
M. W. Tate
G. Geary
G. Duckworth
L. Ames
H. Larwood
A. P. Freeman
S. J. Staples
(Manager: Sir F. Toone)

1932–33

D. R. Jardine (Capt.)
R. E. S. Wyatt
G. O. Allen
The Nawab of Pataudi
F. R. Brown
W. R. Hammond
H. Sutcliffe
M. Leyland
H. Verity
W. E. Bowes
E. Paynter
G. Duckworth
L. Ames
T. B. Mitchell
H. Larwood
W. Voce
M. W. Tate
(Managers: P. F. Warner and R. C. N. Palairet)

1936–37

G. O. Allen (Capt.)
R. W. V. Robins
R. E. S. Wyatt
K. Farnes
W. R. Hammond
H. Verity
M. Leyland
L. Ames
W. Voce
C. J. Barnett
J. Hardstaff
T. S. Worthington
W. Copson
J. Sims
A. E. Fagg
L. B. Fishlock
G. Duckworth
(Manager: R. Howard)

To South Africa

1905–6

P. F. Warner (Capt.)
H .D. G. Leveson-Gower
Capt. E. G. Wynyard
F. L. Fane
J. N. Crawford

L. J. Moon
J. C. Hartley
D. Denton
S. Haigh
J. H. Board
A. E. Relf
E. G. Hayes
W. Lees
C. Blythe

1909–10

H. D. G. Leveson-Gower (Capt.)
M. C. Bird
F. L. Fane
G. H. Simpson-Hayward
N. C. Tufnell
Captain E. G. Wynyard
W. Rhodes
D. Denton
J. B. Hobbs
H. Strudwick
G. J. Thompson
F. E. Woolley
C. Blythe
C. P. Buckenham

1913–14

J. W. H. T. Douglas (Capt.)
M. C. Bird
Hon. L. H. Tennyson
J. B. Hobbs
C. P. Mead
J. W. Hearne
F. E. Woolley
W. Rhodes
M. W. Booth
H. Strudwick
E. J. Smith
A. E. Relf
S. F. Barnes

1922–23

F. T. Mann (Capt.)
A. W. Carr
P. G. H. Fender
V. W. C. Jupp
A. E. R. Gilligan
G. T. S. Stevens
F. E. Woolley
C. P. Mead
A. Sandham
A. Kennedy
G. Brown
G. G. Macaulay
G. Street
A. C. Russell
W. H. Livsey

1927–28

Captain R. T. Stanyforth (Capt.)
R. E. S. Wyatt
G. B. Legge
E. W. Dawson
G. T. S. Stevens
I. A. R. Peebles
W. R. Hammond
H. Sutcliffe
E. Tyldesley
S. J. Staples
W. E. Astill
A. P. Freeman
G. Geary
H. Elliott
P. Holmes

1930–31

A. P. F. Chapman (Capt.)
J. C. White
R. E. S. Wyatt
M. J. Turnbull
I. A. R. Peebles
M. J. C. Allom
W. R. Hammond
E. Hendren
M. Leyland
M. W. Tate
T. W. Goddard

W. Voce
G. Duckworth
W. Farrimond
A. Sandham

1938–39
W. R. Hammond (Capt.)
K. Farnes
B. H. Valentine
H. T. Bartlett
N. W. D. Yardley
P. A. Gibb
E. Paynter
L. Hutton
W. J. Edrich
L. Ames
H. Verity
D. V. P. Wright
T. W. Goddard
R. T. D. Perks
L. L. Wilkinson
(Manager: Flight-Lieutenant A. J. Holmes)

To West Indies

1911
A. F. Somerset (Capt.)
T. A. L. Whittington
S. G. Smith
B. H. Holloway
D. C. F. Burton
D. S. G. Burton
H. L. Gaussen
A. C. Somerset
J. W. Hearne
G. Brown
H. Young

1912–13
A. F. Somerset (Capt.)
A. C. Somerset
T. A. L. Whittington
D. C. F. Burton
A. E. Relf
E. Humphreys
W. C. Smith
S. G. Smith
S. G. Fairbairn
M. H. C. Doll
B. P. Dobson
Captain G. A. M. Docker
A. Jaques

1925–26
Hon. F. S. G. Calthorpe (Capt.)
Hon. L. H. Tennyson
Captain T. O. Jameson
H. L. Dales
L. G. Crawley
C. T. Bennett
W. R. Hammond
P. Holmes
F. Watson
E. J. Smith
W. E. Astill
R. Kilner
F. Root
G. Collins

1930
Hon. F. S. G. Calthorpe (Capt.)
Major R. T. Stanyforth
N. Haig
G. T. S. Stevens
R. E. S. Wyatt
W. Rhodes
G. Gunn
E. Hendren
W. E. Astill
A. Sandham
L. Ames
J. O'Connor
L. Townsend
W. Voce

1934–35

R. E. S. Wyatt (Capt.)
E. R. T. Holmes
D. C. H. Townsend
K. Farnes
W. E. Harbord
W. R. Hammond
E. Hendren
M. Leyland
L. Ames
J. Iddon
G. E. Paine
J. Smith
E. Hollies
W. Farrimond
(Hon. Manager: T. H. Carlton-Levick)

To New Zealand

1906–7

Captain E. G. Wynyard (Capt.)
J. W. H. T. Douglas
P. R. Johnson
W. B. Burns
N. C. Tufnell
G. T. Branston
W. P. Harrison
G. H. Simpson-Hayward
C. C. Page
R. H. Fox
P. R. May
W. J. H. Curwen
A. A. Torrens
C. E. de Trafford
P. F. C. Williams

1929–30

A. H. H. Gilligan (Capt.)
K. S. Duleepsinhji
E. W. Dawson
G. B. Legge
M. J. Turnbull
M. J. C. Allom
G. F. Earle
E. T. Benson
F. E. Woolley
E. H. Bowley
M. S. Nichols
S. Worthington
F. Barratt
W. Cornford

1922–23

A. C. MacLaren (Capt.)
A. P. F. Chapman
G. Wilson
Hon. F. S. G. Calthorpe
T. C. Lowry
C. H. Gibson
W. W. Hill-Wood
C. H. Titchmarsh
J. F. Maclean
Colonel J. C. Hartley
A. C. Wilkinson
Hon. D. F. Brand
A. P. Freeman
H. Tyldesley
(Manager: H. D. Swan)

1935–36

E. R. T. Holmes (Capt.)
Hon. C. J. Lyttelton
A. D. Baxter
S. C. Griffith
J. H. Human
N. S. Mitchell-Innes
A. G. Powell
H. D. Read
W. Barber
J. Hardstaff
James Langridge
J. H. Parks
J. Sims
D. Smith

To United States and Canada

1905

E. W. Mann (Capt.)
H. J. Wyld
L. J. Moon
F. A. H. Henley
G. G. Napier
V. A. S. Stow
F. J. V. Hopley
R. T. Godsell
R. C. W. Burn
H. C. McDonnell
C. H. Eyre
M. W. Payne
K. O. Hunter
Hon. R. B. Watson

1907

H. Hesketh-Prichard (Capt.)
Captain E. G. Wynyard
K. O. Goldie
R. O. Schwarz
L. P. Collins
G. T. Branston
S. J. Snooke
J. W. H. T. Douglas
G. H. Simpson-Hayward
G. MacGregor
F. H. Browning

To Canada

1937

G. C. Newman (Capt.)
N. G. Wykes
J. C. Masterman
K. A. Sellar
A. G. Powell
C. H. Taylor
J. F. Mendl
H. J. Enthoven
A. P. Singleton
J. M. Brocklebank
N. M. Ford
D. W. Forbes
J. T. Neve
(Hon. Manager: Captain T. Carlton-Levick)

To India

1926–27

A. E. R. Gilligan (Capt.)
R. E. S. Wyatt
Major R. C. Chichester-Constable
G. F. Earle
M. L. Hill
P. T. Eckersley
M. Leyland
A. Dolphin
J. H. Parsons
M. W. Tate
G. Geary
G. Brown
W. E. Astill
G. S. Boyes
J. Mercer
A. Sandham

1933–34

D. R. Jardine (Capt.)
C. F. Walters
B. H. Valentine
C. S. Marriott
J. H. Human
W. H. V. Levett
C. J. Barnett
L. F. Townsend
James Langridge
A. H. Bakewell
A. Mitchell
H. Verity
R. J. Gregory
H. Elliott
M. S. Nichols
E. W. Clark

To South America

1912

Lord Hawke (Capt.)
A. C. MacLaren
M. C. Bird
E. R. Wilson
C. E. de Trafford
W. Findlay
C. E. Hatfeild
A. J. L. Hill
N. C. Tufnell
L. H. W. Troughton
E. J. Fulcher
Captain H. H. C. Baird

1926–27

P. F. Warner (Capt.)
Captain T. O. Jameson
Captain R. T. Stanyforth
Captain L. C. R. Isherwood
M. F. S. Jewell
G. J. V. Weigall
G. O. Allen
G. R. Jackson
J. C. White
Lord Dunglass
H. P. Miles
T. A. Pilkington
(Hon. Manager: Captain T. Carlton-Levick)

To Holland

1928

P. F. Warner (Capt.)
R. H. Twining
G. T. S. Stevens
E. R. T. Holmes
C. D. Kemp-Welch
N. G. Wykes
M. A. McCanlis
M. J. C. Allom
H. P. Hunloke
T. A. Pilkington
E. H. Tattersall
E. P. Warner

1933

R. P. Keigwin (Capt.)
N. G. Wykes
R. H. J. Brooke
A. W. G. Hadingham
Captain M. S. H. Maxwell-Gumbleton
J. W. Greenstock
E. G. Holt
J. G. W. Hyndson
Dr T. C. Hunt
Sub-Lieutenant G. V. Prowse
Dr J. H. Doggart

To Denmark

1922

R. P. Keigwin (Capt.)
O. H. Bonham-Carter
P. N. Durlacher
Lieutenant-Colonel P. G. Robinson
H. N. Kent
F. W. Mathias
V. T. Hill
J. C. Clay
M. Ll. Hill
P. B. Martineau
K. K. Homan
E. M. Grace

1925

R. P. Keigwin (Capt.)
Lieutenant-Colonel A. C. Johnston
A. C. Huson

F. H. Hollins
Lieutenant A. R. Cadell, R.N.
P. T. Eckersley
A. P. Scott
H. C. McDonnell
Captain J. G. W. Hyndson
D. S. Milford
J. S. Hartrop
W. Andrews

1939

G. C. Newman (Capt.)
R. Aird
N. M. Ford
C. G. Ford
G. E. B. Abell
P. M. Studd
J. G. W. Davies
J. H. Nevinson
E. Bromley-Davenport
G. Cornu
F. A. Instone
(Hon. Manager: Sir Pelham Warner)

To Egypt

1909

Viscount Brackley (Capt.)
Captain E. G. Wynyard
Captain A. C. G. Luther
G. T. Branston
C. H. M. Ebden
B. P. Dobson
R. M. Bell
E. J. Metcalfe
G. H. Simpson-Hayward
Lieutenant-Colonel H. C. Moorhouse
K. L. Gibson
A. V. Drummond

APPENDIX XII

Some Lord's Statistics[1]

(First-class Matches only)

Most Runs[2]

	Inns.	Not out	Runs	Aver.
E. Hendren	589	75	25,097	48·82
J. W. Hearne	469	52	15,844	37·99
P. F. Warner	385	35	14,110	40·31
W. G. Grace	364	19	12,690	36·78

Most Wickets

	Wkts.	Runs	Aver.
J. T. Hearne	1719	28,242	16·43

Most Runs and Wickets

	Runs	Aver.	Wkts.	Aver.
J. W. Hearne	15,844	37·99	883	22·54
W. G. Grace	12,690	36·78	654	14·73

Most Centuries

E. Hendren	74	A. E. Stoddart	13
P. F. Warner	32	W. R. Hammond	12
W. G. Grace	29	W. J. Edrich	11
J. W. Hearne	28	C. B. Fry	10
F. A. Tarrant	18	B. J. T. Bosanquet	10
H. W. Lee	17	D. Compton	10
J. B. Hobbs	16	K. S. Ranjitsinhji	10

Highest Individual Innings

316, not out, by J. B. Hobbs, for Surrey *v.* Middlesex, 1926.
315, not out, by P. Holmes, for Yorkshire *v.* Middlesex, 1925.

[1] I am indebted to the late F. S. Ashley-Cooper for the figures of W. G. and myself and to Mr E. L. Roberts for the remainder of the figures.

[2] In judging these figures it must always be remembered that W. G. played on many rough and fiery wickets. The wickets in my time were very good, except on a few occasions in 1904 and 1909, when they were pretty 'lively.' Hendren and J. W. Hearne batted in every season on beautiful wickets, except in 1935, when the 'leather-jackets' invaded Lord's.

Ten Wickets in One Innings

E. Hinkly, for Kent *v.* England, 1848.[1]

J. Wisden, for North *v.* South (all bowled), 1850.

S. E. Butler, for Oxford *v.* Cambridge, 1871.

A. Shaw, for M.C.C. *v.* North, 1874.

A. Fielder, for Players *v.* Gentlemen, 1906.

G. O. Allen, for Middlesex *v.* Lancashire, 1929.

Four Wickets with Consecutive Balls

J. Hide, for Sussex *v.* M.C.C., 1890.

F. Martin, for M.C.C. *v.* Derbyshire, 1895.

A. E. Trott,[2] for Middlesex *v.* Somerset, 1907.

Highest Totals at Lord's[3]

729 for 6 wkts. by Australia *v.* England, 1930.

612 for 8 wkts. by Middlesex *v.* Nottinghamshire, 1921.

609 for 8 wkts. by Cambridge *v.* M.C.C., 1913.

Lowest Totals at Lord's

15 by M.C.C. *v.* Surrey, 1839.

16 by M.C.C. *v.* Surrey, 1872.

18 by the B.'s *v.* England, 1831.

18[4] by Australians *v.* M.C.C., 1896.

19 by M.C.C. *v.* Australians, 1878.

Groundsmen at Lord's

D. Jordan 1864–74

P. Pearce 1874–98

T. A. Hearne 1898–1910

H. White 1910–36

A. Martin[5] 1936–

Size of the Ground

186 yards long by 145 yards wide. The slope in the ground from north to south is 6 feet 8 inches.

[1] His first match at Lord's.

[2] Trott also did the hat-trick in the same innings.

[3] In second-class matches the highest totals are 735 (9 wkts.) by M.C.C. *v.* Wiltshire in 1888 and 695 by Norfolk *v.* M.C.C. in 1885.

[4] One man absent.

[5] Martin was called up for police duties during the whole of the War, and H. Gladwell acted as Head Groundsman. Gladwell came to Lord's on June 11, 1896, the day the M.C.C. got the Australians out for 18, a period of service of fifty years. He is still at Lord's.

A Short Bibliography

ALTHAM, H. S.: *A History of Cricket* (Allen and Unwin, 1926).
ASHLEY-COOPER, F. S.: *Eton v. Harrow at the Wicket* (St James's Press, 1922).
—— *Gentlemen v. Players* (Arrowsmith, 1910).
—— *M.C.C. Cricket Scores and Biographies*, vol. xv (Longmans, 1925).
—— *M.C.C. Match List* (London, 1930).
ASHLEY-COOPER, F. S., and HARRIS, LORD: *Lord's and the M.C.C.* (London, 1914).
ASHLEY-COOPER, F. S., and WARNER, P. F.: *Oxford v. Cambridge at the Wicket* (Allen and Unwin, 1926.)

"Badminton Library of Sports and Pastimes": *Cricket* (Longmans).
BARLOW, R. G.: *Forty Seasons of First-class Cricket* (Heywood, 1908).
BETHAM, J. D.: *Oxford and Cambridge Scores and Biographies* (Simpkin, Marshall, 1905).
BETTESWORTH, W. A.: *Chats on the Cricket Field* (Merritt and Hatcher, 1910).
BRADMAN, D. G: *Don Bradman's Book* (Hutchinson, 1930).

CAFFYN, W.: *Seventy-one Not Out* (Blackwood, 1899).
CARDUS, N.: *Days in the Sun* (Grant Richards, 1924).
—— *English Cricket* (Collins, 1945).
Cricketer, The.

DAFT, R.: *Kings of Cricket* (Arrowsmith, 1893).

FOLEY, C. P.: *Autumn Foliage* (Methuen, 1935).
FRY, C. B.: *Life Worth Living* (Eyre and Spottiswoode, 1939).

GRACE, W. G.: *Cricket* (Arrowsmith, 1891).

HARRIS, LORD: *A Few Short Runs* (Murray, 1921).
HARRIS, LORD, and ASHLEY-COOPER, F. S.: *Lord's and the M.C.C.* (London, 1914).
HAWKE, LORD, HARRIS, LORD, and GORDON, SIR HOME: *The Memorial Biography of Dr W. G. Grace* (Constable, 1919).
HODGSON, Rev. R. L. ("A Country Vicar"): *Cricket Memories* (Methuen, 1930).

JESSOP, G. L.: *A Cricketer's Log* (Hodder and Stoughton, 1922).

LAMBERT, W.: *Instructions and Rules for Playing the Noble Game of Cricket* (Lewes, 1816).
LENNOX, LORD WILLIAM: *Celebrities I have Known* (London, 1876–77).
LILLYWHITE, FRED: *The Guide to Cricketers* (1853, etc.).
—— *Cricket Scores and Biographies* (1862 *et seq.*).
LILLYWHITE, JAMES: *Cricketers' Annual.*

M.C.C.: *The Laws of Cricket* (London, 1939).
M.C.C., 1787–1937. (Reprinted from *The Times* M.C.C. Number, May 25, 1937.)

NOEL, E. B.: *Winchester College Cricket* (Williams and Norgate, 1926).
NYREN, J.: *The Young Cricketer's Tutor* (Gay and Bird, 1902).

OSBALDESTON, G.: *Squire Osbaldeston: his Autobiography* (Lane, 1926).

PULLIN, A. W. ("Old Ebor"): *Talks with Old English Cricketers* (Blackwood, 1900).
PYCROFT, J.: *The Cricket Field* (St James's Press, 1922).

RUTTER, E.: *Cricket Memories* (Williams and Norgate, 1925).

SALT, H. S.: *Memories of Bygone Eton* (Hutchinson, 1928).
SHAW, A.: *Alfred Shaw, Cricketer* (Cassell, 1902).
SLATTER, W. H.: *Recollections of Lord's and the Marylebone Cricket Club* (1914).

TAYLOR, A. D.: *Annals of Lord's and History of the M.C.C.* (Arrowsmith, 1903).

WARNER, P. F.: *The Book of Cricket* (Sporting Handbooks, 1945).
—— *Cricket between Two Wars* (Chatto and Windus, 1942).
—— *My Cricketing Life* (Hodder and Stoughton, 1921).
—— *The Fight for the Ashes in 1926* (Harrap, 1926).
—— *The Fight for the Ashes in 1930* (Harrap, 1930).
WISDEN, J.: *Cricketers' Almanack.*

INDEX